D0402713

ALATIN AMERICA COMES OF AGE

THOMAS J. KNIGHT

The Scarecrow Press, Inc.
Metuchen, N.J., & London 1979

Library of Congress Cataloging in Publication Data

Knight, Thomas J   1937-
    Latin America comes of age.

    Bibliography: p.
    Includes index.
    1. Latin America.   I.   Title.
F1408.K56   980   79-18702
ISBN 0-8108-1243-6

FOR BARBARA

CONTENTS

III. LATIN AMERICA'S IMPACT

ACKNOWLEDGMENTS

Those whose ideas have found their way into this book will probably recognize what I have borrowed better than I can. But my information and opinions about diplomacy, the Hapsburgs, Latin America, ethnicity, and the frontier owe much to professors W. A. Fletcher, Robert A. Divine, Thomas R. McGann, Harold A. Deutsch, R. John Rath, J. Harry Bennett, Walter P. Webb, and Joe B. Frantz.

Colleagues who have exerted a major influence are Wayne Selcher, Leon Lyday, Terrence Peavler, Gerald Moser, Michael Meyer, Robert Lima, Les Rout, Robert Graham, Mihailo Dordevic, James McAree, Irwin Richman, Tom Hale, Oliver LeGrone, Jo and Jack Searles, Mark Dorfman, Clem Gilpin, Ray Buck, Charles Ameringer, John Martz, and Richard Schulz.

I have also gained greatly from the annual Latin American conferences sponsored by Temple University and St. Joseph's College of Philadephia and from discussions with students at The Pennsylvania State University, especially Roy Perez-Daple, Sylvia Ruggeri-Ochs, Jane Millar, Raymond Albright, Daniel Zimmerman, Flora Werner, Alice Krull, Lucia del Valle, Emily Chase, and Arturo da Silveira.

Preparation of early fragments of the manuscript fell to Doris Whitman, Claire Davies, and Madeline Craig, and Susan Eberly typed the full and final version. Patricia Dunklebarger helped with the editing, and Sandy Stelts did the index. My wife Barbara and my children Russ and Karen accepted being widowed and orphaned with good grace.

Then there are the nameless shadows of a Texas childhood. I am deeply in debt to the truckers and rodeo people, the campesinos and cotton pickers, the tamale vendor on the corner of the square, the three "witches" from Haiti, the storytellers on the courthouse lawn, and the bounty hunter with the red wolf across the fender of his jeep, to mention only a few. Sensibilities developed on the fault where the United States South and Southwest meet show on every page.

Finally, there remain the Indian-German great grandmother, the dirt-farming paternal grandparents, the missionaries to Latin America on the maternal side, and the adventurers in friendship from across the great human divides of class, caste, and creed.

Thanks to all.

INTRODUCTION

This is a book about Latin America for North Americans. It aims at dispelling some of the persistent myths about Latin America, the most important of which is the myth of backwardness. The degree of development varies in Latin America but is generally mid-range and in many cities quite remarkable. Latin America is youthful but increasingly strong when taken as a whole. It has "come of age" or is at least well on toward doing so.

The second myth is that there is a simple interpretation of Latin America, that it is "Latin, " or "New World, " or whatever. Hence the attempt here to describe the complexities of "Latin" America by including all the Caribbean islands, giving more attention than is usual to sub-cultures of African or Indian or Asian origin, and treating matters, such as food and habits, in which the variability shows most. Hence also the frequent comparisons and contrasts of Latin with North America. There are more than twenty Latin Americas--and, in another sense, only one. The Americas do have a common history of colonial status and revolution-- and do not share a history of wealth. The mix is crucial.

The "Latin spirit" is also, at least partly, a myth. Just how Latin--Catholic, Iberian--is it, and how much the product of Western Hemisphere and world experiences? A persistent theme in Latin America, as in North America, is the struggle against "cultural imperialism" by Europeans. The Latin American elements, the so-called creole culture, have sometimes been emphasized, and sometimes the Indian elements (indianismo) or the Blacks' cultures (négritude). But again the combinations are what matter--the complexities, the day-to-day feelings and actions.

Another myth is that of limited Latin American influence in world affairs because of weakness or a willingness to follow along in the wake of the North American man-o-war. That is no longer true--if it ever was. But this does not mean Latin Americans have declared their independence of Western Hemisphere interests. Rather they have declared their interdependence in the hemisphere and the world. They will continue to be influenced--and to influence. And they have long influenced even the United States, especially its South and West. Two-way influences in matters of race and culture as well as diplomacy are of the essence in a world grown small in television's glare.

This work compliments both Latin and North Americans, the former because it recognizes their considerable accomplishments and the latter because it assumes their ability to deal with the complex social and emotional realities behind such confusing terms as "Latin Americans" and "North Americans." Latin Americans, for example, consider the habit of calling citizens of the United States "Americans" an act of arrogance and instead say "North Americans" (norteamericanos) despite their recognition that Canada and Venezuela are actually north of the equator. "North Americans" is used in the Latin American sense here to symbolize this book's intent: that we United States citizens should learn to see ourselves as others see us and thus better comprehend all the Americans.

PART I

SOUTH AMERICA

Chapter 1

CITY IN THE WILDS

President Juscelino Kubitschek dedicated Brasília, the new capital of Brazil, on April 21, 1960. To get to the ceremonies he had to jet across six hundred miles of near-wilderness between the new capital and the old, Rio de Janeiro. Brasília was worth the trip. The Presidential Palace shone like a jewel reflected in nearby fountains, and the Congress Hall's half-spheres lay ready to house the two branches of the Brazilian legislature. Above all soared tho National Cathedral, whose shape was that of an upside-down vase open from God to Man.

Outside the capitol grounds, however, all was chaos. Most of the minor government buildings were unfinished, and housing was almost non-existent. Mud alternated with dust. And just beyond the city were the frontier wilds of Goiás State. Brasília was so primitive, in fact, that Kubitschek and the other officials returned immediately to Rio to continue the business of governing Brazil. There they found the politicians and people fearful, with good reason, that Brasília might bankrupt the country. The church hierarchy refused to sanctify the cathedral because the architect, Oscar Niemeyer, was a Marxist.

Yet planner Louis Costa had caught the spirit of this fabulous pioneer venture in his design for the city--a soaring bird or plane. Never mind that the materials, including stone and steel, had to be ferried in by plane. Never mind that some of the workers building roads to connect Brasília to the rest of the country had to arm themselves against Indians. Never mind the cost or the opposition. The long-dreamed-of March to the West had been launched. Kubitschek's idea was to bring Brazil into its birthright, the untamed half-continent within its borders. To do that it was necessary to populate the interior, since only one-third of the people lived farther than one hundred miles from the Atlantic in a country over two thousand miles wide.

3

Brasília's story is that of South America in small compass. For the whole continent is forging the fabulous from the primitive. Portuguese-speaking Brazil alone is potentially as powerful as the United States, and some of the Spanish-speaking countries, such as Argentina, might well outstrip Britain or France. South Americans need only a decent amount of investment capital, improved education, more people--difficult as that is to believe--and hard work. Within a very few years Brasília has become a city of well over half a million. Its fate augurs well for the future of South America, a continent emerging from the wilderness.

The development of Brasília also symbolizes how South American history has accelerated in the last few decades. Yet the taming of the South American continent dates back to at least the founding of the "high culture" of the Incas. In that sense, South American history is all of a piece. Its institutions and aspirations are rooted in the exhilarating climb toward modernization. Pioneer restlessness permeates everything--politics, art, whatever. Like North America and other "frontier" areas, South America has embraced change. Indeed, to Americans--South, Middle, or North-- history and change are almost synonymous.

Chapter 2

THE HISTORY

Indian South America

The Indians discovered America over ten thousand years B. C., and Columbus, or Leif Ericsson, discovered the Indians' America nearly twelve thousand years later. Most Indian immigrants traveled to South America down the long mountain chain from Siberia and Alaska through North, Central, and South America to Patagonia. Archaeologists have found a chain of inhabited sites of progressively younger age from the far north to the far south, for instance. Some Indians may have come across on the trade winds from island Asia. The discovery of Jomon-style pottery like that of Kyushu, Japan, in Ecuador indicates this could be true, as does the successful recent crossing of the Pacific by anthropologist Thor Heyerdahl in an ancient-style Asian boat named the Kon-Tiki. Heyerdahl was attempting to prove that waterborne Polynesians could have sailed to the West Indies, and later tried to prove Phoenicians could have come via the Atlantic, too. Anyway, the Indians, Mongoloids from somewhere or even several places in Asia, were the first to discover America.

The Indians scattered unevenly across the Americas. Generally speaking, the western mountains were more heavily populated than the plains and islands farther east. Everywhere the land was virtually empty by modern standards. However, by the time Europeans arrived on the eastern coast of the Americas, there were probably twenty or more millions of Indians from Alaska to Patagonia, most of whom were in the two advanced farming cultures, the Aztec-Mayan in Mexico and the Inca in Peru and Bolivia. Perhaps twenty per cent of the Indians lived in intermediate farming cultures of the forest zones or in hunting-gathering or fishing cultures on the grasslands and coasts.

The history of Indian South America is therefore mainly

5

the history of the Inca empire. European "discoverers" saw the Incas as the Romans and the Aztecs as the Greeks of Indian America because the Aztecs lived in squabbling communities while the pragmatic Incas excelled in law and government. The Incas were indeed good at governing. Their political and class structure was based on conquest and blood kinship and led from the royal caste of the Inca, or emperor, and his family down through the caciques, or nobles, to the commoners and, finally, the slaves. The tribes taken into the Inca's empire or "family" were then related by the intermarriage system of the royal and high noble families, which, over time, became one. Rebellion became sacrilege against the Inca, the father and god-king of the whole empire. Family, state, and religion melded into one.

This elaborate political organization, an almost unbelievable system of roads and commerce, military and administrative efficiency, and collection of substantial taxation or tribute allowed the Inca--meaning either the emperor or the "family, " since they were apparently seen as one--to extend the empire for over two thousand miles from north to south. On the order of the emperor, his "children" trudged the cobbled road of the Incas from Cuzco, the capital, to present-day Tucumán in the Andean piedmont of Argentina or went as far in the other direction into present-day Colombia. Orders, goods, brides, and taxes passed along those roads and into Cuzco. The Inca used the taxes to finance terracing, more roads and irrigation, and such projects as the "hidden city" of Machu Picchu. The slaves and commoners worked the maize and ran the animals, the Inca and the caciques governed well, and the empire grew rich. And then, in 1532, came Francisco Pizarro at the head of his ragged band of Spaniards--and the whole empire collapsed.

Pizarro caught the Incas at a bad time. The curse of monarchies, hereditary succession, had led to civil war when the last great Inca, Huayna Capac, died in 1527 after dividing the empire between Huáscar in Cuzco and Atahualpa in Quito. Huáscar, legitimate son, claimed the whole empire, and Atahualpa, illegitimate, did not scruple to take Cuzco and execute his brother. Then Atahualpa, still weak in authority, was confronted by an emissary from Pizarro who refused to dismount, even in the royal presence, and requested that the Inca go to Pizarro's camp at Cajamarca. Once in Cajamarca, the Inca was ordered to submit to the Catholic Church and the King of Spain and, when he refused, was put under house arrest. Atahualpa, so the story goes, bribed the Spaniards with a roomful of gold and a roomful of silver, but was killed when he threatened Pizarro for reneging on the promise to release him in return for this ransom. The Inca empire was leaderless, and the Spaniards soon conquered the capital. The Inca's "family" broke up, and the empire fell to pieces.

Many of the Indians yearned for a new Inca to lead them against the Spaniards, and "pretenders" appeared, the last, Tupac Amaru, in the great Indian revolt of the 1790s. But what Pizarro had begun in 1532 with 62 horsemen, 106 foot soldiers, and a few cannons progressed inexorably until the Europeans dominated the Inca lands. Spain's conquistadores had triumphed over the Indians. Indian culture began to die in the Andes. Pizarro had done to the Incas in the 1530s what Cortez had done to the Aztecs fifteen years earlier.

The Indian cultures of the forest zones and grasslands lasted longer, and some remain even now in out-of-the-way places. The intermediate-level farming cultures of the forest zones of Indian America were second to fall before European inroads. The Tupí-Guaraní cultures of Paraguay and surrounding areas were no different than the Iroquois-Algonquin cultures of North America in this respect, except that in South America some localized cannibalism gave these agriculturalists a fiercer aspect to Europeans. Juan Díaz de Solis, the first conquistador in Uruguay, was captured and eaten, for instance. Brazilian movement westward was similarly retarded by the fierce opposition of cannibals in the interior. In Paraguay, however, the Tupí and Guaraní were converted after 1608 by the Jesuit Reducciones or missionvillages, partly because the church promised protection from the slave-hunting conquistadores. This enabled the slavehunters to make a large haul of relatively defenseless Indians when the protection of the Church was forcibly removed by the government in the eighteenth century. By that time the Indians in Uruguay and Brazil had also been subdued.

Finally, there were the hunting-gathering and fishing Indians of the grasslands and coasts. The fishing cultures were accessible and easily subdued, but the nomads of the grasslands were another matter, especially once they acquired the horse from the Europeans. The Abibones and Puelches of Patagonia were quite as formidable as the Comanches or Sioux of the North American plains, and the Araucanians of

southern Chile were not unlike the Nez Percé in their mixed
nomadic-settled culture and their implacable opposition to the
Europeans. Neither the Incas nor the Spaniards ever subdued
these tribes. One Argentine president, General Julio A. Ro-
ca, made his reputation as the conqueror of Patagonia in the
1860s and 1870s just as Andrew Jackson had done in Florida
and Tennessee half a century earlier. The Araucanians were
not subdued in Chile until 1883, just seven years before the
last battle with the Apaches in the United States. Indian nomadism died hard, and with a bloody finish.

The Conquest

The European conquest of South America resembled a
backyard brawl more than an invasion. In Europe it was the
time of the Reformation, and Spain and Portugal were rivals
for defender of the Catholic Church against the Protestant
English and Dutch and the wavering Germans and French, not
to mention the "heathen" Turks. Spain's claims were pushed
by Ferdinand and Isabella, "The Catholic Monarchs," and
then by the Hapsburg "Universal Emperor" Charles V and his
son Philip II. Portugal was far less forceful and later even
fell under Spanish control for a time (1580-1640), but under
King João III, a contemporary of Charles, Portugal kept up
the pace set by the great Spanish monarchs who commissioned
Columbus (Cristóbal Colón), Cortez (Hernán Cortés), and Pizarro.

Columbus made his first landfall in 1492; Cortez conquered the Aztec capital in 1519-21; and Pizarro laid low the
Incas in 1532-35. So in under a half-century the Spaniards
toppled the Indian leaders. By mid-century Pizarro's men
going down the west coast and into Chile met with conquistadores coming up the La Plata and into western Argentina.
The south was Spain's, as was the west.

Yet Portugal had begun to catch up as early as 1500,
when one of her Africa-bound captains, Pedro Alvares Cabral,
was blown across the Atlantic onto Brazil's coast, establishing Portugal's claim. By 1530 the agent of Portugal's King
João III, Count Martim Affonso de Souza, was exploring the
coasts from the Amazon to the La Plata seeking sites for
trade and settlement. He established an outpost at a spot
near presentday São Paulo, about half-way between the two
great rivers, to control the coast in both directions. The
Portuguese had begun to make good their claims to the east.

The fact is, however, that Spain and Portugal could not have held South America had the British, French, or Dutch been seriously interested in challenging Iberian claims. The voyage of Francis Drake around South America on a plundering expedition for the British navy proved that. So did the periodic French and Dutch conquests in Brazil and on the La Plata. The north European states were simply more interested in the Caribbean and North America than in South America, chiefly because plantation profits were higher there and trade lines to north Europe were shorter. So the Iberians kept South America, with the exception of the strategically important British, French, and Dutch Guianas lying near the entrance to the Caribbean.

The Spanish Empire

Spanish America was geared to the arrival and departure of ships. The galleons arrived with men and supplies and departed with bullion and men "going home" to Europe. The most famous of the ships was the Manila Galleon which touched port in Spanish America en route from the Spanish colonies in the Philippines. The half-way houses between Manila and Madrid were the two great Viceroyalties of New Spain (Mexico) and Peru. The cargoes gathered in the empire were most often freighted across the isthmus in Mexico or Panama rather than risk the stormy passage around Cape Horn. Present-day Argentina thus had to send its trade west to Lima in order to get it forwarded to Spain--or the Philippines.

The reason was that Lima was to South America what Mexico City was to the Caribbean. Lima's Plaza de Armas was the heart of this part of the Hapsburg empire, as was Escorial Palace in Spain or Schoenbrunn Palace in Austria. On the plaza stood the Viceroy's Palace, the point of origin for colonial government. Nearby were the cathedral and the residence of the archbishop, plus the houses of conquistadores turned landed grandees. The three pillars of colonial life therefore rested on this city founded in 1535 to take out the Inca treasures. The government officials, the churchmen, and the landowners scattered over South America looked toward Lima for guidance--when they were not in rebellion, that is. The House of the Indies, the office set up by the Hapsburg Emperor in Spain to run the empire, also looked to Lima--to keep law and order, to christianize for the greater glory of God, and to keep the bullion flowing. From Lima the orders passed into the Andes, and through Lima the bullion came out.

For three centuries Hapsburg policy was to take much and give little, although in reality things turned out somewhat differently. The mines did in fact pour out their treasures to pay for the famous Spanish armies fighting for the True Faith--and Hapsburg power--around the world. But so much bullion made its way to Europe that Hapsburg power itself was undermined by inflation, so American gold led to the rapid decline of Spanish strength in the 18th and 19th centuries. As for the empire, it was cursed with the aftermath of the encomienda, the grant of Indian land and labor to Spanish Colonials. Because of the Hapsburg desire to make the colonies as self-sufficient (that is, as cheap) as possible, the encomienda, eventually amounted to a revolution on the land in South America. The generally poor conquistadores became fabulously rich through the use of Indian slave or tenant labor on land they soon claimed as their own. In this way the European upper class, which even today owns much of South and Central America as haciendas or estancias, emerged at the expense of the Indians.

The other two powerful forces in Spanish South America, the government officials and the churchmen, generally supported the landlords, who, after all, were kith and kin and adherents of the True Faith. Even when they did not agree with the landlords, the officials and churchmen could do little because Spanish and Church law were confined in practice to the towns. The local government (cabildo) and the local church (iglesia) had a profound effect on the political and cultural traditions of South America, so much that in their combined form of a colonial "mission" they may be considered among the most effective colonizing or frontier institutions ever devised. Yet outside the towns the law of the hacendado--"boss" or "patron"--prevailed, and the encomienda or hacienda was the primary colonizing instrument.

The most acrimonious quarrels in the Spanish colonies were usually caused by the rivalry of the townsmen and the hacendados, with the House of the Indies acting as interested arbiter. The most famous of the townsmen-reformers was Bartolomé de las Casas, the defender of the Indians against the holders of encomiendas. After years of campaigning against the landlords' lobby in Spain, this conquistador-turned-churchman succeeded in having the Indians declared Children of God (and thus capable of civilization) and in getting the more glaring abuses of Indian slavery under encomienda removed.

Despite his blind spot concerning Negro as opposed to Indian slavery, las Casas serves to illustrate the reformist spirit to be found in the best of the Spanish colonizers, including some viceroys of Peru and Mexico. This reformism generally arose out of the Catholic Reformation in Spain, at least until the French Enlightenment tradition came to Iberia with the Bourbon Dynasty after the War of the Spanish Succession (1702-14). The essential idea of the Catholic Reformation was that all civilized or Christianized men must treat each other with "justice" as outlined by Saint Thomas Aquinas. No one could neglect to pay a decent wage or refuse to work a fair amount without committing mortal sin. Hence slavery was as great a sin as theft if those enslaved were Christians. Some colonial officials and churchmen wanted to do their sacred duty in this respect, as did some of the Hapsburg monarchs, but economic self-interest and the power of the colonial landlords stood so firmly in the way that little was accomplished.

When Louis XIV of France forced his Bourbon relatives onto the vacant Spanish throne instead of an Austrian Hapsburg, he not only ended Hapsburg rule in Spain and the Spanish empire. He also opened the Spanish lands to three Enlightenment ideas which soon began to change the nature of Spanish imperial administration: local self-government, economic incentives, and scientific social planning. In the century from the Bourbon accession (1702) until the Spanish American Revolutions broke out (1806), these ideas profoundly affected Spanish South America. The first led to the establishment of two new viceroyalties, one on the Spanish Main and one on La Plata, thus depriving Lima of its monopoly on Spanish government in South America. Even then the people of Caracas and Buenos Aires remained restive, however, because they felt Lima continued as the privileged son of Madrid while they acted the parts of poor relatives.

The idea of freeing the colonial market so as to give incentives to local South American commerce and cause the empire to prosper took root less readily, especially in Spain. But the Europeans born in South America, called criollos to distinguish them from the peninsulares born in Spain, seized upon the notion as readily as the merchants of North America --and for the same reasons. Smuggling, always rampant, became respectable trade in South American eyes, and even the House of the Indies eased trade restrictions when it saw the wealth to be had from lower tariffs on a larger volume of trade. Nevertheless, Caracas, like Boston, seethed with discontent over the trade issue and the dominance of planters over merchants in colonial government.

The notion that social planning was a rational and not a moral activity was a direct challenge to the Church and the theological view of things. So the Bourbon officials themselves set out to submit the church to state authority in the manner of Europe's enlightened despots. The activities of the Inquisition were curtailed and the churchmen subjected to government discipline or, in the case of the irreconcilable Jesuits, expelled. The state then controlled the information sources as best it could, which failed nonetheless to prevent the doctrines of the American and French Revolutionaries from infecting the South Americans. Sedition spread via the words of Thomas Jefferson and Napoleon Bonaparte. It was from these sources that Francisco Miranda caught the revolutionary fever and gave it to the other South Americans.

Portuguese America

The Portuguese Empire was different in degree if not in kind. The Spanish had haciendas for the most part, the Portuguese true plantations worked by slave labor. Sugar rather than gold was king, and Portuguese colonial peoples-- Black, Red, and White--were its servants. Portuguese colonial history is the story of the struggle of interests other than sugar to break out of the round of slave ship, sugar ship, ad infinitum. The sugar interests were centered in the Northeast, in Pernambuco and Bahía, where the plantation system took deep roots after the kings of Portugal had granted lands to the so-called donatarios and the latter had driven off cannibalistic Indians and brought in African slaves. The "plantation house" and the "slave shanties," the gruelling sugar economy, and extensive miscegenation left their marks on this region. A cattle industry was even developed in the backlands to feed the coastal population and furnish hides.

Glorious colonial cities like Salvador in Bahía became the showpieces of Portuguese colonialism in America. A babel of languages--African, Mediterranean, and North European--marked every corner of the region, and religions, like peoples, mixed as the Africans added their Islam and Macumba to the relatively gentle Portuguese brand of Catholicism. The Portuguese grandees gloried in their successes and wealth, and Dutch, British, and French adventurers tried to take it all away from them--and sometimes did, as is the case of the Guianas. Portuguese kings prided themselves on the productive nature of their colonies as opposed to the "exploitative" Spanish system, and plowed back some of the profits to reap an even greater harvest of wealth.

But Bahía was not Brazil, though it thought so. To the south, where the trade winds did not blow, was the then hard-to-reach area of Rio and São Paulo, the future center of the country. The Paulistas limped along, neglected by Lisbon, until gold was discovered in the central backlands in the eighteenth century and the Portuguese kings and grandees got gold fever. Heretofore the central backlands had merely been slave-raiding quarters for the frontier adventurers known as bandeirantes, but now a gold rush to Minas Gerais and eastern Goiás drove back the frontier and made the coast a transshipment point to Europe.

The North began to lose its edge to the Center, as was indicated by the transfer of the colonial capital to Rio in 1763. The retreat of the Portuguese court to Rio to escape Napoleon (1808-1814) only added to the pace of the change. Coffee further magnified it in the nineteenth century, as did the influx of European immigrants and the development of the new cattle-raising centers in the South to compete with those in the interior Northeast. Rio de Janeiro and São Paulo replaced Bahía and Pernambuco as the heart of Brazil, and the proud Northeast fell behind. The end was marked after the fact by the progressives' long-delayed establishment of the republic and abolition of slavery in 1888-89.

The progressive fever had begun in Portuguese America at the same time as in Spanish America, and in the same manner, namely, with the introduction of reforms by progressive royalists led by the favorite of the Portuguese monarchs, the Marquis of Pombal (1750-77) and his disciple, the Viceroy Lavradio in Brazil (1769-79). They had as their aim the creation of a progressive commercial economy less dependent on the plantation system. They were encouraged by the threatened end of the slave trade on the one hand and by the growing incidence of slave revolts and establishment of quilombos, or free-African settlements, on the model of the famous seventeenth-century Republic of Palmares in Alagôas.

Reforms could not allay the tension of the shift from North to Center, however, and agitation grew as the North granted less and the Center wanted more. The leader of the Brazilian revolutionaries of 1789--Tiradentes, or tooth-

puller, because he was a dentist--was executed for his part
in the conspiracy, for example.   Only the arrival of the Royal House in Rio (1808) and the elevation of Brazil to the status of a kingdom (1815) served to calm the pressures for self-
government and enable the Brazilians to ride out the storms
shaking the Spanish American empire.

The Revolutions

The year was 1806; the place, Boston; the man, Francisco Miranda; the mission, revolution--in Caracas, his home,
against the Spaniards, his ancestors.   Miranda had fought in
the French Revolution only to lose French support under Napoleon; had approached everyone from Pitt in England to Catherine the Great in Russia for help; and had finally found some
support in the fledgling United States, though his greatest ad-
mirer, Alexander Hamilton, had died in a duel before he could
help much.   Miranda sailed anyway.   But the Spanish were
ready for revolutionaries and the Venezuelans were not, so
Miranda was defeated and later captured and imprisoned in
Cádiz, Spain.   There he died, long after.

Tiradentes was dead, Miranda in prison, but the fire
would not go out.   One reason was that Napoleon was now
pouring oil on it, especially after he decided to overthrow the
Spanish and Portuguese monarchies in 1808.   His idea was to
join with the revolutionaries of the United States and South A-
merica to bring down the Old Regime the world over.   Napoleon therefore gave up his plans for a French empire centered
in Haiti, sold Louisiana to the Jefferson government in the
United States, and encouraged Miranda's compatriot and lieu-
tenant Bolívar to take up where Miranda had left off.   And
what Napoleon helped liberate from Spain by 1815 the British,
for reasons of strategy and economic interest, helped to remain free after that date in spite of the desires of the Holy
Alliance to re-subjugate all the colonies that had broken away
from the divine-right monarchies of Europe.

Bolívar was no Napoleonic lackey, having become convinced that the French Revolutionary general had turned into
a tyrannical imperialist himself.   Bolívar, like Miranda, believed in the association of free peoples in a world federation
rather than a centrally directed revolutionary colossus.   Unlike Napoleon, he looked to the strength of revolutionary ideology rather than the violence of revolutionary states to spread
democracy.   He dreamed of a league of all nations as the

structure for a united and peaceful world, with its capital in Panama, the meeting point of east and west, north and south. His European education and his visits to the United States had convinced him that free peoples--those of northern South America, the Peruvian area, and Argentina, for instance--could freely associate with each other as had the revolutionary French, Italians, and Germans or the states of the United States. And so in 1810 the "Liberator" launched his attack on the Spanish in Venezuela.

Bolívar, with the help of General Sucre, fulfilled his part of the dream by defeating the Spaniards at Boyacá (1819) and Ayacucho (1824), thus freeing both the northern states and the Peruvian-Bolivian area. Meanwhile, José de San Martín had thrown the Spanish out of Argentina and with General O'Higgins had captured the Vale of Chile. Only in Lima did the Spaniards still have support, and even there the die-hards gave up after some abortive plots to restore Spanish rule in the 1830s and 1860s.

But the Spaniards in fact proved less dangerous to Bolívar's dream than the South Americans themselves. The plan for a South American federation went down the drain when Bolívar and San Martín could not agree on terms at their famous meeting in Guayaquil, Ecuador, in 1822. The south, the Andes, and the north drifted farther apart, and even Gran Colombia, the union of Venezuela, Colombia, and Ecuador, began to disintegrate. The Pan-American Conference called by Bolívar achieved nothing, though the United States continued to promise help through the Monroe Doctrine and the British held the Spanish at bay because it was profitable. Bolívar, crushed, gave up the presidency to Sucre in 1830 and retired into exile, denouncing the South Americans as "ungovernable." Others, particularly Santander, Sucre and O'Higgins, carried on.

Spanish South America's revolutions were republican, far-reaching, and bloody; Brazil's independence was monarchical, limited, and peaceful. The Braganza royal family had always been the mavericks of Catholic Europe, even going so far as to ally with Protestant England. But this time they outdid themselves. First, João VI moved his court to Brazil to escape Napoleon (1808-14) and made Brazil a kingdom under his heir Pedro when João himself returned to Europe (1815). Second, Pedro refused to return to Portugal when ordered to do so by his father, and instead declared Brazil's independence (1822).

The Braganzas thus flew in the face of the reactionary notion that the New World was too barbaric for a kingdom on the one hand, and the revolutionary view that it was too advanced for monarchy on the other. The British Admiral Cochrane then helped the Brazilians fight off both the Portuguese and the American-style revolutionaries. Brazil remained a kingdom and an empire under Pedro I (1822-31) and his son Pedro II (1831-89). The latter was the "Peter the Great" of America, a benevolent despot interested in science and art as well as economics and politics, and Brazil thus stood as evidence to monarchical Europeans that Americans could be "civilized" after all. Meanwhile, slavery continued and discontent mounted.

Brazil Since Independence

Pedro II reigned in Rio, but sugar still ruled Brazil. The history of the Brazilian Empire under the Constitution of 1824 is the story of this sugar-slave regime, as the Braganzas aided the Liberals and Positivists of Rio and São Paulo in ousting the sugar barons from the seats of power. Laws were passed ending the slave trade (1850), freeing the newborn (1871) and slaves over sixty (1885), and--at long last-- abolishing slavery (1888). The slave-owners of the Northeast abandoned the monarchy as a hopelessly revolutionary institution in Braganza hands. The Church, for its part, had long looked upon the Brazilian Royal House as dangerous experimentalists who refused to accept Pope Pius IX's Syllabus of Errors condemning rationalism, church-state separation, and modern social and economic movements. The armed forces wavered, and the navy actually remained monarchist for a time, but in the end the army of Marshal Deodoro da Fonseca carried out a coup in favor of a republic (November, 1889).

Brazilians celebrated the French Revolution and the drafting of the United States Constitution a century late, but Minister Ruy Barbosa, the foremost leader of the First Republic (1889-1930), moved rapidly to put the doctrines of Liberalism and Positivism into effect. The Constitution of 1891 was republican, federalist, and presidentialist, as was required for free government in Liberal-Positivist theory. The economy shifted from sugar to coffee, and economic strength from Northeastern sugar plantations to Central coffee fazendas. Rubber ballooned for a while in the Amazon, and then burst. Besides coffee, only cattle grew in importance in agriculture--and in the South, not the North.

The fact is that Brazil had turned the corner from old-style plantation agriculture toward modern wage-labor commercial agriculture, but mainly for the benefit of the coffee barons of Rio and São Paulo. The keys to the Brazilian Republic were the "alternation system" in politics and the "valorization system" for coffee. The first provided that men from São Paulo and Minas Gerais would alternate as president and vice president, thus excluding those from all other states, North or South. The second assured that coffee would be subsidized and stockpiled or burned, a process which took up to one-third of the national budget in some years. There was no doubt where the power and profit lay in the First Republic, and much of the nation did not like this regionalism any better than the Northeastern regionalism it had replaced.

Hence the Revolution of 1930, which brought the Rio Grande do Sul "cowboy" (gaucho) Getulio Vargas to power. Vargas and the junta of the Lieutenants' Revolt came to power on a platform of "nationalism" rather than "states' rights," however. The Vargas era, from his seizure of power until his suicide at the end of his second government (1954), thus began the struggle for national development rather than regional porkbarreling. Vargas' plan was to have a kind of nationalist socialism without Fascists, since Liberalism meant colonialism and Communism meant revolution--and both, plus Fascism, meant dependence on a foreign power. Vargas was obliged to put down one plot organized in the backlands by Carlos Luis Prestes, the Communist leader; another by the Paulistas, led by the Liberals; and yet another by the Integralistas, the local Fascists, in the German-dominated portions of his own region, the South. Vargas nevertheless persevered in drawing up the corporate-state Constitution of 1937, nationalizing some foreign properties, and developing the middle sectors while keeping order with an iron hand. His suicide resulted from his disillusionment with the collapse of political order, graft among his closest associates, and the general self-serving of the various interest groups.

Since Vargas, Brazil has been groping toward his aim, a workable model for national, rather than regional, development. For a time the politicians of the new breed, many from the European immigrant-groups of the past half-century, led the way--Kubitschek, Quadros, Goulart, and Lacerda, among others. But since the Revolution of 1964 the scepter has passed again to the generals--Castello Branco, Costa e Silva, Garrastazu Medici, and Geisel, all in a line. Their policies are not essentially different from those of Vargas

because their problem is the same, namely, how to avoid
domination by either the West or the East and bring Brazil
up to its full potential as a near super-power.

The Brazilian flag carries the Positivist slogan, "Order and Progress." The Brazil of the parties (1954-64) emphasized progress as the road to order. There was a kind
of brawling frontier quality to Brazilian democracy, as in
California at the turn of the century. Passionate debate was
the order of the day in politics. Masses jostled classes.
Congress tangled with presidents, legislatures with governors.
Region vied with region, state with state, faction with faction.
But development lurched ahead. Some of it was brought on
by private investment, foreign and domestic. Some came
from foreign aid and technical assistance. Some resulted
from state owned industries such as Petrobras, the oil monopoly. All was expensive--like Brasília. And that caused inflation. The leaders of the "Revolution" of 1964, especially
in the armed forces, felt that high wages and large social
projects designed to improve the lot of the masses were mis-
guided. It was the Populist free-silver types vs. the Republican gold-standard types of the 19th-century United States all
over again, Brazilian-style. Besides, there were fears that
Goulart was close to Marxists in the unions and to Francisco
Julião's peasant leagues in the Northeast--and too willing to
build bridges to the Chinese and, rumor had it, to Castro.
So the generals took over.

Post-1964 Brazil thus set out to control the "revolution
of rising expectations" let loose by vote-conscious political
parties. Order became the way to progress. At first political parties and legislatures were abolished, political leaders
were exiled or deprived of their right to vote or hold office,
and the military junta governed by decree. Then in the late
1960s a series of decrees called "institutional acts" established
a closely controlled two-party system, restored the rights of
some politicians, and revived the congress and the legislatures.
The military junta still selected the president, though, thus
perpetuating itself. Meanwhile, the "Brazilian economic miracle" was built on concern for growth instead of care for the
poor, for rapid increase in investment from any and all
sources, and for financial stability. The approach to opening
up the Amazon was typical. The army and state engineers led
the way and were soon followed by Brazilian and foreign in-
vestors, speculators, prospectors, and settlers. The North
American billionaire Daniel K. Ludwig opened up a timber
project the size of Connecticut, for example, cutting down the

Amazon hardwoods, planting fast-growing tree-farm softwoods, and employing thousands of people. Such has become the tough-minded definition of progress--that the unclaimed land and the industrial revolution constitute a frontier safety valve to prevent planned distribution of wealth.

Praise for the Brazilian miracle has been mixed with criticism, however. Human rights issues have been the most controversial. Dom Helder Câmara, Archbishop in the Northeast, has led liberals in the Church in criticizing the government's contention that it is merely suppressing terrorists and Communists, for instance. Amnesty International, the worldwide organization which aids political prisoners in countries of every ideology, has also uncovered evidence of some official complicity by the Brazilian police in the underground vigilante group known simply as "Kill-Communists." The United Nations has complained that Brazil's reservation program is inadequate protection for Amazonian Indians, who are being dispossessed and massacred in true frontier style.

Issues of economic justice are only slightly less troublesome. Many economists doubt, in fact, that the Brazilian miracle can be sustained without more attention to developing a mass internal market by raising wages, placing greater emphasis on education, and renewing attention to regional differences in wealth. Brazil, they argue, is having its industrial revolution--but has not yet had its New Deal. The Brazilian military government speaks of "institutionalization," by which it means habits of order and hard work. It is building giant projects like the cooperative Itaipú hydroelectric plant to light up its own southern states and parts of the La Plata nations. It believes Brazilians are proud to be approaching super-power status and willing to sacrifice in order to achieve that economic and military status in the next half century. Some inside and outside Brazil think the price may be too high.

The Europeanized South

Brazil's southern states were the least advanced in the country at the time independence was gained but are now among the most advanced, and the same is true of the southernmost Spanish-speaking countries of the continent. Uruguay, Argentina, and Chile are now among the most modern Spanish-American countries in terms of income, literacy, and the like--and the most Europeanized. They are the "immigrant countries" of South America, as the center and south represent the "immigrant states" in Brazil and the East Coast and Great Lakes states do in the United States. The Spanish and Portuguese, the Italians, and the South Slavs have made the modern south of South America. There are next to no Negroes, and the Indians have been exterminated or whitened. Asians, mostly Japanese, are few but important in some commercial and manufacturing centers.

Argentina's checkered history is essentially that of the struggle between the old-style life of the Pampas and the new-style life of Buenos Aires. The country is divided geographically into the mestizo-old Spanish Pampas and Andes and the new-immigrant La Plata Basin. Economically, it is divided into the cattle and commercial interests that have dominated the country almost since independence and the new industrialists and industrial workers brought to the fore in the last half-century. Politically, the struggle between City men and Country men described in Domingo Sarmiento's Facundo has never ceased. In a sense, the gaucho dictator Rosas (1829-52) and the Europeanized intellectual Sarmiento continue their rivalry for the spirit of Argentina long after their presidential rivalries have passed into history.

But Sarmiento is winning--first with Hipólito Irigoyen, then with Juan Perón, and now in the resistance of the labor movement to the military government. Irigoyen (1916-22, 1928-30), a European-style Radical, pointed Argentina toward an industrial revolution by opening wide the gates to immigration, by fostering mass education, and by encouraging foreign capital and expanded trade. Perón (1946-55), who was impressed by the "middle way" Mussolini and Vargas were thought to be following between Imperialism and Communism, went even further and set up a development plan with high tariffs, subsidies for industry, nationalization of natural resources, and substantial welfare programs. Moreover, his political movement, Peronismo, was based on the "shirtless ones" (descamisados), which is to say the sweaty immigrant union men of Buenos Aires who, in the South European tradition, wore no shirts to work.

The drift from the gaucho to the descamisado has continued unabated since Perón was forced into exile in Spain by charges that his justicialista movement was fascist. But efforts to form a cohesive bond for the fractious forces of Argentine life have so far failed. A decade-long European-style parliamentary experiment ended, as in Brazil, in a series of military governments--which did not suppress the political in-

stitutions of the country, however.   The gap between polarized
left-wing forces in the universities, the unions, and the professions on the one hand and the army, the commercial interests,
and the Church even continued to widen.   By the late 1960s
urban guerrillas inspired by Che Guevara's "revolutionary
offensive" and workers in the industrial center of Córdoba,
much nearer Che's Bolivian base, appeared to have forced the
issue with the military, that is, revolution or reaction.
Perón's followers, who had paralyzed politics for years in an
attempt to restore justicialismo, held the trumps.   So Perón
was recalled in the early 1970s as a way of restoring the middle way and, after the leader died, his wife Isabel succeeded
him as president so as to continue the magic of the name.
But it did not work, and another military government drawn
to the Brazilian and Chilean hardline standards was established
by General Jorge Videla.

If Perón had lived longer; if Isabel had possessed the
charisma and intelligence of Perón's first wife Eva, "angel of
the poor" because she came from that class and allied government with Catholic charities to favor the descamisado; if the
times had not been so poisoned by Vietnam and Che--what ifs
might have made Peronism the common bond?   Probably none,
since Perón's remaining models, Salazar in Portugal and Franco in Spain, also gave way to democracy by the late 1970s because the Church turned to a theology of progress.   Then why
has Buenos Aires, "Paris" of Latin America, not become the
center of a European democracy alternating between Social
Democrats and Christian Democrats?   The answer seems to
lie partly in the traditional division of City from Country,
which is deeper certainly than in New York, or even in
France and Spain.   The rest of the answer probably lies in
the lack of an economic miracle in Argentina.   Whether to be
meat-packer and shoemaker to Europe or an industrial cog in
a Latin American machine--or how to combine these--has not
been clearly agreed on.   Meanwhile, Argentines, who once produced more than the rest of South America combined, see themselves outstripped by Brazil and react as the French reacted
to the rise of Germany and the United States, namely, with
the feeling that they are still more "cultured" and "intelligent"
than such materialists.   A dignified cosmopolitan with a limp
--that is Argentina.

Chile's "middle way" between Imperialism and Communism has until quite recently been more libertarian than Brazil's
or Argentina's.   Chile has the same problems, namely, regionalism, maldistribution of wealth, assimilation of immi-

grants, and foreign capital. But Chile's traditions have usually run more to the cultured and the political than to the economic and the military. Hence the Chilean transition from Conservative-Liberal through Radical to modern politics has been only superficially the same as that of Argentina. For what emerged after World War II was a political rather than military rivalry between two essentially democratic forces, the Christian Democrats of Eduardo Frei and the Social Democrats of Salvador Allende. So stable was Chile, in fact, that both the far-left Communists and the far-right Conservatives participated in elections in lieu of making military revolutions and counter-revolutions. Coalition-making tended to cause an alternation of the Christian Democrats and Social Democrats in power and to hold Chilean development and reform to a slow, evolutionary process--until Allende was elected and deposed (1970-73).

The events of the 1960s and early 1970s seemed at first to confirm the Chilean tradition. For most of the 1960s, Frei's Christian Democrats dominated Chile's political life. They followed the "every man his brother's keeper" program of Pope John XXIII, John Kennedy, and like-minded Catholics the world over. This "cooperative strategy" of classes working together toward a consensus led to the half-nationalization of foreign-owned copper companies, paternalistic state-aided self-help programs, and vigorous encouragement of the growth of the "middle groups" of educated Chileans. The aim was to run the gauntlet between the "reactionary rich" and the "revolutionary poor." The symbol of all this in Chile was the Alliance for Progress, which was proposed by President Kennedy at Frei's suggestion as a "middle way" between Conservatism and Marxism. In return for Alliance aid, liberal reforms were to be instituted, and the resulting growth was to make more reforms possible.

Then in 1970 the Chilean voters decided that such a program was not sufficient and elected a mixed Socialist-Communist Popular Front government with Salvador Allende Gossens as president. Despite some threats of a coup d'état, Allende took office and began a Marxist-inspired program of nationalization of both foreign and domestic assets, planning of prices and wages to the benefit of the lower classes, and state-directed projects for development. The major point, however, is that the program was initiated by law, not by revolution. Constitutional liberties were generally preserved, the "revolution" was voted through the congress and executed by the traditional bureaucracy, and--despite leftist pressure

within the Popular Front--compensation for nationalized assets
was to be paid.

The worldwide attention focused on the death of Allende
in the September, 1973 coup led by General Augusto Pinochet
was due only partly to the bloodiness of the overthrow.   For
Allende's Chile represented for many the alternative of electoral revolution in the Third World.   Latin Americans of
"progressive" persuasion remembered that Chile had had an
elected socialist government in the 1930s and thought that
there, if anywhere in Latin America, a revolution in liberty
might be generated.   Europeans, especially Latin Europeans,
remembered their elected Marxist ministers of the early post-
World War II years and thought that Communists were less
dangerous in a legal government than underground.   But both
extreme left and extreme right inside Chile and out saw it
differently.   Russian-line Communists supported Allende, Castro visited, the remnants of Che's defeated Bolivian guerrillas
were given sanctuary.   But Allende did not arm the populace,
form a one-party state, or turn the economy over to workers
and peasants.   The revolutionary left was therefore dissatisfied with the slow pace of progress toward a "toilers' state. "
They believed Allende had stepped only on the tail of the capitalist snake.   They would have preferred to oust Allende's
"Kerenskyists" and form a true workers' state.   And they
made quite a battle of it for a while after the coup--hundreds
were killed, thousands imprisoned in everything from soccer
stadiums to dungeons, and more thousands, including Allende's
widow, exiled.

The Pinochet victory therefore seemed somewhat hollow, both at home and abroad.   At home the hatred of the
far left soon spread to the erstwhile allies of the junta, Frei's
Christian democrats, because of the severity of the repression, embarrassing revelations of United States involvement
in "destabilization" of the Allende government, and inadequate
advances toward "renewing" the economy.   By the late 1970s
the Pinochet government had to reform its secret police, the
DINA, release political prisoners, and hold a referendum
trumpeted as a patriotic vote for "Chile" and "Pinochet" as a
quarterstep toward liberalization.   Abroad the Pinochet hard-
handedness and revelations of CIA involvement brought ostracism by Europeans, an attack on the United States' apparent
spheres-of-influence policy by many Latin American nations--
and a change, however reluctant, in United States policy.
Soon the United States was talking of a "Good Partnership"
with Latin America, accommodating Panama and Cuba, and

criticizing the Chileans on human rights matters. Even efforts to "stabilize" the Chilean economy through World Bank favoritism were so harshly criticized that they had to be altered somewhat. So the Chilean military's closest supporters, including the Brazilian and Argentine juntas, felt it necessary to put some distance between themselves and Pinochet. And the prospect of the Latin European-style "progressive" democracy Chile has long aimed at seemed alive--barely.

Uruguay has for most of its history been the "Switzerland" of South America in everything but geography. The reason is that Uruguay's greatest president, José Batlle y Ordoñez (1903-07, 1911-15) and his Colorado party intended it that way. Batlle talked and legislated Uruguay into the showpiece of South American democracy. A multiple presidency like the Swiss cantonal council was instituted; the army was disbanded and strict neutrality announced; immigration was welcomed; the economy was managed so as to become the "meat basket" of Europe; and one of the most extensive welfare programs in the world was begun. Swiss-like neutrality brought the Montevideo Conference during World War II and the Punta del Este Conference announcing the Alliance for Progress.

Since the late 1960s, however, when the Blanco party made a comeback after a century in opposition, Uruguay has moved in the direction of a more efficient one-man presidency, a more "efficient" economy for trade's sake, and more violence. The once-stable Uruguayan political system has become polarized. Urban guerrillas called Tupamaros (for Tupac Amaru, the "Last Inca," who organized a revolt against the Spanish empire) have pursued Che's strategy for the slums of the Americas. The result has been the same as in the rest of the Europeanized portions of Latin America, a Uruguayan-brand of militarist "discipline." Political stabilization has meant that Presidents Pacheco and Bordaberry have altered the constitution to establish a single-president system, have strengthened the role of the army and the police in Uruguayan life, and have cooperated with the military governments of the south to suppress "international terrorism." Politics exists but is subdued. Economic stabilization has meant an austerity program designed to require more work for less reward--by eliminating pension benefits once available after a mere twenty years of work, and also by holding down real wages for everyone from gaucho meatpackers to Marxist clerks. Uruguay is no longer a "Switzerland." Whether it can become a "Belgium," a densely populated smaller power sandwiched between and selling medium-range manufactures to its larger neighbors and to the world, remains to be seen.

The Indian States

While the South looks to Europe for its inspiration, the Indian states of Paraguay, Bolivia, Peru, and Ecuador look to one or another of the many Mexicos of the 1910 Revolution. It is only natural for countries which are forty to seventy per cent Indian to look to the "Indian Revolution" for guidance. Yet what they see is different. Paraguay and Bolivia make an interesting contrast, for example, because they have so much in common. They are the only landlocked states in South America; they are the most strategic because they lie between the South American great powers and at the heart of the continent; they are the poorest; and they have suffered more from war, including the Chaco War between themselves (1932-35), than any other South American states. Nevertheless, they look to different Mexicos for inspiration.

Paraguay, a swamp with a hill in it, looks to the Mexico of Indian-European assimilation under military leadership. General Stroessner, long its military strongman, rules a country where nearly everyone speaks both Spanish and Guaraní, where differences in wealth are less than elsewhere in South America, and where political oppositionists are spirited, not into prison, but into exile in Brazil, Uruguay, or Argentina. Isolationist in foreign policy, militarist in politics, backward in economy, conservative in culture--such is Paraguay. Or such it has been, for now there are stirrings as the electricity of the Itaipú power project begins to spark the industrial dynamo, Mennonite immigrants come to the Chaco to hide from the world and to ship out the products of their always-considerable labors, and the exiles hunger to return from Montevideo and Buenos Aires. Someday the elite of mestizo exiles may in fact return to establish their Paraguayan version of one-party Mexico.

Bolivia, a sky-high mountain with little water, looks to the Indianismo of Zapata, that is, to Indian dominance of the country's affairs. The Bolivian Revolution (1952) was made by the Indian tin miners for the majority of all Bolivians who are Indian and speak only Indian languages. The governments since the 1952 revolution have oscillated between supporters of Víctor Paz Estenssoro and Hernán Siles, the founders of the National Revolutionary movement (MNR), and the La Paz elite's other arm, the military officers. The miners' unions led by Juan Lechín have not been able to control the La Paz government, but they do control many of the mining areas with their militia, their efficient organization, and their class-conscious politics. The Indian agriculturalists remain generally apathetic.

Hence the factions turn over and over in La Paz--from the MNR to Barrientos to Ovando to Torres to Banzer--as they always have. Meanwhile, the other two Bolivias outside La Paz control, the miners and the Indian agriculturalists, go their own way as much as possible. Neither the pro-Western government of General Barrientos, who spoke the Indian languages though he was "European," nor the revolution led by the "European" Che Guevara (killed there in 1967) has been able to change this basic drift of Bolivian life. Bolivia remains the most divided and the poorest country in the Americas, except perhaps for Haiti.

Bolivians often blame their poverty on their bad luck in losing their seacoast to Chile in the War of the Pacific (1879-83). They did in fact lose the profits from the nitrate fertilizer of the Atacama Desert and are losing whatever might have been gained from the ocean offshore. But the most that can be expected is that treaty provisions providing free transit to the sea for Bolivia may eventually be fulfilled --not much to look forward to except in terms of national pride. The price of tin is more important, and it has suffered because of the plastics revolution. The prospect that oil can be produced profitably in the Bolivian, as in the Peruvian and Ecuadorian, jungles east of the Andes offers what seems the best hope for something approximating large-scale modernization. Meanwhile, class and caste divisions and foreign determination to prevent such a strategic area from tipping the balance of power in Latin America make Bolivia, along with Paraguay and the only sparsely settled Amazon, a buffer between a conservative south and a liberal-to-radical north--a poverty-stricken Zapatista state of mostly subsistence Indians trying to find a formula for national cohesion within a state controlled by the mestizos of La Paz.

Peru and Ecuador resemble each other even more than Paraguay and Bolivia do. These are the classic lands of classical imperialism in South America. The rivalry between "European" coast and "Indian" highlands scars their present as much as their past. In Ecuador this manifests itself as

a rivalry between the outward-looking commercial interests
of coastal Guayaquil and the inward-looking administrative
circles in highland Quito. The two most famous men in Ecuador, ex-OAS Secretary Galo Plaza Lasso and several-times-
president José Velasco Ibarra, represent these two factions,
while the Indian masses have to content themselves with, at
best, benevolent "European"-dominated government like that
of President Calles of Mexico in the 1920s. Ecuador's "military populist" regimes of the 1970s have tried to rise above
these divisions, but apparently have not. Yet Ecuador has a
fairly bright future because of its resources, including oil and
some uranium, and its apparent return to democracy.

For good or ill, Ecuador has staked its immediate future on the jack of commerce--on bananas from the coastal
plantations worked by immigrant Negroes from the Caribbean,
and even more on oil from the east slope. This causes tensions like those of 1920s Mexico: with a conservative Church,
with a government bureaucracy wanting to spread the wealth
around to the masses, with the foreigners who help in development and buy the products. This last is especially important, since otherwise too much of the profit goes abroad.
The United Fruit Company's Chiquita bananas have been brought
under stricter contracts, for example, and Ecuador has even
joined the Organization of Oil Producing and Exporting Countries (OPEC) and, like Venezuela and the Arab oil giants,
manipulated production and prices. Meanwhile, the Indians
sit impassively in the doors of their Andean huts contempla-
ting their lot since Inca times. If they ever become a self-
conscious force as they did in Mexico during the Revolution,
Ecuador will have still more of the tensions which have been
around since the Spanish came--tensions which have already
surfaced in Peru.

Peru, in contrast to Ecuador, has begun to act like
the radical-minded Cárdenas government of 1930s Mexico.
The famous "Forty Families" of Lima, the scions of the colonial aristocracy, have given way since 1968 to the nationalist revolutionaries led first by General Juan Velasco. Velasco and his successors are acting to seize the property of
foreign-owned companies, encourage land reform, and institute
a military modernization of the unbelievably poor highlands.
The leader of the forces favoring the more evolutionary plan
for modernization, former president Fernando Belaúnde Terry,
is in exile teaching architecture in the United States. Yet
the man who started it all in Peru, Víctor Raúl Haya de la
Torre, has never been in power. He announced the founding

of the radical APRA group while in exile in Mexico in 1924, was denied the fruits of his victories in elections on two occasions by the army, and nevertheless forced the governing groups to abandon the "Forty Families" in favor of an all-out national development program. General Velasco is merely the latest of his creations--and Mexico's.

The overthrow of Velasco by other members of the junta in the mid-1970s did not alter the direction of the "Peruvian Revolution" so much as its speed. The "left nationalist" brand of military "civic action programs" still prevails. Experiments with nationalization, as complex as those in Mexico, are still under way. Haciendas in the uplands have been turned into everything from communal enterprises of the peons who have always worked them (compare the Mexican tribal ejido) to state-owned cattle ranches (compare the state cotton farms of northern Mexico), or have simply been left alone if they are well run by local rather than absentee owners and are not too large. State monopolies like those of Mexico (and Brazil, and recently even Venezuela) are promoting the oil industry. Thereby hangs a tale of North American-owned oil firms, which preferred lower profits to no profits, pressing the United States government into accepting nationalization in the mid-1970s.

The contrast with Mexico in the 1930s, when it was the United States government that forced the oil interests to give in, or with the contemporary actions of copper companies when Allende nationalized the Chuquicamata mine, is striking. Still, the United Fruit Company has been going the oil giants one better in selling off its existing property in most of South and Central America with United States government blessings. But all of this does not assure that Peru will soon solve its deepest problem, the division of Indian countryside from the "Spanish" coast and cities. Whether the Peruvian military has hit upon the proper governing principle for Indianist nations by using the military for "civic action" to encourage education and health programs in the mountains and can someday establish at least a "one-party democracy" like that of the Revolutionary Party in Mexico is not yet clear. But it is interesting that the Peruvian experiment has been applauded by radicals such as Castro and accepted by the United States as the Cárdenas experiment was earlier.

The Caribbean Littoral

The lands of the Spanish Main (Colombia and Venezuela) and the Guiana states (Guyana, Surinam, French Guiana) are in a sense Middle American as well as South American. There are, for example, substantial numbers of Africans and East Asians the farther east one goes toward northern Brazil. The United States and other powers have also been more inclined to interfere in all these states than in states farther south and west because of their strategic location. And the curses of colonial plantation economies linger in exaggerated forms--though not quite so obviously in Venezuela, which has "sowed the oil."

Venezuela, like Mexico, has pulled itself up by the bootstraps in the last fifty years, only much farther. The leading Venezuelan party, the Acción Democrática (AD), had led the way to modernization since World War II by accepting foreign, chiefly United States, capital on strictly Venezuelan terms. Its leaders, particularly ex-president Rómulo Betancourt, fought off the challenges of the reactionaries and the Communist guerrillas by beginning to sow the oil wealth all over the country--in an industrial Brasília at Ciudad de Guayana in the Orinoco Valley, in new and better schools, in welfare programs, in subsidies for industry and housing. The victory of the Christian Democrats under President Rafael Caldera, then of AD President Carlos Andres Pérez, actually carried Venezuela beyond the Mexican example, however, by proving that one-party government was not necessary to carry on modernization. Since 1958 Venezuela has had successive democratically elected governments, and for that and other reasons the analogy with Italy implied by the name "Little Venice" seems apt. There is the alternation between Social Democratic and Christian Democratic political forces. There is also the tension between secularism and sacramentalism in social and cultural life. There is the wide gap between very rich and very poor. And town vs. country. And regionalism. And howling traffic in the plazas. And a vast lust for life.

The Italian analogy could be carried even further. Venezuela has something like Italy's South Tyrol territorial dispute with Colombia in the Andes and something like Italy's North African interests in Guyana, with which there is another, and more heated, territorial claim. Problems remain, but Venezuela has clearly reached the relatively high level of in-

come and literacy, the attitude of mind tolerant of class mobility and assimilation of all colors and cultures, and the
political stability typical of the modern state. Whether Venezuela can sustain this character when the Lake Maracaibo oil
runs out remains to be seen, but the prognosis seems hopeful
because of the discovery of iron ore in the Orinoco. The
prospect of developing an industrial heartland in the interior
plains (llanos) is also enhanced by the nationalization of the
oil industry and by the recently renewed commitment to social
investments in education and training.

The "nationalization" scheme is remarkable in that no
state monopoly has been created, merely a kind of state holding company to control and direct the continued efforts of the
multinational oil firms. The social investment scheme is obviously designed to put Venezuela in a position to become a
"Sweden" rather than an Italy--that is, the exporter of specialized manufactured goods rather than shoes and clothing. All
of this is no small achievement for a country which forty
years ago was under the cruel "Tyrant of the Andes, " Juan
Vicente Gómez, the latest of the many dictators who had made
the country the classic case of caudillismo. The fall of Colonel Pérez Jiménez (1950-58), a persecutor of the AD whose
decoration by President Eisenhower led to the stoning of then
Vice-President Nixon in Caracas in 1958, apparently marked
the end of political authoritarianism in Venezuela. The army
is in the barracks. So now the task seems one of further
stabilizing the social order, combining economic growth with
economic justice, and celebrating the creation of a true example of "Latin democracy. "

Colombia is as much a "Spain" as Venezuela is an
"Italy. " Fewer resources, a more conservative Church, less
nationalist feeling make it a society in which subsurface tensions invite suppression to make life tolerable. For Colombia's basic problem is that there is too little common feeling,
so the country teeters at the abyss of political chaos, as it
always has. Bogotá, government center, against Medellín,
industrial center; Church against intellectuals; lowlands against
mountains; cattle against coffee; European against mestizo and
Indian; class against class; Liberal against Conservative--such
was and is the reality behind the endemic fighting known as
La Violencia. Former dictator Rojas Pinilla tried to smother
conflict under army-led modernization, but in 1957 he was
ousted by the politicians who devised the National Front as
another strategy. According to this plan, the Liberals and
Conservatives have alternated in power, thus clamping a

moratorium on the large-scale violence which killed tens of
thousands. They have rooted out the rural "bandits" and
the guerrillas of ex-priest Camilo Torres (killed in 1966) and
their Marxist compatriots, devised a national program of moderate land reform and industrialization, and in general bought
time for tempers to cool.

The possibility of a viable political system built on
old-style Conservatives and Liberals is not unthinkable, as
indicated by the election in 1974 of yet another veteran Liberal, Alfonso López Michelsen. The danger is that such a pa-
tronage-oriented system of local constituencies and regional
loyalties will make reforms too limited or too slow. The
economy is adequate only when coffee prices are high, so the
boom-and-bust cycle of one-crop economies rollercoasters
Colombians frequently. Population growth is among the world's
most rapid as well, so there is also a treadmill effect. Hence
there is a distinct possibility that the impatience will become
so great that the Rojas Pinilla movement, now led by the ex-
dictator's daughter, will begin to win elections with its right-
nationalist development schemes. Or the army could decide
to follow the Brazilian or Peruvian example of nationalist development, that is, move to either the leftist or rightist military alternatives of the Spanish Civil War. Yet it does not
seem very likely that Colombia will soon follow the example
of today's Spain and adopt European Social and Christian De-
mocracy--or that it will adopt Castro's Communism. Here
South America joins Central America in spirit as well as in
fact.

The Guiana states are like Caribbean islands that hap-
pen to be on the continent of South America. They are too
small to develop viable national economies on their own and
must therefore attach themselves to some larger unit. They
also suffer from the low level of skills that comes from decades of plantationism. Hence they have remained colonies
until very recently and are still so closely associated economically with the "mother states" of Britain, The Netherlands,
and France that they might yet be called colonies had they not
gained some political independence in the 1960s. There is no
doubt that many in the political classes of these states, like
their counterparts in the Antilles, would prefer association
with either the Socialist Bloc or, better, an all-Caribbean
federation of small states. The most publicized quarrel over
this issue has been that between former Guyana premier Cheddi Jagan, a Marxist, and his successor, Forbes Burnham.
The East Indians, descendants of "coolie" labor, line up be-

hind Jagan while the Africans, sons of black slaves, stand behind Burnham, and politics becomes a strictly racial matter, as in so much of the Caribbean. Meanwhile, many citizens are still gold prospectors ("pork knockers"), sharecroppers, or employees of foreign enterprises. Here South America joins the Caribbean in fact as well as in spirit.

Chapter 3

THE FOUNDATIONS

Geography and Technology

Shave off all of North America northward of a line from Jacksonville, Florida, to Fairbanks, Alaska, and invert the remainder. The result is much like South America. The Alaska of South America is the Argentine state of Patagonia, nearer the South Pole than Alaska is to the North Pole. The Alabama of South America is the Brazilian state of Bahía, a hot and wet area bordering the Amazon near the equator. Sheep-growing in the northern Rockies is equivalent to that in Patagonia, and problems of the former slave-worked cotton plantations in Alabama are similar to those of the former sugar plantations in Bahía.

South America, like North America, "drifted" away from the landmass of Eurasia billions of years ago. This continental drift produced sky-high mountains in the west of both continents and lower lands nearer the Atlantic. It is no surprise, then, that the American continents are twins, but not identical. The Andes mountains, for instance, are higher and more rugged than the Rockies, but narrower from west to east. Mt. Aconcagua, between Chile and Argentina, is actually a mile higher than Mt. Whitney, as are nine other Andean peaks. Forty-nine Andean peaks are over twenty thousand feet, and only the Himalayas have higher altitudes. Moreover, the entire chain is alive with volcanoes, as the North American Rockies are not. Earthquakes are far more frequent in Peru and Chile than in California and Alaska, as the Andes continue to grow. From the tip of Chile to the border of California the Latin American mountains stretch one and a half times as far as those of the United States and Canada. Transportation and communication, both north-south and east-west, are therefore exceedingly difficult in the western part of South America.

33

The rest of South America is lowland, with the exception of the Venezuela-Guiana and Brazilian Highlands, which resemble the Appalachians in the United States. The coastal plains and river valleys of South America differ from those of North America, however. For one thing, the Andes and the Brazilian Highlands rise so steeply from the Pacific and Atlantic that the piedmont replaces the tidewater plains very near the oceans. The narrow coastal plains nevertheless support the majority of the population. Many of the major South American cities--Rio, São Paulo, Buenos Aires, Santiago, Lima, and Caracas, for example--lie on these plains or just above them on the escarpment. So narrow are the plains that these cities have become notorious for their shantytowns, called barrios or favelas, which climb out of sight up the hillsides.

The river valleys of South America dwarf those of North America but have had less impact on human life than the Mississippi or St. Lawrence. The drainage map resembles a hand. The Plata and the Amazon form the thumb and forefinger surrounding the Brazilian Highlands, while the Orinoco and Magdalena divide the Guiana Highlands and the northern Andes. The hundreds of westward-flowing Andean rivers play little part except where they have gouged out habitable bays and inlets. The Amazon, the world's greatest river by volume, has several tributaries the equal of the Mississippi and drains an area the size of the United States. The Plata system, much like the St. Lawrence, has falls to match Niagara and touches four countries. The Orinoco and Magdalena, like the Rio Grande and Colorado, rush through mountains low and high and into the homelands of cowboys and Indians. And the Andean rivers have carved out valleys like those of central Chile, where Santiago and Valparaiso compare favorably with Sacramento and San Francisco in the valleys of California.

Yet on the whole the river valleys of South America are sparsely settled. Certainly nothing like the densities in the Mississippi and St. Lawrence systems exists outside the lower La Plata and the central valley of Chile. The primary reason is that South America has a less temperate climate, with the frost line falling in southern Brazil. Thus only the lower La Plata and the central valley of Chile are jungle- and mountain-free enough for comfortable and easy habitation. The jungles of the upper La Plata, the Amazon, and the Orinoco and the mountains surrounding the Magdalena have held population proportions relatively low. Instead, the people have clung to the coast or migrated to intermontane basins in the Andes and highlands.

So important are the highland basins, in fact, that Latin Americans have come to use a vertical climatic designation to accompany the horizontal one familiar to North Americans. They call the mountain zones "hot land," "temperate land," and "cold land"--tierra caliente, tierra templada, and tierra frío --to designate their suitability for human habitation. Thus South America really has two climatic regimes in one, the first being the mountain latitudinal one of the lowlands and the second the vertical one of the mountains. The former includes most of the great cities of the coast, whereas the latter also has great interior capitals like Bogotá, Colombia, and La Paz, Bolivia. In lowland South America the Amazon valley has only Belém and Manáus, hardly the equals of New Orleans and St. Louis.

The major impression of South America has always been of its natural wealth. Its size is heroic--the widest plains, the biggest rivers, the highest mountains. Its climate is heroic--the hottest jungles, the coldest pole, the driest deserts. Its plants and animals are heroic--the largest freshwater fish, the most colorful birds, the hardiest plants. Why not a continent heroic in resources as well? Latin America first made an impression on the world because of its gold and silver, for example. So rich were South America's mountains thought to be that Europeans believed there was a golden city, El Dorado, hidden away somewhere in the Andes. Stories that Pizarro took that palace full of gold ornaments from Atahualpa reinforced European notions. Thus the myth of a South America over-rich in natural resources grew up. And the myth of an open frontier to absorb people and fuel economic growth lives on.

The myth is partly true. The supplies of precious metals and stones from Peru in the high Andes to Minas Gerais in the Brazilian interior were and are seemingly endless. Just to the north of Rio de Janeiro lies one of the world's largest deposits of high-grade iron ore, and the Andes furnish tin in Bolivia, copper in Peru and Chile, and many other metals. The Amazon Basin could furnish an almost endless quantity of wood, and the humid Pampa of Argentina is probably the world's best agricultural area for cattle and grains, better than the Great Plains of Anglo-America, the North European Plain, or the Russian Steppes. The cold Peru Current is one of the finest fish-producers in the world's oceans.

But much of the myth is untrue. For one thing, the South Americans have never been able to develop their natural resources themselves. This was true in part because South America's resources are poorly located or combined poorly with other resources. Thus Chile's nitrates and the Peru Current's fish are on the side of South America away from the primary market in Europe, and the Pampas' cattle and grain have had to depend on a poor harbor at Buenos Aires and European refrigeration techniques for marketing. Above all, South America has iron but little coal, so the Industrial Revolution has been delayed and made dependent on outside help. Nothing like the Great Lakes or Rhine River iron-coal complexes could develop without imports of raw materials.

South America's extraordinary flora and fauna have also had quite a reputation, mainly because they served as the crucial specimens for Charles Darwin's development of the theory of evolution in The Origin of Species (1859). Darwin's journal of his trip as naturalist on board the British navy's research ship Beagle in the 1830s was in fact a kind of guidebook to South American plants and animals for several generations of Europeans and North Americans. In Bahía, Darwin marveled that tropical luxuriance could be so very different-- and thus led himself into the mistake of believing that enviroment could be the major cause of species change. While going down the Atlantic coast and up the Pacific coast, Darwin prowled the Pampas to observe rheas and thistles, climbed the Andes to test vertical climatic effects, speculated on problems of survival in coastal deserts like the Atacama, and finally came to the firm conclusion that God did not create the infinite gradation of creatures all at once but over eons. On the Galápagos Islands, Darwin came upon the central mystery of tortoises, iguanas, and finches differing from those of the nearby continent and from each other, island to island. He was especially puzzled by the fact that South Americans could tell him which island their tortoise-shell jewelry came from--until, of course, he hit upon the answer of "survival of the fittest" and knew that evolution could change tortoises rapidly on an isolated island. For Darwin, God's hand had written "evolution" in the natural patterns of South America.

The economic, as well as the scientific, importance of South America became a passion for Europeans and North Americans as a result of the work of an equally great naturalist of the generation before Darwin, Alexander von Humboldt, whose explorations throughout Latin America (1799-1804) inspired the scientists of the Napoleonic era. His contribution to the catalog of life-forms has long since been superseded by those of Darwin and others. But the questions raised by his explorations concerning the importance of the tropics to human welfare continue to be debated. For almost a century after his death in 1859, it was assumed that the tropics were hostile to human habitation and economic growth and that, since South America had much tropical and little temperate land, it was doomed to backwardness. Argentines and Chileans accepted this view as readily as Europeans and North Americans. "Enlightened" thinkers in the tropical countries --as witness Da Cunha's Backlands and Rivera's Vortex-- voiced the same concerns as Hudson's Green Mansions in this respect: the tropic lands were a "green hell" that sweated off the veneer of civilization. But now the equatorial lands are coming to be regarded as a potential asset--a place where heat-energy is much greater than in temperate zones and therefore where food-production may soon rival tourism because of the great efficiency of growth. There is talk that the "green hell" vision of the tropics may be as much a myth as was the notion that the Great Plains were "the great American desert." And many South Americans believe that they need only a few technological breakthroughs in tropical (or alpine) agriculture, health, etc. --the equivalent of barbed wire for the treeless Great Plains--to assure success for the march to the interior in the Amazon or the Andes.

When the Inca's engineers built roads and calculated on counting-strings (quipus), South America was nearly the equal of any continent in science and technology. Now it is not, and many South American scientists are trained in Europe or North America. Such has been the effect of colonization and South American hostility to "materialism." Yet two Argentines have won Nobel Prizes in science, Bernardo A. Houssay for Medicine in 1947 and Luis F. Leloir for Chemistry in 1970. Some of the continent's social scientists have contributed to the understanding of both South American and world culture, as anthropologist Gilberto Freyre has in his study of cultural assimilation under slavery entitled The Masters and the Slaves. Moreover, national universities like those in São Paulo, Rio de Janeiro, Buenos Aires, Santiago, and Caracas are now educating superior scientists and technicians who will soon make their marks on the cultural scene.

The pattern of scientific and technological under-development in South America is in fact best understood as semi-development. To be sure, in many ways South Americans suffer the universal result of inadequate technology: they cannot get at their resources and make productive use of them. There are not enough tractors and threshers for the fields, not enough machines for the factories, not enough trains and trucks to move goods. This is particularly true in the "interior," just as it was in the United States and, to a minor extent, still is. In both South and North America the farming, manufacturing, and transportation systems are focused on the coastal areas where, indeed, most of the people are. In South America settlement has spread inland along the rivers Plata, Orinoco, Magdalena, and Amazon or along the railroads and motor roads fanning out from Buenos Aires, Rio, Caracas, and Santiago. The ship and the plane have their role, but in South America, as in North America, the land machine predominates. At first it was the horse and wagon, but now it is the tractor, truck, bus, or auto- except in the wilds of the Andes and the Amazon. And even there the sound of the bulldozer echoes as vast road projects like Brazil's cut highways into the wilderness.

South Americans are not only more and more able to get at their resources. They are also making better use of them. But "technological society"--the culture of machine production, instant communications media, rapid transportation, and medical manipulation of birth and death--has not succeeded in replacing the earlier social habits to the extent it has in North America and Western Europe. In the Amazon and the Andes, one sees the digging stick and slash-and-burn nomadism; on the Pampas of Argentina, the Brazilian Highlands, and the Venezuelan llanos, large-scale mechanized agribusiness; on old-style haciendas or in Indian villages, handicrafts unchanged for centuries; in the up-to-date factories and skyscraper offices, computers humming away. Similarly, there are witch-doctors and heart surgeons, stone-agers and jet-setters, bow-and-arrow and ballistic-missile warriors, many illiterates and a few sophisticates, tom-toms and televisions. The range of technologies is clearly greater than in North America, where the old is passing fast, or in parts of Africa and Asia, where the new is coming more slowly. South Americans therefore live as "contemporary ancestors" or "contemporary descendants. "

South American science and technology are also only partially self-sustaining. There is room for doubt that even the most sophisticated scientific and technological nation is capable of all the learning required to maintain and enhance technology now. But South Americans clearly "borrow" a great deal more of their technology and of the learning necessary to sustain it than do North Americans and West Europeans. Many Latin Americans would like to manufacture more, do more of their own education, produce enough skilled technicians to maintain the equipment, and invent technologies more suitable for South American circumstances. In addition, the application of technology is proving as difficult as learning it. Only a very few South Americans have an understanding of technology, so they are not able to extend the benefits to all the others. Vast hydroelectric plants may exist, and nuclear plants may be on the way. But many if not most homes, even in some cities, have no refrigerator and, for that matter, no toilet. Technology has increased, not decreased, the gap between rich and poor so far, just as it has in the early stages of industrialization everywhere. Science and technology are therefore actively resisted in some quarters as inhumane, undemocratic, or imperialistic.

What all this means is hard to tell. South American optimists say that once they can get at their riches through technology, poverty will melt away, the southern continent's wealth and power will surpass that of the United States, and a utopia consistent with Latin love of life will emerge. Pessimists argue that South American industrialization is creating the same environmental and social problems seen in already-industrial nations or, worse, that the gap between rich and poor nations and individuals is widening, not narrowing, because of the too-rapid onrush of technologies. The permanent impoverishment of the Amazonian and Andean Indian, or even the permanent overshadowing of South by North America, is a recurrent nightmare. But mainly, South Americans see technology as a new frontier, a new way of getting ahead in the manner of the conquistadores. Meanwhile, technology is impacting population issues as well as development issues by drawing people to the cities, by altering the population growth pattern, and by creating a situation for more extensive modern mixing through social mobility.

Population Patterns

The population pattern of South America is unusual in many ways. In the first place, South America, like North America, still has a relatively sparse population when compared with most of the rest of the world. Brazil, for example, occupies a territory larger than the continental United States or Europe but has only recently exceeded a hundred million people. Second, the settlement pattern is one of isolated clusters of population, rural or urban. Hence very densely populated centers alternate with very sparsely settled regions. One-third of all South Americans live in five population clusters along the coasts and in the high basins. Third, the South American population has of late been growing faster than any other in the world except the Caribbean-Central American. Fourth, there is a very substantial migration under way within South America--from rural region to rural region, from countryside to towns, from coast to frontier and back. Some of this migration is associated with pasturage and transhumance or slash-burn agriculture, but most results from localized agricultural troubles (as in the Northeast dust bowl in Brazil) or from the effects of the Industrial Revolution. Fifth, the South American population is composed of a wide variety of ethnic and cultural groups combined in varying proportions. Race mixture has proceeded rapidly, and more than half the South Americans are of mixed ancestry. The primary elements have been the American Indian, or Amerind; the early colonists, mostly Spanish and Portuguese; the African slaves; and the recent immigrants from Europe and Asia.

The Amerinds probably made their way to South America down the mountain chain from Siberia and Alaska through North and Central America, though they could have come across the Pacific from Polynesia. At any rate, Indian peoples had established their southernmost outpost in the great Inca civilization of Peru long before Europeans discovered the Western Hemisphere existed. The only rivals to Inca civilization among Indian peoples were the Aztec and Maya groups of Central America. The descendants of these Inca peoples, who speak Quechua and Aymará, still make up much of the population of Andean states like Peru and Bolivia, where in many areas more people speak these Indian languages than Spanish. The Indian cultures beyond the Andes area have generally been absorbed into the Latin culture except on the still-primitive upper Amazon, though the Tupí-Guaraní language is widely spoken in and around Paraguay. What remains of Indian influence is found in the mestizo, or Indian-European, racial type and in cultural influences on Latin language and culture. Both the settled agriculturists of the Inca regions and the former nomadic tribes of the plains have in general been displaced and subordinated by European colonists and recent immigrants.

The first Europeans were conquistadores who came in the wake of Columbus' ships after 1492. They were mostly Spanish and Portuguese of lowly but knightly origin known as

caballeros. They were generally working for the government
so as to secure a fixed percentage of the booty, and they usually went back to Europe. Only later did colonists come--
traders first, then planters and farmers, then government officials. Many of them still returned to Europe, leaving Indian concubines and mestizo children. Ever so slowly, however, permanent settlers and their European wives came to
stay, to profit, and to raise children of European stock who
had never seen Europe. These were the criollos or creoles
who eventually made the South American revolution against
the Spanish and Portuguese. Most of the "Europeans" in
South America today are descended from creoles.

Africans were brought to South America as slaves because Indian slaves were unable to endure heavy labor and
were soon considered potentially Christian after the campaign
by Las Casas. Blacks proved physically fit and were also
thought to be cursed with the mark of Cain and so suitable
for slavery. Slavery itself was considered legitimate by European, Indian, and African cultures at that time, so all con-
spired to bring slavery to South America--and Black Africans
to Brazil and the Guianas. Most slaves came from the "hump"
of West Africa or from Angola, though proportionately more
came from the latter. They worked on sugar plantations under conditions much like those of the Caribbean Basin or the
American South. The regular and irregular racial interweav-
ings typical of plantation life produced mulatto and zambo, or
Black-European and Black-Indian mixtures, but in greater numbers than in regions farther north in the New World. Some
slaves escaped or were freed and became "freemen" mixing
with the general population. Along the frontier line moving
toward the interior the mixing was usually more rapid. Yet
another kind of experiment, the Black-founded, mixed-race
Republic of Palmares, existed for a short while in colonial
Brazil. When slavery was finally abolished in Brazil in the
1880s, the mixing of African with other types was speeded up
from its already rapid rate. Some Africans nevertheless
maintained elements of their original culture, the most famous
being the African religions of Macumba, Candomblé, and Xingu
in northern Brazil. Most African influence has occurred through
the assimilation of the Blacks' cultural traits into the local
traditions of Brazil and the Guianas, however.

The Spanish and Portuguese made it illegal for citizens
or subjects of other governments to settle in their empires
and fought several wars to keep out the British, French, and
Dutch, so it was not until after the Wars of Independence that

the immigrant population became diversified. But at the turn
of the twentieth century, several South American states, especially Argentina and Brazil, became concerned about their
relatively small populations and began offering free transportation and other incentives to any and all comers. And so
the Europeans came by the millions, mostly Spanish and Portuguese but also Italians, Germans, Poles, and many other
nationalities. Brazil's southernmost state, Rio Grande do Sul,
became predominantly German, for example, as did parts of
southern Chile. Italians, Slavs, and Jews rose rapidly in government and business in Buenos Aires, São Paulo, and other
cities. Relatively more immigrants were from southern and
eastern Europe than in North America, and they came later
and constituted a greater portion of the population. The Asians
came in lesser numbers, some as "coolies" in the Guianas
but most as Japanese immigrants to the cities of both coasts.
European or Asian, they were, like immigrants elsewhere,
ambitious in business and education, clannish in social relations, and reformist in politics. And they were received as
immigrants everywhere are received--with distrust by nativ-
ist rivals, with disdain by the old order, and with elation by
governments and industries hungry for cheap labor and skilled
hands. Thus the "immigrant communities" often retained their
culture and grew.

   South Americans of "mixed" ancestry come in so many
varieties that terms are not available for all "types. " Nor
do South American governments generally keep census records
of the numbers in any but the European-Indian, European-African, and African-Indian types. So confused is the situation
that hundreds of terms, both insulting and complimentary, are
used to describe the people in any area of South America.
Some of the usual Spanish and Portuguese terms, respectively,
for the three unmixed and the three mixed groups are blanco
and branco for Europeans; negro and preto or negro for African; indio and indio for Indians; mulatto and mulatto or pardo
for European-African; mestizo and mestiço or pardo for European-Indian; zambo and cafuso or pardo for African-Indian.
Even these relatively standard terms mask complex social and
emotional realities, of course. "Europeans, " for example,
could feel themselves to be still-Italian or still-Spanish, Ar-
gentine-Italian or Argentine-Spanish, or simply Argentines.
Pardo ("mixed"), the term used in Brazil's census, is likewise a confession of the impossibility of describing (and of a
lack of desire to describe) the offspring of a quadroon or oc-
toroon (one-fourth or one-eighth African and the remainder
European). And such "mixed" people, not to mention the In-

dians, may or may not want to "integrate" with the "overcul-
ture. " Moreover, these terms often do not mean the same
as their English equivalents, as in the case of "Negro, " which
usually means only the very blackest person in South America
but includes much lighter shades in North America.   Persons
considered "Black" in North America would not be "Negroes"
in Middle or South America, for example.

Some areas of South America are more mixed than
others.   It is true that the west is more Indian, the north
more African, and the south more European.   But such sim-
plification yields less than half the truth.   Four kinds of areas
can presently be distinguished: predominantly European; predominantly Indian; mixed with a large proportion of Negroes;
and mixed with a large proportion of mestizos.   The predominantly European areas are southern Brazil, Uruguay, and the
cities and plains of Argentina and Chile.   The Indian areas
are in the Amazon Basin and the Aymara-Quechua areas of
the Andes.   The heaviest Negroid areas are on the Caribbean
rim and in northern Brazil, and the mestizo areas cover the
rest.

The direction race mixing is taking so far in most of
South America is toward the whitening of the population.   The
immigrants are mostly white, and those who are not, like the
Japanese, have not intermarried to any great extent as yet.
A larger-scale migration from the Caribbean and Central America could lead to darkening, but so far such migration is minimal.   The upper- and middle-class whites who until now have
had as many children as darker people of the lower classes
have begun to limit their families, but more upper-class children survive because of better food and medical care.   Upper-
class, most often blanco, men also continue to have greater
access to lower-class, most often darker, women than the reverse.   Marriage between light and dark is often not frowned
upon in South America.   Not that there is any lack of prejudice.   Biases are simply more cultural than racial, more a
matter of wanting a mate who is "a good Catholic" or "of
good family, " a male who is "manly" (macho) and strong, or
a female with "dignity" (dignidad) and beauty.   These are the
matters which keep indios, negros, and blancos apart in many
areas.

Hence race does seem to be closely associated with
class differences.   In Brazil, among the most mixed of all
South American states, the relationship of skin color and class
position is clear despite Brazil's reputation for tolerance.

The situation in the rest of South America is similar. The darker the skin, the lower the class. A way up for educated South Americans of darker skin can exist through wealth and intermarriage, since there is far less prejudice than in the Caribbean or North America, especially with respect to the mulatto and the mestizo. But the influence of slavery and tenant labor nevertheless lives on in the class structure for most of the descendants of Indians and Africans in all of Latin America. It is possible to visualize the South American system of "social stratification"--the order of castes and classes--as a pyramid. One face of the pyramid is marked horizontally with the classes. On top is an upper class of landed gentry and exporters, new-rich industrialists and bankers, and a transitional lower-upper class group of professionals (high level churchmen, doctors, lawyers) and intellectuals (professors, managers). Next comes a middle class of the remaining intellectuals (priests, bureaucrats, teachers, office workers) independent businessmen and farmers, and skilled workers. At the base is a lower class of unskilled workers, small subsistence farmers and tenants, and tribal peasants. Another face of the pyramid shows the castes via curving vertical lines: a larger proportion of the blancos in the upper than the middle or lower classes; a larger proportion of negros and indios in the lower than the middle and upper classes; and the "mixed" filling the middle-class bulge but extending into the upper and lower classes. Blacks and Indians are more likely to be unskilled laborers or tenant farmers, mestizos and mulattos more likely to be priests and industrial workers, "Europeans" more likely to be bishops and bankers.

Ostensibly the South American social structure does not seem all that different from that of North America, in which North European Protestants tend to be upper class, Mediterraneans and East Europeans middle class, and Blacks, Indians, and Spanish-speakers lower class. But there are major differences with respect to "social mobility" within both classes and castes. The South American class structure simply has not provided the mobility familiar to many North Americans. The chief reason is that fewer places have been open in South America's upper and middle classes because economic development has been slow. Whether the "feudal system" of landed oligarchs has prevented progress in South America or there have been other causes, the upper class has remained minuscule and the middle class nothing like the vast center of North American life. The "middle sectors" are thus still fighting for their economic, social, and political lives in South America in the way they were in the United States in the mid-19th

century.   They and the lower classes are "revolutionary" because they see too little progress to provide social mobility
for everyone.   They tend to think that the rich must become
poorer for the poor to become richer because the gap is so
very, very wide in most parts of South America.   Yet they
tend to believe that an enlightened elite must lead the masses
until "development" takes hold.   Expansion has only just begun to act as a safety valve for these pressures, which are
felt by a far wider range of South than North Americans because the mass consumption society has not yet arrived.

"Minorities" in South America feel this pinch most, as in
North America.   But the "castes" of North America are in one
sense closer to the center of life, and in another sense farther
from it.   In South America, the Africans and Indians share a
nearly universal need for further development with the "mixed"
and "white" castes but are not generally in the forefront of demands for social change, whereas in North America Blacks and
Spanish-speakers are somewhat more isolated in their need for
further development but are frontrunners in the demand for social change.   Minority self-consciousness also seems less pronounced in South than in North America at this point--either because the situation is better, according to some, or because a
sense of roots has yet to develop, according to others.   Many
South Americans like to argue that there is less ethnic prejudice,
less alienation, and therefore less resistance because of the good
habits Iberians developed in their proximity to Africa or because
of the fraternité implicit in their French (as opposed to English)
Revolutionary heritage.   Recently liberal North Americans--and
increasingly some Marxists--have come to contend that South
Americans have simply been blinded by their continued belief that
they have no "race"problem" and that elsewhere conscious attempts to reform out such prejudices have made for greater progress.   Meanwhile, the South American presumption is that what
minorities require is "integration" when in fact the Indians have
always preferred "separation. "

Two population patterns are obviously affected by the
changes under way in the social structures of South America,
namely, migration and growth.   In one sense, the South American migration pattern demonstrated the successful beginnings
of modernization and mobility.   "Pre-industrial" or frontier
migration--immigrants from abroad, emigration from the
coasts to the interior--has in most countries given way to
"industrial" migration to the cities.   The immigration incentives of the generation of Irigoyen have not yet been torn down,
and the populating of the Amazon, of the Pampas and llanos,

and of the Andes goes on. Yet how far it can go in such jungle and mountain "wastelands" is uncertain. The good land on the "frontier" is in any case fast disappearing, and the dominant result of migration is urbanization. At present rates the populations of the Caracas, São Paulo, Rio, Buenos Aires, and Santiago areas could double and re-double by the end of the century. So in another sense South American development could well be distorted by the mobility it generates. Many formerly food-sufficient countries such as Venezuela are already importing foodstuffs because City need is outdistancing Countryside production. Yet "ruralization" programs seem a false hope despite heroic efforts like those of Brazil. All of this means that the "industrial" population pattern of South America--population increases from internal growth, movement to the cities--can be accommodated only by increasing agricultural efficiency, by paying for more imported food, or by controlling population growth.

Population growth is also closely related to development, of course. On the one hand, development provides the means of reducing death rates before citizens are conscious and capable of and willing to respond to the need for reducing birth rates. The result is the familiar rapid rise in population during early industrialization. Hence Latin America's highest-in-the-world population growth figures. Even Venezuela, with the highest per capita income in Latin America, has a rate that requires doubling the number of houses, schools, hospitals, and jobs every twenty years just in order to stay even. Since Venezuela is oil-rich, it can buy food and still invest in progress the way Britain was able to until World War II. Venezuela has a chance of staying ahead of its baby boom, in other words. Brazil may have enough of a safety valve in its frontier lands to do the same. Others, however, must run harder or reduce population growth. And even Venezuela and Brazil have too large a "dependent population"-- too many non-working young or old--for healthy development, since over half the population is in its teens or younger.

But at least two disagreements concerning South America's population-growth problem persist. First, will development not induce an automatic reduction in growth as it proceeds, assuming it does proceed? After all, say some, the better-educated, socially mobile, urban "moderns" have fewer children in South America just as they do elsewhere. The extent to which government ought to encourage family planning rather than merely proceed with development planning is therefore quite controversial throughout Latin America. North

Americans were lucky not to have faced the issue of whether
to pursue a government-sponsored birth control program because their industrial development preceded the saturation
point in population growth. But Latin Americans have to confront the issue of "free choice" more directly--despite the notion that fecundity demonstrates virility or femininity, despite
the feeling that it may be an act of selfishness rather than of
social responsibility to prevent conception, and despite the existence of powerful opposition to population planning in the
Church and the social structure.

The second debate, which is viewed as an evasion by
advocates of population planning, is whether birth control will
inhibit development, at least in nations with a still-open frontier. Revolutionaries argue that population control is merely
the way the status quo powers prevent challenges from newer,
radical nations growing stronger. Churchmen argue that population control is merely a way of evading responsibility toward the poor by shifting the burden to the unborn when sacrifice or sexual restraint by the living is more moral. Given
such disagreement as to whether population growth is part of
the problem or the solution, there is little wonder that creation of a "high industrial" or "post-industrial" population pat-
tern--stabilized numbers, reasonable distribution among urban,
rural, and suburban areas--is not generally one of the goals
of development planning. Many South Americans, who in this
respect have a greater margin for error than most Middle
Americans, believe that they can play the wealth strategy as
an alternative to population control.

Development Issues

South American institutions retain the flavor of a frontier society. The economy is underdeveloped and largely agricultural. Wide gaps in wealth and social prestige persist,
while standards of education are generally low and rates of
illiteracy high. But the economic and social order is not
stagnant. Great cities like São Paulo rival those of North
America in the splendor of their skyscrapers and the squalor
of their slums. Production and real wages are up, illiteracy
and disease rates are down, more in the cities than in the
countryside. Yet the "rural sector" still predominates, with
too many on the land producing too little because of poor methods. Over most of South America, two agricultural systems
exist side by side, the giant estate or plantation (called the
hacienda in Spanish and the fazenda in Portuguese) and the

village farming community. In some areas, however, recent European immigrants and governmental reforms have created a third type, the individually owned farm.

The greatest amount of arable land is in large estates, but their number and their size are diminishing. Some five per cent of the population has half the land, and three-fourths of the good land. This state of affairs came about during the Colonial and Revolutionary periods, when the great landowners absorbed first the village lands of the Indians and then, in some areas, the Church lands. This was done in spite of attempts of many governments, both colonial and independent, to prevent landowners from gaining too much strength. The power of the hacendados has until recently set them beyond the reach of the government and the Church, not to mention the laborers working on the haciendas. Even now the great estate owners retain much of their influence because their lands produce the sugar, coffee, and cattle without which South American economies would collapse. But few of the benefits of the great estates go to the laborers working on them.

Efforts to improve South American agriculture are related to the landholding systems. Few governments have tried to restore the village farming communities. To do so would probably lead to lowered production, as when Mexico tried to re-establish the Indians' collectively-owned tribal ejidos in some areas after the 1910 Revolution. The problem is that the peasants would produce only enough for themselves and not furnish food to the cities. Most governments are working toward individually owned farms by dividing up large estates among those who work on them and by encouraging immigrants to open up frontier lands. In this way southern Brazil and scattered areas in Chile, Argentina, and Venezuela have become pioneer-type farming areas. Sometimes increased production has resulted, sometimes not, depending on the skills of the new farmers. Communists, and some non-Communists, say a collective farm with all the former laborers working together with equipment furnished by the government would be better. So far no South American country has tried this solution to any significant degree, though many, especially Bolivia after the 1952 revolution, have considered it. The Cuban example in the Caribbean has given new popularity to this plan in much of South America, however, and the government of radical Socialist Salvador Allende began such a program on a small scale in Chile before being overthrown in 1973.

Besides landownership the one-crop economy and agricultural inefficiency are the most serious problems. "Monoculture" is best illustrated by Colombian coffee production
and Argentine cattle herding. Dependence on overseas markets, the interests of the great landowners, and the government's need for development capital make one-crop economies
difficult to change. Any drop in the price of coffee on the
world market damages Colombia severely. International pric-
ing agreements would help, but diversified agriculture would
help more. What modernization for efficiency's sake there
has been in agriculture is found in the commercial economy.
Coffee plantations and cattle ranches are sometimes run efficiently, but more often they are not. Mechanized equipment
is not widely used because hand labor is cheap. The "new
farmers" of Brazil, Argentina, Chile, and Venezuela have the
highest yields and the most equipment. They grow truck crops
for the cities and high-profit commercial crops such as soybeans, and offer the best hope so far for a diversified and
efficient agriculture As for the agricultural laborers on the
great estates and the Indians in the villages, they are desperately poor, uneducated, and inefficient. They often farm with
digging sticks. Some are so hungry that they chew narcotic
leaves or drink tea made from pain-killing plants.

The other "primary" economic activity, extracting resources, is also different in South than in North America.
The Roman Law used in Spain and Portugal says that water
and mineral rights belong to everyone. Thus the mines of
the Iberian empires belonged to the king to lease to those who
would work them for the state monopoly. Those who leased
the mines often claimed to own them, but the kings usually
kept control. The ore also belonged to the king, except for
the part contracted for by the leasing individual and his workers. The independent governments of South America still follow this law but are not always clear as to what it means.
For a time after independence foreign companies and local individuals were allowed to get "titles" to mines, oil deposits,
and the like. But recently most South American governments
have reclaimed the state's ownership rights to mineral wealth.
They have insisted that foreigners and citizens alike re-nego-
tiate contracts for the exploitation of these resources on terms
more favorable to the state. Some have re-created state monopolies over mining, expelling the "owners. "

This law is important because the mineral wealth of
South America could pay for modernization if properly exploited.
South American nationalists feel that Europeans and North

Americans have benefited more from the wealth of the continent than South Americans themselves. Foreign investment is welcomed, but only on South American terms. Nothing like the past practices of "foreign ownership" is tolerated. Most new contracts retain over half the profits for the host country and require smelting or refining to be done locally in order to encourage South American industry. The great multinational oil companies now must refine Venezuelan oil in Venezuela, for instance, rather than in the Netherlands Antilles as before. Native concerns usually must follow the same rules, and export of capital is often forbidden.

South American Socialists and Communists--and many nationalists as well--argue that progress would be faster if the government itself undertook to run the mines and oil fields, and some countries have made a start in this direction. Brazil, for example, has created the oil monopoly of Petrobras, and Bolivia has instituted nationalized tin production. Most governments still favor nationalization of all means of production in the Marxist sense only as a last resort, however, and before its fall the Allende government in Chile even agreed to pay compensation for the foreign copper companies it had nationalized. The tendency is to nationalize foreign but not domestic investments. Several countries--such as Chile, Peru, and Bolivia-- have oscillated to nationalization and back.

The difficulties with nationalized production are greater than is sometimes imagined, since the population usually demands more consumer items from a "popular government" and foreign investment evaporates. Thus the "popular governments" are often obliged to become more restrictive in machinery and improvements. Still, both Marxist governments like those of Cuba and Allende's Chile and nationalist regimes like those of Mexico, Bolivia, and Peru seem to be leaning toward increased nationalization as at least a temporary solution to the problem of capital for modernization. The problem the leadership is trying to avoid is division into a "dual society" of the old and the new.

The very rich and the very poor live in the countryside and engage in agriculture or mining. They represent the old order. The new South Americans are the middle groups of the cities who engage in the production of goods and services. They are the industrialists, the wage workers, the doctors, the teachers, and the government administrators. Their concerns are those of urban groups everywhere, that is, the cost of living, education for their children, national well-being, and world affairs. Some are native, some foreign; some very rich, some very poor; some well-educated, some almost illiterate; some happy, some desperate. But they have in common a hope in the urban frontier of the modern money economy. Whether they are able to build such an economy will probably determine the future of South America.

The problems they face are disillusioning. The Biblical saying that the rich get richer and the poor poorer is an everyday reality. Most often this is blamed on the fact that South America has a "dependent economy" or, as Marxists call it, a "neo-colonial economy." The industrial nations of Europe and North America simply got the jump on South America and the rest of the under-developed world. This makes South American development harder. It is not just that many of the profits of early industrialization have gone out of South America to pay for the foreign capital necessary to develop mines, communications networks, and basic industry. That can be remedied by an equitable division of profits in the future. A more basic problem is the necessity for selling low-priced agricultural products to buy increasingly higher-priced manufactured articles and machinery. South Americans are thus always running too slowly on a treadmill. They work harder and take lower real wages to modernize, only to find that the price has gone up. Modernization becomes more costly every day. The rich do get richer and the poor poorer.

Another problem is just as maddening for the middle groups of South America. That is the exaggerated inflation caused by the early stages of industrialization in every part of the world. Advanced industrial economies like those of the United States and the Soviet Union make ends meet by simply producing and selling more goods and services, but South American states cannot do that. There just are not enough middle-group people to buy the increased production. South Americans therefore have to make ends meet by raising prices. Everybody gets squeezed in the ensuing inflation, the economy gallops away, and development costs still more. Political tensions often result, too. After all, when the cost of bread doubles in a year, everyone wants a raise.

The only way out is to make some hard social decisions and carry out some reforms, however difficult that may be politically. In the first place, governments must insist on help from abroad in the form of high prices for exports and low prices for imports. This is more important than outright foreign aid, though such aid is helpful if the political price is not too high. The primary requirement, however, is a wider internal market. Only a "mass market" will allow local producers to flourish. And of course the growth of the middle groups will require government aid in education and training, the building of a transportation and communication system, and the funding of new enterprises. Hence either private or public middle groups must of necessity replace the estate owners and mining magnates as the main influence on the government.

The lower La Plata valley, central Chile, the São Paulo-Rio de Janeiro complex, and northwestern Venezuela have already made this transition, as have isolated areas in Colombia and Peru. British trade and investment set Argentina and Chile on their way in the late nineteenth and early twentieth centuries. For the most part the Chilean middle group was of local European extraction, but in Argentina the more recent immigrants, particularly the Italians, have played a large role. Venezuelan industrialization has begun more recently with the help of a flood of United States investment, as was also the case in the industrial centers of the Andean countries. Brazil has received aid from both European and United States sources. The middle groups in all these countries are mixed, though local people of European and mixed extraction predominate.

The nationalism of the middle groups has so far enhanced moderization by encouraging investment at home, education, and public works. But this can only go so far. Naturally the success of industrialization in these few areas makes it harder for other regions to do the same, unless, of course, aid is given to the underdeveloped parts through national or regional projects. Furthermore, the desire of most nations to produce the widest possible range of products could become self-defeating. A South American common market in which Brazil concentrated on coffee and automobiles, Argentina on meat and washing machines, and Peru on copper and television sets would be better in the long run. But efforts in this direction have not been especially successful because of ideological differences and rival economic interests among the members of common market organizations. Nationalists find it difficult to persuade local workers--and themselves-- that it is more efficient, even if jobs are scarce, to import autos from a neighboring country.

Yet South Americans, indeed all Latin Americans, know that their only real chance for modernization is income through trade. The Latin American Free Trade Association, formed in 1960, reflects their concern. Both South and Middle American states belong, but the greatest volume of trade takes place among South American states. The aim of the association is to reduce the tariffs among the member states in order to build up wider markets inside Latin America itself. There is some talk of eliminating tariffs completely, as the Andean Common Market and the Central American Free Trade Association are trying to do. Meanwhile, the two major trade problems remain: the too-small internal market resulting from general underdevelopment, and the adverse balance of trade with Europe and North America. There is little likelihood that South American industry will be able to widen its share of the world market rapidly enough, so El Dorado, if it is to exist, must be built on the vast population still outside the money economy. Only tariff protection and economic development can offer a solution to this difficulty.

The key is thus the development plan. By now virtually every country has one. There is everywhere an emphasis on agrarian reform--on elimination of monoculture, on improvement of production through mechanization and modern agronomy, and in most cases on redistribution of the larger landholdings, foreign and domestic, to the landless and near-landless peons. The problem of marginal minifundia has not been tackled in most places because that means "The Revolution," as it is universally called in Latin America, must devour some of its own children. In the end, however, the way up for the rural poor is the way out--to the city. Hence the attention to industrialization.

Generally, the plans depend on a combination of private and public capital to build the factories that generate urban employment and increased production. National development may be managed, for example, by a "development corporation" like those of Chile or Venezuela so that public influence always outweighs private in management decision-making. Thus even Inter-American Development Bank and International Monetary Fund capital is under the control of the country's leaders whether or not resources have been nationalized. This is done because South America cannot do without foreign capital as yet, but also wants to avoid the manipulative foreign influence of the past. A "mixed economy" somewhere between laissez-faire market enterprise and a nationalization for which the administrative resources are not available is the usual answer. Most plans also follow the three-step development plan so popular in the Third World:

first, make production of crops and raw materials efficient
and profitable; second, process the products native to the region or the country; and last, use the profits for starting
heavy industry and high-profit, skilled-level production.

Two points in every plan are inevitably controversial.
One is how much "social investment"--education, housing,
medical care--it is necessary or desirable to provide for the
millions who are moving from the rural-agricultural to the
urban-industrial economy.   On the one hand, such social
overhead is expensive and benefits some people more than
others, thus creating a "meritocracy" of technicians, bureaucrats, and intellectuals.   On the other hand, only a healthy
and contented population that is relatively well-educated can
or will execute the development plan over the long haul.
Most planners have opted for more rather than less social
overhead, particularly in more radical countries.   But since
1964 Brazil has taken the opposite direction.

The second critial issue is whether a country can be
force-marched toward economic development while practicing
a political democracy complete with elections, congressional
haggling, and lobbying by special interests like the landlords,
the army, the unions, and the Church.   For this puzzle many
solutions have been tried: one-party dominance on the model
of Mexico in Bolivia and Brazil; army directorship like Perón's
in various places; bureaucratic planning by the intellectuals
here and there; or, at least for a while, traditional coalition
politics in Uruguay, Venezuela, and Chile.   Indeed, the political factor is one of the weakest points in the economic development schemes, since the instability of the political sphere
makes long-range planning specious in many countries.

Nations and Parties

One of the most striking contrasts in history is the
comparison of the political development of North and South
America since the beginning of the nineteenth century.   In
1815 the United States of North America had just won the War
of 1812 and confirmed its independence.   The North American
revolutionaries did not succeed in their aim of liberating Canada and joining it to the United States, but neither did the
Europeans succeed in dividing the continent into rival western
and southern states via the Aaron Burr Conspiracy or the
Civil War.   Hence when the Southern secession was crushed
in 1865 and a united Canada achieved autonomy in 1867, a
two-nation North America emerged.

The South American liberators, Bolívar and San Martín, had the same vision as the North American revolutionaries. In 1822, at the height of the South American revolution, they met at Guayaquil, Ecuador, to coordinate efforts for a United States of South America. But the odds were against them, and they failed. For one thing, the hot-headed Bolívar and the moderate San Martín did not get on well with each other. For another, the gap between Gran Colombia in the north and west and the Argentinian-Chilean area in the south was already too wide to bridge. The population centers were much more localized and self-interested in South than in North America, where the Appalachian mountains held the eastern core of the United States stable and scattered people going west. In South America the La Plata, Chilean, Andean, and Venezuelan settlements were separated from each other by vast expanses of uninhabited lands and so broke apart. And there was always Brazil. Canada lay alongside the United States, but Brazil was between the Spanish-speaking portions of the proposed United States of South America.

So South America dissolved into independent republics. Generally, these republics were based on the divisions imposed by the Spanish and Portuguese in colonial times. In the Spanish colonies, there were four vice-royalties in New Spain (Central America and the Caribbean), New Granada (Venezuela, Colombia, and Ecuador), Peru (Peru, Bolivia, and Chile), and La Plata (Argentina, Uruguay, and Paraguay). Administration was effective near the cities but weaker with increasing distance from the capitals of Mexico City, Bogotá, Lima, and Buenos Aires. Thus the captaincies-general and presidencies in places like Chile and Ecuador developed the habit of governing themselves and refused to give it up after independence. The Portuguese empire did not break up to the same extent because the crown maintained unity of a sort until independence in 1889, and because the population was more centralized on the east coast, as in North America. Thus the United States of Brazil emerged intact, whereas the Spanish-speaking part of the continent divided into separate republics. The Guianas remained under British, Dutch, and French rule until the mid-twentieth century.

One blessing has accrued to South Americans along with the curses of their state system. Since borders run in mostly uninhabited areas, there have been few wars. The one densely inhabited border area, between Argentina and Brazil, did cause wars in the early nineteenth century. But the creation of the buffer states of Uruguay and Paraguay put an end to those conflicts. Other wars were caused by the existence of valuable resources in border areas, as in the case of the War of the Pacific (1879-83) between Chile, Peru, and Bolivia over possession of the Atacama desert. The Chaco War (1930s) between Paraguay and Bolivia was a nationalist aberration with little gained and much lost by both sides. Despite today's relative peace among South American states, border disputes persist between Argentina and Chile, Venezuela and Guyana, and several others. Borders are not well-defined, and that could prove a problem when the interior is settled in the future. Still, the chief curse is instability, not war.

The political instability of South America is legendary. Several countries have had literally dozens of revolutions and constitutions. Since independence Venezuela has had a new constitution every six years, Ecuador and Bolivia one every ten years. Argentina and Chile were the most stable of the Spanish-speaking countries until Venezuela achieved stability and the southern states fell into instability after World War II. Brazil's disorderly politics occurs most frequently at the state level, whereas national politics have, except for the turbulent postwar period, been somewhat less chaotic, and many would say less democratic, than in Spanish-speaking America. It is no accident that the richest countries are the most stable; or, if one prefers it the other way round, that the most stable are the richest. Internal stability remains a problem for even the most prosperous South American nations, however. Caudillos--Strongmen, especially military strongmen-- are still the most common form of government in South America.

The chief cause of political instability is economic and social inequality. Changes in the locus of power, wealth, and prestige resulting from the Democratic and Industrial Revolutions are transforming the character of South American politics. In the nineteenth century political instability was caused by rivalries between factions of the landowners. Caudillismo had the character of a blood feud. Yet even the Blancos (Whites) and Colorados (Reds) in Uruguay, the most clearly delineated parties of the last century, fought over government patronage more often than over their stated principles of "conservatism" and "liberalism." Most politicians and their followers often dispensed with party labels altogether and became known by the name of the leader, a custom held over in such terms as Peronistas, the designation for followers of the Argentine politician Juan Perón. Perón ac-

tually represented a new phenomenon hidden under the old label, however. For he based his movement on the newly de-
mocratized and industrialized groups of white- and blue-collar
workers in the towns. Like Vargas in Brazil, he was impressed by the economic successes of Mussolini in Italy and
Lenin in Russia, and perhaps not sufficiently impressed by
their political failures. Without the emergence of the middle
groups of the towns, whose interests are not like those of the
landowners or the peasants, modern party movements would
not have been possible.

The political order is presently disrupted by the struggle between the representatives of the landowners on the one
hand and of the middle sectors on the other. Every political
institution is troubled in this way. The armed forces, the
Church, and the state bureaucracy, long the pillars of oligar-
chical control, are shaking or crumbling. In the armed forces, the navy is usually the most aristocratic, the air force
next, and the army least. This is true because the army is
conscripted from all national and social groups and often has
national consciousness. Rivalries within the army and among
the services are therefore often severe and occasionally break
out into open fighting. Some of this results from personal rivalries as before, but increasingly it has taken on the character of national as against local concerns. The generals who
have governed Peru since 1968 are radical nationalists, for
example, whereas the generals who have recently governed
Brazil and Argentina are much more traditional. The Church
hierarchy, generally conservative, has also been challenged
by modernizers from the middle groups who serve as local
priests. One archbishop, Dom Helder Câmara of northern
Brazil, has encouraged such priests against the wishes of
the Pope. As for the state's bureaucracy, most of the people who now work in it are educated professionals rather than
the sons of the wealthy, at least in the southern part of the
continent. Yet on the whole the oligarchy retains greater control over these institutions than over the parties and legislatures, chiefly because it takes education to become powerful
in the armed forces, the Church, or the bureaucracy--and
education is still confined to the wealthy more often than not.

The parties, politicians, and political institutions have
hardly inspired confidence, however. The apple of liberty
plucked by Bolívar and San Martín quickly turned to ashes in
the mouth. The Enlightenment theories derived from the American and French revolutions led to the creation of constitutional governments with executive, legislative, and judicial branches,

but the functioning of these political institutions has been very different in North and South America. The presidency in South American republics is invariably weaker than in North America. The president is usually forbidden by the constitution to run for a second term, which means that opponents need only wait out his first term in order to thwart his program. National congresses and especially local governments are therefore much stronger in South America than in the United States. Government is also less effective, which slows development and encourages coups d'état by the Strongmen. Many a revolution has been started when a South American president, out of personal interest or genuine national concern, has tried to succeed himself.

The legislative branch is not much more effective than the executive, partly because of election procedures and partly because of partisanship and political patronage. South American election laws generally provide for both proportional representation and disenfranchisement of illiterates. Proportional representation means that each party gets the proportion of legislators corresponding to its percentage of the vote, so that no one votes for a man, just for a party. The number of parties always increases under this arrangement, since the smaller parties are assured of some representation. Thus there are dozens of parties in most South American countries, as in west and south Europe, where the proportional representation system is also used. The advantage of this system is that, theoretically, no one's opinion remains unexpressed, as it can in a two-party system like that of the United States or a one-party state like the Soviet Union. But of course the disenfranchisement of illiterates over most of South America leaves much of the population without a political voice anyway. The question of enfranchising illiterates is a serious problem in the Indian states and in Brazil, whereas the mostly literate south and Venezuela suffer less from it.

Only after the legislature has been elected does the real business of politics begin. The presiding officers of the legislative houses and, in most places, the government ministers have to be selected by the legislators. The parties, not the president, select the executives. Partisanship then comes into play, with the legislators wanting to know what patronage will come their way if they vote for so-and-so. Party coalitions emerge to do the business of government. In Uruguay until 1966 the "presidency" was a committee of several men, as in Switzerland, but in most South American countries the cabinet is more like those of France and Italy --when the Strongmen are not in power.

The parties have a difficult time making stable coalitions because of their different interests and ideologies. Party systems have oscillated between two-party, multi-party, and single-party alternatives. In the nineteenth century the two-party alternative was the most frequently used as Conservatives and Liberals vied for the support of those few who could vote. The Conservatives favored strong government, mercantilist economics, and religious education and damned the Liberals as potential "democrats" who threatened to let loose the political forces of the incapable, illiterate masses. The Liberals, on the other hand, argued that society would remain forever backward if the military men, the large landowners, and the priests continued to govern. The educated classes, the "natural aristocracy," should therefore develop parliamentary government, free enterprise, and science as an alternative. Politics took on the character of a struggle between Countryside and Town, Church and Freemasonry, Conservatives and Liberals. Until the beginning of the twentieth century partisan politics consisted of a debate as to which elite should guide the country. Conservatives and Liberals alike looked with disfavor on the "anarchy" of the French experiment with multiparty coalitions and wider franchises.

Yet the new century brought new conditions. The Democratic and Industrial Revolutions made the masses politically conscious and economically valuable as factory workers. Multi-party democracy became the rule rather than the exception. The traditional Liberal parties lost their support to parties more radical in interest and program and in many places disappeared altogether, while the Conservative parties remained the home of the interests of the military, the landowners, and the Church. The Right (Conservatives) was then opposed by new parties of the Center and Left, parties wider in scope and interest. The politics of Europe spilled over into South America in Radical and Social Democratic, and later Communist and Fascist, parties, and native nationalist experiments emerged as well.

Radicals and Social Democrats favored multi-party parliaments with stronger powers than the executive branch--in other words, governments like those of France, Italy, and the Spanish Republic. Christian Democrats and Christian Socialists, who believed in charity and just treatment by employers and workers toward each other, got a late start in South America but became strong after World War II in several places, particularly in Chile and Venezuela.

Local South American nationalist parties emerged with something of the same approach of the European-derived parliamentary parties. The first South American nationalist party was the APRA of Peru, founded after World War I by Victor Raúl Haya de la Torre. Acción Democrática of Venezuela and experiments by Perón in Argentina, Vargas in Brazil, and the revolutionists of Bolivia and Peru have been of the same character. All these nationalists were influenced by the success of the Mexican government party after the revolution of 1910, whether or not they thought in similar one-party terms. Most South American governments at present are supported by some form of multi-party coalition of these Center and Left parties--if the Strongmen are not in power.

The same disgust with electoral and parliamentary politics which motivates the Strongmen and the Conservatives drives the adherents of the single-party state, the members of so-called totalitarian parties, the Fascists, the Communists, and the Castroites. The Fascists were strong so long as the fortunes of Hitler and Mussolini were growing in the 1930s and 1940s, but their appeal is now gone. They flourished in Brazil and Argentina, where the German and Italian immigrants sometimes found them attractive. Yet Vargas outlawed the green-shirted Integralistas in 1938, and the Argentine government was only slightly less hostile to the Fascists there during World War II. The Fascist view was that both Liberalism and Communism were self-interested middle-class and worker-class movements, whereas the Fascists were interested in "total" or "integral" national movements to benefit all classes equally. Fascists were crushed nevertheless because they were thought to be foreign-dominated by the Brazilian and other governments. Yet Vargas and Perón had to become more "nationalist" and "socialist" in order to counter their appeal. Fascism is no longer a viable organized political movement in South America.

Communism is viable, organized, and growing. Marxist ideology has appeal because it promises inevitable progress toward a world "community" in which everyone knows where his next meal is coming from. In the Marxist view, despotic kings once held all property until the feudal nobles cut themselves in on the deal. Then the bourgeois industrialists and bankers grew in wealth and strength until they pushed aside the plantation owners and turned the serfs into wage-workers, a process sanctified by the American and French Revolutions. Now the wage-workers of factory and farm, the proletarians, are being provoked by the bourgeois with low wages and high prices for food, housing, and other necessities. Hence the second, or workers', revolution is inevitably coming because the selfishness of the ruling classes always makes so many enemies that an eruption occurs. This "dialectic" has carried humankind from a system in which only one owned property and all others were slaves (despotism) to systems of a few free (feudalism) and many free (bourgeois democracy), and soon such "progress" will mean that all are free--because of public ownership of "the means of production" through nationalization of the property of the rich. All Marxists argue that enough capital will be released by expropriation to fund moderization. Besides, "the people" will then work harder because they will, at last, be working for themselves.

But Communism goes beyond its Socialist cousin in promising a shortcut to the "common good"--by skipping the capitalist stage. The "people's party" will, as in Russia and China, hasten modernization by turning peasants into engineers without first making them shopkeepers. Most Communists in South America presently follow the Russian argument that the workers in the cities are the proper focus for Communist organization. The Chinese or Maoist claim that the peasant masses are the real revolutionaries has recently gained on the Russian-dominated official parties, however. Hence in many countries there are now two Communist parties, one of which works within the unions according to the Russian plan, and one of which attempts to organize guerrilla groups among the peasants, as Mao Tse-tung would have it. One or both of these parties may be legal, depending on the country, though in most of South America both are illegal.

Even more radical is the Fidel Castro-inspired guerrilla movement whose hero, "Che" Guevara, was killed in 1967 while leading a small revolutionary band in Bolivia. Their idea is that the peasants and workers cannot start a revolution without the leadership of dedicated, armed insurrectionaries in the mountains. Generally they will have nothing to do with the "soft" Communists of the Maoist and, especially, the Russian variety. These Guevaristas, and their urban descendants such as the Tupamaros in Uruguay, form one of Latin America's unique contributions to the would-be Marxist-Leninist "world revolution." Like all other Communists, however, they agree that a single-party dictatorship of the proletariat must follow the revolution.

The Socialists, in contrast to the Communists, accept the possibility of a Marxist revolution by ballot rather than bullet. They believe truly democratic elections will bring the people to power and that the welfare state is not a bribe to the working class to prevent revolution but a step toward the workers' state. They do not believe that provoking "reaction" --oppression by the classes, frustration of the masses--is necessary to produce "revolution." Hence South America's other major contribution to the Marxist movement has been to prove that a Socialist-Communist "popular front" could elect a still-revolutionary Socialist, Salvador Allende, in Chile-- that a revolution by ballot might in fact prove possible, especially in a Third World country. The overthrow of Allende in 1973, which "proved" to Marxist radicals that the alternative of "people's democracy" would not be tolerated by the "bourgeois democrats," thus restored the hostility of Socialists and Communists. But Allende's government also raised questions among South Americans of a parliamentary persuasion as to whether the Socialists' first commitment was to workers' revolution or to democracy, and whether the Communists in a popular front would be willing to surrender power at the next election.

This issue has a different quality in South than in North America, however, because of the powerful role of Catholicism and the deep divisions within Catholic opinion. Conservative Catholics view all modern materialism, capitalist or socialist, with horror. They believe that "the brotherhood of man" can be enhanced by organizing the state according to "Christian principles," which is to say principles of self-sacrifice, "just" rather than maximum prices, and treatment of everyone as a member of the "family" of God. Hence the need for church-state cooperation to teach morality in the schools. Hence the necessity for laws to prevent landowners or industrialists or workers from taking advantage of each other. Hence the role of the Church in setting a moral example of "poverty, chastity, and obedience"--of economic, sexual, and political restraint.

At first these sentiments led South American conservatives to oppose democracy, secular education, and economic development, which created the same conflict between Church and Freemasonry as existed in Latin Europe. But the Papal encyclicals Rerum Novarum (1891) and Quadragessimo Anno (1931) eventually made peace with modernism on the basis of "justice," meaning a concentration on the good of all rather than selfish personal good. In Spain and Portugal, this produced the "corporate states" of Franco and Salazar, but in Argentina it took on a character which resembled that of

Mussolini's Italy in Perón's Justicialismo. The Catholic rich and the Catholic poor were to be drawn together on the basis of "justice" and "brotherhood," according to Peronist theory.

Since World War II this conservative Catholicism has given ground to more democratic Catholic opinion in both Latin Europe and Latin America. The rise of the Christian Democrats as an alternative to the Marxists was sanctioned, in fact, by the encyclicals Mater et Magistra of Pope John XXIII and Populorum Progresio of Pope Paul VI in the early and late 1960s, respectively. Pope John declared that not even atheistic Marxists were beyond the ecumenical love of the Church, and Pope Paul made the non-violent elimination of colonialism and poverty--the "Development of Peoples," as the title of the encyclical says--the duty of every Christian. Such has been the inspiration of the Christian Democrats such as Archbishop Câmara of Brazil and Eduardo Frei of Chile, no less than those of France, Italy, or, for that matter, the "Kennedy democrats" in North America. "I am my brother's keeper" is their motto.

But some of their more radically democratic brothers and sisters have adopted a so-called "theology of hope" or "theology of liberation." Their "revolution for God's sake" has taken the form of non-violent resistance like that of Martin Luther King and César Chávez in the United States or, in a few cases such as that of Camilo Torres in Colombia, of guerrilla priests. The Church hierarchy would not go that far, however, and excommunicated Torres long before he was killed in battle. Still, the "worker priests" have joined the production lines with the workers in many areas, and many parishes are centers of "social Christianity"--and of resistance to the Strongmen.

The appeal of both Socialism and Catholicism rests only in part on their acceptance of some kind of "revolution," however. There are also elements of one-for-all-and-all-for-one idealism which have likewise conditioned the "liberalism" of South America. The so-called "Latin spirit" simply seems much less amenable to the individualist approach to politics than is common in North America. Even in the nineteenth century South American Liberals sought the "positive state" of August Comte rather than the "negative state" North Americans derived from John Stuart Mill and Herbert Spencer. The Mill-Spencer doctrine of states rising from savagery (anarchy, poverty, superstition) through monarchy (tyranny, mercantilism, state religion) to liberty (representative government, free enterprise, science) had little appeal in Latin America, in part because it placed Latin Americans in frontier anarchy or statist tyranny.   Yet the main appeal of Comte's influence came from his claim that nations must be led by their elites from "theology" to "philosophy" and finally to the science of society or "sociology. "   This "positivism" has continued long after political parties espousing its doctrine have disappeared. South Americans expect their leaders to lead, not to follow; they expect citizens to be helped by their leaders, not protected from them.

Today South Americans still believe, then, in a public philosophy that values a "positive state. "   But the political infighting of all the ideologies and the fragility of national institutions often make "positive" action extremely difficult.   South Americans' twentieth-century answers to this problem of unity and effectiveness have been those of other developing countries in times of crisis.   Sometimes they have tried to stir up revolutionary or nationalist fervor to create a common purpose. In this respect Betancourt or Allende was little different from Jefferson or Jackson.   Sometimes they have resorted to one-party or dominant-party governments for decades at a time. In this respect Vargas and his nationalists were little different from Lincoln and his dominant post-1865 Republicans dealing with slavery and industrialization.   Sometimes they have relied on charismatic leaders to inspire them to unified action.   Remember Wilson and World War I, Franklin Roosevelt and the Depression.   And sometimes they have resorted to disciplined management--to Strongmen.   Recall the United States occupation and "reconstruction" of the defeated Confederacy.   The greater the threat of disunity, the greater the efforts at unification.   The greater the need for development, the greater the efforts of the positive state to do something about development.   Rightist generals in Brazil, leftist generals in Peru--both doing the same thing, namely, responding to South Americans' expectations that leaders will do something "positive" about development.

South Americans' public philosophy also differs somewhat from that of North America with respect to personal security and personal liberty as a result of the greater favor accorded the positive state.   The attitude toward security and liberty is summed up by the statement, "Life is struggle. " Security is difficult to come by, partly no doubt because poverty always undermines security, but also partly because, as Europeans have always said, "frontier" societies of the Western Hemisphere are all more violent than the "civilized" states of the Old World. Crime is indeed endemic throughout Latin America. Crimes against persons are probably more frequent even than in North America. Crimes against property are more serious still--everything from theft to official corruption. But the attitude is that protection is a private rather than a public matter. The judicial branch, it is believed, cannot create an objective legal standard because of political pressures upon it, and the police agencies often enforce even just laws in a partisan fashion. In this respect the Military Strongman who overthrows a legally-elected government--or the CIA which aided in Allende's overthrow--is just an oversized example of many a local judge or police chief. Workers are treated unfairly in one area, owners in another, depending on whose party dominates the region. It is usually assumed that friends in high places (connections) are necessary for political protection, and that going armed is the best assurance of personal safety.

This traditional South American view that personal welfare is dependent on influence or strength seems to be receding, however. "Law" rather than "politics" or "revolution," the formal rather than the informal acts of state, have gained considerably in South America since World War II. The rich may still be kidnapped for ransom or revolution on a not-infrequent timetable. The poor may still suffer from official corruption or brutality. Political assassinations may continue. Crime may flourish. Riots and coups may come and go. But enough stability has been achieved to allow for more than a little personal and political liberty. Venezuela is presently most advanced in this respect. There are few parties and citizens without full political rights--the Communists being the glaring exception. There are few proscribed activities, those having to do with divorce, abortion, and other sexual taboos being the notable exceptions. No one is kept from an education because of his creed or origin--though religious and class preferences exist, of course. To be sure, Venezuela is the richest and relatively the most stable state in South America now, and elsewhere the competition of ideas and toleration of diverse practices is less. Toleration may even have slipped a bit in the tense '60s and early '70s, when Chile, for one, succumbed to Left, then Right conformity. But the long-term trend seems toward more personal liberties, albeit with less nonconformism than in North America. South Americans, like other "Latins," fear they would "lose face" if they were so nonconformist as to insult or outrage their neighbors. This dignity (dignidad) is socially, not politically, enforced, though.

The wide range of personalities among South America's leaders, past and present, is obviously a result of the regional, ideological, and behavioral complexities of the political order. The leadership comes from every caste and class, though more from the blancos and the rich; from every region, though more from City than Country; from every ideology, though more from left than right. But in personality they are as different as the pistol-toting Vargas, the urbane Kubitschek, and the fiery Lacerda; the stiff Stroessner and Pinochet and the open Frei and Allende; the idealist Haya de la Torre and the realist Betancourt; the ascetic Câmara and the hedonistic Perón. The small influence over circumstances of even the most powerful leaders is also the result of the same complexities. Cooperation is lacking. Citizens often fail to do--or lack the skills to do--what seems necessary. Capital flees the country. Resources are unavailable. Skills are inadequate. Taxes are evaded. Decisions are ignored. Justice is hard to come by. Politics remains unstable. Events are out of control. The world's powers seem unsympathetic. Modernization lags, and popularity sags. So the temptation to build up the "positive state" and create "order and progress" is real. Still, there is more order than before--and more progress--despite the resistance of bedrock social realities.

Social Realities

The politicians may propose, but the family still disposes in South America. And by "the family" most South Americans mean something very different from what most North Americans do. South Americans think "horizontally," whereas North Americans think "vertically." To South Americans it is still very important not only to live close to one's parents, brothers, and sisters but also to uncles and aunts, cousins, nieces, nephews, and godparents and godchildren. What the president of the republic is doing is less important than that one's uncle's godson has just acquired a job in the post office and can get married. North Americans are more interested in the "vertical" figure of the president than the "horizontal" figure of the uncle, not to mention the uncle's godson, if he even has one. Only in the middle groups of the big cities, and often not there, has this extended family structure begun to give way to the nuclear family. Many a city worker, educated at the expense of the family and the patrón back on the farm, is still sending money "back home" to help a cousin or niece.

The tenant farming or sharecropping system of the hacienda rests on the family structure as much as on the hard facts of economic exploitation. The relationship of the patrón, or landowner, and the peón, or tenant farmer, is often very intimate. The patrón is the godfather of the peón, or the peón's children, which makes him "family." The oldest son of the family is sometimes given release from work for schooling and, if bright, aided to get a secondary education. Sick peones are sometimes cared for by the patrón's wife, who is, after all, "family" too, and usually feels her responsibility deeply. Tenant farming is thus debt bondage, abject poverty, and hard work--and "social security." The city often seems cold compared with the warmth of the Big House.

Hence the love for the land. The "little homeland"--patria chica in Spanish--seems far more important than the nation as a whole. Parties matter little to most outside the cities, but our politician, our man, the guy from our little homeland matters a lot. He's almost "family" too. And what has he done for us lately? Has he got a sewer for his "family," or a government job for that first son we've all worked so hard to educate? If he hasn't, he probably will, for he feels the appeal of the "family" connection too, and knows the value of the votes as well. Thus are caciques (local bosses) born, and caudillos (larger bosses) in their turn. That Vargas was a gaucho from Rio Grande do Sul mattered to southern Brazilians because it meant a challenge to the "bigwigs" of São Paulo and Minas Gerais. It meant something like the South against the North or the West against the East in United States politics.

Yet the cities are beginning to change all this a great deal. The city worker may send money to cousins in the country and visit there often, but will his children? Probably not. Their new extended family will be the neighborhood, and the second urban generation will live with spouse and children, and perhaps parents, without as much regard for uncles, cousins, and others. Godparents and godchildren there will be, but the state now guarantees the future of children more than godparents do. There are millions of second-generation urban people in South American cities, and someday they will be in the majority. Rural South America is becoming urban and modern, and is paying the price West Europe and North America have paid, namely, the loss of the security of the extended family. Union leaders, politicians, teachers, and friends stand in the emotional universe where uncles, patrones, priests, and cousins used to. Meanwhile, the tension between the still-rural majority and the new urban middle groups divides South America.

The bridge between the urban and the rural is the "community"--the village in the rural area, the neighborhood in the cities. Its heart is the parish church, its head the local school, whether parochial or secular. The political powers in the community run a poor third in respect. The priest baptizes and buries, confesses and consoles, and guards the moral and, through charity, the material welfare of his flock. The "conservative" Church is therefore still sometimes at odds with the "liberal" schoolmasters, whose function is to "modernize" the children so that they can enter the wider world. The warfare between small town and mass society has thus intruded into most villages of Latin America the way it has in the dispute over Darwinism in North American schools. Moreover, the coming of the mass media--the movies in medium-sized towns, TV in the local cantina, transistor radios almost everywhere--has accelerated the process of shaking up the community and setting it on the road to "progress." Migration out and back has also loosened family and community ties.

But even the urban areas still have "communities" of a sort, that is, neighborhoods with the church and the school as focal points. The poor suburbs especially--favelas in Brazil, ranchos in Venezuela, barrios in many places--are the home of millions who are neither "traditional" nor "modern" but "transitional." The priest and the schoolteacher are part of the community there, but the national and urban politicians are scarcely visible except on TV and are considered to tax and police too much while providing no water, sewers, streets, and other social services. When all this is added to the geographical, ethnic, economic, and political divisions in South America, it becomes obvious that the two major social realities involved in the evolution of a common bond of nationhood are diversity and change--and that South Americans' beliefs and behavior are shaped by these realities. Almost any aspect of daily life shows the pattern.

Perhaps nothing reveals South America's diversity better than its eating habits, however. Every heritage shows. Iberians have contributed not only the style of the typical kitchen, all tile, copper, and earthenware. They have also added a variety of cuisines as broad as the north-European ethnic groups' contributions to the foods of the United States: from Castille, a taste for roasted meats, stews, and sausages;

from Catalonia and the Basque country, a seafood palate second to none; from the Levantine provinces, a cuisine featuring rice and fruits; from Andalusia, the cowboy cookery which
has now spread so widely; and from Portugal--not Spain, as
is commonly believed--a taste for the spicy. The monks
brought their talents with wines and spirits, the nuns their
winning ways with dulces (sweets) for holy occasions, and every Iberian an appetite for milk products and sauces. The
Africans added more tropical flavors--recipes for more spices,
more tropical fruits and nuts, more and different kinds of ce-
reals. The Indians gave potatoes, special beverages, and tobacco. Later arrivals added Italian, German, Mideast, and
North American elements.

The result is a variety of foods equal to such a varie-
gated population. Take Brazil's feijoada completa as an instance of assimilation of traditions: half a dozen spiced meats
and sausages; toasted manioc meal (farofa); rice with onions
and tomatoes; rum with lemon or some cachaça (sugar-cane
brandy); and of course some fruit, a cocoanut pastry, and
coffee. Or you could have the simpler vatapá (fish and shrimp
in ginger-and-peanut sauce) and get the same impression, or
experience what has happened to North Africa's couscous (cuscuz) in the Northeast (tapioca, sugar, and cocoanut) and in
São Paulo (cornmeal or manioc and anything). Farther south
Brazilians' and Argentinians' tastes merge in a yen for fired
bife which is shared by cattle cultures in Venezuela, Central
America, Texas, and Andalusia. Argentines can do things
with beef--the stew-in-a-squash called carbonada criolla, the
beef-around-vegetables called matambre or "kill-hunger"--that
go far enough beyond a barbeque (asado in Argentina, barbacoa
in Mexico) to make a French chef blush. The Pacific and
Caribbean-coast peoples perform the same magic with seafood
--as in ceviche (lemon-"cooked" fish) in Peru, caldillo de
congrío (fish soup) in Chile, or sancocho (fish-and-potato po-
tage) in Venezuela--without being any more behindhand with
beef than Brazilians and Argentines are with fish. Iberian
delicacies such as paella or chorizo sausage can be found almost anywhere.

The land helps history provide a basic tradition and a
number of variations. Corn, beans, squash, and spice are
basic. Corn becomes not only cuscuz in Brazil and tortillas
in Mexico, but little tamale-like meatpies called humitas, hal-
lacas, or empanadas. Sometimes empanadas, which originated in Galicia, are served filled with fruit instead of meat,
like French crêpes. Rice substitutes for or mixes with corn

in many places such as north Brazil and lowland Peru, and
potatoes carry more of the caloric burden in the high Andes,
where they are known as papas--and whence they have descended to become elegant fare when covered with excellent spiced
sauces such as hot-pepper ají. In south Brazil and the La
Plata region, wheat bread is favored, and in the tropical regions manioc flour is laboriously made by squeezing the juices
out of cassava roots. Beans are so numerous and varied
that they find their way into everything from black beans and
rice in the African-influenced areas to porotos granados (cran-
berry beans with corn, squash, and rice) in Chile. Squash
finds its way into everything from a casserole to a squash-in-
honey dessert (calabaza enmielada) but is sometimes replaced
by more exotic substitutes such as yuca roots. Authentic
South American cooking, high or low, depends in large measure on these basics of Indian America, then, though everything from French grand cuisine to a burger-and-Coke quick
lunch is available for a price in the large cities.

South Americans--indeed, most people in Latin Amer-
ica--have more in common with the French than the North
Americans when it comes to meals, however, because eating
is a social occasion, as in Iberia. Even in the Caribbean
tea-time is much like the Spanish merienda, a light meal a-
round six o'clock, which to Iberians and Ibero-Americans is
mid-afternoon because from one-thirty to three they have had
their large midday meal (comida) and have taken a siesta.
The day thus revolves around the midday period in Latin
America, partly because of tradition and partly because of
climate. Schools are out, the family is together for the comida, or the individual is shopping or relaxing, as in Europe.
Other meals, like merienda, are unimportant--cafe con leche
for an early-morning wakeup (desayuno, or breakfast), a few
empanadas and coffee, perhaps, for elevenish brunch (almuer-
zo), and a medium-sized meal at nine or ten at night (cena).
Latin Americans and Europeans understand each other on
these matters (except that many Europeans eat heavily at
night instead of at midday) and think North Americans are
rat-racing through their meals. North Americans consider
such meal arrangements inefficient, slow, and late.

If mealtimes reveal South American diversity, the epic
biological events of life, death and sex, show the changes being wrought by modernization. Death is not sanitized in any
"traditional" Latin culture. The ancianos (elders) are not put
out of sight but revered--for their experience, to be sure,
but also for their courage in facing the ever-nearing "intrud-

er. " Nor is death a taboo subject to be camouflaged with eat-drink-and-be-merry chitchat: ancianos talk of "when I am dead, " and their grandchildren of "when you are dead. " Death must be confronted with dignity by all. Family and friends must keep vigil with the corpse, walk with the procession to the burial, go through a lengthy period of mourning, and pray for the soul of the dead to pass through Purgatory to Paradise. The honor of the family depends on the dignity with which the dying confronts demise and the manner in which everyone masters grief and fear. This traditional world is "alive" with the spirits of the dead--of ancestors as well as saints. But the fear of fiendish hell typical of Protestant cultures is not the aim; rather, it is self-control in the face of the certainty of ultimate adversity. Dying is not separated from living as in much of North Europe and North America, not shut up in old-age homes, undertaker-parlors, and saccharine sanctimony. Not that Latin Catholics court death, for that would be the sin of suicide, the ultimate arrogance and lack of self-control. But their moral code demands that they not shun death either--as the matador dare not turn his back on the bull, nor the soldier on an enemy. Better to die well than to live dishonored.

Modernization is changing much of this, of course. South American moderns are much like their counterparts anywhere. The quick-step of change has undermined some of the respect for the "ignorant" ancianos, the illusion of human progress and power has glossed over the inevitable, the industrial order has shaken the extended family and Church discipline, and societies two-thirds youthful think the future is forever. The "youth cult" has, in this sense, come to some of South America. Death is noble or accidental, not a common curse or a Christian liberation. Death has lowered its profile somewhat, as in most future-oriented "modernizing" societies. But life is still cheap enough in much of South America--because of natural dangers, privation, crime, or social conflict --that most people lean to the face-death-with-dignity side of the question. The Catholic tradition is still very much alive in this respect, and there is as yet little inclination to use euphemisms such as "passed away" or to abandon the emotion-charged rituals for the "coldness" South Americans believe they see in North American "funerals. " Reactions to death are demonstrative but controlled.

Traditional relations between the sexes, in contrast, are undemonstrative--but also very controlled. Marriages are arranged between the families after an elaborate court-

ship-from-afar involving letters, chaperoned meetings, and
both-families get-togethers with the "suitors" (novios). Boys
should have many novias because it is manly (macho); girls
should not have too many novios because it is crazy (loca).
Flirtation is one thing for both sexes, but courtship is quite
another. Everyone is pluperfectly conscious that marriages
should be made between people of "good family" because both
family names will appear in a bridegroom named José Martínez González (Christian name followed by father's and mother's
family names) and a bride named María López Alvarez whose
married name will be María López de Martínez (Christian
name followed by father's and husband's family names).

The bride is aware that vivacity, expression of emotional needs, expectations of affection, questioning will not be
tolerated. An honorable, orderly, "good family" household
should be her goal. The Christian ideals of virginity and
chastity are interpreted to mean strict supervision before marriage. Loose women are even worse than pushy ones. And
childless women are the worst. The bridegroom is aware
that he must choose a woman of honor, maintain his authority in the household, and yet prove his macho in conferring
sexual pleasure. Receiving pleasure is nothing, since a cas-
ual conquest or a prostitute, a woman who must always be
paid and never loved, can provide that for a gift or a fee.
Several especially "Latin" themes emerge from these somewhat contradictory standards: the independence of mistresses
and prostitutes; the rebelliousness of adolescent males; the
protection of the family's female "honor"; the ostracism of
illegitimate children; the "masculine" female head of the family trying to control rebellious sons and incautious daughters;
and the masculine fear of aging.

There have always been ways around these strict "Latin" sexual mores--elopement followed by belated "blessings"
from the families, or discreet miscounting of the months
from elopement to giving birth. Furthermore, in out-of-the-
way areas the Church has always tolerated, even encouraged,
stable free unions or common-law marriages until they could
be "regularized" and the children declared legitimate. With
modernization new cracks have been added to the wall of sexual self-control, however. The "leveling" in relations between
the sexes that is typical of industrialization has clearly started
among the elite and the middle sectors in South America.
"Modern" women do expect love and a voice in family affairs.
Duels in defense of the honor of one's sister have virtually
disappeared in the cities. Chaperonage and isolation of ado-

lescent girls have declined considerably. Arranged marriages, bride-prices, and dowries are less consequential. The stigmas attached to illegitimacy, pre-marital and extra-marital sex, and "barrenness," though still much, much greater than in present-day North America, are weakening.

In short, the habits associated with "romantic love" are spreading in South America, just as they did in early-twentieth-century North America. And that includes sex for pleasure in wedlock. Divorce is still illegal in most of Latin America, however, and contraceptive devices, even where they are legal, are strictly controlled, so teenage pregnancies are numerous. Sterilization is taboo for theological reasons. Abortion is sinful. Homosexuality is unnatural. Yet the pressures are building for legislation permitting divorce and for greater freedom regarding contraception, if not for the more radical sexual practices. The crucial point is that practices vary widely class to class, ethnic group to ethnic group, country to country.

It is possible to see in all this the famous "Latin character" which Cervantes embodied in the two chief figures of Don Quixote. On one side of the "Iberian soul" is the Don--idealistic, mystical, selfless, almost naive. On the other is his squire Sancho--realistic, suspicious, selfish, almost cunning. Cervantes was contrasting Spain's south and north, the rich and the poor, and all humanity's mix of romanticism and cynicism. But the Man from La Mancha's tilting at windmills seems to fit with the South American tendency to see no faults in one's family, friends, and associates, and to expect that one's "cause" will suddenly prevail through God, fate, luck, or The People. Sancho's tough-mindedness likewise fits the competitive attitude toward "outsiders"--toward another's women, another's party or region or country, another's "cause." In this way the "Latin temper" comes clear: the distaste for compromise, the fear of losing face, the forthrightness in the face of death, the competitive machismo and its female equivalent, and the lust for life in both the Don's hereafter and Sancho's right here. Above all, it explains the "passion" of South American character, since both the Don and Sancho are constantly proving themselves in the eyes of the world and in each other's eyes. Unlimited loyalty to friends, unfailing hostility to foes, and Doubt at war with Belief in the same mind--such is the self-image supposedly seen by many Latins.

But this view of the Latin temper must be qualified in two ways. The famous intellectual historian Germán Arciniegas, a Colombian bearing the name of the ancient hero of his German ancestors, has pointed out that the Iberian soul has been reshaped by hosts of other spirits and by its New World abode. What of the stoic Indian sitting taciturn and unbowed by centuries of Iberian civilizing? What of the extroverted African more moved by joyous Voodoo gods than the introspective Christian saints? And what of the Americanization of the Latin spirit? Loyalty and generosity toward friends, caution and cunning toward two- or four-legged foes--those elements of the Spanish mind fit the frontier lands. Closed social systems, the penchant for oscillation between authority and anarchy--those do not. Hence the influence of the great American-Latin thinkers like Miranda, Bolívar, and Martí. Besides, the Portuguese are less "Iberian" than the Spanish in introspection, crisis orientation, and religiosity. And the new immigrants, whether Germans, Italians, or Japanese, are certainly "modern" rather than "Latin." The impact of this second non-Latin character influence, modernization, is even harder to describe than that of the non-Iberian "traditional" cultures. The usual approach is to call modern culture "voluntary" because one is not born to it but chooses it. Cultural alternatives have opened up because of the two "Ms" of the twentieth century--migration and modernization. And South America's "Catholic culture" is well into this process.

South America is indeed the most Catholic continent in the world. There are, however, a few Jews, Muslims, Buddhists, and Protestants. The Jews are mostly immigrants to Uruguay, Argentina, and Chile; the Muslims, partly descendants of West African slaves in Brazil, partly Lebanese or other Arab immigrants in the southern countries, and partly East Asians brought to the Guianas as indentured laborers; the Buddhists, primarily Japanese in the south and on the west coast. The Protestants, partly Germans from Europe, partly Mennonites from North America, and partly Fundamentalist converts from Catholicism, are scattered throughout. In addition, there are the adherents of African-derived religions like Candomblé and Macumba--that is, the practitioners of so-called Voodoo--in North Brazil and the Guianas. A few unconverted Indians in the Amazon and on the offshore islands round out the picture. Together these non-Catholics number less than five per cent of the population. Popes, archbishops, bishops, and, above all, parish priests are therefore very important people everywhere--and the most important people in many places.

There are Catholics and Catholics, however. In the cities and larger towns are those familiar to Europeans and North Americans, people who attend Mass and Confession, revere the Sacraments, and affirm the Credo, "I believe in God the Father Almighty. . . . " But in the smaller towns and out-of-the-way rural areas, particularly where Indian or African influence is strong, there are people who, though called Catholic, have little contact with the Church or the Sacraments, believe in the magic of charms, in the influence of sun, moon and stars, and in the "super-magic" of the Church. Finally, there are "modern" Catholics in the big cities, who go through the rituals of Catholicism but march to the beat of the philosophic traditions of post-Enlightenment Europe. Generally speaking, the higher the class, the more modern the religion, among either the Catholics or the other religious groups. The carrier of these modern attitudes is that other pillar of South American beliefs, the school, especially the public school.

Education reflects the value-systems as well as the social circumstances. From grade to graduate school, church and public education exist side by side. The elite and the middle classes favor the private elementary schools, although children of all classes and colors are found in most schools. The public school system is thought of as an instrument of national and continental development, and of "modernism." An Argentine president and writer of the nineteenth century, Domingo Sarmiento, became the father of public education in South America after witnessing its helpful effects in the United States. Today most South American states have extensive public school systems and compulsory attendance laws, but in many areas neither teachers nor schools are available. Illiteracy rates run from near zero in the south to over sixty per cent in the Andean states, depending on how effective the public elementary school system has been. Most countries still have large literacy programs, like Brazil's much ballyhooed "alphabetization" effort in the backlands.

Secondary and higher education reflect the environment even more faithfully than primary schools. Famous Catholic universities such as San Marcos in Lima or Córdoba in Argentina are now being challenged by public universities modeled on Mexico's National University in virtually every South American country. Yet fewer than five per cent of South American students reach the university level, and most who do so enter the arts or the liberal professions rather than economics or science. The more privileged follow the elites' tradition of a European, usually French or Spanish, educa-

tion. Government scholarships encourage study of economics
and science, often in the United States since South American
universities have too few such programs. Teachers are generally trained at the high schools rather than the universities
and are often not highly paid or respected. In a word, South
America's educational system is still oriented toward educating country gentlemen rather than skilled professionals, although some countries, especially Brazil, Argentina, Chile,
and Venezuela, are actively seeking change. São Paulo University is in the forefront of such nationalist and developmental education.

One striking feature in higher education is the political activism of students and faculty. Several factors have
contributed to this activism. One is the tradition of university self-governance, which goes even beyond its European
original in degree of autonomy. Police and other agents of
the government are often not permitted on campus at all, even
where the state pays the bills. Another is the "Latin" respect for the Man of the Word--the poet, the philosopher, the
orator--in politics. Most important, however, are the shock
waves of the so-called University Reform set off in the 1920s
and 1930s by Haya de la Torre and his generation of students.
The aim of those "revolutionaries" was to make the universities independent of both Church and State so that they could
become the spearheads of social change. Some of the more
radical elements of the University Reform, such as the street
academies run by students and faculty to eliminate poverty,
have eroded over time, but the notion of a revolutionary university elite endures. Yet the major source of the unrest is
simply that the universities represent the apex of the pyramid of modernist beliefs--a break with the past or, from another point of view, a corruption of the youth.

The most influential of the modernist philosophies are
the Neo-Thomism of South Europe, the Liberalism and Positivism of West Europe, and the Social Democracy of West
and Central Europe. Neo-Thomism, particularly in the form
advocated by the twentieth-century French Catholic philosopher
Jacques Maritain, is especially influential because it reaffirms
the importance of the Catholic Church and of Christian charity as substitutes for individual striving and class conflict.
The Christian Democratic Parties and their leaders, such as
Eduardo Frei of Chile, are convinced that a just social order
can be created by appealing to the consciences of good Catholics inspired by the Neo-Thomist notion that "Life is growth."
Laymen's groups similar to the Opus Dei (Work of the Lord)

in Spain have grown up to carry out the principles of the two
most respected foreign Neo-Thomists, Pope John XXIII and
President Kennedy of the United States.   This movement
should not be confused with Italian and Spanish Fascism, which
used the same language but turned a deaf ear to pleas for
charity and instead invested resources in military hardware.

    Liberalism and Positivism were more popular in the
nineteenth century than now, but many in the middle classes
still adhere to such doctrines because of distrust of the "conservatism" of the Church, by which they mean the Church-
landlord alliance.   The principles of progressive government,
industrialism, and science seem to these people to promise
a brighter future than either Neo-Thomist charity or Marxist
socialization.   The epic battles between Church and State over
control of schools and land reform have been fought on this
basis.   All over South America the Freemasons have set up
lodges to counter Church influence and encourage "free" governmental and business methods.   Few advocate the free enterprise doctrines of the English and Americans, however.
Instead, most favor the doctrines of Auguste Comte, the nineteenth-century French founder of Positivism.   Their basic argument is that where there is only a small educated elite, it
is necessary to have efficient scientific planning--or "positive"
planning--by lawyers, doctors and administrators rather than
harum-scarum development by businessmen.   Ambitious people thus go into the "liberal professions" in South America
rather than into business as they might in North America.
Businessmen are deemed less "successful" than government
civil servants in South America.   Advocates of an "Anglo-
Saxon" emphasis on business incentive rather than planning
have little influence, partly because of a South American solidarity with "Latin methods" but mainly because the South
American business class is so small.   Enterprise, growth,
and progress are notions shared by Liberals and Positivists,
however.

    Marxists argue that human brotherhood and fellow-feel-
ing cannot be achieved by either charity or enterprise because
no one in the elite is generous and open enough to ignore differences in rank and position.   Only the government can do
that because only the government belongs to all the people.
Hence public education is not enough, and public management
of housing, industry, and commerce must be added to the
social program.   Communism--as distinguished from Social
Democracy--is generally opposed by South Americans on the
grounds that a Communist party does not allow opposition and

one cannot tell if it really does represent the majority of the people in its distribution of national wealth. So far, Communism has less appeal than the democratic brand of Marxism, partly because the German or Russian philosophic ideas behind Communism are less real to South Americans than French, Spanish, or Italian ideals.

Modern philosophies have an influence out of proportion to the numbers who adhere to them because their adherents belong to the literate elite, a state of affairs which would seem to threaten a conflict between the value-systems of the elite and the masses. What eases the tensions, however, is the widespread continuation of subsidiary attachments to more fundamental customs even among the elite. The extended family system is one. The male-centered life in which the woman is much subordinated is another. The concept of machismo or he-manliness leads to emphasis on masculine leisure and comfort, a dual standard of sexual morality, and a demand for dignidad or saving face. The unique sense of space and time is another. Many a North American has unknowingly insulted a South American by arriving too early for an appointment or by standing too far away when chatting, since the vast majority of South Americans, low and high, seldom arrive promptly or stand farther apart than a foot and a half to talk. Latin Americans are "formal" in public and not all that "informal" in private and are therefore often shocked by North American informality when in public. Finally, there is the respect for emotion, for the poet over the scientist, for the man of the spirit over the man of the mind. These things matter in South America, for they often count for more than all the philosophies put together. In fact, they account for the "cooperative" or "collective" orientation of both academic and popular philosophies of life--for the borrowing of Marxism, Positivism, and Neo-Thomism rather than the individualistic Utilitarianism of North America, and for the local development of a vitalist like José Enrique Rodó rather than a pragmatist like William James.

One thing that is certain is that the South American is not a "loner." Life is lived in the kitchen or parlor--or in the streets. A South American generally does not like to be alone, work alone, live alone. He does not strive to get away from the rules of the family and the community in order to "be himself." To exist in a "state of nature" is not an ideal. Instead, he would like to be the champion at something--bullfighting, boxing, art, politics, life, anything--in order to gain the respect of the community. His is a populated world. He therefore does not strive to "get ahead" or "get away" but to "get respect. " So "showing off" is bad, "self-control" good. To see and to be seen--and to keep face throughout--is the nature of the South American code of honor. Similarly, South Americans are confused by the long hours North Americans devote to the isolated task of working to get on, just as confused as North Americans are by the South American tendency to be doing a dozen things at once instead of concentrating on the business at hand. For North Americans, work is work and play comes later; but for South Americans, as for Middle Americans and most Mediterraneans, work and play must go together to prevent boredom and alienation. And that is also why the Man of the Word is important, for he enlarges life and holds the community together. Literature is thus more important than business.

Literature and Arts

Since in South America education is a literary pursuit, literature is strong. This is a land where poets, novelists and historians are elected president, honored with state funerals, or both. The Man of the Word is king. He is internationally, as well as nationally, revered. Themes vary, but several recur: triumph of civilization over barbarism, attachment to the plains and mountains, triumph of the individual and collective spirit over seemingly insuperable odds. Anyone reading two famous nineteenth-century South American prose epics, Domingo Sarmiento's Facundo and Euclides da Cunha's Os Sertões, will instantly recognize the first of these themes, for instance.

Sarmiento's theme is the rivalry of civilization and barbarism--of moderns versus Indians and Indian fighters--for the soul of Argentina. Facundo is a lightly veiled diatribe against the Indian fighter, Manuel Rosas, by his citified successor as Argentine president. Sarmiento treated the Pampas as James Fenimore Cooper did the prairies: they made the Indian noble and the European brutal, while cities degraded Indians and upgraded Europeans. Sarmiento modeled himself after the great East Coast reformers in the United States and depicted Facundo as some vicious, Indian-slaughtering Andrew Jackson corrupted by the brutal gaucho existence of the Argentine frontier. Such debunking never quite erased the image of the gaucho and his Indian peers as nobler and more Argentine than their city compatriots in Buenos Aires, however. The Argentine national epic, Hernandez' Martín Fierro, continued to be read and gave rise to a nostalgic frontier-based "gaucho literature" later. One such work, Güiraldes' Don Segundo Sombra, or Second Shadow, explored the loss of the frontier, of childhood, and of national innocence in almost the same terms used in Huckleberry Finn.

Da Cunha's subject in Os Sertões, or Backlands, is the rebellion of a spiritualist sect in the Brazilian Northeast, but the theme is the same as Sarmiento's--human degradation because of uncivilized natural and social circumstances. Da Cunha's engineering background and Positivist sympathies led him to the conclusion that emotional religion, the tyranny of the leader of the rebellion, and the crushing poverty caused by the São Francisco River valley's recurrent droughts went together inevitably, "scientifically." Moreover, bringing civilization to the frontier outback seemed extremely difficult to Da Cunha, since he thought anarchy, poverty, and superstition to be rooted in the mixed racial complexion and horrid natural circumstances of the wilderness as well as its social backwardness. No wonder that the armed forces sent to restore order perpetrated a massacre equivalent to Wounded Knee in North America. Backlands dehumanize everyone. Da Cunha's only hope lay in the slow spread of civilization from the coast to the interior under the leadership of the Positivist elite of the newly-formed Brazilian Republic.

Needless to say, Da Cunha's vision, which was not unlike the Social Darwinism of Theodore Roosevelt and Woodrow Wilson, eventually gave way to a greater sympathy for a nationalism that included the masses. The literati continued to favor such Portuguese classics as The Lusiads, Camões' epic of the conquest, or the classic style of Machado de Assis' nineteenth-century novels of fashionable Brazilians. But after World War I the wider reading public turned to a "regionalism" akin to the New England, Southern, and Western schools in the United States. Jorge Amado's Dona Flor, for instance, turned the "rise" of the mulatto cook in the Northeast into a hymn to the Brazilian love of life, racial tolerance, and general good humor. The theme of modernization in Brazilian works thus illustrates the struggle for identity--cultural, national, and personal--in most Latin American literature.

Despite the elegance of his Portuguese, Machado de Assis himself tried in a sense to "rise above" Iberian "backwardness" by imitating French culture, that is, the Parnassians in his poetry and the Realists in his novels. His poem "Blue Fly, " in which a rough hand crushed a resplendent dragonfly, is as close to Gautier as the more famous modernismo of Rubén Darío in Spanish America. And Braz Cubas and Dom Casmurro, though Brazilian in theme, are psychological novels à la Balzac and Flaubert. Azevedo's The Mulatto went a step further and imitated Zola's Naturalism in the same way Da Cunha did.

Finally, in 1922, Graça Aranha, poet and novelist of Brazil's French school and second only to Da Cunha in influence on Brazilian literature, issued a Modernist Manifesto renouncing all Europeanism in favor of an indigenous national literature. In one sense, these modernists have failed because regional schools which preceded the modern state thrive. In the Northeast regionalists have produced Deep South-like works such as poet Jorge de Lima's "That Negress Fûlo, " José Lins do Rego's plantation novels, and Gilberto Freyre's famous social study of slave culture, The Masters and the Slaves. In the West the most notable contributions have been historian Vianna Moog's The Bandeirantes and such sequels to Da Cunha as Ramos' Dry Lives. In the Brazilian southland, a kind of American Midwest provincialism has emerged in Erico Verissimo's novels of Porto Alegre, works which, fittingly, owe much to Hemingway and Dos Passos in the United States and to Shaw and Huxley in Europe. Yet Verissimo is evidence that there is a truly Brazilian style despite the continued tug of regional influences below and global ones above.

In fact, Verissimo, along with Amado and the poets, can be said to represent the three basic ideas of Brazilian culture--destiny, openness, and uniqueness. Verissimo lauds those who refuse to be crushed by destiny or, for that matter, deluded by successes. His A Place in the Sun and Saga therefore capture the sense of proud confidence and intolerance of weakness felt by most Brazilians and, indeed, by most pioneer peoples. Brazilians are like Americans and Russians in believing that they have a manifest destiny to improve themselves and the world, though Verissimo himself has some doubts as to the wisdom of such habits.

Amado's picture of Brazilians as open, optimistic Dona Flors is repeated in the equally famous Gabriela, all "clove and cinnamon. " Hedonism over hatred, inclusion rather than exclusion, Carnival more than Lent--such is the Brazilian's self-image. Hence the outrage at dry lives on the frontier. Hence the generally high opinion of the "fun-loving" African culture and the hostility toward the "stolid" Indians. Hence the emphasis on variety as opposed to the "narrow-mindedness" of North American and of Spanish and Spanish-American culture, or, for that matter, any other culture. Hence the fact that Raquel de Queiros presents feminism in Tres Marias and other novels by mocking machismo the way Amado does. Brazilians think it is healthy not to take oneself too seriously--in politics, religion, race, whatever.

The poets, meanwhile, have been struggling to reverse the prejudiced statement that Portuguese is "the tomb of thought, " that is, too uncivilized to be taken seriously. From Aranha and the Generation of 1922 through the Generation of 1945 to João de Melo Neto and beyond, they have had the aim of making a unique language worthy of being the tongue spoken by more Latin Americans than any other. Brazil will soon be, in their view, a political and cultural super-power, at which time Portuguese will become a "world language" like English and Spanish.

In Spanish America, as in Brazil, works of so-called "creole literature" (criollismo) were becoming as passé as the classicism of Iberia by the time Romulo Gallegos published Doña Barbara in 1929. A more revolutionary generation after World War I saw the confrontation of the "barbarous" Doña with the "enlightened" Señor Luz on the llanos of the Venezu-uelan interior as an outdated version of the struggle for civ-ilization, no matter how inspiring Gallegos' ultimate amalgam of love of land and love of law--of past and future--might be. The intellectual public's younger members therefore turned from Doña Barbara, the Colombian Rivera's Vortex, and Se-cond Shadow to two more forward-looking approaches.

The first was the avant garde movement, which be-came associated in all of Latin America with a "cultured" re-sistance to North European and North American "coldness" and "materialism. " The somewhat different modernisms of the Nicaraguan Rubén Darío in Spanish America and of Graça Aranha in Brazil had in common the twin notions of Latin cul-tural superiority to Anglo-Saxons and of Latin Americans as the saving remnant for Latins in the face of the disasters of the 1898 and 1914 wars. The attitude was captured in the Uruguayan Rodó's designation of Latins as "Ariel" and Anglo-Saxons as "Caliban, " the blithe spirit and vicious brute of Shakespeare's The Tempest. Latin American, and especially South American, intellectuals thus absorbed the surrealism and other isms of Dalí and Picasso and García Lorca in a spirit of cultural superiority as well as intellectual rebellion against a rising authoritarianism in Salazar Portugal and Fran-co Spain. Soon exiles poured in to reinforce experimentalist attitudes already deeply held. Literature and revolutionary politics merged in Latin America as did literature and coun-ter-revolutionary politics in the Iberian states.

The other movement was engagé or socially committed literature. The Spanish American version included the indian-

ismo borrowed from the Mexican Revolution and best expressed
in the Bolivian Arguedas' Race of Bronze and the Peruvian
Alegría's novels. The implied question was: "Why not a continent of Bronze nations from Patagonia to Alaska if white
domination can be pushed back?" This concept of Bronze or
Red Power obviously held less appeal in urban or less Indian
areas than the Andes and Mexico, so elsewhere the "radicalism" of both Fascists and Communists had some appeal as a
response to "Anglo-Saxon cultural imperialism. " In Brazil
and Argentina the Fascist appeal found favor among German
and Italian immigrants and sympathizers of Salazar and Franco, but elsewhere Marxist sympathies were stronger--and
everywhere the nature vs. nurture, Hitler vs. Stalin argument
had an impact on literature, journalism, and the new popular
arts of radio and film.

The appeal of committed Leftist writers of Europe,
especially Sartre and Camus, was seconded by the influence
of intellectual friends of revolution, among them the Chilean
poet Pablo Neruda and, in the post World War II generation,
such novelists of the sudden "Boom" in Latin American literature as Gabriel García Márquez of Colombia and Carlos
Fuentes of Mexico. And for many of the most recent writers
the joining of the avant garde and the engagé is seen as necessary if the stultifying cultural habits contributing to oppression are to be overcome. They therefore favor a kind of
Castroism of culture, designed to root out every vestige of
the "classical" and the "creole" in the arts--except, of course,
the hard discipline of creativity.

The "classical" tradition never quite disappeared in
either Portuguese or Spanish America, however, and in the
latter it produced Jorge Luis Borges. The nearly-blind Argentine poet, teacher, and national librarian has managed to
universalize and modernize the standard themes. He has seen
two World Wars, the competition of totalitarianism and revolution, the agonies of underdevelopment, and the watering-down
of intellectual standards in the popular arts--and yet continues
to stress insight into the central mysteries of life. South
Americans revere European literary figures, such as Kafka
and Sartre and García Lorca, who talk of turning inward, but
even Borges, who is most like them, has transmuted this into a temporary check on the irrepressible growth of human
life. Borges writes of "labyrinths, " not as places to get lost
in but places to find the true self. His parables make "dream-
tigers" into magical new friends rather than nightmarish monsters. In his poem "Guitar, " the heart follows the last dy-

ing chord into the ever-opening Pampas. Borges' question
has always been: "What is the best thing we could stand for?"
For him the quest for a "more civilized" life is more noble
precisely because it is endless and universal. Like William
Faulkner, one of his favorites, Borges has made the national
and continental themes into the story of everyone's search for
eternal esthetic and moral meaning. And it is for this reason that many see Borges, not the revolutionaries, as the inspiration for the post-World War II "Boom," and in particular for the young novelists whose pioneering, like Borges',
takes them into the universal human quest for expanded meaning and significance.

Pablo Neruda is to poetry what Borges is to prose--a
sum of more than all the parts. One part of Neruda leads
back to the odes, lyrics, sonnets, and eclogues of Iberian,
Italian, and Latin poetry the way Borges' work draws on classical satires and fables. So Neruda produced an "Ode to the
Dictionary" in which each word, one after the other, expands
the human horizon by multiplying the possibilities of self-ex-
pression. Another part draws on the fecund upward sprawl
of nature and man in the Americas, particularly where men
try to tack settlements ever higher in the still-rising Andes.
"The Heights of Machu Picchu" thus celebrates the Incas'
drive toward progress which still inspires moderns. A third
part is rooted in a kind of democracy of the senses which
sees humankind as most noble when most united by common
feelings. Hence Neruda's emotional "Communism"--or better,
"communalism"--was based at first on Whitman's universal
urges, then on the Latin pride of culture Darío and other modernists offered as a counter to Yankee materialism, then on
revolutionary solidarity, and finally on an almost pantheistic
universal empathy of man and nature. "The Dictators," in
which rebellion builds like a tropical storm until a cloudburst
of swamp water pours out, really has the same theme as
"Tides," in which the waves do not undermine Neruda's beach
home Isla Negra but instead form him as if he were a shell.
But above all there is the Chilean part of Neruda. With his
countrywoman, likewise a Nobel Prize poet, Gabriela Mistral,
whose poems inevitably delivered her child or herself into a
comfortable oneness with some larger meaning, Neruda sings
of a very Chilean kind of promise. He sings more of gusto
than of struggle. For his hope is based, like that of many
South Americans, on a faith in the latent energies awaiting
liberation in man and society.

The South American may be sick and poor, then, or oppressed, but is whole and not hollow. And the Man of the Word, and sometimes Woman of the Word as well now, is the keeper of this healthy spirit. Perhaps that explains why film, a kind of literature in action, is a South American passion. Black Orpheus, a Brazilian film based on a novel by the eminent poet Vinícius de Morais, is among the best movies ever made. It draws on the Greek myth of Orpheus, who tried to rescue his sweetheart Eurydice from the grave, and on the events of Carnival time in northeast Brazil. A black man from the favelas, who plays the guitar, dies while cheering the Carnival crowd, only to have his guitar taken over by a small neighborhood boy, who also has the gift of inspiring the hopeless. And so the theme passes to the assembled masses in the movie houses: only a man of civilization, a man of the land and people, a man with the gift of the spirit is needed to fulfill the promise of South America.

This theme appears as the grandiose and the elaborate and the up-to-date in architecture and sculpture and as the amalgamation of African, Indian, and European cultural traditions in painting and music. The soaring majesty of the baroque churches and palaces of north Brazil and the coasts of Ecuador and Peru look back to the grandeur of the Inca palaces of Cuzco and Machu Picchu and forward to the hustle and bustle of city-building in the republican period. Such frontier cities as Brasília and its Venezuelan equivalent, Ciudad de Guayana on the Orinoco, are the logical outcome of a vigorous tradition that carries architects like Fernando Belaúnde Terry to the presidency of Peru. The most famous native sculptors, like the crippled Brazilian "Aleijadinho" who decorated Brazil's baroque churches in the colonial era, communicate an untamed energy hidden in the human forms of saints and sinners alike. Modernist sculptors are strongly influenced by the Spanish vigor of Picasso's twentieth-century works.

The painters of South America cannot match those of Mexico, with whom they share, however, the theme of cultural liberation and amalgamation. Hence the Indian-inspired murals of the Mexicans Diego Rivera, Orozco, and Siquieros have had as much influence as European and North American styles. Candido Portinari of Brazil painted the starvation on the land, the crushing burden of ethnic division, the savagery of God and man--and the promise of the future--in starkly simple forms and primary colors resembling those of African and Indian styles. The theme of cultural unity was most obvious, however, in the greatest of South American musicians, Brazil's Heitor Villa-Lobos, whose symphonies, operas, chamber music, and songs put into elaborate European form both the folk music (choros) of Brazilian street-singers (chorões) and the throbbing rhythms of popular South American dances like the tango and bossa nova. Some of his compositions for the guitar made it a respected instrument for serious musicians after it had long been neglected as a plaything of the musically illiterate. A South American culture is evidently being born in sight and sound.

Yet South America still has a cultural world to win. Its folk handicrafts and folk culture are succumbing to rapid modernization and urban homogenization. Efforts are now being made to preserve the ancient and colonial heritages and to fuse them with modernism to make a unique South American culture. The export of art objects is illegal in most of South America, and archaeological and historical commissions are at work restoring and recording the treasures of the past. Intellectuals are convinced there is more to South America than Hispanidad, but as yet they are uncertain what it is. Some are impressed by the theory of the Mexican writer José Vasconcelos, who says that all of Latin America represents the newest of new cultures, a world culture or La Raza Cósmica made of Black, Red, and White ingredients. Others prefer the Peruvian political philosopher Haya de la Torre's idea of an "Indo-America" from the Rio Grande to Tierra del Fuego. All know what they do not want, but as yet many do not know what they want. They are still pioneering.

Pioneer Outlook

South America's pioneering spirit has long been compared with that of North America and contrasted with that of old, settled areas like Europe or China. In the simplest and broadest terms: To what extent might Frederick Jackson Turner's "frontier thesis," that the open continent known as the American West determined the character of North Americans, hold for South Americans as well? Or, translated into the terms of Turner's Latin American counterpart, Clodomir Vianna Moog: Are the heirs of bandeirantes and pioneers alike in outlook? The answer is probably "Yes!" with respect to the notion of "civilizing" nature and native peoples. Conquistadores, bandeirantes, pioneers--all saw glory, God, and gold just over the horizon.

"Gold" still lures Brazilians and Venezuelans and Chileans to mine and lumber and cultivate as if their environment's resources were limitless. The hostility toward materialism inherent in the Iberian traditions may have buffered the acquisitive urge slightly more than the Anglo-Saxon shopkeeper tradition, but the frontier still seems to have produced an attitude far more like that of North America than of Iberia or other parts of West Europe and the Mediterranean. Expansion equals opportunity equals progress equals civilization. Backwardness--even as represented in the traditions of indigenous peoples--is bad. Eventually, the melting-pot of peoples will bubble happily because of the heating-up of economic opportunities, unless, of course, "oppression" keeps the lid on too long. South Americans, like North Americans, live for the future. El Dorado still exists in their minds.

"Glory"--individualism--is not so clearly a result of the South American frontier experience. Iberian habits and Catholic tradition de-emphasize individual in favor of collective effort. Isolation, in Latin minds, invites aberration, crime, sin, anarchy. Solitude seems to threaten South Americans. Mentally, theirs is an inhabited world of missions and villages rather than isolated Daniel Boones, of civilized rituals and conduct rather than outback devilries, of family and Church and laws rather than noble savages and mountain men. They would find it hard to explain the successes of Robinson Crusoe in the wilds. Other factors besides tradition may also have contributed to this mindset. Nature may in fact be more difficult to conquer in South than in North America. A South American Lewis and Clark would have found the Amazon twice as wide as the Great Plains and the Andes twice as high as the Rockies, for example. And native peoples were definitely more difficult to conquer in most of South America. The Incas were not the Sioux. The proper analog for South America is probably Russian Asia rather than the American West, since in the vast expanse of Siberia extremely hostile nature and organized Muslim peoples of high culture led to more collective than individualist pioneering.

The free-booting bandeirantes of Minas Gerais were therefore, in a sense, exceptions, whereas the pioneers of Iowa were not. North Americans carved out farmsteads before government reached them; in contrast, South Americans usually set up municipios, then settled the region. No doubt the influence of individualist pioneers has been exaggerated in North America's continental conquest in view of the many army, land office, and commercial efforts, but the difference

between North and South American "frontier individualism"
still seems crucial. The South American man-in-a-state-of-
nature expects something of the community and knows it will
require something in return. He is not like the North American Adam out in "virgin land, " but is a pioneer nevertheless.

The conquest of the Americas for the sake of "God"
may have set the scene for belief in a revolutionary "manifest destiny" as well. There may be a direct inheritance
from Puritans to Founding Fathers, or from conquistadores
to Che Guevara's legions. The Frenchman Alexis de Tocqueville remarked in his mid-nineteenth century Democracy in
America that the United States and Russia were alike in their
expansionism, which he attributed to the lack of deep cultural
roots and to bad habits acquired in seizing the West and Siberia. Might he now add South Americans, especially Brazilians, to his list of peoples believing that anything is possible, indeed inevitable? There is probably a sense in which
South Americans, and particularly Brazilians, do believe they
were born free and are destined to free others as well.

Many North Americans believe themselves "chosen" to
spread electoral democracy, industrial enterprise, and scientific advance. Many South Americans likewise feel anointed
to bring about multi-racial democracy (Brazil), Indianist democracy (the Andean revolutionaries), or Latin-style democracy (Peronists). Do the South Americans have as serious a
case of the expansionist turn of mind as the Russians and
North Americans? Once the conquest of their continent is
truly complete, will they have an imperialist phase or subli-
mate their drive into economic and scientific advances as the
two present super-powers seem destined finally to do? And
can such expansive habits, even in the economic and technical spheres, be reconciled with the "limits to growth" implicit in a world in which every nation will eventually become
more or less developed? Will some Tocqueville from a sta-
bility-oriented society like, say, China, soon add Venezuela
or Brazil to the list of those nouveaux riches states too blinded by pioneering successes to see their own limitations?

Or is such speculation merely the sour-grapes grumb-
ling of those hostile to the frontier's chief product, namely,
openness of mind, willingness to experiment, "democracy" in
the broadest sense? Turner's notion that the United States
would become staid and conservative like the Old World when
the safety valve of escape from the bureaucratized East to
one's own land in the West was closed has been proved at

least partly false by the opportunities opened by industrial growth. Yet this idea gains credence because of the relative conservatism of the United States compared with attitudes in still-frontier areas of South America, where not only "progress" but also "revolution" and "conquest" are good words.

On the other hand, it is possible to argue that South Americans have never been as "open" in terms of class and caste mobility as North Americans--with the possible, but debatable, exception of the Brazilians. Or perhaps South Americans are as open in many civic rights but much less so in economic and private life. If true, is this the result of different stages of development, so that South America should be compared with the United States of, perhaps, the 1920s? Or is it the result of the confrontation of social groups--Iberians and Indians, masters and slaves--rather than of individuals? Or is it the result of the Iberian tradition, in which the Church and the Roman law are for all but property and family are jealously guarded? In any case, pioneer "democracy" seems to exist in South America even though it differs from that of North America and takes various forms depending on the region.

The farther north one goes, the more South America is like the American South rather than the American West. The tradition is deeper; the races and classes are farther apart; the economic growth is slower--except, in many such matters, for Venezuela. Venezuela, like Argentina and the interior of central and southern Brazil, is "western," frontierish; the plantation areas of Brazil and, to a lesser extent, the fazenda and hacienda areas of central Brazil and the Andes are "southern"--the domain of gentlemen lawyers and politicians, impoverished Black and Indian sharecroppers, and a deep sediment of paternalism. Most of Middle America, in contrast, is southern in this sense, with only northern Mexico being western--in fact, the original American Southwest. Northern Mexico has a legacy of Indian nomadism, conquest by friars and fighting men, and all the rest of the cultural apparatus of what the North American historian Eugene Bolton called the "borderlands" of the Spanish Empire. The Caribbean islands and the narrower and tropical parts of the isthmus of Central America are plantation or hacienda areas like northeast Brazil or Peru. The three Americas are "American," then, but with a different emphasis on the ingredients in each case, which makes Middle American attitudes as different from South as from North in many ways. For most Middle Americans, life is more like a heroic tragedy than the hopeful chronicle of South American pioneering.

PART II

MIDDLE AMERICA

Chapter 4

THREE REVOLUTIONS

1917

The Mexican Constitution passed the constitutional convention with ease, despite the continuing chaos of the revolution which had begun in 1910. Zapata in the south and Villa in the north still retained their strength, and the Carranza government in Mexico City was shaky. But Mexico now had a revolutionary constitution declaring that all the land belonged to the nation through the government. In Mexican eyes, this meant that Mexico was the first non-European and non-Europeanized nation to become master of its own destiny. For the Indians, the majority of Mexicans, could now "get their land back" from the Europeans or "get the benefits of the national wealth" instead of having the profits go to Europe or North America.

In short, the Mexican Revolution was seen as superior to either the American and French Democratic Revolutions or the then-in-progress Russian Bolshevik Revolution, all of which were European-centered, white-oriented movements. The supporters of the pre-revolutionary Díaz government, which had tried to create a modern economy with American and European capital, and the Mexican Socialists and Communists, who favored the Russian example, were equally rejected and suppressed by the Mexican Revolutionary Party, which began slowly to distribute land to the Indian peasants and to seize the foreign-owned capital for developing the country. The United States, meanwhile, had begun to terminate its interventions of the past three years and was accepting the verdict.

1940

Luis Muñoz Marín, son of the líder máximo of Puerto Rican resistance to United States control at the turn of the

93

century, and his newly founded Popular Democratic Party won the elections on a platform of change in the dependent status of the island under the Organic Act drawn by the United States Congress in 1917. United States President Franklin Roosevelt responded by appointing a member of his New Deal "Brain Trust, " Rexford Tugwell, as governor. Tugwell was to work with Muñoz, who was leader of the Puerto Rican Senate until he himself became governor in 1948, in order to move Puerto Rico toward economic and political viability so as to prevent Axis infiltration. Muñoz thus began "Operation Bootstrap" to make Puerto Rico the "Showplace of Democracy" in Middle America and, indeed, in the whole developing world. Using the Five Hundred Acre Law written into the Organic Act by U. S. legislators and an Industrial Incentives Act, he seized overlarge plantations and funneled American capital into small-goods industries in an attempt to diversify Puerto Rico's sugar economy and develop a small-holding farmer class. Among the alternative political relationships with the United States-- independence, statehood, or the in-between "commonwealth status"--Muñoz chose commonwealth status as the most likely to encourage investment and assure internal political stability. Despite Cold War tensions in the United States and violent opposition from independentistas in Puerto Rico, commonwealth status was offered by the United States and accepted by Puerto Rico in a referendum in 1951.

Puerto Ricans and their industries thus gained exemption from U. S. taxes and also profited from ducking under most of the tariff restrictions imposed on outsiders. They paid higher shipping costs and felt threatened with the loss of their Latin culture, so not all was on the plus side. Puerto Rico's economy boomed because of tourism, new industry, and special prices for agricultural products. Muñoz became very influential in Pan-American affairs, in the Organization of American States, and in hemisphere affairs, where he often acted as spokesman for the "democratic way" along with Figueres of Costa Rica, Betancourt of Venezuela, and Frei of Chile.

1959

Fidel Castro made his way by jeep through the countryside toward Havana. The crowds on every hand celebrated the departure of Fulgencio Batista, the Cuban strongman off and on since 1933, and hailed the accession of the leaders of the 26th of July Movement--and their new líder máximo, Castro. This most middle-class of Middle American states thus accepted this middle-class deliverer from the Sierra Maestra on the eastern end of the island, while the lower classes, particularly the dirt-poor tenants, remembered the talk of land reform by Fidel's brother, Raúl, and the Argentine-born Che Guevara. The Eisenhower government in Washington waited apprehensively to see which route the 26th of July Movement would take--toward the Mexican model or toward the Russian model--since it was obvious Cuba would never again be as close to the United States as was Puerto Rico.

Fidel himself wavered. He instituted land and rent reforms which only half-seized the property of Cuban and foreign owners, showed independence of both the United States and Russia in the United Nations, and promised elections. The United States, fearful of Russian penetration into the Caribbean at the height of the Cold War, began to make ready for the worst, threatened an embargo if the land seizures were carried out, and started preparations for the Bay of Pigs invasion two years later. Castro raised the ante by flirting with the Russians and by actually seizing some property, including U. S. property. The confrontation worsened until Castro demanded the immediate return of the Guantánamo naval base and announced that he had become a Communist--and until the United States turned to anti-Castro exiles in the Bay of Pigs invasion (1961) and nearly came to nuclear war with the Soviet Union in the Cuban Missile Crisis (1962).

Despite their great differences in political focus, these three competing revolutions of modern Middle America have an essential similarity in their struggle against harsh lands and hard times. For one thing, no vast continent exists to serve as a safety valve as in North and South America. Moreover, national division is typical--much more typical than in Canada, the United States, and Brazil, and somewhat more than in the Spanish language republics to the south. Foreign political, economic, and cultural influence, even domination, is also more extensive than anywhere else except, perhaps, other in-the-middle regions such as the Middle East, Southeast Asia, East Europe, and the Lowlands. Middle America is pulled three ways--east by European and African interests, north by United States interests, and south by Latin American interests. The result is that Middle America's history has led to a spirit of uprising instead of pioneer conquest. The expectation of success is the same as that of South or North Americans, but the mechanism is different:

sudden insight and ecstatic action, resistance or revolt, liberty or death. In defeat, defiance; in victory, vitality--that has been the outlook of the majority of Middle Americans from before the Aztecs until after Castro.

Chapter 5

THE HISTORY

Indian Middle America

Middle America was the stage for the most exciting
show of American Indian history. From the fifth to the fif-
teenth centuries only China, India, and some Mediterranean
cultures could compare with the Mayas and the Aztecs. The
Spanish meant to compliment these Indians when calling
them the equals of the ancient Greeks, but they were actually
more advanced than the Athenians in some ways. The Mayas,
whose city-states came together as an empire about the fourth
century after Christ, had already begun to decline by the time
the Spaniards reached southern Mexico. But their scientific
achievements lived on in the Aztec culture farther north. The
Maya had in fact devised a 365-day calendar more accurate
than any created by the Greeks, the Romans, or any other
European people, not excluding the Gregorian Calendar implemented by the Catholic Church in 1582. They had built impressive pyramids at Chichén Itzá and Tikal from which to
observe the heavenly bodies and natural forces of the sky
which they regarded as divine interventions. They had made
the transition from pictographic to ideographic writing, but
not to the alphabet.

Their hieroglyphics, carved on temples and stellae, reveal that their society had highly-developed social, political,
and religious philosophies related to the growing of the corn
for tortillas. Their religion, summarized in the sacred text
known as the Popol Vuh, was central to the culture. The
Mayas, again like the Greeks, lived in city-states associated
with each other by means of a general cultural bond of ritual,
sacred games, and moral philosophy. They looked with disfavor on outsiders as intellectual inferiors and barbarians, a
not unfair assessment by people who invented the zero and a
base-ten mathematical system as much on their own as the

97

Asians did. Yet such arrogance cut them off from their neighbors and caused divisions within, and the Old Empire (400-1000) gave way to the weaker New Empire (1000-1500) and eventual civil war. Hurricanes, smallpox, and Spaniards finished the job of destroying Maya civilization.

What the Mayas invented, the Aztecs often improved but just as often corrupted. The Aztecs were to the Mayas what Alexander the Great was to the Greeks, the borrower who extended the culture but watered it down. Just as the ruthless Macedonian Alexander extended his sway over the northern Greek tribes, the fierce Aztecs from northern Mexico conquered the Toltec empire of central Mexico and pushed the Moctezuma's influence into the fringes of Mayaland. From the Toltecs and the Mayas they absorbed Indian high culture. But the Aztec calendar, represented in the splendid Sun Stone, was mathematically inferior to the Mayan. Likewise, the Religion of the Sun took on a much fiercer aspect in the hands of the Aztecs. Ritual sacrifice, in the form of scapegoating to fend off taboos and in the execution of captured enemies after a perfunctory war-crimes trial, was practiced by these recently nomadic peoples, as it apparently had not been by the more sedentary Mayas. But the Temple of the Sun Stone in Tenochtitlán, the sacred capital on the islands of Lake Texcoco, not only provided the place for the ghastly excision and burning of living human hearts; it also embodied the extraordinarily advanced Aztec social and political ideals.

Aztec philosophy was based on the twin ideas of the oneness of all things and the brotherhood of all men, both of which were symbolized in the all-seeing Sun. This sun worship or fertility religion is not so very different from that of the Semites, the Indo-Europeans, or the Incas and Mayas, but the Aztecs seem to have drawn different conclusions about social rules from it. Unlike the Inca empire, for instance, the Aztec empire was in theory a federation of city-states that had freely chosen to live together, not something one was born into by being the child of a certain father or the distant "child" of the father-emperor. In a way this "Greek" idea was far more democratic than the "Roman" idea of the Incas (and of the feudal states of Europe like Spain). The state (politics) and the land (economics) were held "in common," since all men are one with each other and with nature.

In practice, it did not work out quite so neatly as the ideal would have it, and some of the taxes and tribute from outlying tribes, such as the Tlaxcalans, were not freely given by believers in the universal religion of sun worship but rather extorted by force. Yet the notion that gods and people and things which seem different are really at bottom the same thing enabled the Aztecs to take into their "empire" all sorts of tribes without destroying the various religions and cultures. In three centuries (1200-1500) the Priest of the Sun, the Moctezuma, had built a great "empire" whose center was the Sun Stone in Tenochtitlán. From it "radiated" the aqueducts, the causeways and roads, and the laws that gave life to the Aztec peoples. The throbbing heart on the Sun Stone's altar symbolized this "pumping" of vitality to the parts of the body politic.

But the heart was soon to die, for the Spaniards came down the causeways in 1519-21 and put out the Sun. The Aztecs, the Moctezuma no less than the others, were confused. They knew that they were living in a world of pain, with the Sun dying and coming to life every day, with some men dying and others being born, with corn dying and growing again. Their chief gods of this world of pain, Huitzilopochtli and Tezcatlipoca, were gods of pain and war--and wealth. But the god of the coming world, Quezalcoatl, the Serpent-Bird, would fly in on the rising Sun from the east and put an end to pain. Could Cortez, who came down the Sun's rays from the east, be Quezalcoatl? He announced a new era with a new ruler, Charles VI, and a new religion, Christianity. Yet he demanded the destruction of the old gods. Who could tell? Moctezuma talked, then fought, and the Aztec peoples did, too. Cortez, unlike Pizarro fifteen years later in Peru, came upon a viable, fully functional Indian culture that died hard. Or perhaps it lives on in the indianismo of modern Mexico. Cuauhtémoc, the last Moctezuma, stands proudly in bronze on the main street of Mexico City--looking toward the rising sun.

As in South America, most Indian history in Middle America has been made by the high agricultural societies, in this case the Aztecs and Mayas of central and southern Mexico, Guatemala, and Honduras. They have preserved what indianismo remains. The semi-settled tribes of southern Central America and the Caribbean succumbed within a century of Columbus' landing to the rigors of slavery and the ravages of disease. Almost no trace remains of the original three cultures of the Caribbean--the Ciboney of western Cuba, the Arawak of the Greater Antilles, and the Carib of the Lesser Antilles. The relatively advanced Arawaks had conquered and pushed back the primitive Ciboneys and were suffering from the newest island-hopping invasion from South America by the cannibalistic Caribs. The Europeans were thus able to play the Indians off against each other and conquer all but the Caribs rather easily, despite the fact that the Caribbean, then as now, was relatively heavily populated. The same process of conquest was followed after Balboa's first lodgment of Europeans on the mainland at the Isthmus of Panama in 1513. The northern Chibchas were subjected rather easily to Spaniards there.

The nomadic Chichimecs of northern Mexico were a different breed, however. Like the original Aztec conquerors, or the Apaches or Abibones, they had never been subdued by other Indians and had no intention of surrendering their nomadism to the Spanish missions either. They took the Spaniards' horses and then began to take Spanish lives by the thousands. Only the joint efforts of the Mexican and United States governments finally brought these small bands of wide-roving hunters to heel in the late nineteenth century. One could even argue that the warlordism of Pancho Villa was a revival of this tradition of mobile resistance to the encroachment of the Mexican and United States governments. And men still migrate back and forth across the border, legally or illegally, to work as field hands (braceros) in the American Southwest. Nomadism dies hard.

The Spanish Empire

Columbus made his second trip to Española (Hispaniola) in 1496, looking for Navidad, the settlement he had founded just after his "discovery" of America in 1492. He found the place in ruins and the people dead from Indians or disease, and so went on to found Santo Domingo, the first permanent European habitation in the Americas. His passengers and men spread out to farm the land themselves, or to enslave the Arawaks and the newly imported Africans, or to gather booty. In this way the linchpin of the three-stage Spanish conquest was locked into the Americas at the closest spot to Spain on the trade winds. Hispaniola, Puerto Rico and Cuba were to serve as the jumping-off point for Balboa and Cortez, the conquerors of the Isthmus of Panama and the heartland of Mexico, respectively. The offspring of the pigs and horses Columbus unloaded in Santo Domingo fed Balboa and Cortez and carried them to their conquests. And from Panama and Mexico the Spaniards eventually launched their conquests of much of South and North America. But in the first century after Columbus' startling discoveries, the Spaniards' success-

ses were invariably dependent on the food and supplies provided by the Antilles.

The man who profited most was Cortez, who was supported by the Governor of Cuba in the conquest of the Aztec
empire in 1519-21. Bernal Díaz del Castillo, one of Cortez'
men, chronicled the whole affair. Cortez landed on the Mexican coast, burned the ships to prevent his men from deser-
ting, and named the region Vera Cruz (True Cross) in honor
of its being the first Mexican region "liberated" from pagan-
ism. He then "converted" the Tlaxcalan peoples by booming
his cannons and racing his mounted horsemen to prove the
power of his God and his King--and, perhaps more important
to the Indians, ended the tribute Moctezuma, the Aztec god-
king, had forced upon them. The Tlaxcalans then secured
his line of march into Tenochtitlán, where Cortez came face
to face with the Moctezuma himself. The Moctezuma was not
unwilling to welcome a new god to the Aztec pantheon, but
Cortez was adamant in demanding that all gods but Jehovah
must be destroyed.

While Cortez returned to the coast to subdue a Cuban
force sent against him, the pacific Moctezuma was replaced
by Cuauhtémoc, who chose to resist all the Spaniards by force
and seized most of those still in the city for sacrifice on the
Sun Stone. When Cortez returned to the city, he found all
the causeways closed and well defended. After a half-year
siege in which Aztecs and Spaniards contested every span of
the causeways and many a house of the central city, the
Spaniards made their way to the Zócalo, captured Cuauhtémoc
and the last defenders, and became masters of Moctezuma's
empire. The Temple was razed and the Cathedral of Mexico
begun on the same site. The Aztec idols were smashed or
buried, and the gold ornaments were melted down for ship-
ment to Cuba and Spain. The causeways and roads were soon
mended so that tribute flowed in and orders out, as before.

Balboa had already anchored the third point of the
Spanish conquest in Panama. In 1513 he had sighted the Pacific ocean from a peak in Darién, and by the time Cortez'
conquest of Mexico City was complete, Panama had taken its
place as one of the major trans-shipment routes in world
trade. The Spanish court had immediately recognized Panama's value as a shortcut home to Spain from the Philippines
and was busy securing its approaches by conquests in Venezuela and Colombia, the famous Spanish Main. Soon Spaniards
crossed the Isthmus and scrambled onto the western mountains of Central America. The most famous of the conquis-

tadores-in-residence, however, was Francisco Pizarro, who
was outfitting an expedition to conquer the Inca empire in
Peru. So the Spanish conquest of Middle America was well
along just thirty years after it started with Columbus' landfall in Hispaniola in October, 1492.

The Golden Age of the Spanish empire in Middle America extended from Cortez' conquests to the independence of
Mexico and Central America in the 1820s, exactly three centuries. The Viceroyalty of New Spain, as it was called, followed almost the same course as the Viceroyalty of Peru.
The House of the Indies in Spain, following the theories of
Las Casas and the enlightened Bourbon despots, tried to run
the empire as humanely and profitably as their vision would
allow. But the conquistadores, hacendados, and padres who met
face-to-face with the Indians were sometimes less than law-abid-
ing and humane. Together they superimposed on Indian culture many of the same institutions carried to South America--
the Roman Catholic religion, the hacienda system, and the
Roman Law. In some ways, the Spanish empire was more
helpful in Middle than South America because there was a
lower ratio of Spaniards to Indians and because Spanish cattle culture opened up a much greater percentage of waste
land in the Middle American deserts. Still, the basic features
were the taking out of silver and gold and the production of
plantation crops, both of which primarily benefited the native-
born Spaniards (peninsulares) rather than Europeans born in
the empire (criollos), not to mention the other castes and
classes. Hence the revolutions of Father Hidalgo and Augustín Iturbide in Mexico (1810-21) and of Morazán in Central
America (1820s and 1830s) were extensions of the campaigns
of Bolívar and San Martín in South America in their political
and social origins.

But in Middle America Spain did not lose all its empire in the first wave of revolutions. Instead, it held onto
most of its colonies in the islands and lost only the mainland
states. The second, less glorious, period of the Spanish empire (1821-1898) was marked by concentration on plantation
agriculture in Cuba and Puerto Rico rather than on mining.
So long as the profits of the Mexican mines and haciendas
rolled in, the House of the Indies neglected the small tobacco
and coffee farmers who had replaced the Indians in the Greater Antilles. But when the Mexicans revolted, the Spanish
government began to convert these islands to sugar plantations
by driving back or buying out the Spanish dirt farmers and
importing Blacks from Africa and the other Caribbean islands.

In half a century the social and racial complexion of Cuba and
Puerto Rico changed drastically, which contributed to the tensions surfacing in the abortive Cuban Revolution (1868-78) and
the revolts that led to the Spanish American War (1898). The
United States intervened, drove the Spanish out of the Caribbean, and assumed control over Cuba and Puerto Rico--and
the Philippines--by the Treaty of Paris (1898). This was
merely the latest example of a predominant theme in the history of Spain's "second empire" in Middle America, namely,
that Spain's dominance gave way to the dominance of northern
Europeans. This process went back to the rapid conquest of
the sugar islands in the Lesser Antilles by the British, French,
and Dutch in the sixteenth century, and soon came forward to
the growing influence of the United States in the areas near
the Panama Canal.

Northern Europe's Colonies

The Lesser Antilles, Trinidad, Jamaica, the Bahamas,
and western Hispaniola had little gold and therefore few Spaniards when the English, French, and Dutch began their penetration early in the seventeenth century. Until that time the
northern Europeans had contented themselves with privateering.
The royal navies outfitted pirates and paid them part of the
booty they took from the Spanish galleons tacking upwind from
Panama and Vera Cruz to Havana to catch the trade winds en
route back to Spain. Not even the "convoy system" (1561-
1748) could protect the bullion from the likes of Francis Drake,
though it made privateering less profitable. The British,
French, and Dutch therefore decided to cut out the pirates
and directly involve their navies, particularly since they
feared each other as much as they wanted Spanish pieces of
eight.

The naval bases the north Europeans conquered from
the Spanish soon expanded into slave-worked plantations for
tobacco, indigo, and sugar. They "grew the gold"--or rather
their slaves did--and were so proud that their colonies were
"productive" that their propaganda started the Black Legend
(leyenda negra) that Spanish colonies were "exploitative."
So valuable were these specks of land that the French gave up
all of Canada to England after the French and Indian Wars
(1756-63), to keep just a few of them. The richest and most
powerful men in Europe after the kings were the merchants
who processed and traded the goods produced on these Caribbean plantations and their East Indies equivalents. So fierce

was the competition between Europeans for the islands that
every one except Barbados changed hands at least once. Every European empire in the Caribbean was first of all a
string of forts like El Morro in Puerto Rico, bastions hang-
ing over the volcanic cliffs to bombard the approaching inva-
ders. Slowly, however, the north Europeans pushed the Spanish out of those forts, the most notable conquests being the
seizure of Haiti by the French (1763) and of Trinidad by the
British (1797).

The name of the game was trade in slaves coming in,
rum and tobacco going out, and supplies coming back. This
"triangular trade" among the island colonies, north Europe,
and Africa was the bread and butter of the Caribbean empires.
The over-large plantation population could not have supported
itself adequately even if the slave owners had not taken almost all the production for themselves. Food was constantly
in short supply, but the "slavocracy" was perpetuated because
it was so profitable that food could be imported if necessary.
A constant influx of slaves was also required to make up for
the horrendous death rates caused by maltreatment, insuffi-
cient food, and overwork. The lush era of Caribbean colonialism therefore lasted until the abolition of the slave trade
by France and Britain (under the influence of the American
and French revolutions) and later by the Dutch and Spanish
as well. The success of slave revolts in Haiti (1791-1822)
and the abolition of slavery in the British Empire (1834) accelerated this decline of the colonial plantation. Yet in fact
the plantation system persisted in its traditional form until
very late in the nineteenth century, since contraband slaving
and sharecropping replaced the legal trade and legal slavery.
When former slaves were not available, the government often
subsidized the importation of contract laborers--pejoratively,
"coolies"--from Asia.

Nevertheless, the influx of European and North American capital did eventually convert the Caribbean economy to
one of large-scale commercial agriculture based on seasonal
wage labor. The modern sugar estate replaced the old plantation around the turn of the twentieth century. But the profits to be had from steel, as compared to those from sugar,
lured the smart money to Europe and North America and left
the former jewels of empires pale by comparison. The Caribbean islands were no longer quite so profitable, relatively
speaking. In fact, they were usually a losing proposition so
far as the "home government" was concerned. Indigenous
independence movements and international hostility to colo-

nialism have made "dependencies" politically costly as well. The history of the twentieth-century Caribbean is therefore the story of the decline of the European empires, as elsewhere in the world.

Since World War II, many of the Caribbean colonies have achieved their formal independence without the bloodshed attending the birth of Haiti, the Dominican Republic, and Cuba in earlier years. The political situation remains very fluid, however. For one thing, the Europeans have seldom surrendered their control gracefully and have therefore left a greater heritage of bitterness than necessary. The British, for example, tried in the early 1960s to establish a Caribbean Federation which would also have made the preservation of British economic domination easier. The result was that Jamaica and Trinidad left the federation because they wanted to follow a more nationalist policy--and because each wanted to be the capital. The French and Dutch made the citizens of their colonies full citizens of France and the Netherlands as a means of pacifying them, but independence-minded West Indian politicians have pushed on anyway. The second reason the situation is so tense is that the internal problems left by colonialism have scarcely been touched as yet. Some accommodation on the vital matters of class and caste will have to be reached before the islands can develop a viable state system. And finally, there is the continuing rivalry for Middle America in international affairs, now in the form of the Cold War. The influence of the United States is the dominant element in this rivalry, though Castroism grew for a while and several national and international forms of Middle American autonomy have been proposed.

United States Influence

Because of its anti-colonial tradition, the United States has undertaken a curious kind of imperialism in Middle America. The key to the United States' position has been the Monroe Doctrine and its later "corollaries" by Theodore Roosevelt and Lyndon Johnson. President Monroe said in 1823 that United States influence was better than European influence because the United States was an anti-colonialist republic and the European states were colonialist monarchies. Americans-- North, Middle, and South--should therefore work together to eliminate colonialism and backwardness. That has been the official United States position from then to now--against the British, French, and Spanish in the nineteenth century and against the Fascists and the Communists in the twentieth. In United States eyes, the free peoples of the Americas are working together to prevent the growth of dictatorships in the Western Hemisphere, and the Organization of American States is just the latest manifestation of Bolívar's dream of a Pan-American Union for Democracy. And many in Middle America support that view.

In many other Middle American eyes, however, the United States has defaulted on the moral obligations enunciated by President Monroe. Such people indict the United States on three charges of acting contrary to the principles of democracy and international law. First, the United States has annexed territory that formerly belonged to Middle American states or, as the Middle Americans see it, ought to have belonged to them. The present-day states of the American Southwest, for example, were taken from Mexico in the Texas War (1836) and the Mexican-American War (1844-48). Similarly, the Panama Canal Zone was ceded to the United States after the United States-financed revolution detached Panama from Colombia (1903). There is no agitation in Mexico for a reconquista against the United States, but resentment burns so fiercely that President Johnson made much of the return of the tiny El Chamizal district in El Paso, Texas, to Mexico. The struggles over revision of the Panama Canal Treaty (1964-78) indicate the division of opinion between Latin and North Americans on such issues.

The urge to protect the approaches to the Panama Canal has led the United States into the special territorial arrangements which constitue the Middle Americans' second objection to United States policy. These range from the Platt Amendment (1901-1934), giving the United States a veto over the Cuban Constitution, to the Organic Act (1917), giving Puerto Rico "commonwealth status" within the United States. The Virgin Islands, acquired from Denmark during World War I, are even more like colonies. The most curious of these arrangements, however, are the "leases" of military bases like Guantánamo in Cuba. Increasingly, Middle Americans are challenging these leases, especially if they were signed by the former colonial government, as is the case with those acquired via the Destroyer Deal between Winston Churchill and Franklin Roosevelt in World War II. The Guantánamo lease is being challenged by Fidel Castro on the grounds that no government can alienate national territory by contract. The United States has been turning some of these bases over to friendly governments since World War II. But Guantánamo?

Middle Americans also object to United States military interventions as an infringement on national sovereignty. Such interventions have come in three overlapping waves. The first was the late-nineteenth-century period of "dollar diplomacy" when the United States threatened war against the Europeans in Mexico (1867) and Venezuela (1894-95) and actually went to war to drive out the Spaniards in Cuba and Puerto Rico (1898). The occupation of the Panama Canal Zone (1903) and the declaration of the Roosevelt Corollary (1904) marked the culmination of this period. The end of such intervention was marked by the Good Neighbor Policy of Franklin Roosevelt, which cancelled the Platt Amendment in Cuba, withdrew the Marines everywhere, and prevented intervention in Mexico when U.S. citizens' property was nationalized (1934-38). Meanwhile, the second wave of interventions--in Mexico (1914-17), Nicaragua (1910-25), Santo Domingo (1916-24), and Haiti (1915-34)--was occurring because of the German threat in World Wars I and II. The culmination of this phase was that Destroyer Deal by which the British leased the United States bases at strategic points in return for fifty ships (1940). Finally, there have been interventions since World War II in Guatemala (1954), Cuba (1961), and Santo Domingo (1965) to prevent Communist penetration or, in the case of the Bay of Pigs invasion of 1961, to remove it. The United States contends that the Organization of American States has sanctioned these post-World War II interventions, but in the Dominican Republic crisis of 1964-66, President Johnson added a "Johnson Corollary" to the effect that the United States had a unilateral right to protect itself against "another Castro." Many Middle Americans resent this view.

The problem for Middle Americans, as they view it, is to find an acceptable alternative to European and American influence without falling under the influence of yet another outside force. Since independence, they have experimented with various forms of nationalism, federalism, and internationalism to move toward Middle American unity, but so far without conspicuous results--except, perhaps, in Mexico.

Independent Mexico

Modern Mexico was born on September 16, 1810, with the cry of Father Miguel Hidalgo y Costilla: "Mexicans! Viva Mexico, viva independence, viva the Virgin of Guadalupe!" For his hearers answered with, "And death to the gachupines!" The criollo and mestizo revolt against the peninsular Spaniards (gachupines) was then begun by priests and peasants under the leadership of Father Hidalgo, a criollo of impassioned Catholic conscience, and Father Morelos, a mestizo of pronounced Enlightenment leanings. Neither was to see the revolution through, but the terrifying example of Hidalgo's head hung high in a cage in Guanajuato failed to still the Indian peasants.

The victor over Father Morelos, Colonel Augustín de Iturbide, therefore gathered around him the frightened remnants of creole power and declared himself Emperor Augustín I of Mexico in 1821. He had come to think of himself as the Napoleon of the New World, a man fending off the forces of tyranny (the gachupines) from above and the forces of anarchy (the mestizos and Indians) from below. He was the middle way between the monarchists of Europe and the Jacobins of America, an alternative to the reactionary Concert of Europe and the revolutionary mobs of Jefferson and Bolívar. Already the Mexican Empire stretched from Yucatán to Yosemite, and Augustín I had plans to extend it farther. But the dream lasted only a year, for Iturbide was overthrown and driven into exile, leaving behind him the shattered remains of the "crown of Mexico."

Then began the period of struggle between these two revolutionary traditions, that of "enlightened" European-style moderism and that of peasant-based Indian "nationalism." In the nineteenth century, these forces were represented by General Antonio López de Santa Anna and Benito Juárez, respectively. General Santa Anna, who helped oust Iturbide, was president no less than eleven times up to 1855. His internal political program was supported by the landowners, the Church, and the army and designed to encourage benevolent creole leadership. His foreign policy was designed to fend off the encroachments of the United States in Texas and California, but it failed. The loss of the Texas and Mexican-American wars (1836, 1844-48) removed Mexico from the rank of geographical giants like Russia, China, and Brazil and elevated the United States in its place. The oligarchy was so discredited as a result that Juárez, a Zapotec Indian, took over the presidency on a program of Liberal reform.

The Juárez period (1857-72) was one of the most confused in Mexican history, but it represented the first emergence of the indianismo that was to dominate Mexico's future. The Reform Constitution (1857), which Juárez designed to break the power of the hacendados and the Church, set off a civil war. The creole oligarchy at first contained the Juárez

forces but then made the near-fatal mistake of siding with
foreigners. In 1862 the French, British, and Spanish came
to restore order and collect on their loans, and the French
stayed to put Maximilian of Hapsburg and his wife Carlotta
on the throne of a renewed Mexican Empire. Napoleon III of
France was glad to find that the creole program of Iturbide
lived on in the minds of the Church and the landlords. What
none of them counted on was the persistence of the Juaristas
and the success of the United States in the Civil War with the
Confederacy. The threats of the American government forced
the French to leave, and Juárez executed Maximilian in 1867.
From then until he died in office 1872, Juárez went about
opening up opportunities for his mestizo and Indian followers
through programs like those of his idol, Abraham Lincoln.
Having fought for the ideals of freedom and nationalism,
Juárez set out to legislate them into existence through home-
stead acts, separation of church and state, and political hon-
esty. Mestizos rose a lot, indios a little. The creole oligarchy dug in its heels and waited.

Porfirio Díaz, one of Juárez' mestizo generals, came
to power in 1876, and, save for one four-year period behind
a stand-in, remained president until the Revolution of 1910.
Originally, Díaz came to power to protect the Juárez Reform
from the reviving oligarchy, but soon he changed direction.
He not only changed the Reform Constitution to allow himself
to remain in office and fix the political process but also began to raise capital by mortgaging the country to foreigners.
His program was much influenced by the Positivists of Mexico, the Cientificos, who argued that a country with a small
educated elite needed scientific management in order to modernize. Scientists and industrialists would lead Mexico out
of the wilderness, not the Indians.

Mexico did in fact make progress under Díaz--at a
great price. Internal peace, the Pax Porfiriana, was secured
by unleashing a newly created rural police force made up
chiefly of former "bandits. " Economic growth was achieved
by selling over one-fourth of the country's land and mineral
rights to foreigners, chiefly North Americans. The object
was to replace the Indians' communal subsistence agriculture
with a modern commercial and industrial economy. When
tribes like the Yaquis of the northwest revolted, they were
suppressed and shipped off to be sold for labor in the mines
of Yucatán. The countryside seethed with discontent, but
Mexico City grew in wealth and splendor--and Díaz in the reputation of the "civilized world. "

Then came the clash. Franciso Madero, a rich humanitarian from northern Mexico, objected to Díaz' succeeding himself yet another time and was thrown into jail, then released after Díaz' re-election. Madero went to the United States, called for a "second revolution," and got more than he had bargained for. The Indians erupted in the Revolution of 1910 and swept Old Mexico forever into the dustbin. The Mexico of Iturbide, Santa Anna, and Díaz crumbled under the impact of the Mexico of Hidalgo, Juárez, and the Revolution. Mexicans are proud of the fact that they were "the first to restore America to the first Americans" and emphasize the indianismo of the events from 1910 to 1921. Actually, there were several revolutions going on at the same time. There were those who, like Madero, wanted to get rid of the Díaz dictatorship and restore constitutional liberties. Others, such as Victoriano Huerta, were at bottom warlords leading bandits in search of booty from whatever source, rich or poor, native or foreign. Some, especially the legendary Emiliano Zapata, were saviors of the Indians out to restore the communal lands of the ejido. Most, and notably Pancho Villa in northern Mexico, were a bit of each. Almost all wanted to punish the rich Porfiristas and the foreign oilmen and ranchers. The result of all of these conflicting claims was a bloodbath from which the Constitution of 1917 and the Carranza government eventually emerged.

Both the Constitution of 1917 and the politics of the Revolutionary Party reflect the struggle between the "Europeanized nationalists" in Mexico City and the "Indian nationalists" in the hinterlands north and south of the central plateau. In 1917, the Carranza government represented the former, and the followers of Villa and Zapata, who did not attend the Constitutional Convention, the latter. The Constitution nevertheless made a nod toward indianismo in its claim that all the land belonged to the people of the nation and could be expropriated where necessary. After 1917, expropriation of land and formation of ejidos became the chief cause of rivalries within the Revolutionary Party (soon called "PRI" after its initials). The Church question complicated matters, however, since the Indians were as Catholic as they were land-hungry. Attempts by the early PRI governments to suppress Catholicism led in the 1920s to a serious revolt, the Cristero movement, and revealed to the Party the lack of appeal of the anticlerical issue among the Indians. Only the "Europeanized" intellectuals and workers of the plateau and coastal cities thought that the Church had to be subdued in order to modernize. So President Cárdenas (1934-40) patched

up the quarrel with the Church and began seriously to expropriate and redistribute the land. Thus Indian agriculturalism
and modern industrialism have become the twin poles of PRI
policy since World War II.

Still, the constitution and the Party have been over-run
by deep currents of Mexican history. The social promises
of the Constitution have been implemented on a localized basis because of regional differences in climate, culture, and
habits. The foreigners have been expropriated in the main,
and the land belongs to the people through the state. But in
actual use patterns it is in large haciendas and communes in
the dry north, small individual farms and commercial farms
in the plateau and coastal areas, and tribal communes in the
Indian south. Modernism and Indianism exist almost side by
side, with modernism gaining as the Mexican version of the
Industrial Revolution draws workers away from the land.

The political promises of the Party likewise remain
largely unfulfilled because local politicians are often allowed
to enforce the laws or not in accordance with regional customs. The anti-clerical laws remain in effect but are generally ignored, and few dare challenge the local governor and
tax-gatherer. It cannot be otherwise because the sense of
national destiny is not yet sufficiently strong to allow a truly
national policy. Moreover, the unions of workers and of peasants sometimes make irreconcilable demands upon the Party
and force a shifting pattern of administration. Until the almost equal division of Mexico's people moves in one direction
or the other, the PRI has no alternative but to move with
caution. In the long run, the modernist pole is likely to
draw most of the people, but Mexico's aim is "Indian modernism." Zapata still lives, but he looks more like Madero now.

Recently Mexico seems to have begun another of those
periodic shifts within the Revolutionary tradition. Because
the changes are taking place within the Party, they are often
overlooked by observers who are accustomed to the parliamentary traditions of West Europe and North America. But
it is the essence of the PRI tradition to act as a magnet for
all disruptive forces on the Right or the Left--to offer Party
positions to their leaders, to take over their programs, to
move in their direction if they are popular enough. Thus in
the Carranza-to-Cárdenas period (1917-40) the Party emphasized the class conflict elements of the Revolution because
the Peasant Leagues and the Labor Confederation of Vicente
Lombardo Toledano were very strong. Only the "alien" ele-

ments were kept outside the Party coalition--the Communists, the Sinarquistas or local Fascists, and the big businessmen who favored "Gringoism." The Churchmen, once considered alien, were soon redefined as non-hostile elements and tolerated if not admitted to the Party. Land reform, nationalization of oil, labor legislation--in a word, class-conscious nationalism--marked this period.

The government turned Rightist under President Alemán, however, and remained that way for twenty years (1940-60). From one point of view, it appeared that Mexico had abandoned the Revolution to secure United States capital and had joined the anti-Communist crusade of the Organization of American States. From another perspective, it seemed that the Party had chosen to emphasize a different strain of revolutionary thought, not unlike Arab or African Socialism, namely, developmental nationalism. The idea was that before class-conscious nationalism could work there had to be more wealth to share. Hence the vigorous industrialization program --at the expense, to be sure, of social services. "Development first, distribution later" seemed to be the motto.

In the 1960s pressures began to build for a third approach to the Revolution. Mexicans sometimes view the changes as a struggle to "return to the Revolution," to displace the Alemanistas and revive the Cárdenas approach. Certainly there is some of the older revolutionary tradition about, as recent troubles among the Peasant Leagues of the northern Mexican states indicate. But now there are two new elements: first, the middle sectors enriched and educated by the Revolution; and second, the advocates of a second revolution in the Marxist manner--but this time following a Latin American model, Castro. The Party has already begun to show signs of re-thinking its stance in the selection of presidential candidates, alternating the moderately conservative Díaz-Ordax with the quite radical Echeverría and then returning to the moderate López Portillo. The Party has not decided whether the second revolution will be advanced industrialism under a mixed economy or Castro's new radicalism. As usual, the Party is waiting to see which forces become dominant before moving to absorb their programs and capture their followers. To date, despite student riots and serious peasant and worker dissatisfaction, there is little indication that changes will take place outside the Revolutionary Party. The battle between the Nationalist Revolution in Mexico and the Marxist Revolution in Cuba has been joined, and all Middle America is awaiting the outcome.

Two elements of the Mexican Revolution besides one-party nationalism should also be mentioned: development strategy and foreign policy. Mexican development strategy is remarkably non-ideological. In agriculture, it utilizes Indian communes, state farms, and private ownership. In industry, it mixes private and state enterprises. Capital comes from every available source. Labor runs from subsistence farmers to Communist oilfield unionists to highly educated civil servants. Resources are owned by the state or not, depending on how efficiently the private owners operate. There is some evidence for the radicals' contention that the Mexican Revolution has stagnated and accepts a dual society of new-rich and still-poor. The eastern and western ends of the old trail for freighting the Spanish galleons' wares across the Mexican isthmus are now anchored by oil-rich Vera Cruz and tourist-rich Acapulco, for example, while much of the in-between area is a vast rural slum of Indian villages sending their excess population the thousand-plus miles to the United States to find work. The smokestacks of industrial Monterrey in the north contrast with the hardscrabble lands and adobe or sandstone huts nearby. The splendor of the elegant Pedregal or Las Palmas suburbs of Mexico City stand out all the more because of the slums across town. One could also cite the evaded taxes, the necessity for mordidas (bribes), the conspicuous consumption. Yet there is also evidence of dedication on the part of doctors and teachers in the backlands and the slums, of Church-state cooperation in producing justice and order, and of improved circumstances for body and soul --evidence, in short, that development has begun to take hold. Mexico seems head-to-head with Cuba in this respect, despite different, and perhaps more difficult, circumstances.

Mexican foreign policy, in contrast to Cuba's, is neutralist, almost isolationist. Mexican leaders have avoided any hint of a challenge to United States interests since Pancho Villa crossed the border into New Mexico in 1916 and provoked General Pershing to move into Mexico to restore order. The Zimmerman Telegram (1917), in which the Germans offered to help Mexico regain the lands lost to the United States in 1848, was not even seriously considered, and Mexicans have seen no reason to change their policy in this respect, especially after seeing the results of the Castro confrontation with the United States. Efforts at allying the Mexican and United States Communist parties after World War I were initiatives by the North American party and have never been revived since their failure. Mexicans prefer United States tourists and trade despite a long, long history of conflict in

the first century of independence. But on the other hand the
Mexicans also refuse to do the bidding of the United States in
the OAS or the United Nations, on the oil issue, or with respect to "the Latin American Revolution. " Nor has Mexico
given an inch on the issue of Mexican ownership and control
of national resources, even though the rules are often flouted
by Mexicans adding North American "silent partners. " Still,
the result is much more like the United States-Canadian relationship than the United States-Cuban one. Recent settlements regarding Colorado River water and the sharing of
electric power augur well despite Mexico's "revolutionary"
heritage and its refusal to ostracize Castro in the OAS.

Central American Disunity

Nationalism has been a healthy force in Mexico, a potential great power of well over fifty million people. But in
the six small nations of Central America, with twelve million
people altogether, it has been a curse that keeps them divided
and weak. Since independence Central American leaders have
attempted to combat this problem with projects for unification
and federation, generally without success. The present-day
Central American Common Market is therefore merely the
latest chapter in the struggle between nationalism and federation.

The struggle between central authority and local leaders began in colonial and revolutionary times, when the entire region, except Panama, was theoretically governed from
Guatemala City but actually run by local interests. On September 15, 1821, the leaders of the Captaincy-General of
Guatemala declared themselves independent and soon joined
Iturbide's Mexico. But El Salvador, more radical than the
rest, seceded from this "new imperialism" and sent an emissary to Washington to apply for admission to the Republic of
the United States. Iturbide's general, Vicente Filísola, conquered San Salvador for the Emperor, only to become isolated by the overthrow of Iturbide's government in Mexico
City. The Guatemala City leaders then came over to El Salvador's point of view and decided to call a National Assembly
to create a federated republic.

The National Assembly met on June 24, 1823, and
formed the Central American Federation. The Constitution
abolished slavery but, as in most republics then, left government to the rich by restricting suffrage. The first president,

the moderate Manuel José Arce, was unable to enforce the federal laws on the local level, and civil war erupted between the Conservatives and the Liberals. The Liberals, led by the Honduran Francisco Morazán, won over the creole areas and began to extend the power of the state into the more conservative Indian and Spanish regions. But his rival Carrera rallied the Indians with a program of religious solidarity. Morazán was executed by a firing squad on the twenty-first anniversary of independence, September 15, 1842. Meanwhile, in 1838 the Federal Congress had declared that secession was legal, and the modern national states had begun to take form. The death of Morazán, the last effective force fighting for the federal republic, merely confirmed the demise of the Central American Federation. Morazán's statues remain in Central America today to show that the ideal of unity is not dead, but beside them are the statues of nationalist caudillos like the Somozas of Nicaragua. The nationalist rivalries and foreign entanglements emerging from the Federation's civil war have plagued Central America for over a century. Guatemala, Honduras, Nicaragua, El Salvador, and Costa Rica go their separate ways. Panama, until 1903 part of Colombia and since then bifurcated by the Canal Zone, is a state like no other--but Central American nevertheless. Add to all this Belize, which was known as British Honduras before planning for independence began in the 1970s, and which both Mexico and Guatemala claim, and quite a scrambled puzzle is created.

There are simply too many divisions for Central America to get together easily. Costa Rica is over ninety per cent European, has a high literacy rate, lives relatively well off the profits of its small farmers, and governs by means of a functioning democratic state. Guatemala, at the other extreme, is more Indian than not, remains overwhelmingly uneducated, lives an abysmally poor existence off mixed subsistence and plantation agriculture, and suffers under political habits that have brought to power dictators like Carrera, Justo Rufino Barrios, and Jorge Ubico. El Salvador, Honduras, and Nicaragua resemble each other in their mixed populations, their plantation agricultures, their middle-range educational level, and their political instability. They are different in that El Salvador and Nicaragua have wealthy elite families like those of Guatemala, whereas Honduras, like Costa Rica, has more nouveaux riches than "society" types. Moreover, Nicaragua differs from most of the other states in that it is a potential route for a canal and so resembles Panama in being more involved in external matters. And so, with Guatemala as a too-large "Germany," Panama as a stand-offish "England,"

and the rest as squabbling in-betweens, Central America
crawls along--divided. Only a renewed threat from a "Russia" like Mexico, strong but not overwhelming, could unite
these countries firmly, and that is not a likely event.

The greatest hindrance to Central American unity has,
in fact, until recently come from the outside rather than the
inside. As the focal point of Atlantic-Pacific shipping, Central America has been encouraged in its weakness in order to
prevent a local threat to the canal routes in Panama, Nicaragua, and elsewhere. In the nineteenth century, the rivalry
between Great Britain, headquartered in British Honduras,
and the United States, represented by the shipping interests
of Cornelius Vanderbilt in Nicaragua, was so fierce that it
often set off brushfire wars in Central America. Occasionally United States citizens, such as the famous "filibusterer"
William Walker, would "intervene on the side of liberty"
against the British-backed Conservatives and revive the disorders that destroyed the Federation. At one time Walker
got to the point of petitioning the United States Congress to
admit Central American slave states to balance the free states
being admitted to the union after the Mexican-American War.
The Congress refused. At other times, the Conservatives
would set out with British support to give the Royal Navy control over the area. Skirmishes often resulted, and war between the United States and its former colonial masters was
threatened more than once. But in the end the American-
backed revolution of 1903 which gave Panama its independence
and the United States its canal, settled the issue in America's
favor. Not even the rival Nicaraguan route remained for the
British, as the United States had tied that up by a treaty in
the 1850s. Actually, the British government had already come
to an entente with the United States that left the Central American
sphere to the North Americans. Throughout the twentieth century, this entente has held and challenges to the United States'
strategic dominance in the area have come from the Germans
and Russians on the one hand and local radicals on the other.

It is these latest challenges from without and within
that have produced the renewed program of minimal unification
in a Central American Common Market. The Spanish-speaking elites in all these countries have always been determined
to preserve their Latin heritage against all comers, Indian or
foreign, and recent events have caused them to rally around
that heritage. No sooner had National Socialist appeals to
sympathizers in Guatemala been headed off than the Communists began to appeal to the landless poor and the Indians.

This threatened to throw the Central American elites more than ever on the mercy of the United States, as was the case when the left-oriented Arbenz regime was ousted in Guatemala in 1954 with American help. The lines were even more tightly drawn when Fidel Castro came to power in Cuba and Nicaragua furnished support for the Bay of Pigs invasion. President José Figueres of Costa Rica spoke for educated Central Americans of the 1960s when he said he did not want to make a choice between Castroism and dependence on the United States. The United States, seeing in this movement some promise of economic growth and greater stability in the region of the Panama Canal, began to support a middle way between Castroism on the one hand and old-style elitism on the other.

The Central American Common Market was formed in a series of commerical treaties signed between 1951 and 1962. All the independent states except Panama belong, and it is hoped that Panama will soon join despite the fact that its higher wage and production costs will put it at a disadvantage in selling its goods. The market's aims are so far limited to reducing tariffs, developing a common transportation network, and setting up methods of clearing and payment. There is no doubt that in time the Central American Common Market will return to the idea of a political federation and begin debates like those now going on in the European Common Market. For the moment, the Honduran-Salvadorean War (1969) makes that seem very remote, though.

In the meantime, Central America has its hands full trying to carry out reforms sufficient to satisfy its people and prevent insurrections. The United States has put at Central America's disposal some Alliance for Progress aid--and some Green Beret counterinsurgency forces. The less adjustable landowners and foreign plantation managers continue to resist fundamental land reform, however, and the Indian insurgency seems to be gaining, too. Naturally, the Costa Ricans, who need reform least, have done the most. Nor is it certain that the United States would look with such favor on a Common Market which moved left or offered a threat to the Canal Zone. For the whole question of the external relations of the Central American Common Market remains very unclear. Will it remain associated with the Western economies or, like Castro, turn eastward? Will it find a place in the Latin American Common Market, as Mexico has? Or will Middle America have a market all its own? The future remains very uncertain.

What that future will become probably depends on the outcome of the by now hackneyed struggle between the forces represented by the Somozas in Nicaragua, Figueres in Costa Rica, and the more revolutionary groups among the politicians and the guerrillas. The Somozas, who came to power as modernizers during the United States occupation, have become new-style caudillos whose hope of success lies in the support they can garner from the United States' fear of Communism. They own much of the land, grant many concessions to such interests as the United Fruit Company, and control the still-backward population with an iron hand. The fact that Nicaragua could furnish an alternative route for a canal strengthens their claim on United States support. It is hard to tell whether they are more afraid of Communism or of a switch of United States support to something like Figueres' plan.

For a time, the Somozas and Figueres were in a toe-to-toe struggle that led to attempts on Figueres' life and near war between the two states. What precipitated the whole episode was the onset of Figueres' reforms in Costa Rica during his first term as president in 1948. He vigorously attacked the problems of plantation agriculture, set in motion the development of a democratic welfare state, and in general challenged the Somozas' band of Central American politics. As time went on, the United States, under the threat of the growth of radical movements in Guatemala (and later Cuba), began to heed Figueres and even to insist that private American firms like United Fruit give up some of their properties in Central America. The Central American Common Market was one result, Alliance for Progress aid another. Soon MacDonalds' hamburger beef was being raised mainly in Costa Rica, but on terms very favorable to Costa Ricans. Figueres, along with Betancourt in Venezuela and Frei in Chile, came to symbolize United States support for reforms without revolution. The culmination came in 1959-61 when Figueres, invited to Havana by Castro, condemned the Cuban drift toward Communism--and then denounced the Bay of Pigs invasion.

The crisis had long been coming from the left. Guatemala set the tone when Juan José Arévalo became president and began a left-nationalist reform program that culminated in the near-Marxist regime of Jacobo Arbenz in 1952-54. The intervention of the United States to displace the Arbenz nationalists in 1954 merely drove the revolutionaries underground. Nor did the fact that the Bay of Pigs invasion was launched with the tacit support of Arbenz' American-backed successors endear the United States to the radicals. More

and more reformers on the Figueres model began to drift toward the guerrilla solution of which Fidel Castro was to become the symbol in the whole of Latin America. New-style
guerrillas took as their model either César Sandino, the mur-
dered hero of the Nicaraguan armed resistance to the United
States interventions of the era of dollar diplomacy, or Che
Guevara, the professional revolutionary fighter who even tired
of desk jobs for Fidel and went underground once again in
1965. Whether Guatemala--indeed, all of Central America--
will belong to those inspired by "Che," "Pepe" Figueres, or
the Somozas is yet to be seen.

Panama will almost certainly remain unique whatever
happens. The problems are generally the same, that is micro-statism, nationalism, political instability, modernization.
But the Canal changes everything. It makes Panama a pawn
in international relations and gives the country potential economic viability. The "Canal question" overshadows all others.
Three alternatives to the 1903 arrangement have been proposed over the years: first, turn the Canal over to Panama
and return the Canal Zone; second, "internationalize" the
Canal and the Zone; and third, make the Canal an open wa-
terway like the High Seas. Panama has always insisted on
sovereignty over the Zone, more of the Canal tolls, and the
illegality of the coerced 1903 treaty. The United States has
concentrated on the strategic questions of defense of the route
connecting New York and California. In the meantime, the
Canal approaches obsolescence as many ships--the largest
tankers and some aircraft carriers, for instance--go round
the Horn because they are too large for the Canal. Plans
for a new sea-level canal in Nicaragua or Colombia, or a
railroad in Mexico or Costa Rica, have begun to be formulated. In this way Panama might someday lose its uniqueness,
unless, of course, the sea-level canal or the railroad is built
in northern Panama, as some argue would be best.

The United States separated Panama from Colombia and
eventually persuaded the latter to recognize the new state.
But in general the United States did not intervene in Panama
as it did in Cuba and Puerto Rico, Haiti and the Dominican
Republic, Nicaragua and Honduras. It simply held the Canal
and the Zone. Small treaty changes to alter toll payments to
Panama was about all the action there was--until 1964, that
is. The 1964 riots, which were precipitated when the Stars
and Stripes were raised above the Panamanian flag on a Zone
high school to flaunt North American "sovereignty," resulted
in twenty-one dead and new negotiations. The seizure of pow-

er from the elected government of Arnulfo Arias by the military-nationalist General Omar Torrijos in 1968 accelerated the process. Torrijos claimed to admire Castro--and continued to suppress the Communist party of Panama. He claimed to hate Yankee influence--and kept Panama tied to the dollar, welcomed the branch banks of Wall Street, and encouraged private investment. Meanwhile, he gained support from other Latin Americans until the Panama Canal issue, like the Cuban blockade issue, became a symbol of North Americans' willingness to be "good neighbors." So in 1973 the United States accepted the principle of eventual Panamanian control of the Zone and the Canal, and in 1977 a new treaty was signed to "return" them--although the United States could intervene, if necessary, to keep the Canal open after it is returned to Panama at the turn of the century. Such is the growing independence of even the most sensitive strategic areas of Latin America, including Central America and the Caribbean.

Caribbean Struggles

The Central Americans have a strong Spanish heritage to give them hope for unity, but the Caribbean peoples have only their misery. The sad fact is that many Caribbean people dislike each other more than they do outsiders. Hence, the persistence of colonialism and the difficulties when it has been overturned in this region. To date there have been three great surges of anti-colonialism. The first, during the Revolutionary era, gave rise to the states on Hispaniola, Haiti and Santo Domingo. The second, before and after the Spanish-American War of 1898, saw the emergence of Cuba and Puerto Rico. And the last, since World War II, led to the independence of most of the remaining colonial possessions of Britain.

Hispaniola was freed by slave revolts while its French masters were engaged in the French Revolution. This was a shock to French plans, which included the separation of North America from Britain in the American Revolution and the conquest of the whole Caribbean with Admiral de Grasse's fleet. By 1782 almost the entire American region was in the French sphere, with the British holding only four islands. Then came the French Revolution of 1789--and Toussaint's slave uprising in Hispaniola in 1791. Pierre-Dominique Toussaint, called Toussaint l'Ouverture, took charge of the slave forces, put an end to the random slaughter of the white planters, and

restored the economy on a wage-earning basis rather than
slavery, only to have Napoleon's forces invade to regain the
French empire. Toussaint died in a French prison, but malaria and yellow fever won the day and left the country free
of colonial rule.

Toussaint's successors then decided to "liberate" the
rest of the island, inhabited more by Spanish-speaking smallholders than plantation slaves, and succeeded in unifying Hispaniola for a time (1822-44). The Santo Domingans never accepted Haitian rule, however, and a Black-White civil war
drove people of like color together at the opposite ends of the
island or killed them off. Eventually Santo Domingo--led by
Juan Pablo Duarte--emerged as a relatively underpopulated
"White" nation looking for a patron and for White immigrants.
The United States and Spain both refused annexation. Meanwhile, Haiti became an overpopulated "Black" state, an isolated Black ship in a White-ruled sea.

Haiti has paid a high price for its isolationism. The
economy has been permanently damaged by the fight of the
Haitian peasantry against plantationism. Not only did the majority of the population cut itself off from the sugar market
by shifting to coffee production; the early governments par-
celed out the land in very small plots which have since been
subdivided until they are uneconomical producing units. This
might be overcome in the usual way of government reform
programs, except that the Haitians have good reasons not to
trust their government. In the first place, the government is
generally made up of French-speaking, Roman Catholic, light-
skinned members of the Haitian elite, while the masses are
mainly very dark Voodoo worshippers who speak the dialect
known as Creole. Secondly, the government has never been
excessively concerned with much besides its own affairs.
The elite drags the government back and forth from anarchy
to repression, and wise men stay out of politics. Jean-
Jacques Dessalines won independence and was assassinated; Hen-
ri Christrophe and Alexandre Pétion fought it out for spheres
of influence north and south; Jean Boyer reunited the country
but invaded Santo Domingo--and so on to the present, with an
interlude of occupation by American Marines (1915-34). Since
1961 President Francois ("Papa Doc") Duvalier, and his son
and successor Jean-Claude, have perpetuated the suffocating
political order while Haiti continues to record the lowest figures in the Americas in literacy, health, and income. "Baby Doc" has attempted to lessen the influence of the secret
police and to draw more European and North American tour-

ists, but many Haitians are still leaving to become illegal aliens in New York. The Duvaliers are, however, more dark-skinned than most of the elite, which may be a sign that things are changing. So far, however, Haiti is a tragic example of what happens when a small nation has to go it alone for racial or other reasons.

If Haiti's "Black nationalism" has caused it to become too isolated, the Dominican Republic's "White nationalism" has made it too dependent on foreign powers. Throughout the nineteenth century the country shifted from a White colonialism that promised aid against Haiti to a White independence that meant freedom from the plantationism of colonial policies for Santo Domingo's "poor white" farmers. After the Haitian occupation (1822-44), the Dominicans actually approached Britain, France, and the United States before becoming the only Latin American country ever to return voluntarily to Spanish rule (1861-65). The victory of the United States in the American Civil War and the expulsion of the Hapsburgs from Mexico by Juárez coincided with the permanent changeover of "Santo Domingo" to "The Dominican Republic"--and the failure of President Grant's effort to get the United States Senate to annex the country by treaty. Since that time Dominican history has been marked by the rise of the modern wage-labor sugar plantation and the growing influence of the United States. In fact, the resistance of the Dominican poor whites to the creation of plantations led to the first United States intervention (1916-24), from which Leonidas Trujillo emerged as dictator of the country (1930-61).

Trujillo's aim was to make the Dominican Republic indispensable to American interests in economic and foreign affairs, particularly after the European sugar market collapsed in World War II. Trujillo's rigidly anti-Communist line covered his own dictatorial methods, so that after the Castro Revolution the Dominican Republic gained the former Cuban sugar quota at subsidized United States prices. After Trujillo was assassinated, Juan Bosch, a Socialist, was elected president on a platform of land reform and industrial growth-- in short, a plan to combat plantationism. Yet Bosch did not criticize the "White nationalist" elements of Trujillismo, such as the massacre of Haitians who strayed over the border, the creation of White border settlements, or the encouragement of exclusively White immigration from Spain and Spanish-speaking countries. When Bosch was overthrown by the army, the ensuing civil war brought on the second United States intervention (1965-66). The Americans thought they were fighting to get rid of plantation agriculture, with the result that Joaquín Balaguer won the presidency several times but presided over a divided country. Democracy depends on whether Balaguer and his more radical successor, President Guzmán, have found a middle way between Right and Left dictatorship.

The second wave of independence washed over the Caribbean in the wake of the Spanish-American War. But in 1898 the United States did not show restraint as it had in Central America and Santo Domingo in the 1850s and 1860s, and thus became intimately involved in the affairs of Puerto Rico and Cuba. The twentieth century has witnessed the progressive disengagement of the United States from President McKinley's imperialist ventures via the elevation of Puerto Rico and Cuba to a more and more independent status. This political retreat has not been matched by an equal withdrawal in economic and military affairs, however, as the continued existence of Guantánamo Naval Base and the growth of American investment in Puerto Rico indicate. Nevertheless, Franklin Roosevelt's Good Neighbor Policy of returning political control to the Puerto Ricans and Cubans--and hoping for democracy and friendship toward the United States--has been abrogated only in the case of the Bay of Pigs invasion against Fidel Castro.

Puerto Rico has responded, at least in part, to American hopes and become the Caribbean's Showplace of Democracy. The success of Muñoz Marin's Operation Bootstrap in 1940 seems all the more remarkable when the magnitude of the economic and social problems is understood. For Puerto Rico was ten times more densely populated than the United States (599 per square mile), more seriously divided ethnically (one-quarter negro in the Spanish sense), and infinitely less well endowed with natural resources (no important industrial raw materials) and social skills (near 100% illiteracy in 1940). In these circumstances Muñoz decided to make a virtue of the necessity of dependence on the United States and persuaded President Roosevelt to appoint a governor, Rex Tugwell of New Deal fame, who sympathized with Operation Bootstrap.

Muñoz set out to build up the economy by re-directing the sugar economy and encouraging industry in accordance with the dreams of nineteenth-century Puerto Rican nationalists such as his father, Using some provisions of the United States laws governing the island, the Foraker Act (1900) and the Organic Act (1917), Muñoz reduced the holdings of the sugar planta-

tions, over sixty per cent American-owned, to the legal limit
of five hundred acres. He then used some of the land seized
to create sugar cooperatives and some to establish individually-
owned truck farms. Thus the Jíbaros (peasants) could get
land and begin to solve the food-import problem. The excess
population still had to be removed from the land, however,
and Muñoz determined that they should be taken into local industry or, as a far inferior choice, go to the United States
mainland and work for a while. The faster the industrialization, the fewer families would be split up.

Hence Muñoz devised a plan for industrial incentives--
tax credits, free building space, cheap labor--to get United
States industry to locate on the island. The plan was partly
successful, and Puerto Rico was able to encourage some
firms that would train some of the skilled personnel that were
badly needed--medical firms, small-goods industries, and the
like. By the time Muñoz retired in 1964, Puerto Rico could
partially feed itself, process its own rum and clothing, and
even perform some specialized industrial operations. Per
capita income was up from about two hundred dollars to nearly a thousand per year, which masked the fact that as many
as one-third of all workers were unemployed at certain times
of the year. Muñoz could afford to ignore charges that he
was a "communist" or an "imperialist," though he did seize
property on the one hand and accept United States military
bases on the other.

What Muñoz could not ignore were the feelings of
Puerto Rican nationalism among his people. And there was
enough bad in the relationship with the United States--restric-
tions on prices and shipping charges, language and racial
prejudices against Puerto Ricans on the mainland, the military draft, the growing materialism--to obscure good points
like exemption from income taxes, several billions of dollars
of welfare and social security payments coming in each year,
and Constitutional guarantees. In the early 1950s Muñoz arranged to have Congress pass Law 600 allowing Puerto Ricans
to choose their status so long as United States bases remained, and then argued for a continuing commonwealth status
rather than independence or statehood. Puerto Ricans voted
for commonwealth status and wrote a constitution setting it
up in 1952. After Muñoz' retirement in 1964, Luis Ferré,
an advocate of statehood, won the presidency, but the independence movement received nearly one-fifth of the votes.
Since that time, the percentages of Puerto Ricans favoring
statehood, commonwealth status, and independence seem not

to have changed much. Meanwhile, the number of Puerto
Ricans returning from the mainland nearly equals, and in
some years exceeds, the number going there. Whether the
United States Congress would reverse the half-century retreat
from imperialism and make Puerto Rico the fifty-first state,
should the Puerto Ricans petition for statehood, is uncertain
But an increase of Castroism in the Caribbean would make
that tempting, since Puerto Rico is in the strategic center of
the area.

Cuba is like Puerto Rico in its relatively "White" ethnic stock, its relatively advanced economic and social systems, and its history of neglect by Spain. But conflict was
greater than in Puerto Rico, and in one sense Fidel Castro's
1959 revolution was just a rerun of the Ten Years' War
(1868-78), the First Cuban Revolution (1895-98), and the Sergeants' Revolt that put Batista in power (1933). In the Ten
Years' War, the Cuban Forces, led by the mulatto Antonio
Maceo, fought the imposition of the slave plantation on the
previous small-farm economy by the Spanish. Despite their
promises of amnesty and reform, the Spanish delivered
neither, although slavery was finally abolished (1886). Cuba
became more and more a land of sugar plantations selling to
the United States. When the Spanish tried to impose higher
taxes on sales of sugar the Cuban plantation owners themselves went over to the side of the revolutionaries. José
Martí, the poet who was now leader along with Maceo, returned from exile in the United States when violence erupted
in the mountains of eastern Cuba (1895). With the help of
almost all groups in Cuba, the guerrilla bands fought the
Spanish to a standstill despite the new concentration-camp
tactics used by the Spanish commander, "Butcher" Weyler,
against the civilian population. Yet the rebels could not
throw Weyler out.

Then came United States intervention and the expulsion
of the Spanish. Most people in the United States were no
longer thinking, as John Quincy Adams had in the year of the
Monroe Doctrine, that Cuba was an apple that had to fall in
the United States lap by "political gravity," but they did resent Spanish "backwardness" and the sinking of the battleship
Maine in Havana harbor. Martí's revolutionaries relished
such help but resented the fact that American owners were
also building plantations and aiding Cuban plantation owners.
So when the treaty of Paris (1898) failed to get the Americans out of Cuba, the intervention turned sour. After four
years of occupation by the marines (1898-1902), the com-

bined opposition of the Cuban revolutionaries and the anti-
imperialist Democrats in Washington forced President McKinley to withdraw from Cuba. But the Republicans insisted on
keeping Guantánamo Naval Base near the revolutionary hotbed
in the Oriente mountains and passed the Platt Amendment
reserving the right to intervene in case any anti-American
laws were passed by the Cuban government.

Once again the Cuban revolutionaries felt cheated,
particularly since the movement toward a modern plantation
economy picked up speed as American investment flowed into
this safe market. By the nineteen thirties half or more of
the Cuban economy was owned by United States firms, just as
in Puerto Rico and the Dominican Republic. In such circumstances it was very difficult to convince Cuban radicals of
the helpfulness of American programs for the improvement
of Cuban health and education standards. The good done in
the elimination of yellow fever and the building of schools
was obscured by Cuban hatred of the American-backed plantation and tourist industries.

Thus the Sergeants' Revolt (1933) brought to power
Fulgencio Batista, a poor boy who rose to sergeant in the
army by becoming a good secretary. Batista showed that he
was a "man of the people" by firing all the generals and
abolishing the title itself, himself becoming merely a colonel--
and by appointing a Cuban radical, Dr. Grau San Martín, as
president. When Washington rejected Grau under the provisions of the Platt Amendment, Batista, mellowing with power
and wealth, responded by appointing a more conservative individual in order to get the Platt Amendment repealed by
President Franklin Roosevelt. The radicals felt that the
Good Neighbor Policy failed to meet the problems of economic
and social backwardness but began to regain hope when President Roosevelt encouraged the Muñoz regime in Puerto Rico.
Unfortunately, Roosevelt's representative in Cuba, Sumner
Welles, was not as successful with Batista as Rexford Tugwell
was with Muñoz, mainly because Batista was less forward-
looking. Because it was wartime, and because Grau was
elected when an effort to move toward parliamentary rule
was tried, the 1944 Constitution was thwarted. Batista returned as president and soon turned repressive and self-
seeking. In so doing he probably destroyed whatever hope
there had been for making Cuba another Caribbean showcase
for parliamentary democracy.

Next came Fidel Castro. First, there were his years

of exile and struggle. From his father's sugar plantation in Oriente Province he carried his radicalism to the University of Havana and led an attempted coup against the Moncada army camp, only to be imprisoned, amnestied, and exiled to Mexico by Batista. With the support of Cuban exiles in Mexico and the United States, his 26th of July Movement landed in Oriente to renew the revolution and was so decimated by Batista's troops that only eleven, including Castro's brother Raúl and Che Guevara, reached the mountains. There, among the poorest and most radical people of Cuba, Castro became "Fidel," the new Martí. Little by little, many Cubans of every class came to sympathize with the man who had everything they admired--physical strength, a gifted tongue, courage, and feeling for the common people. He had acquired in Cuban eyes the very attributes Batista had possessed when he deposed Machado. Batista fled because he had lost support, not because Castro had deposed him. Second, there were Castro's heady first months of victory. The jeep ride from Oriente to Havana was like a triumphal procession reminiscent of times past. In the same way, the political imprisonments, drumhead military trials, and summary executions were repeat performances of Cuban and Caribbean traditions. So were the rapid-fire reforms and the hostility toward foreigners, particularly Americans. Finally, there came the realization that Cuba was still much the same, still dependent on foreigners--this time the Russians.

The Russian connection is what makes the Fidelistas different from past Cuban and Caribbean radicals. The fact is that this connection changes the century-long growth of United States power at European expense. How it developed is still hotly debated. It is true, as one view holds, that the Castro government seized Cuban and foreign property, that Raúl and Che were radical Marxists, and that the United States government did little to stop the fall of Batista and the progressive radicalization of the Cuban Revolution. Yet it is also true that Castro, though very radical, was not originally Communist- or Russian-dominated, that the Cubans tried to follow the Puerto Rican land reforms and even promised to pay for United States properties if Americans bought more sugar, and that the Eisenhower government was much more conservative in the Cold War situation than the Roosevelt administration had been during the Axis threat. Whether it was the Russians manipulating Castro or the Trujillo sugar interests tricking Eisenhower, Cuba ended by becoming a Communist state and the first successful challenge to United States dominance in a century.

The measure of United States distress was seen in the Bay of Pigs invasion, planned by President Eisenhower and carried out by President Kennedy. With the collapse of that invasion, the United States retreated to the position that so long as the Castro government did not represent an offensive threat to other American states the Organization of American States would impose only economic sanctions. The only time the Big Stick in this policy has been used was in the case of the Cuban Missile Crisis (1962), when the United States threatened to invade Cuba to prevent the deployment of Russian missiles, thought to constitute an offensive threat to the United States and other American nations. A 1970 diplomatic confrontation when the Russians were thought to be creating a submarine base at Cienfuegos reaffirmed the United States stance, however.

All this has made Castro's Cuba a somewhat unusual type of Communist state. References to Cuba in Russian and Chinese publications give Castroism a special label to indicate it is somewhere between capitalism and communism. One reason is that Fidel does not follow either the Russian or Chinese strategy against "United States imperialism" but tries to unify with other Latin American radical movements such as those in Mexico and Peru. Che Guevara's "theory of guerrilla warfare, " which carried him into his revolutionary venture in Bolivia and led to his death, caused the whole Cuban movement to argue that the Russian- and Chinese-style communists of Latin America were too conservative because they played politics in the cities and villages rather than taking to the countryside to fight it out.

Another reason is that the Cuban economy has not been completely nationalized and converted to Russian-style industrialization and modernization. In the early years, Castro tried to push Cuba in that direction, but poor management led to the importing of raw materials at a higher cost than finished goods could be bought in Europe or the United States. Since 1964 Castro has concentrated on higher sugar production and on industrial goods Cuba can use herself rather than sell. This makes Cuba somewhat less dependent on Russia, except for sugar sales, and leaves Castro free to rejoin the Latin American community of nations should it become "anti-imperialist. " Finally, Castro's social policies have not always moved toward the Communist model. The health, housing, and education programs aim at "an anti-imperialist society, " but they also aim at preserving the family traditions of Cuba while upgrading the quality of life for its citizens. Children have a lot of contact with their parents, and most families live in individual houses rather than in "collective living units" like apartments.

In short, Castro seems to the Russians and Chinese merely a near-Communist, whereas to Cubans he seems more radical than other Latin American Communists. To the United States government he seems to threaten Caribbean security, while to Caribbean radicals he seems to be a new democratic force taking up where Mexico and Puerto Rico left off. Meanwhile, Cuba's "strategy of world revolution" has gone through several incarnations of its own. From 1953 to 1960 a "democratic front strategy" (which in Marxist terms means an alliance with Liberal Democrats, as when Stalin joined with Churchill and Roosevelt against Hitler) led to cooperation with any "democrats" against Batista and United States "reactionaries." From 1961 to 1972 a "revolutionary front strategy" (Communist revolutionaries only) led to attempts at "exporting revolution" to Haiti, Puerto Rico, Venezuela, and Bolivia in alliance with the Russian or Chinese parties, or, most especially, with Vietnamese and Latin American guerrillas. From 1972 on, United States-Russian-Chinese détente led to a "popular front strategy" (Communists and Socialists only) in cooperation with Chilean, Peruvian, Jamaican, and other "radical" governments to create "a Latin America for Latin Americans" and to "liberate Africa" using Cuban troops. Whether this latest Cuban strategy will succeed in doing anything more than ending the isolation of the 1961-72 period, or whether a genuine détente with the North Americans could emerge, is hard to say. Which way the wave of the future runs depends in large measure on events in the "Black Caribbean."

The third wave of Caribbean independence movements began after World War II and is still rolling across the island colonies of the north European nations--the Black Caribbean where populations are often more than ninety per cent Negro. Until recently, there has not been a coherent revolutionary movement, but an evolutionary arrangement between Caribbean colonial elites and European governments. In the French and Dutch colonies this has taken the form of "full citizenship without annexation," in the manner of Puerto Rico's commonwealth status. Thus the citizens of the French West Indies have deputies in the French parliament and those of the Dutch West Indies in the Netherlands parliament, on the theory that these are specks of Europe in the Caribbean island-chain. And in a sense French and Dutch culture have been transplanted deep in the colonial soil of Guadeloupe and Curaçao, but racial and economic differences probably go deeper still. The British experiment with political independence within the Commonwealth has grounded on the same shoals. The essential change is that a new "Black Power" movement that cuts across traditional political boundaries has grown up under the influence of revolutionaries drawing on the ideas of the Jamaican Marcus Garvey. There is some substance to the latest Black Power idea that, like the Indian or "Red Power" states of Middle and South America, the Black states of the Caribbean will have their turn, although such a view ignores the revolutions of the "White states" of Cuba and Puerto Rico in between--that is, the Marxist and Liberal alternatives.

The complexities of the Black Power revolution in its Caribbean homeland can be seen best within the former British colonies. By 1958 the British Colonial Office was convinced that it had hit upon a scheme for emancipating the "Little Seven" islands by joining them to the larger Trinidad, Jamaica, and Barbados in a Federation of the West Indies. Trinidad seemed to be the key. It was one-third East Asian, one-third Black, and one-third mulatto and therefore might feel threatened by a Black-majority state. Oil had made it richer than the others, and it might be disinclined to share the wealth. But the mulatto Eric Williams, elected prime minister after the granting of self-government in 1956, agreed to take the plunge. By 1962 negotiations had reached a point where Britain was preparing to give independence to the remaining colonies to complete the Federation.

Then Jamaica withdrew. Contributing factors were geographical isolation, the fact that Jamaica had half the Federation population and Trinidad only a quarter, economic disadvantages similar to those of Trinidad, and jealousy because Jamaica, self-governing since 1944, was losing the capital of the Federation to Trinidad. But the feeling that Jamaica was the capital of Black radicalism was also influential. As the home of Marcus Garvey, who in the 1920s created the Universal Negro Improvement Association, Jamaica had developed a sense of Black nationalism. Garvey's notion that God was black, that Negroes had once ruled the world until White-ruled Babylon had overthrown them, and that God had returned Emperor Haile Selassie of Ethiopia to the throne of the world had caught on even among some Jamaicans who did not belong to the Black Power movements of the Kingston slums. Africa was to be the Promised Land

and Negroes the Chosen Race, and the Federation was therefore too mixed and too British. With the votes of Black nationalists, Alexander Bustamante defeated Norman Manley, the prime minister, on an anti-Federation platform and became the first leader of the independent Jamaican nation.

The Federation then collapsed. Eric Williams took Trinidad out within weeks. Barbados, whose oil fields were supporting the "Little Seven," withdrew in 1966. All the independent states remained members of the Commonwealth and received tariff preferences and citizenship privileges, and the mulatto elite remains in power. Yet the Black Power movement continues to expand. Some of its supporters, like Trinidadian Stokeley Carmichael, have gone to the United States to arouse "Black consciousness" there, and others to Brazil and Venezuela. But the main effort is concentrated on the Caribbean, and the main aim is to overthrow White economic and social domination and the power of the Whites' supposed allies, the mulatto elite. By now there are Black Power advocates in the French and Dutch islands as well, and there were riots in Martinique and Curaçao as well as Trinidad in the late '60s and early 1970s. When the unrest subsided, however, the mulatto-White alliance remained. Eric Williams was re-elected in Trinidad-Tobago on a platform of evolutionary reform, and Michael Manley won election on a program of "social engineering" in Jamaica despite the opposition of Marcus Garvey, Jr.

Still, it is evident that Black Power ideology cuts across all the older alternatives, colonialist and modernist. For one thing, there are Black Power adherents throughout the Black Caribbean, islands and coasts--Garvey in Jamaica, Geddes Granger in Trinidad, Elton Motley in Barbados, Lincoln Charles in Grenada, Evan Hyde in Belize, Aimé Césaire in Martinique, Stanley Brown in Curaçao, and, for that matter, Rap Brown in the United States South. The older Black leaders--Bradshaw in St. Kitts, Bramble in Montserrat, Bird in Antigua, Pindling in the Bahamas, Williams in Trinidad-- have clearly been thrown on the defensive, so much so that many have switched from European-style clothing to fatigues and dashikis. They are nevertheless damned as "Afro-Saxon"--the Caribbean equivalent of "Uncle Tom" or "Oreo"-- by Black Power adherents determined to end the "busboy economy" in which Blacks serve White tourists. In Evan Hyde's words, "Tourism is whorism," a powerful slogan in areas where unemployment is over twenty-five per cent and one per cent of the population (usually White) owns half the property.

There are, however, several important differences between the Caribbean and the North American Black Power movements. First, Blacks constitute far larger percentages in the Black Caribbean that in even the "Black counties" of the United States South--in fact, from sixty to ninety per cent. Second, Black Muslims have almost no influence in Caribbean Black Power movements because Orthodox Muslims from the Mideast and East Indies form the shopkeeper class in many areas, making Islam a threat instead of a source of liberation. Third, opportunities for Black social and economic mobility are less in the Black Caribbean because of the more rigid social structure, the under-development, and the closing off of migration to other Commonwealth countries or the United States. Black Power thus looks more attractive in the Caribbean than in North America--and more feasible.

Which way will the Caribbean go? Might it move toward improved relations of some sort with the northern-hemisphere Europeans and North Americans? In that case, the question is: "What will replace colonialism?" Only Bermuda and a few other British fragments, the Virgin Islands, and the French and Netherlands Antilles are still strictly "colonial." Might commonwealth status, like that of Puerto Rico and some of the English-speaking islands, satisfy more than the elites if economic rewards can be generated? The curtailment of immigration from the Black Caribbean by both Great Britain and the United States in the 1960s threatens this alternative, though Puerto Ricans still have special access to the United States mainland. Nor have land reform and industrialization schemes yet been sufficient to show the viability of the economic dimension of the commonwealth alternative, unless Puerto Rico is to be counted as a success despite the fact that the United States pours in six billion dollars per year in tax credits, welfare, social security, and food stamps. More likely versions of this alternative would seem to be special aid and trade agreements.

Or might the Caribbean move toward the Marxist alternative? There are certainly Marxist forces in the Caribbean outside of Cuba--Bosch and the Constitutionalists in the Dominican Republic, Aimé Césaire in Martinique, James Milette in Trinidad, and perhaps Michael Manley in Jamaica. But there is no indication that any of these movements accept the Cuban notion of separate Marxist development aided by Russia or China. In fact, most Caribbean Marxists are democratic socialists, not revolutionaries, at least so far. An interesting point is that Cuba sees Black Power as a step toward true revolution, while many other Marxists, such as Cheddi Jagan in Guyana, oppose such "racism" as contrary to "revolutionary brotherhood." Jamaica and Trinidad have actually banned the works of Black Power advocates like Malcolm X, Stokeley Carmichael, and C. L. R. James.

The Black Power movement's aim is apparently to lean on the ethnic heritage of Black Africa, rather than the political brotherhood promised by Marxism, in the unification of the Caribbean. Whether this approach will lead any further than the Puerto Rican or the Cuban alternatives seems problematical. Yet whatever happens to the Black Power movement, the Caribbean peoples will remain powerless so long as they cannot unite with each other for mutual gain. Until then they will be pulled apart and used as pawns in a game that is not of their own making. In this respect, Black Power is nothing new. The Caribbean Free Trade Association of the early 1960s attempted to create a common market of Liberal Democrats. Cuba's efforts at exporting revolution in the mid-1960s aimed at a Communist Caribbean. By the late 1960s, the Black Power alternative seemed on the rise. Yet in the early 1970s a conjunction of alternatives seemed to be emerging--in a "Southern strategy" involving an all-Latin American, or even all-Third World, unity. Jamaica led the way for other Commonwealth nations to join the OAS, but then voted with the Latin American majority to force a lifting of the OAS quarantine of Cuba. Hence the original speculation that the Jamaican move into the OAS presaged Canadian entry and an alliance to modernize gave way to equally feverish speculations that the OAS might become a Third World alliance against the Europeans and North Americans. The proper analogy for the Black Caribbean in all this is probably neither Canada nor Cuba, however, but Mexico, whose "Red Power" is the equivalent of Caribbean "Black Power," that is, a search for a principle of unity. But then Liberal and Marxist approaches promise the same goal of common interest. And every attempt at unification is flying in the face of island geography and a history of division.

Chapter 6

THE FOUNDATIONS

Geography and Technology

Middle America consists of two mountain ranges ce-
menting South and North America together. One range is
nearly submerged--the Caribbean islands. The other is
exposed--Central America and Mexico. In the Caribbean,
the taller the peak, the larger the island--the Greater and
Lesser Antilles. In Central America, the range starts narrow
and low in Panama and ends wider and higher as it merges
with the Rockies at the Mexican-United States border. Both
land and air are alive. The "shaking earth" produces earthquakes and volcanoes in plenty, and in 1943-44 it threw up a
new volcanic mountain, Paricutín, in southern Mexico, one
of only two or three such instances in recorded history.
The whole area is also "hurricane alley." Like the hurricanes, rain comes from the east with the trade winds. So
the farther east, the wetter, and vice versa for the deserts
of Mexico and the drier western coast of Central America.
The rains divide Middle America into an Island-Coastal culture of former plantations like the Deep South and a Mainland-
Mountain culture of ranches and poor farms like the American
Southwest. The former is African and European, with a few
mulattoes. The latter is European and Indian, with many
mestizos.

The natural resources of Middle America are meager--
the silver and gold of the mountains and the oil of the Mexican coastline, some oil and bauxite on the Caribbean islands,
a climate favorable to tropical agriculture and tourism, and
the geographic position on the north-south and east-west communications routes. Such circumstances invite foreign involvement and tie Middle America to outside powers such
as the European colonists, the North Americans, and now,
in Cuba, the Russians. The desire of most Middle Ameri-

cans for an independent economic and cultural base is therefore hindered by geography as well as history. Both arable
land and the iron and coal for industrial development are in
short supply. An adequate diet is virtually impossible because most of the islands are too small, much of Central
America is too wet, most of Mexico is too dry, and everywhere the land is too hilly and over-populated.

The whole area thus depends on imports of food and
a starvation diet to balance the mouths and the nourishment.
Mexico's attempts to increase agricultural yield have made
some progress, but what can be done when one irrigation
reservoir in the arid northwest goes dry and another on the
Isthmus of Techuántepec threatens to burst because of too
much rain at one time? Likewise, Mexico has made the
transition to modern industry, but only by importing many of
the necessary raw materials on stringent terms. The rest
of the area remains dependent on outside markets and, unlike
Mexico, cannot hope to develop heavy industry on its own,
even with imported raw materials. The nations of Middle
America, except perhaps Cuba, look first to Mexico, then to
South America, and only in the last resort to the United States,
Europe, or Russia as permanent partners in progress. They
want to build a Middle American culture on the ashes of a
plantation economy, but they have little in the way of resources to work with.

Water craft dominate Middle America's technology--
except, of course, in the interior of Mexico--as completely
as land craft do in South and North America. Boats come
in all descriptions. Mingling with the Canal-bound hulks are
the tour boats ferrying tourists to sun and fun. Yachts chug
in and out of idyllic havens. Shrimp and fishing trawlers
comb the warm blue waters for commercial catches, while
their smaller kin carry sportsmen and subsistence fishermen
into the traffic jam. The really large ships crowd into the
few ports adequate to berth them or wait to transit the Canal.
And in the ports of medium and small dimension the smaller
craft of every type elbow each other in berth or at anchor.
Some of the press has been eased by jets setting funsters
down near Playboy Clubs, Hiltons, or Clubs Méditerranées.
But skiffs worthy of Hemingway's The Old Man and the Sea
still ply the hurricane lanes or enter the rivers where, in
a few isolated places, they may brush gunwales with log ca-
noes.

Yet for all the differences with the tractors and trucks

of the vast land-areas to the south, the purposes are the
same--to conquer isolation, forward development, and, though
only adequate land transport can really complete the process
except in the smallest islands, encourage national feeling.
Two curious features: first, port-to-port communication is
still usually easier than road or rail travel; and second, the
Pan-American Highway makes north-south land travel easier
in Mexico and Central America than east-west travel. Tech-
nologically, in other words, colonialism is still easy, nationalism hard.

Middle America, in contrast to North and, to a lesser
extent, South America, needs tropical science and technology.
Middle Americans certainly encounter South Americans'
problems with technology, namely, the necessity for borrowing
it, the inadequacy of the social and educational structure to
support advanced technology, and the dislocation of some citizens' lives to assure "progress." Yet Middle Americans
must also wait for an adequate tropical-zone technology unlike
the temperate-zone technology of North America and Europe.
The problems of tropical medicine in the building of the
Panama Canal, for example, are well known--yellow fever,
vipers and scorpions resentful at the invasion of their prem-
ises, snail fever, debility from heat and humidity, and the
like. But over the years folk remedies such as the use of
cinchona bark in some liqueur to produce quinine for malaria
have slowly been improved upon and a genuine tropical medicine has been created by the Cruz Institute in Brazil and
similar laboratories in Middle and North America.

In like manner, a large-scale effort is proceeding
under United Nations auspices to create a tropical agriculture.
The international research institute that produced the special
"flour" Incaparina in Guatemala, along with other experiment
stations in Puerto Rico and the Philippines, is struggling to
produce a cereal as good for the tropics as winter wheat
has been for the Plains and the Pampas. And at the other
extreme the Nobel Prize-winning creator of "miracle rice,"
the Iowan Norman Borlaug, is still working at his Rockefeller-
funded institute in Mexico to create a wheat as good for the
deserts as his rice has been for tropical lowlands. In South
America, the south and most of Brazil can borrow European
or North American crops, but the Amazon and parts of
Venezuela and Colombia must wait with the Middle Americans
for many a tropical miracle, and the Andean states could
use a dry-land miracle or two from Borlaug.

A third notable feature is that the effects of technological progress also became more evident faster in the islands and peninsulas of Middle America than in mainland North or South America. Middle America's niche has less of nature's bounty, so technology's impacts are more visible and vital, with fewer alternatives and less margin for error. Even with the best of technology, Middle America will certainly have as much trouble feeding itself as have other island-peninsula areas such as West Europe and Japan, and probably more. Again, even with the best of technology, Middle Americans will be hard pressed to export more than they import so as to make jobs for themselves the way the West Europeans and Japanese have. It is one thing to talk of three to four per cent population growth in South America, where-- for a time, at least--technology might be able to help produce twice as many jobs, houses, clothes, and doctors every twenty or so years. Ecologically, it is another thing altogether to talk of doubling production in Middle America.

North Americans have the necessary technology and resources to balance human needs and production. The West Europeans and Japanese (and increasingly the oil-rich Middle East nations) have the technology but not the resources. South Americans (like the Russians, the Chinese, and many Africans) have the resources but not the technology. But Middle Americans (like the Mediterraneans and island Asians) have neither the resources nor the technology. Some Middle American nations such as Mexico (with its oil) or Panama (with the Canal) may be able to join the Britains and Japans and Irans in industrial progress but probably cannot match Brazil, the United States, the Soviet Union, or even Argentina. Middle America's babies are held hostage by a stingy land, no matter the technologies or development strategies so far devised to rescue them.

The technological prognosis for Middle America is thus less hopeful than for most of South America except the Andean states, which are poor in arable land. But must Middle America forever struggle along with under-productive technologies, with too many citizens born and too many dying too soon, with a vast gap between rich "moderns" and poor "traditionals"? Or can a dependent economy that is not demeaning or destructive--a genuinely interdependent economy-- be created on the basis of specialized trade and tourism? In other words, can a relationship as healthy as that between The Netherlands and the United States be created? Can the tendency of "industrials"--nations and persons--to pull away

from "agriculturals" be controlled? The United States puts
billions of dollars into Puerto Rico per year, the Soviet Union
a billion into Cuba, and so on with the British, French, and
Arabs, a circumstance which cannot continue in spite of the
fact that quite a bit is taken out, too. The Middle Americans, on the other hand, watch the growing gap and the con-
sequent hemorrhage of people and treasure caused by under-
production of wealth and over-production of population--and
resent it as much as the Poles and Italians did when they
found themselves in the same situation in the late nineteenth
century. Populations too numerous for their niches either
die off or move out, and Middle Americans are now too soon
dead or too soon off to North or South America.

Two other outcomes have recently been suggested.
The hopeful one is that new strains of corn and wheat and
soybeans and rice, and new techniques of dry and wet farming, will make the deserts of Mexico and the swamps of the
Caribbean coasts bloom; that sun, wind, water, and nuclear
energy will make fuel plentiful; that the Caribbean seabed
will be mined and its waters farmed; that improved machines
and improved minds will make production efficient enough to
support ten times the population per unit of land; that control
of birth will make postponement of death less damaging--in
short, that the future predicted by the technological optimists
will come true. The other future is one of ecological pessimism in which the industrialized nations exhaust their resources and either collapse, resume imperial conquests to
secure resources, or at any rate cease foreign aid and trade
and force out all foreign workers and thus set off a world
depression. Everyone, according to this doomsday forecast,
sinks back to a subsistence level, and the regime of ignorance, disease, and poverty reclaims those who had tempo-
rarily escaped. The epic dimension of these predictions is
perfectly suited for Middle America, where life has always
been lived at the level of crisis. But most Middle Americans, along with most North and South Americans, would
prefer a cooperative, interdependent solution to their problem
rather than shouting across the growing gap of rich and poor.
Hence the scientists and technologists of the agricultural
stations, industrial schools, and medical laboratories see
Middle America as a crucial test case for interdependence--
and themselves as part of the solution.

The People

As there are too few resources, there are too many

people. With more than seventy million people in 1970, Middle America has about one-third the population of North or South America on one-eighth the land area. Moreover, the population jumped from fifty to sixty million from 1950 to 1960 and is increasing even faster now. The settlement pattern magnifies the problem by crowding the people in the most habitable areas--the drier western part of the islands, the highlands of western Central America, and the central valley of Mexico. Densities in these areas approach and in isolated cases exceed rates in East Asia or The Lowlands of West Europe. Despite the migration of Puerto Ricans, Mexican braceros, and Cuban refugees to the United States, and of Black Caribbeans to Europe, sufficient population outflow to ease these pressures probably cannot be anticipated. Venezuela and Colombia now take some immigrants from Middle America, but still not enough to ease the pressure.

Two demographic themes have thus dominated the Middle American scene since World War II, migration and population growth. For two decades millions left Middle America for the United States and Europe. Much of this was technically not "migration" at all, since Puerto Ricans are United States citizens, Martiniquers citizens of the French Union, and Jamaicans and Trinidadians citizens of the multiracial Commonwealth headed by the British monarch. Indeed, it is possible to argue that Mexican braceros in the United States are merely following a nomadic pattern that was established by Coronado's exploration of Colorado sixty years before Plymouth Rock and has been maintained even after the United States absorbed the Spanish West in 1848. There has also been some "brain drain" migration as Middle American citizens become educated in Canada, the United States, or Europe and stay on, thus "beheading" their homelands. These intellectuals are usually welcomed in the host countries. But the rest of the migrants have taken menial jobs in the developed countries. They have moved into the barrios of the United States Southwest and the "Spanish Harlems" of its East Coast cities, or into the East End of London with the migrants from Pakistan or Malaysia or India. Many "brain drain" professional personnel from Middle America (or from East Asia) actually serve these communities in the United States and Europe because of the language needs and cultural affinities. And they often become spokesmen for the community in the tradition of the "liberal professions" in Latin America.

Cuban migration into Florida is special. Though

menials arrived both before and after Castro, most of the
Cuban professionals received an exemption from the growing
United States immigration restrictions as "refugees from
Communism. " That exemption and the Puerto Rican exception
stand in stark contrast to the end of the bracero program
(1964), the imposition of quotas on Western Hemisphere immigrants (1968), and regulations regarding "illegal aliens"
(the late 1970s). Thus only special political considerations
like those affecting Puerto Rico and Cuba seem able to with-
stand economic and cultural (or racial) sentiments that run
counter to the Western Hemisphere "open frontiers, " once
considered inviolable. Effective restrictions in the United
States would obviously exacerbate the population-density problem of Middle America which, along with economic opportunity (Mexican-Americans) or freedom issues (Cuban-Ameri-
cans), fueled the migrations in the first place. And if Britain sacrifices the Commonwealth citizenship ideal to rising
"racialism" and depression-born union hostility toward cheap
labor, the problem could become catastrophic in every quad-
rant of the Caribbean.

Unlike South American governments anxious to occupy
their share of a vast continent, Middle American governments
are acutely aware of the need for population control even if
"pronatalism" is still rooted in the general culture. All the
obstacles to family planning inherent in developing cultures
and Latin cultures, plus one, are present in Middle America.
The "plus" is the visibility of North Americans and West
Europeans practicing birth control--and the fact that hatred
for such "oppressors" rubs off on population control itself.
It is considered revolutionary not to practice contraception,
since that way the revolutionaries will come to outnumber
their adversaries more and more. The ultimate "betrayal"
would be for a wife to practice birth control without her
husband's consent, for example. Hence the fact that the
first female contraceptive pill was tested by volunteers in a
Puerto Rican health center in the late 1950s because such
devices were illegal in Boston is often interpreted as "cultural imperialism" or "destroying the moral fiber of Puerto
Rican women. " Yet contraception is more and more widely
practiced, though the spread is slow. Meanwhile, another
complicating factor has emerged: voluntary return of Puerto
Ricans, Mexicans, and others, so that the net migration of
some groups is toward Middle America. Better medicine,
lessened migration, slowness of birth control--just add them
up. Densities increase astronomically.

After numbers, the next most important demographic factor in Middle America is still race. Racial divisions are indeed baffling. In the simplest terms, the four great continents are all represented--in the Indians of America, the Europeans, the Blacks from Africa, and the East Indians from Asia. In the Island-Coastal culture, the American Indians were either killed or died of disease in the early stages of European colonization and importation of African slaves. The essential complexion of the population was therefore determined by the interaction of Europeans and Africans in a plantation environment, with the admixture of East Asians in the British- and Dutch-held islands in the last century of colonialism. What emerged was a relatively unmixed population of Whites (blancs in French), mulattoes (jaunes, or yellows), and Blacks (bruns, browns, or noires, blacks). There were very few Whites, small numbers of mulattoes, and vast numbers of Blacks in the British, French, and Dutch colonies. The mulattoes were generally descended from adulterous relationships between White male slave owners and domestic household slaves, the Blacks from the field hands of the plantation era. The importation to islands like Trinidad and Curaçao of wage-laboring East Asians after the abolition of slavery in the nineteenth century added more weight to the in-between caste rather than the lower because many Asians became shopkeepers and handicraftsmen.

On the Spanish islands of Puerto Rico and Cuba, a variant of this situation arose because the Spanish were more interested in taking gold from Mexico than producing sugar in the Caribbean. Sugar plantations and a substantial "African" population (largely from Jamaica) therefore came only in the nineteenth century, after the loss of Mexico and the abolition of slavery. Hence the Spanish-speaking islands are the most "European" in the Caribbean, and the Africans there are not treated with the same degree of prejudice encountered in the other islands. Hispaniola, the island housing Haiti and the Dominican Republic, is a very special case, since Haiti is over ninety per cent negroid and the Dominican Republic almost as firmly caucasoid. But this is the result of a difference in French and Spanish colonial policies on the one hand and the early-nineteeth-century racial wars between the Haitian Blacks and the Dominican Whites on the other. The general population pattern remains "white," "yellow," and "black."

In the Mainland-Mountain Culture, many Indians survived and few Africans arrived, so the familiar Latin Amer-

ican caste system of European, mestizo, and Indian emerged.
In Central America, the cities and the highlands of the Pacific coast are now European and mestizo, while the volcanic
mountain spine and the humid Atlantic coast are more Indian.
Guatemala is sixty per cent pure Indian because the Spaniards
found only the Atlantic piedmont around Guatemala City attractive, but Costa Rica is almost a European country because the poor Spanish farmers took to the equable highland
climate as well as they did in Puerto Rico and Cuba. Belize,
El Salvador, Honduras, Nicaragua, and Panama are more
mixed, but on the same pattern. The Africans brought to the
Atlantic coast to work the banana trees and build the Panama
Canal have added an unassimilated element, which causes internal divisions in states like Nicaragua and Honduras. These
Atlantic coastal areas have thus become a shatter belt between
the Island-Coastal and Mainland-Mountain cultures and are
among the most destitute and volatile places in the Americas.

In Mexico, the caste problem has influenced every
struggle since Cortez defeated Moctezuma. Even now, Mexico
calls itself Indian but is governed mainly by mestizos and
owned essentially by mestizos or people of European stock.
The modern history of Mexico is marked by the effort to get
the castes to work together for the good of all. Generally
speaking, the south from Morelos to Yucatán is Indian, the
central valley and plateau around Mexico City mestizo, and
the north and west more European. In historical terms,
this means that the Mayas and the peripheral tribes of the
Aztec empire successfully resisted European encroachments,
the core of the Aztec peoples amalgamated with the descendants of Cortez' captains, and the nomadic tribes of the north
and west succumbed. No one should ever forget that Zapata
was a Zapotec from Morelos State, or that the Revolution
granted the Indians of the south a special form of tribal landholding, the ejido. There is even a Yucatán Independence
Movement at present. But on the whole indianismo is little
more than a word, since the languages and folkways are
gradually giving way to Spanish-language schools and to laws
passed in Mexico City.

The Mainland-Mountain culture therefore rests on an
Indian core in northern Guatemala and southern Mexico and
tapers off to less-Indian areas in northern Mexico and southern Central America. The Island-Coastal culture darkens,
then lightens again, north and south from the somewhat
Europeanized island of Cuba until it reaches Texas on the
north and Venezuela on the south. But culture is not coter-

minous with race, either in fact or in the self-image of the majority of the people. Most of the racial terms also have cultural connotations, since language, folkways, and occupations determine one's caste as much as skin color. In Mexico, a non-Indian is one who dresses modern and speaks Spanish, and in Central America such persons are usually called "Latins" (Ladinos) whether they are caucasoid, mongoloid, or negroid. In the Caribbean, color means a lot more, but even there one finds differences. In the Spanish islands, one is "white" (blanco) unless he is very dark brown or black (negro), as in South America. In the other islands, caste is partly determined by the ability to read and write a European language and partly by adherence to a European religion. Thus Voodoo and Creole, the religion and language of the majority of Haiti, are considered "backward," whereas Roman Catholicism and French are considered "civilized." A Black (brun, nogro) who has adopted these European ways is therefore often considered to be in the upper caste.

It is evident that neither race nor language lead toward a unitary culture in Middle America. How would people speaking Spanish, English, French, Creole (French-based Haitian), Dutch, Papiamento (Dutch-based West Indian), various East Indian languages, and hundreds of American Indian languages even communicate with each other? Indeed, Middle American language mirrors the fractious realities. Besides the usual degrees of literacy, semi-literacy, and illiteracy associated with the class and caste structure of any developing area, Middle America has more than its fair share of the linguistic tangles of both pluralist and colonial areas. This is a shatter belt where languages clash and contend because peoples do. As Black English is to American Standard English, so Creole is to French, calypso English to the King's English, Papiamento to Dutch, Indianized Spanish to standard Spanish. As so-called Tex-Mex is to American Standard English, so Maya is to Spanish, or, for that matter, the English of descendants of Black freemen who escaped to the Dominican Republic in the 1850s is to Spanish there. There are nationalist elements, too, so that Mexican Spanish, whose official form is maintained by officials in Mexico City, compares with the Spanish demanded by Madrid officials about the way American English does with British. Finally, there are revolutionary elements: abandonment of the "polite" form of addressing "superiors," use of the terms "comrade" and "brother," and similar leveling tendencies. Still, the Latin languages have a "class consciousness" inherent in tu ("thou," for family and infe-

riors) and él ("you," for the public and superiors), and it
reinforces the division which plagues Middle America most--
the rural abyss between patrón and peón, "estate" owner and
field hand.

In short, there are also obstacles to development's
serving as a force for unity as it has in North America, and
those obstacles lie mainly in the backward rural regions.
The land and the land-use patterns work people extremely
hard in Middle America. By far the most common agricultural patterns are those of large-scale commercial agriculture. The encomiendas became haciendas in Middle as in
South America, but often with a difference. Only the relatively fertile regions heavily populated with Indians could sustain the classic hacienda system, so it predominates mainly
in the Central Plateau of Mexico and in parts of Central
America. There the peón-patrón pattern developed as it did
in Colombia, Peru, or Chile. There the settled agricultural
population has eked out an existence and supplied cattle and
food to the mining camps and administrative cities of the
colonial and independent states. Elsewhere, however, the
character of the land and the relatively low numbers of Indians produced the "ranch" and the "plantation."

The ranch was a response to the dry land of western
Mexico and the once-Mexican American Southwest. Its economic importance was minor compared with the hacienda and
the plantation, but it kept open the vital communications
routes and made use of otherwise virtually useless waste
lands as cattle ranges. What is not often recognized is that
it imparted a gaucho-like social and political character to
the regions where it predominated. For the charro's (cowboy's) was a "male society" more often than not, with few
women, few marriages, and few legitimate children--in short,
without much of a traditional family life. The men moved
from bunkhouse to bunkhouse or, if they did have families,
migrated to follow the cattle. The cowboy and the migrant
worker thus emerged as the main character types along with
the ranch owner. The owner was likely to have a wife and
family, control social and political affairs, and look down
upon the "immorality" of the cowboys and migrants. The
relative stability and security of the peón-patrón relationship
of the hacienda was therefore missing on the ranch. The
peón was less settled and secure, and the patrón more isolated and fearful. The fact that the rancher was more likely
to be Spanish or creole while the cowboy and the migrant
were Indian or mestizo added to the complications. Violence

was endemic, and it is no accident that Pancho Villa emerged in this region.

The plantation covers the humid coasts of islands and mainland alike, but the Caribbean is its homeland. The arc of plantation culture that stretches from Brazil to Texas is anchored in the Lesser Antilles. Whatever existed on the cotton plantations of Alabama and the sugar plantations of Bahía was magnified there. The profits were larger, the social disorientations were greater, and the racial mixture was more explosive than farther north or south. In economic terms, the Caribbean plantations were and are means of producing for foreign markets a single crop, usually sugar, with cheap human labor. But there have been two forms of plantations: the slave plantation which lasted until the mid-nineteenth century, and the modern wage plantation using seasonal laborers and sharecroppers who are unemployed the rest of the year. Even in their modern form, the plantations produce large profits for a few individuals and leave most workers poor and unskilled. They also make the region dependent on the marketing of a single crop and thus subject to catastrophic economic disorders in the event of a price decline or ill will on the part of a customer. This monocultural economy curses the "banana republics" of Central America almost as much as the "sugar islands" of the Caribbean.

The Central Americans have nevertheless escaped many of the social consequences of the plantation system because only the modern wage-labor plantation has existed there. The Caribbean people, on the other hand, have reaped the full fury of the whirlwind sown by plantation slavery. Recalling the situation on a slave plantation shows why. To say that the few whites who lived in the plantation house gained from the labors of many slaves in the slave quarters at the bottom of the hill is to tell only a part of the story. The far more damaging results came from the fact that slaves were looked upon merely as stored-up labor, not as persons. Thus "chattels" had their social ties completely broken by the plantation experience. As long as the slave trade continued, it was cheaper to import a full-grown field hand than to raise a slave child, so women and children were an unprofitable burden in most cases. When slave children were wanted, they were very often bred like cattle and not produced by a stable union. In any case, the family ties were not allowed to exist during the daytime, when there was work to be done by both parents.

The exceptions to this rule were the "house servants," those who attended the family of the plantation owner. They were often encouraged to have stable family relationships and to train their children to become domestic servants in their turn. In between were the slave foremen, White or Black, who guarded the slave quarters. They were usually unattached and lived in close proximity to their charges. Hence it does not take too much imagination to see the source of White-Black and domestic servant-field hand hatreds, sexual fears and rivalries, the breakdown of the family structure, and the predominance of the woman in slave culture. These feelings have come down in Caribbean culture in almost undiluted form and remain to plague the construction of a viable social system there.

The most important event in Middle American history since the arrival of the Spaniards was therefore the abolition of slavery, for it promised an end to the domination of the plantation system. The Mexican Revolution's attack on the hacienda and ranch pointed in the same direction. On the whole, however, the experiment in creating a small-holding class of skilled farmers has failed in Middle America. The oldest smallholders, the tobacco and coffee growers of the highlands of Central America and the Caribbean, are being pushed out by the large modern plantations after having survived colonial times. Only in Costa Rica, where they were numerous, and in Haiti, where foreigners could not own property until the American intervention, have they retained substantial influence. In Costa Rica they have become commercialized farmers and relatively well-off, while in Haiti the peasant continues to isolate himself from the world and remains very poor. Trujillo's experiment with smallholding colonies of Santo Domingan Whites near the Haitian border was more an attempt to keep out the Haitians than a serious economic program. In the Dominican Republic, as elsewhere, the modern plantation grinds away at the status of the small farmer and forces him down to the subsistence level or into the cities in a manner reminiscent of Steinbeck's The Grapes of Wrath. Puerto Rico is about the only small country to have made any headway in fighting the obvious economic advantages of the corporate plantation. But these social successes were possible only because the United States Congress passed the Five Hundred Acre Law and made it possible for Muñoz Marín to expropriate the estates of some of the plantation owners. Other Middle Americans cannot dispose of their oligarchies' control so easily.

Even in Mexico the attempt to create a yeoman farmer group has slowed considerably since World War II. To be sure, the land reforms of the thirties and forties have made their mark. The old-style small farmers, the <u>rancheros</u>, were left untouched when the large estates were seized, and many of the seized properties of the Central Plateau were made available for sale to individuals as small farms. But there was no social commitment to individualistic agriculture, and much of the seized land was made into "individual <u>ejidos</u>," where a person owned the land but worked it with others and could not sell it, and "collective <u>ejidos</u>," where the people on the collective owned the land communally. Likewise, the subsistence agriculture that often emerged on the <u>ranchos</u>, the individual <u>ejidos</u>, and the property left to the <u>hacendados</u> encouraged the government to establish more and more "collectives," especially in the irrigated oases of the north and northwest. What emerged from all this was Mexico's present mixed agricultural system in which much of the commercial production is done by the collectives on the one hand and the <u>rancheros</u> on the other.

Mexico's non-ideological experimentation was apparently what Fidel Castro had in mind when he came to power in 1959, but by 1961 he had gone much farther in the direction of "collective farms" of the Soviet type. What made his program different from the Mexican was, first, that he tried to force the small tobacco and coffee farmers into it and, second, that he wanted to move much faster in getting agricultural production up and freeing peasants for work in the new industries being established. On a purely economic basis, this made as much sense as the Mexican collective or the modern plantation in Puerto Rico because more could be produced with less labor. But the speed with which it proceeded and the hostility that developed in the United States caused Cuba to have lower production and to lose its sugar market. The result was an economic disaster which made Cuba more dependent than ever on sugar and a foreign market, this time in Russia. Whether Castro's Agrarian Reform Law will eventually pay for its social costs as did the Mexican Constitution and the Puerto Rican Five Hundred Acre Law remains to be seen. But after nearly a quarter century Cuban sugar production has resumed its upward spiral, and the next order of business in Cuba will have to be to get other profitable commercial and food crops, whether by individualistic or collective production methods. Nevertheless, Cuba like the rest of Middle America will have to depend on successes in industrialization to guarantee something more than equal shares of rural poverty.

The New Industrialism

    The differences between Middle American and South American industrialization are as instructive as the similarities. In the first place, Middle Americans must run even harder than South Americans to compete with industrialized countries. There is no virgin continent to conquer in Middle America, and what natural resources existed have been wasted through overpopulation and the plantation economy. Tourism is a greater advantage than in South America, and tourists, unlike investors, leave their money and go home. But tourism is really "monoculture without a crop" because, unlike industry, it requires seasonal, non-self-renewing, and low-skilled work. A densely populated area like Middle America cannot live--cannot feed, clothe, and house itself--without making up for a lack of resources with superior human skills, as The Lowlands or Japan clearly show. Hence the hearts of Middle American planners may be in South America, but their heads are in The Hague and Tokyo. They are trying to move from plantation agriculture to internal-market agriculture and from internal-market industry to specialization in high-yield products for the world market. It is no accident that the Dutch and the Japanese have done the same, while Brazil and Argentina, more like the United States than Costa Rica is, can afford more widespread development programs. Only Mexico has the critical mass for grander schemes, and even there arable land is extremely scarce.

    Middle American planning has therefore naturally had an even more localized and elitist pattern of modernization and urbanization than that of South America. The centers of industrialization are located either near administrative centers like Mexico City or close to the market sources as is the case with Monterrey, near the United States, or Tampico, near the water. This is the pattern in Puerto Rico and Cuba or anywhere else--in short, whatever the ideology. Attempts to take industry to the interior are still rare, though Mexico has had some success in the cotton region of the north-central mountains. The result of all this is the catastrophic overgrowth of Mexico City, Guatemala City, Panama City and almost any other city. There is simply not enough work in industry to take care of all who come down from the hills, and barrios become vast hives of people looking for work or welfare. Cities become more administrative than industrial, bureaucracies get costly, and development of industry turns into development of government. There is little wonder that government elites fear that the voting mechanism will create

make-work jobs, spur inflation, and retard the growth rate.
Single-party planning is considered a hedge against unwise
acts of desperate peasants and slum dwellers. Thus politicians, unions, and the masses usually have even less involvement in development planning in Middle America than in South
America, for good or ill.

The new classes of Middle America therefore resemble
their South American counterparts in education, social concern, and style of life. But they are even fewer in number,
still more professional than business-oriented, and almost
totally of native rather than immigrant stock. Mexico and
Guatemala are much like Indian South America in that the
major social problem is the integration of the Indians into
modern, urbanized life, although there is not quite such a
large proportion of Indians. The Caribbean is a waterlogged
Brazil, a patchwork of peoples, some of whom predominate
in one area and some in another. The difference is that
Negroes are found in larger percentages than anywhere in
Brazil. Central America resembles the South American littoral in its mixture of cultures and conflicts. But there is
no equivalent in Middle America of the Europeanized part of
South America, unless it be Cuba, Puerto Rico, and the
Dominican Republic, or perhaps Costa Rica. But even in
those countries "new immigrants" are few because of over-
population, and almost all those are Spanish. Meanwhile,
the grinding-down of the extended-family structure into a
nuclear-family, socially-oriented middle group that serves
modernization proceeds under the pressure of governmental
reforms. Whether the ethnic barriers will give way as the
family structure has is not yet clear. But it is clear that
the middle sectors--the industrializing groups of managers
and workers--face special problems in Middle America, and
particularly in the Caribbean.

For one thing, the "ladder of success" is still very
rickety for social reasons. It is obviously hard to move
from campesino (peasant) to obrero (worker). That transition
requires, as it always has in early industrialization, not only
new habits and skills but also a move to where the work is.
Dispersed industry is too costly for the first stages of modernization, so industrial-city slums, labor oversupply, and
knocked-down wages are typical. And because of the rigid
class and caste structures and the lack of a frontier safety valve
in Middle America such conditions exaggerate the tendency of
obreros to "identify down" (with their peasant cousins) rather
than "up" (with the "employees," or empleados). As yet

workers do not expect to get ahead, or to have even their
children become empleados or own their own businesses. The
"ladder" therefore tends to break between empleado and obrero,
too.

This tendency has two major consequences for labor
relations. First, it confirms the anarcho-syndicalist tradition
of labor movements in all Latin countries. Essentially, that
means that unions (gremios) are committed to striking for
political as well as economic reasons--for lifting radical
governments as well as wages. This does not necessarily
mean that the unions are following Marx, since Sorel's ideas
of a general strike are perhaps as powerful. But it does
mean that the unions are definitely radical and that North
America's AFL-CIO devotes a great deal of attention to combating such syndicalist tendencies and to encouraging "free
labor development." Conversely, the Cubans have set up an
international union structure to encourage Marxist radicalism.
Middle America is therefore the main battleground of a "labor
war" that has spilled over into the United Nations' International Labor Organization.

The second consequence of the obrero-empleado gap is
that both sides insist on strict formal codification of work
rules in a "labor law" (derecho del trabajo). The labor relations of North America emphasize union-management negotiation on wages and working conditions, but Latin Americans
prefer the European method of statutory determination of
minimum wages and workplace safety. That diminishes the
in-the-shop conflict while emphasizing the adversary relationship. But it also leaves the process at the mercy of forces
outside the shop. The shop steward is often less important
than the union leader. The plant manager is sometimes less
important than the government inspector. The potential for
politicizing grievances and sparking labor unrest is therefore
considerable. So is the potential for personal favoritism and
bribery. "Sweetheart" relations between managers and labor
leaders, mordidas for inspectors, mutual suspicion, and lost
production--such are the all-too-frequent penalties of excessive attention to the competitive aspects of the industrial
labor scene. Some of the tension comes from the stage of
development Middle America is in. Early industrialization
tempts managers to squeeze workers for every bit of production in order to hurry progress, and workers strain for
every centavo of wages in order to keep up with skyrocketing
prices. But some of the tension also comes from the culture of work typical of Latin, and indeed of most formerly
colonial, areas.

Empleados themselves may or may not "identify up, "
however. For the ladder is also broken where the "what
you know" of the tecnicos clashes with the "whom you know"
of the old elite. Many a bright engineer or manager of humble family finds promotion blocked by someone of "good family. " Many a dedicated civil servant finds advancement cut
off by political patronage. On the other hand, the children
of the old elite may have become jefe (chief) or dueño (owner)
through the advantages of a superior education. And exacer-
bating the entire situation is the fact that the lower ranks of
educated empleados, such as clerks and teachers, are filled
with ambitious people whose income barely allows them to
make ends meet in an inflationary situation. Empleados are
therefore socially schizophrenic. One group--the lower-
ranked, the frustrated, the humble of background, the ideal-
ists--sympathizes with, and often joins with, the workers and
the liberal professions to push for Indianist, nationalist, or
socialist solutions. Another group--the upper-ranked, the
rising stars, the well-born, the pragmatists--identifies with,
and often cooperates with, the elite of landed and industrial
wealth. But as yet cohesion among the technical, industrial,
and landed elites is much, much less than in North America,
or even South America.

The notion that Middle America is a particularly
striking example of the "dual society" of early-industrial
Third World countries therefore needs refinement. There is
clearly a dual society in the sense that the gap between the
very rich and the very poor is wider than any except perhaps
Africa's and Asia's--much worse than the gap between reservation Indians or Mississippi sharecroppers and New York
cosmopolites, certainly, and probably worse than anywhere
in South America except the Amazon and the high Andes.
The underclass includes the ranchero or Indian of the Mexican desert. His house is adobe or wattle. With luck, the
roof is castoff corrugated tin from the nearest village. There
are no appliances. There is not even a floor. His clothing
and that of his family is homemade and traditional--calzones,
rebozos, etc. Their food is some combination of corn,
beans, and cactus beer (pulque). Their water is inadequate
and probably owned by someone else. Their land is the
same. Their possessions consist of a bed, a table with
benches, a few utensils, some farming implements, and an
animal or two. Their life expectancy is forty or so years.
Two-thirds of the children have died. There is no school.
Nor are there books. Nor a radio. Nor a road or a bus.
Income is nonexistent except for a day's wage here and there

for manual labor. And there is no way out save, perhaps, via a stint as a bracero in the United States or a scramble for work in Guadalajara or Monterrey. The rest of the underclass merely plays out variations on this theme. Thus there is the Central American in jungle hut, the Haitian in mountain hovel, even the slumdweller in cardboard-box shanty around almost any Middle American city.

The Middle American rich are, in contrast, very rich indeed. The "estates" in Middle America support townhouses in London, Paris, or Madrid--and private jets for weekend trips, a Mercedes at either end of the transatlantic flight, and private European educations for the children. Some Middle Americans live in Europe or North America and commute the other way for business. The stay-at-home Middle American elite, and probably the absentee rich as well, may not be a match for the super-rich of the oil states or for European or North American magnates, but their wealth stands out all the more because of the surrounding squalor. And that's the rub. To become rich in a rich society is one thing, but to become rich in a poor society is quite another. So the Middle American rich, like the rich of Asia and Africa, are not evidence of general advance but of special advantage. Even in South America, where development is generally more advanced than in Middle America, this dual society phenomenon persists because the number of citizens benefiting from the new industrialism is still small. When Venezuela's per capita income exceeded $2,000 per year in the 1960s, for example, it was still not possible to argue that the country was developed in the sense that modern living standards had spread to large numbers of citizens outside Caracas. And the generality of Middle Americans, like most South Americans, are nowhere near the Venezuelan mark and so do not look on their rich as a bearable expense. The negative economic impact of the rich therefore seems much greater in Middle America than in highly industrialized countries.

This vision of Middle America as a dual society of voracious rich and helpless poor is the heart of radical doctrines for modernization, be they nationalist, leftist, or electoral. Only vigorous reform or revolution can end such "dependency" (dependencia) according to quite a few Middle Americans. Their view is that the middle rungs of the ladder of success are missing because the rich have removed them. The fact that all the moderns taken together--the landed old rich, the industrial new rich, the managerial jefes,

the educated empleados, even the semi-skilled obreros--make
up no more than a tenth to a fifth of Middle American societies strengthens their appeal. But the same fact that
creates revolutionary urges mitigates against revolutionary
advances. Successful revolutionaries find themselves face to
face with the same nasty realities: the inability or passivity
of the masses makes it nearly impossible to sustain economic
and social advance; the hostility or flight of the rich cripples
the country unless it can be prevented; and the professionals
may or may not stand for rubbing elbows with campesinos
and obreros. Hence there is a tendency for a revolutionary
party to slide back into the embrace of the professionals or
to coerce them into revolutionary action. Only a relatively
advanced and externally-supported country like Cuba could afford to allow so many professionals to leave after the Revolution, for example.

There is an alternative to this interpretation of the
Middle American condition as one in which the long-term
meaning of development is elimination of the dual society.
Perhaps the creation of a large and satisfied and socially-
committed middle sector group is the key to development.
Perhaps the chasm between rich and poor is a temporary
phenomenon of the "robber baron" period every modernizing
country goes through. Perhaps the Mexican, Puerto Rican,
and Cuban--and for that matter the American, French, Russian, and Chinese--revolutions have had in common the process of the professionalization of society. If modernization
means ousting the landed elite from control of the society,
all have tried and to some extent succeeded in doing that.
If it means trying to raise the level of skills in more and
more of the population, they have done that, too, and succeeded in varying degrees. In other words, the minimally
productive rich and the minimally productive poor have been
inspired, coerced, cajoled, seduced, or scared into greater
productive endeavor. Besides agreement on these basics of
development in all the modernizing revolutions and evolutions,
however, there remain two profound disagreements: how to
reward and how to control the new industrial classes. Too
little reward and too much control causes fight or flight--as,
some argue, was evident in the Mexican Civil War and the
Cuban exile phenomena, respectively. Too much reward and
too little control causes a new class and a slowing or even
an end of modernization--as, some argue, recent Mexican
and Puerto Rican experiences have shown. Yet stutterstep
progress is still progress.

In Middle America the development of middle sectors
full of dedication, commitment, and wisdom may prove particularly difficult, however. The colonial experience has
left a legacy of hostility and mistrust among the masses and
a low level of national commitment on the part of the elite
or, for that matter, the masses. So long as elites and
masses remain alienated, little is to be expected. Furthermore, the idea that revolutionary urges are a panacea for
lack of commitment and effort has so far proved untrue,
save, perhaps, in Cuba. Revolution has not provided much
of a shortcut to modernization, though it can bring about the
necessary "religious conversion" of the elites to modernization. The prime problem is neither the inertia of colonialism
nor the inadequate momentum of revolution, though. It is
the brain drain. Enough Middle Americans are probably
trained for middle sector positions at the University of the
West Indies, the University of Puerto Rico, the University
of Mexico, or abroad. But there is a magnetism in the ac-
cessibility of the United States and Europe and the relative
attraction of careers there. Upward social mobility for
trained Middle Americans often means a career outside their
own nations, since social or economic barriers exist at
home. There is some indication, nonetheless, that many of
these obstacles to formation of nationalist middle sectors
are being worn down. Modern nationalism is taking form,
though whether its form should be revolutionary or evolutionary, multi-racial or ethnic is hotly debated.

Still, modern aspirations, once developed, may not be
fulfilled as easily in Middle America as they were in North
America and probably will be in South America. The uphill
climb is simply steeper. An analogy with the United States
South and with East Europe may illustrate the crucial difference. The South, for example, has had most of the problems now faced by Middle America. It has been subject to
outside economic forces, that is, to the industrialized North
with the riches, the population and political weight, the superior skills--and the profits from the South. Its population
has fled north to menial jobs in the core cities or to become
New York or Washington wizards. Its politics have been
one-partyish to head off the potential race and class violence
and to protect the modern interests of the thin elite. Its
people have been stereotyped as incurably lazy, hickish,
bigoted, and violent. But the South's political stability has
finally paid off in sufficient governmental aid, and its cheap
labor in sufficient runaway industry, to put the "sunbelt"
into a nearly competitive position with the "snowbelt." The

South's per capita income ($6,000 or so by the 1970s) has thus reached about two-thirds that of the North ($8,000) and the dual society gap has begun to inch closed. The same phenomenon is evident in East Europe: per capita incomes ($2,000-$3,000) have begun to close in on West Europe's ($3,000-$7,000) after a century of East-West, and for that matter South-North, divergence. The point is that Middle America ($500-$1,000) is the tropical depression between its neighbors in South America (except for the very poorest, such as Bolivia, about $800, up to Venezuela's $2,500) and, more especially, in the North American South and Southwest. And tropical depressions often spawn hurricanes.

They also drench the earth so that if the winds are not too violent, luxuriant growth follows. Underdevelopment near development--again the United States South comes to mind--has traditionally meant late but rapid growth. Proximity may be Middle America's saving grace if the resource and population problems are not insuperable, and if the political instability is not too great, and if the dependency is not too damaging--a lot of ifs. The formal development plans reflect Middle American leaders' consciousness of this "good neighbor" alternative. Indeed, Britain's decision to enter the European Common Market forced Commonwealth nations in the Caribbean to move toward this alternative. Three emergent elements of Middle American economic strategies are crucial. One might be called "Caribbean first." Aid to and from and trade with Caribbean and rimland states is emphasized: Venezuela provides aid to several Central American states with oil money, and Cuba runs an agricultural aid station in Jamaica, for instance. Of course this principle has political fallout: an end to Cuban isolation despite North American objections, pressure against the Somozas during the late-1970s uprisings in Nicaragua, and other evidences of centripetal tendencies. The second principle might be called "several baskets." Middle Americans insist that development "eggs" have no political genesis. They try to achieve such independence by diversified two-country agreements (with Poland, Sweden, Czechoslovakia, Rumania, Canada, Nigeria, and China as well as the United States or the European Common Market) and by emphasis on truly international efforts (the United Nations agencies, the World Bank, and the Inter-American Development Bank).

The third element is, no doubt, "out from under"--meaning, of course, a change in the traditional relationship with the United States and West Europe. Some of this so-

called "Southern Hemisphere strategy," aiming at a "new
economic order" in which the Northern and Southern hemispheres are in a more coequal relationship, could be con-
strued as anti-United States or anti-European or revolutionary.
Most, however, is merely aimed at a better deal in the traditional dealings, since Middle Americans are acutely aware
of the absence of alternatives to their relationship with the
"industrial north." Their aim is to negotiate good tariff arrangements with the Common Market, to alter the United
States Trade Act of 1974 to their advantage, or, better yet,
to get a guaranteed market for their products at a good price.
The era in which Middle Americans were chiefly concerned
with getting the United States and colonial Europe to accept
the principle that there exists no right whatsoever to intervene to protect the property of foreigners in Middle America
seems to be passing. The Middle American preoccupation
has become one of undermining the most-favored-nation principle of trade treaties. Their contention is that small, developing nations cannot build up their "infant industries" if
they have to give the United States or the Common Market
the lowest (most-favored) tariff rates. Even the United States,
they argue, threw up tariffs against foreign goods in the
1870-90 period--as has every other developing country. In
short, Middle Americans want a grace period in which they
can put up their own tariffs while still having access to
northern markets. Call it "indirect aid," if you will, or
"equity" if you are of another mind.

Concentration on the formal economy will distort the
picture of Middle American possibilities, however, because
every developing area has a large so-called "other economy."
Portions of this underground network are unhealthy for Middle America, her neighbors, or both. The most obvious are
the drug traffic of the Colombian, Mexican, and other "connections," the prostitution of big cities and tourist areas,
and the quickie-divorce mills of Mexico, Haiti, and the Dominican Republic. Several points need to be made about
this crime empire. First, it is a two-sided arrangement
involving organized crime in the United States and Europe--
or South America--as well as shady types in Middle America.
Miami and Marseilles simply moved their business from
Havana to other areas when Castro cleaned house. Second,
crime is hard to resist where low national and personal incomes increase temptations and desperations. Middle American mobbery got its start the same way North American
mobbery did--running rum during Prohibition in the United
States. Mexican and Colombian campesinos cannot resist the

poppy any better than good ol' boys could resist the still.
Third, crime thrives because the national and international
cohesion to resist it is lacking. United States-Mexican efforts to destroy the poppy farms of the sierra with helicopter-
hopping squads of federalistas has not met with wide acceptance in or outside Mexico, nor with wide success.

The most important point is that parts of the underground economy have official sanction or acquiescence. Some
of the problem is just venality. Thus it was with Batista,
for example. Hence also the allegation that Colombians make
more from cocaine than coffee and that Panamanian President
Torrijos' family is drug-trafficking. Yet the larger difficulty
is that the distinction between "legitimate" and "illegitimate"
is sometimes hard to make. It is debatable how unhealthy
some underground elements are, not to mention whether they
are unique to Middle America or more excusable in an under-
developed area. Are the numbered-account tax havens in the
Bahamas more reprehensible than Switzerland's? Is the
cockfight or dogfight gambling more damaging than the legal
casino's? How harshly shall we condemn the sharecropper
for bartering his vegetables or the cantina owner for skim-
ming a little to avoid taxes and fixed prices on the formal
economy? Is the Mexican front man for foreign companies
to be applauded for increasing investment in his depressed
patria chica, or berated for selling out his country? Or
look at it from a slightly different angle. Is the North American retiree to be condemned for moving to Mexico (or even
back home to Puerto Rico) to stretch his Social Security?
What of the San Diego or Tucson consumer--or the tourist--
who stretches his dollar south of the border? And what of
the TV manufacturer who builds his factory where labor is
cheap? Does he exploit Middle America if the parts are
made there and the TVs assembled in Ohio? Does he exploit
Ohio if jobs are exported to Middle America and TVs are
sold north of the border? Again, this is like the United
States South: the underground economy remains strong, what
is unfair competition remains relatively undefined, and competitive advantage, the drive train of development, continues
to run down the map and into Middle America.

The Mañana Ethic, that supposed opposite of the
Puritan Ethic, can now be placed in the same sunlight as
earlier Yankee stereotypes of Rednecks. The comfortable
assumption that laziness begat poverty, that poverty begat
crime and violence and ignorance and bigotry, and that these
four in turn begat repression and a whole host of other back-

wardnesses deserves to be dismissed as the New England
myopia it is, whether one is talking about the Confederacy or
the Caribbean. The genealogy is far, far more complicated
than that. It might be "Colonialism begat..." Or it could be
"A late start begat..." Or "A harsh land begat..." Or
"Political fragility begat..." There are, of course, cultural
differences in attitudes toward work, upward mobility, and
the like. But it seems much less likely that they are
Protestant-Catholic, Nordic-Latin, White-Black, or temperate-
tropic differences than that they are feudal-modern, or, better yet, hopeless-hopeful, differences. The North American
West developed faster than its South for the very same
reasons.

The real differences in Middle American (or Latin
American) and North American attitudes toward work lie not
so much in how hard the work may be, but in its value.
Latin Americans have not, or at least not yet, internalized
the materialist strivings North Americans associate with
modernism. Instead, they look to the dignidad in work--to
the relations it gives with family, community, and nation.
Materialism is antisocial, selfish in their eyes, damaging to
self and to society. Tomorrow will take care of itself if the
individual has done his part, but not done so much as to
embarrass his neighbors. Honor in one's work is what matters. Which Middle American leaders would have it otherwise? Certainly not those who make political and moral
law. And who is to judge them less wise than the puritanical
materialists?

The Political Scene

Hard as it is to believe, Middle America is more
underdeveloped politically than economically. Two problems
have been a constant plague: micro-statism and political
dependence. Middle American political leaders have long
recognized these problems but have been unable to overcome
them. The scattered island-states of the Caribbean and the
mini-states of Central America are best compared with the
Balkan countries of Europe and the Indochina states. Too
small to act on their own in the world arena and too hostile
to work together, they have become dependent on one or
another outside power for support or have remained colonies.
So whereas European empires have crumbled, the power of
the United States, though lately challenged by the Russians'
influence in Cuba, has risen. Attempts by various small

states to go it alone have usually either been crushed by imperial power or have failed in all but formal independence. The whole economy is still dependent on foreign markets, and the entire region is tied to the United States' defense network through the OAS. Mexico, which is on a par with the ABC powers of South America, is the sole exception. But even Mexico remains divided by an internal micro-state-like regionalism and has refused to give a strong challenge to the United States in Western Hemisphere affairs. Until the problem of micro-statism is overcome, there is little likelihood that Middle Americans can develop their political power sufficiently to prevent outside intrusions. Yet the micro-state problem can be overcome only by the final disappearance of imperialism, which is now being completed, and by the development of new principles of organization to replace both colonialism and nationalism, a process that is only beginning in the Central American Common Market and various Caribbean Federation schemes. Nationalism may be an asset to the rather large states of South America; in most of Middle America it is a threat.

This situation has always been tailor-made for Strongmen, whether buccaneers, imperialists, caudillos, or modern dictators. Those with power felt impelled to use it; those without power thought the imperial or national leaders too far away and weak to prevent a golpe. The security of the population caught in the middle was nil. Men who could command the allegiance of wide segments of the population were few, and most were old-line caudillos until the Mexican Revolution. After that the Strongman usually was backed by a party or an army, or by both. There have been many old-style dictators such as Duvalier of Haiti, Trujillo of the Dominican Republic, and the Somozas in Nicaragua. But many countries now follow either the Mexican, Cuban, or Puerto Rican "revolutionary" model.

The Mexicans have one party, the Mexican Revolutionary Party, which always wins over token opposition with huge majorities. Neither the presidency, the congress, the important Mexican states, nor the military and bureaucracy have ever been controlled by other forces for any extended period since the Revolution. There is good reason for single-party rule in this case, as Mexico was fearfully divided by civil war and needed stable government. Other nations, with a less healthy governing party, have tried the same thing with less success. Cuba, for instance, is attempting its revolution with Communist guidance, and all ideological opposition is forbidden, though other Marxist parties are allowed. Those who look to this solution over the Mexicans' pragmatic (but still one-party) approach do so because they believe Marxism will appeal to many more Middle Americans because it is non-nationalist.

The adherents of the Puerto Rican system of two-party government of the Anglo-Saxon type argue that both Mexicans and Cubans have to give up "one-party dictatorship" for "democracy" sometime, and should simply start there. This approach is the rule in Puerto Rico and the former British colonies like Trinidad and Jamaica. Opponents point out that even Muñoz was a kind of "democratic dictator" despite two-party government, and argue that multi-party government in any form is inefficient for developing countries. Finally, there is some question whether the Black Power movement represents a new model of potential importance for Middle America. If so, its idea of a government by and for Blacks would represent a fourth force challenging the old caudillo tradition.

The implications of all these forces were seen in the Dominican Crisis of 1964-66. The old-style dictator, General Trujillo, had been assassinated in 1961. He was replaced by his vice president, Joaquín Balaguer, a nationalist who tried to form a Mexican-style party to modernize the state. The opposition, under Socialist Juan Bosch, won the election but was pushed by its Communist supporters in the Cuban direction. The military, under General Wessín y Wessín, then tried to go back to the Trujillo system by throwing out Bosch--and civil war led to the intervention of United States marines. Supervised elections resulted in a Balaguer victory in 1965, but the multi-party system left Bosch and his followers so dissatisfied that they drifted from their previous parliamentarianism toward a program favoring "democratic dictatorship." The situation has remained extremely volatile because, unlike the Anglo-Saxon countries, the Middle American nations do not equate democracy and parliamentary government. Meanwhile, the Negro-majority governments of countries like Jamaica have favored Bosch. Such are the complexities of Middle American politics and ideology that make future unity and strength a far-off hope.

But ideology is only one of the means of seeking political unity in Middle America. Indeed, Middle Americans have relied on the "charismatic leader"--the Juárez, the Cárdenas, the Muñoz, the Castro, the Garvey--far more than on the political creed. Middle America's leader-heroes are somewhat different from the distant and aloof Perón types of Spanish South America, however. Folksy, man-of-the-people styles are more typical. Castro not only forbids statues and titles. He also plays dominoes and baseball, swings a machete in the sugar harvest, and mingles with the street crowds. He is good old Fidel in fatigues. In South America only the Brazilians are so first-namish with their leaders-- in the case of Vargas, for instance, who was always "Getulio." This is not Europe with its titled Fuehrers, Duces, and Caudillos, or even its underground-name Lenins and Stalins. Nor is it the pomp of African charismatic leaders. Rather it is a world where leaders draw citizens close to themselves and to each other by patriotic or revolutionary symbol-making. It is the difference between the leaders North Americans remember by nickname or by initials--Andy, Abe, Teddy, FDR, JFK--and those they do not.

In developing countries it is extremely important to create this feeling of a common bond with the leader. But there are also anti-democratic dangers in this approach. The leader can go bad, as with Batista. Or momentum can be lost with the leader, as may have happened after Muñoz stepped down. The temptation for the charismatic leader to believe that the revolution or progress has been fulfilled in himself is certainly real. That way lies a "personality cult" (as the Marxists call it) or absorption by the older elite, though the latter result usually occurs in the second generation of any modernizing movement--as has almost certainly happened in post-World War II Mexico. All this said, however, it is certain that the rise of Black Power leaders wearing African or peasant garb and presenting as their heroes the leaders of slave revolts is in the mainstream of Middle American politics. And North American experience with a strong executive in time of crisis--Washington during the Revolution, Lincoln in the Civil War, Franklin Roosevelt in the Depression and World War II crisis--indicates that such an approach is not necessarily incompatible with democratic progress. The results are what count, at least in developing-country eyes. Backwardness with freedom seems no virtue.

There has always been one additional danger in charismatic leadership, however, and that is "statism." Middle American modernizers have generally worried less about this "Napoleonism" than about the possibility that their leader will be deflected before he roots out the corruption and favoritism benefiting the old elite. Yet there are two forces inclining

toward excessive bureaucratization in an area such as Middle
America: the leadership wants to hurry modernization along
by means of centralized planning, and the movement's followers expect early rewards that can only be provided in the
government sector because of economic inertia. Many Middle American revolutions have lost their momentum in this
fashion. Robespierre's "Terror" cleans out the corruption
of the previous regime only to find that a Napoleon's "Ther-
midor" has created a "new class" enriching only itself. The
Mexicans and Puerto Ricans and Cubans insist that what
Napoleon did in France, and what Trotsky said happened in
Russia and Mao tried to prevent in China, just must not
come to pass in Middle America. So the Mexicans emphasize
indianismo, the Puerto Ricans look to the jíbaro, and the
Cubans lionize the campesino. Nevertheless, the statist tendency remains so long as self-sustaining and spreading modernization has not caught on, and critics contend that no Middle American revolution is still spreading in this sense.

Yet Middle Americans continue to believe that inspiring
leadership offers their best opportunity for reconciling development and democracy. North Americans are likely to be
skeptical of the notion that such "Latin" leadership amounts
to "a constant election" because it embodies the will of the
people. And in principle Middle Americans, indeed most if
not all Third World modernizers, would agree that open
elections and complete civil rights represent the ideal--for
the future. The quarrel rages over "political stability."
North Americans argue that it flows out of elections involving
all democratic (but not Fascist or Communist) parties. Middle Americans of the Left and the Right contend that their
political systems are not sufficiently cohesive to risk open
competition.

There is some mutual misunderstanding here. North
Americans fail to see that the coups and counter-coups of
Middle American politics constitute a kind of "election." The
ousted leaders receive sanctuary in the embassies of sympathetic Latin American states, or go into exile, or even go to
jail and are amnestied. Miranda, Madero, and Martí prepared their new deals in the United States, after all, and
Castro readied his in Mexico. At any moment dozens of
would-be presidents and ex-presidents are scattered throughout
the Caribbean islands and rimlands awaiting their chance.
So the news reveals Bosch in Puerto Rico waiting to replace
Balaguer, Arias returning from Florida in hopes of turning
the tables on what Torrijos did to him in 1968, and even one

of Fidel's sisters, Juanita, leading the anti-Castro exiles in Florida in a campaign to prevent United States-Cuban détente Similarly, some Middle Americans think electoral politics of the North American--or Puerto Rican--sort constitutes false competition because they fail to understand the role of the utilitarian consensus in such arrangements.

The vexed issue of personal freedom and security in Middle America remains, however. Middle Americans believe that much has been lost from time to time through such external intrusions as European colonialism, North American intervention, and Communist machinations. Radicals believe that much has also been lost to the entrenched elites of land and capital abetted by conservative external forces, and cite Díaz' Mexico, Batista's Cuba, and Trujillo's Dominican Republic as modern examples. Conservatives believe that much more has been lost because of radical agitation among the impressionable masses, and cite Castro's Cuba as an example of what happens to freedom of choice after successful revolutions. All, interestingly enough, agree that the major loss has been due to lack of "institutionalization." The psychological meaning of development is, after all, to enlarge the ingroup, to include castes and/classes in the modernizing effort. Where development reaches a certain stage, caste and class violence diminishes.

As yet Middle America seems not to have reached that point, since the exile-and-amnesty system for political change has broken down. The number of political assassinations, political prisoners, and political uprisings is on the increase in both radical and conservative countries. The United States Central Intelligence Agency is blamed by Middle Americans, but the cloak-and-dagger warfare of Castro's Cuba and Pinochet's Chile indicates that the newer political style has been internationalized. The central role of the exiled Venezuelan "Carlos" (Ilich Ramírez Sanchez) in the international terrorist or guerrilla bands supporting world revolution by skyjacking and kidnapping has added yet another dimension.

The Organization of American States has not been able to deal with the freedom-and-security issue in Middle or in South America for the same reasons it has not seen fit to become involved in civil rights matters in the United States: division and lack of influence. In the mid-1970s the OAS was able, however, to agree that terrorist attacks (individual acts) were not a human rights issue, whereas torture and imprisonment (acts of state) were, a decision conservatives took to indicate a drift toward radicalism. But the OAS has not been able to agree on a position regarding press and electoral freedoms. The United Nations, meanwhile, has begun a human rights campaign that calls into question the rights records of several Latin American states (Brazil, among others) a decision conservatives thought too gentle with Cuba and other leftist states.

The United States governments of Presidents Ford and Carter have nevertheless supported the human rights efforts of the OAS and the United Nations. In South America arms shipments have been suspended, aid and trade pressures put on, and public criticism broadcast, with the result that Brazil has refused North American military aid. The Brazilians, like the Russians and Cubans, argue that such pressures are a sublte form of intervention and an infringement on national sovereignty. The United States argues that they promise to enhance democracy in the face of totalitarianisms of Right and Left. Whether the majority of OAS states will see such efforts as democracy or intervention--and apply the principles to Nicaragua and Cuba--is the point of issue.

The Nicaraguan case is the least troublesome. The notoriety of the Somoza regime has grown since its inception in the 1930s. The wealth of the ruling family, the neglect of reforms, the management of elections, the repressive security machinery, the involvement as staging area for the Bay of Pigs fiasco--all have contributed to the obloquy heaped on the Nicaraguan government. But until recently Nicaragua's proximity to the Canal has assured the United States support which brought the Somoza family to power in the first place. The United States marines were always thought to be available again, if necessary, to hold down the Sandinistas, guerrillas named for the hero of the armed opposition to North American occupation forces in the pre-Somoza days, César Sandino. Thus when the United States in the 1970s turned away from the Cold War doctrine of "containment" and in the direction of the "mutual security" of Good Neighbor days, it clearly meant that opposition to Somoza's methods had become nearly unanimous in the OAS. The assassination of the Somozas' chief above-ground opponent, the newspaper editor Chamorro, led in 1978 to rioting in Managua, a general strike throughout the country, and further isolation of Nicaragua as Venezuela, Mexico, and the United States actually made diplomatic protests. The ouster of the Somozas by Sandinistas in 1979 was supported by Cuba,

Costa Rica, and Panama, encouraged by the OAS, and acqui-
esced in the United States. But will the United States see a
threat to security if Nicaragua drifts to the left in its quest
for human rights?

The Cuban case is more volatile. The United States
insists that so long as the Castro regime exports revolution
in Latin America and Africa, keeps thousands of opponents
incarcerated, and stifles criticism (by jailing the poet Padilla,
for example), Cuba deserves to be ostracized and punished.
Hence North American reluctance to move toward détente with
Cuba until Castro ends his playing at Cold War, too. There
has been Latin American criticism of the same sort--by
Venezuela, Costa Rica, and sometimes Mexico, among others
--but also a greater willingness to lift the 1964 OAS sanctions
against Cuba. Is this a Latin American blind spot concerning
revolutionary as opposed to reactionary statism? A case
could be made, certainly, that Latin America is still a "hot"
(new, radical, open) area and the United States is growing
"cold" (closed, conservative, old). But might this also be,
at least in part, a difference between a seductive and a co-
ercive strategy for "mellowing Communism"? The West
Europeans have certainly interpreted the Latins' pushing the
United States and Cuba toward détente as a positive development akin to their own seductive approaches aimed at drawing
Spain and Portugal away from radicalism, approaches which
also contrast with the United States' hard-line stance against
"Eurocommunism. "

Meanwhile, Middle Americans are preoccupied with the
character of their leaders. There is nearly universal agreement at this point that outside involvement in the "recruit-
ment of elites" is intolerable, though Commonwealth nations
still accept appointment of governors-general by the British
monarch. United States financial support for parliamentary
parties in elections, to say nothing of C. I. A. involvement or
military intervention, is execrated. Connections with North
American or European political forces, or investment abroad,
is probably a detriment at election time, in fact. Connections with Leftist countries and parties is probably less damaging, though still frowned upon and usually not openly tolerated or admitted. Connections with the Vatican are a plus
in many places, though priests and bishops are expected to
"stay out of politics. " The Medellín Statements (1968) of the
Latin American bishops have not led to as much "radical
Catholicism" as they did in South America, for example.
There is of course still much external influence on the

leadership-selection process in Middle America: Puerto
Rican Governor Ferré was a partner in a Miami-based construction firm, and Fidel was first a dollar, then a ruble,
revolutionary. But leaders are less and less likely to be
placed in power with direct foreign help as in the case of
Joaquín Balaguer in the Dominican Republic. They may share
the sentiments of external groups, of course, but more and
more they must come to power on their own because the
Russians do not want to anger the North Americans, and the
North Americans do not want to anger the Middle Americans.

There is less Middle American agreement on the
proper role of the masses and the classes in the choice of
leaders. Participation in elections is often limited by pro-
scription of parties and individuals, restriction of the fran-
chise to the literate, or circumvention of the electoral process by Strongmen. Nevertheless, a "status revolution" has
begun. The old landed elite is being challenged by the newer
group. This is not precisely like the Confederate plantation-
ists vs. the Rockefellers in the United States, but it is close.
The difference is that the landed grandees, even of the enlightened Adams-family sort, are being shouldered aside by
centralizing nationalists rather than market-enterprise Rockefellers. At first these nationalists were relatively untrained
politicos like those of the Mexican, Puerto Rican, and Cuban
revolutions. They had trouble rewarding their citizens because the motor of modernization could not be kept running
at high speed. Now, however, many of the nationalists are
skilled tecnicos--engineers, physicians, managers--who believe they could move the country save for the politicos' foot-
dragging and self-interest.

One school of thought, led by the Marxists, contends
that the politicos are closer to the people and that the tecnicos will become a new class of oppressors unless the unions
and other revolutionary bodies resist. Another school believes the tecnicos have more interest in truly national development than the old-style revolutionaries or the self-
interested workers and peasants. Hence the argument that
has divided Mexico for over a century--between Juárez's
populism and Díaz's cientismo--continues throughout Middle
America. But now there are more tecnicos than before and
the social arrangements are more amenable to them. If the
North American Republicanism of the 1870s-1920s period can
be said to be the equivalent to the three great Middle American revolutions in changing political leadership, it is just
possible that Middle Americans are on the verge of another

status revolution that will bring them a "brain trust" and a
New Deal. Still, the Middle American elite remains smaller
and less open than in the United States at the beginning of
of the century.

Social Arrangements

Don Quixote and Sancho Panza are alive and thriving
in Middle America, but they have different neighbors than in
South America. The somewhat weakened Iberian influence in
Middle as opposed to South America is reflected in food and
drink. To be sure, the elegance of the Iberian grandees of
Central America and Mexico is second to none in the New
World. Here also is cowboy (charro) cooking little different
from that of the gauchos of Argentina and South Brazil, the
huasos of Chile, or the vaqueros of interior Venezuela and
Brazil. But here the Maya and Aztec peoples have left a
more indelible imprint on cuisine than could the Inca peoples
on their spare mountains. Tortillas are the key, for in
Middle America they are the round corncakes familiar to
North Americans, whereas in much of South America tortillas
are omelettes, as in Spain. This ancient staple of the Middle American Indians, along with beans and peppers (chiles),
dominates the diet of the Mainland-Mountain culture.

Tortillas appear as tostadas, enchiladas, tacos, flautas
(overlong flute-shaped tacos), chimichangas (giant wheat-based
tacos from Sonora), and quesadillas (tortillas around chiles),
or as the poor man's chilaquiles (tortilla-and-anything casserole) or sopa seca ("dry soup"). Corn meal dough (masa
harina) appears around meat as tamales or, in more dis-
criminatory kitchens, in gorditas or any of the empanada-like
meat pies of Ibero-America. Indians still eat atole (the corn
gruel once known from Patagonia to Alaska) or pozole (hom-
iny) as well. Chiles come in dozens of varieties, and beans
in more varieties still. Mole poblano, a hot sauce which
includes a bit of chocolate, is a Mexican addiction whose fire
is far too much for most Iberians or Ibero-Americans, with
the probable exception of Chileans raised on pebre sauce and
Caribbean-shore peoples influenced by African and East Asian
affinities for ginger. South Americans often consider Central
American food crude by comparison with their own, more
Iberian dishes.

The Caribbean islands and Central America, like
Brazil and Venezuela or Florida and California, revel in a

taste for tropical fare. Pineapples, coconuts, yams (not sweet potatoes), and bananas (or their larger cousins, plantains) are used everywhere, and citrus fruits, cocoa, papayas, guavas, mangoes, avocados, and peanuts almost everywhere. Almost any area in and on the tropic seas has a special scent ranging from jaca (jack fruit) and palm oil (dendê) in the Brazilian Northeast to the akee and the ugli (cashew) in many of the islands. And almost every dish has a hint of Africa or, to a lesser extent, the East Indies and the Mideast areas of hot-land cuisine. The flat, pan-fried cakes of West Africa have become Jamaican coo-coo (cornbread with okra), Brazilian cuscuz, and the United States South's cornbread. The Asians' tastes have mixed with the Africans' leanings toward ginger, nutmeg, and saffron, so that a kind of culinary border between basically African and basically American Indian food lies just beyond the waterline in Central American and Mexico.

The overlay of cultures in the Caribbean is mirrored in the mix-and-match of food habits. Cheeses baked with shrimp and peppers (keshy yena, Papiamento for queso llena, filled cheese) in the Dutch area, tea time of coconut or banana bread in English-speaking islands, traditional Spanish sofrito sauce in formerly Spanish regions, and elegant fish soups in Haiti or the still-French colonies--these show the colonial influences and only half-attenuated European tastes of the upper classes. Pelau (pilaf) reveals the Asian influence, cassava biscuits the African contribution, and a few exotic dishes the Carib Indian cultural remnants in the islands nearest South America. Most interesting, however, are the mixtures: picadillo (ground beef with spices, olives, and raisins) in Cuba, piononos (plantain-wrapped meat) in Puerto Rico, poulet rôti a la Créole (banana-stuffed roast chicken) in Haiti, calypso pork roast (seasoned with rum and half the Orient's spices) in Jamaica, chutney in Trinidad, and "fritters" (deep fried something) in every culinary language of the region.

More beef, olives, and garlic in the Spanish-influenced areas, a bit more fish where the French have been, a touch more lamb and pork because of the British, a dash more sweets and spice from the Africans and Asians or corn and yams from the Africans and Indians, and a lot of kneading and stirring make the Caribbean fare. Such variability has also spread its influence: first, to the lower classes of the United States South, where it met Mexican cuisine, French cajun cuisine, and British cuisine in Louisiana and made

New Orleans a kind of all-Caribbean city; second, to the
lands of the colonizers and the tourists, giving the whole
Atlantic region and much of the rest of the world a sweet
tooth.

By now it is impossible to say whether the Old World
or the New has most influenced the other--as typified by
sugar cane, an Old World product through which the New expanded its impact and, say some, increased its own misery.
Then there is coffee, which is so nearly universal in Latin
America that British-island teasippers seem as exotic as
gauchos sucking their bitter yerba mate tea through bombilla
straws out on the Pampas. Café con leche for breakfast, an
after-dinner demitasse of sugared potency--it is the same all
over the Spanish-speaking world and in much of the rest of
the Americas and Europe as well. But Latin Americans high
and low are connoisseurs and snobs: they can tell where
coffee is from, whether it has been picked, shelled, and
dried properly, how it was brewed--in a word, the same kinds
of things a Frenchman can about French wines. Except where
real coffee is rationed to increase exports, Latin Americans
imbibe tintos, the potent demitasses, most all day and half
the night. African coffee is considered putrid, and the instant Nescafé North Americans make by combining African
brands with inferior Latin American brands merits only one
remark: "No es café"--"It's not coffee." The class differences show in drink as they do in food, but mainly in alcohol
rather than coffee.

The good wines of the Andes and the not-so-good ones
from Central America are not the everyday drink of the
masses as in Iberia, but the occasional indulgence of the
relatively well-to-do. German- and Dutch-trained brewers,
and interaction with the United States, have made beer somewhat more popular in Mexico and parts of the Caribbean.
But the masses still lean to coffee, fruit juices, and strong
spirits, particularly cane spirits, and most especially rum.
As beer is to Bavaria and Milwaukee, or wine to Paris and
Rome, so rum is to tropical and semi-tropical Middle and
South America. In Middle America, all classes and almost
all regions bake plantains in rum and sugar and cinnamon,
mix rum and citrus juices, and drink rum or cañita straight.
It has no serious competitor except, in the Mexican desert,
cactus-made pulque (near-beer) and tequila, or, in parts of
the Caribbean, ginger beer. Cane spirits (including Brazilian
cachaça) predominate until one reaches the wines and the
brandies far south of the equator--the pisco (grape brandy) of

Peru, for example--or the High Andes equivalent for pulque, called chicha (corn near-beer). The upper classes everywhere generally prefer European wines and imported Scotch or gin and look down their noses at local liquors.

Drinking is convivial, as in south Europe, and alcoholism seems less of a problem than in North America or West Europe because it brings "loss of face"--and because the real passion is for sugar. Latin Americans drink the milk from coconuts, papaya milk shakes, and soft drinks so sweet that people in the southern and western parts of the United States, who share this sugar-syrup addiction, cannot stomach them. In the Caribbean, a lot fewer people have had lobster creole than frío-fríos, called "snowballs" in Jamaica and "snowcones" in the United States. Then there are coconut ice creams and sherbets, banana cakes of many descriptions, and, especially at Carnival and other holy times, pasteles (pastries) and dulces (sweets) shaped like every human, animal, and thing ever seen or fancied. Nor can one forget caramel pudding, which is to Latin America as "pie" is to North America, whether it be called flan, natillas, or leche quemada. A little rum, a heavily sugared demitasse, and tobacco complete the culinary picture. This penchant for sugar sets most Latin Americans off from North Americans as surely as do such exotic foods as gusanos de magüey (cactus grubs), nopales (cactus leaves), tunas (cactus pears), vers palmiste (palm-tree catepillar), monkeys, and parakeets, or on the North American side, raccoon, quail, and caviar. What the Americas share is a taste for the common yield of New World lands, such as the cucumbers in gazpacho, a cold soup of Andalusian origin. Otherwise, they are very different.

Social problems naturally arise from such diversity. They are more or less the same in kind as those of South and North America--cultural pluralism, social dislocations, historical hatreds. But they are different in degree; that is, worse than in South America, and far, far worse than in North America. The crucial factors seem to be lack of geographic and economic outlets. Middle America is more Old World-ish than South and North America on this measure. When the coastal areas became closed societies in Brazil or the United States, the restless moved on or, by threatening to, got a raise and better treatment. Middle Americans, like West Europeans, live on islands and peninsulas and cannot do that. Society is therefore tighter. In the United States, moreover, and in West Europe, industrial wealth also encourages social mobility and makes either up or out a

safety valve for discontent. Middle America is more like
southern or eastern Europe, then, and perhaps most like the
Balkans in its poverty and weakness in relation to a colossal
northern neighbor, its rigid rural social structures, and its
revolutionary politics. South Americans, by way of comparison, have generated slightly more economic energy than
Middle Americans in the south and in Venezuela and about
the same or slightly less in the Amazon and the Andes. The
consequences for Middle America? Classes, castes, and
communities close ranks. So-called middle institutions--
family, church, and village--command more respect. And
in the face of such glacial social change national politics becomes mere fluff, even in the most revolutionary, change-
minded countries.

The Mexican Revolution, for instance, has altered the
much-studied village of Tepoztlán very little in over half a
century. As late as the 1950s the famous North American
anthropologist Oscar Lewis found the villages of this Zapata-
country area doing mostly what they had been doing for hundreds of years. The mestizo inhabitants farmed their tiny
fields of corn and beans, grew vegetables and fruits and
chickens in their yards, and usually went hungry for a month
or so before the harvest. Only during fiestas and Carnival
did people really eat well. Cornstalk houses (jacales) still
existed, but most lived in adobe houses, and the rich in
Spanish colonial "mansions." Only one private house and a
tourist stop had a flush toilet, however. There were no
streetlights because there was no electricity. Medicine
meant home remedies provided by curanderas (healers).
Birth was aided by midwives using Indian-era charms and
implements. The priest and the patrón, the local cacique,
and one's compadres (godparents) were the people who counted
in one's life. Family relations were conservative in the extreme. Men worked in the fields, women at home. To live
and die with dignity was the be-all and end-all of existence.
But there was change then and has been more since: white
bread available in nearby towns, increased population because
of advancing life-expectancy, a few children in nearby schools,
and a fifth of the men as braceros in the United States. Despite all that, the norm was stability, even in this much-
Latinized village a mere sixty miles from Mexico City. Relations with the municipio, the state of Morelos, and the
Mexican nation counted for next to nothing.

Lewis discovered almost the same thing in the early
1960s in La Esmeralda, a seafront slum in San Juan, Puerto

Rico. There, however, the weight of city life above had
pressed jíbaro culture out of the inhabitants to a certain extent. Hard against the wall of El Morro, for example, stood
the headquarters of Muñoz Marin's Popular Party--and the
public television set provided by the government. There the
work was less regular, less self-sufficient, less self-
rewarding. The women worked as domestics or as menials
in the hotels, or owned cantinas, or left for the United
States Mainland. The men worked in construction or were
unemployed--or left for the Mainland. Elements of the stable
jíbaro culture of the rural Puerto Rican interior remained,
however. There were the curanderas, and there was the
machismo, and the attachment to Muñoz as a kind of patrón.
There was the Church, the Carnival spirit of hope, the preoccupation with honor, dignity, and saving face. And above
all there was the family, for Lewis was tracing the changes
wrought in the extended Ríos family by Muñoz' progress.

Fernanda Fuentes, the Negro mother, was still living
in La Esmeralda with her sixth common-law husband, and
Cristobal Ríos, a light-skinned Puerto Rican, had long since
disappeared from the free union which produced three daughters and a son. Fernanda's adult daughter, Soledad, and an
adult son, Simplicio, were in New York with their spouses
and children, and the two teenage daughters, Felicita and
Cruz, were with their mother. The striking point is that
the Caribbean extended family was functioning despite the
separations and privations. Connections between the grandparents of the interior, the matriarch of La Esmeralda, and
the third and fourth generations in New York and San Juan
were affectionate. Trips to and from New York and the
jíbaro homeland were frequent. And in the end, Cruz, the
youngest daughter, having turned nineteen, secured steady
work and moved up to a San Juan public housing project--
yet remained attached to the matriarchal family so typical of
the Caribbean.

The most revealing case of cultural inertia is probably
to be found in Cuba, though. The tendency to concentrate on
the exodus of the middle sectors in the face of the Castro
Revolution has obscured the "other revolution"--the extent of
change in Cuban villages. But in the mid-1960s José Yglesias,
a Cuban journalist who grew up in Florida, visited a rural
area in the Sierra Maestra near where Teddy Roosevelt rode
up San Juan Hill and Fidel started his uprising. There
Yglesias found that the United Fruit Company sugar mill had
been nationalized but that rural life and work had changed

little. Commercial labor was still mostly seasonal--a fury of work during the harvest (zafra), little at other times. Subsistence labor on one's own spot of land to make ends meet was therefore the major activity. The government had converted the other United Fruit Company buildings into public housing and schools, but there were too few maintenance personnel and teachers. Above all, Havana seemed far away and foreign, however real the newspapers and the radio at the cantina made Fidel. Youth were less concerned about revolution and education than with sex and sports. The family still counted for much. So, for that matter, did the Church. Fidel's revolution remained more political than social.

In short, when revolutionaries try to flesh out the history of Middle America, it proves very difficult to add to the bare bones of political change. There is, nonetheless, one element of social change that does seem crucial, relations between the generations. Middle America, like all areas of rapid population increase, has a skewed "population pyramid," since in most places half the population is under twenty as compared to an average age of thirty or so in North America. Moreover, the "generation gap" in attitudes seems to be widening in all of Latin America. The young are more likely to be modern--to use the media, to be mobile, to have industrial skills, to sanction rapid change, and to look to peers rather than family for their values. They seem to use the familiar tu with their elders, their teachers, indeed almost anyone; to simplify their names even more than the rest of the Ibero-Americans have; and in general to face the future rather than the past. They expect more from their lives. They dress mod, talk mod, think mod. They are on a first-name basis with the world. Elders think the young are losing face and lack dignidad. Family, confessor, and school are mobilized to halt the passing of the ancestral order. But the elders are outnumbered, the middle institutions overwhelmed, the ancestral values undermined. Middle American youth, like South American youth, are undergoing the rites of passage that late-nineteenth-century North American youth experienced: they are becoming grown-up nationalists with identities quite unlike those of their parents. They are not breaking the family ties, but they are transforming them. Cruz Ríos in her San Juan apartment represents the Middle American majority--young, ambitious, frustrated, impatient.

So the word for the social growth of Middle America is "luxuriant," that is, fecund and strong but stifling, like

the jungles. Layers of history mat down on and intertwine
with each other. No Middle American lives on the flat utilitarian plains of the mind associated with the United States
Midwest. Instead, his light is filtered through layer upon
layer of history, geography, and culture. His formal rituals
are instructive in this respect. There are the holidays of
the Christian calendar--one's saint's day (the day of baptism
and naming, far more important than one's birthday), the
great holidays of Carnival, Lent, and Holy Week, and, of
course, Christmas. There are the holidays of nationhood--
in Mexico, September 16, the anniversary of the 1810 grito,
and in the Commonwealth nations the official birthday of the
British sovereign. There is probably less celebration of
Hispanic Day (Dia de la Hispanidad or de la Raza) than in the
rest of the Iberian-culture areas, however. But there seem
to be far more local and ethnic fiestas and fairs than in
North or even in South America. African (and increasingly
slave-revolt) celebrations, remnants of Maya and Aztec rituals,
and political-party rallies such as May Day flourish in tropical profusion.

Equally revealing of cultural connections, however,
are the Middle American's sports. Hunting and fishing, the
sports of still-frontier societies, appeal to every class and
region. Baseball and boxing join Cuba, Puerto Rico, Panama
and Venezuela to United States culture. Mexico and Central
America are tied to Spain and Peru by the bullfight (corrida),
whereas Venezuela and Colombia are less enthusiastic and
the La Plata states actually forbid bullfighting. Horseracing
(carreras de caballos) and soccer (fútbol) reveal the influence
of Europe, whereas the Caribbean addiction for jai alai
(pelota) and cockfighting shows localized Basque and West
African influence. Middle Americans are willing heirs to a
strenuous existence in which they are tugged this way and
that in a culture now threatening to collapse inward, then to
fly apart. Middle American life is therefore hard but certainly not dull.

Hence it is no accident that the Middle Americans
value the heroic. Theirs is a harsh land with a harsher history, and the heroic struggle to wrest a living from nature,
to conquer or prevent conquest, and to master fear in oneself is woven into the fabric of life and art. The heroic
artistry of the Mexican bullfight, in which a man sets out to
conquer nature by transforming his fear of death into grace-
ful brushes with danger, symbolizes the mood. This is the
mood that launches the search for El Dorado or the everyday

hacking at a stingy land for meager fare. It is also the mood that leads to conquest of Indians and enslavement of Africans on the one hand, and wars of independence on the other. This is the mood of a dark Catholicism that seeks to subdue the demons in man or a dark Voodoo that tries to ally with the spirits of nature in the struggle for human existence. It is also the mood of the frenzied rhythms of Caribbean dances or the epic murals of the Mexican painters. This is life and art on the edge of existence. This is the Cuban cockfight with one winner, alive, and one loser, dead. This is Man Alone in mortal combat with Nature, Men, and Self.

The aim is not so much machismo as dignidad. The unique capacities one has, the position one has inherited or merited, the honorable conduct one displays--these are the important matters. Money and success are secondary in comparison. Better a good matador or novelist than a nouveau riche businessman or governmental official. Better unflinching dignity than skill or progress. One must never permit a loss of face or an embarrassing slip. The matador who slips loses his dignidad--or his life. Anyone who slips loses his soul, his position, his wealth, and the respect of his fellows. Here is the fierce determination to triumph found in South America, but without the confidence of success. The tense matador rather than the loose Carnival reveler is the Middle American prototype. Courage is all-important.

This explains why Middle American religion is more a matter of passion than of doctrine. Seeing Mexicans walking on their bleeding knees to venerate the Virgin at Guadalupe explains a great deal about the Catholicism of this area. The fine-spun theories of the theologians were as nothing to the simple faith of the Indian masses. This made the amalgamation of Christian and Indian religions easier, and only the nomadic Indians offered much resistance to conversion. The Aztecs and Mayas joined their old and new faiths in a passionate amalgam designed to subdue the evil in nature and men. Juan Diego was not the only Indian to see the Virgin of Guadalupe, for many had been looking for something like her for a long time.

The Maya peoples of Guatemala, for instance, still come down to Chichicastenango from the highlands to light their votive candles for the Holy Mother as well as the remaining Indian gods, and though the Aztec altar has disappeared from the Zócalo in Mexico City, the Cathedral of Mexico has risen on the same site. In the Cathedral and

many other Spanish baroque churches scattered over Middle
America the dark interior chapels still symbolize the hell of
this world which only faith and courage can lead us through.
And the veil of the Virgin of Guadalupe a few miles from the
Zócalo symbolizes the miracle of the light which comes to
those who persevere. Moreover, what the Virgin does for
the Indians of Mexico and Guatemala the Voodoo spirits do
for the Haitians. The "medium" ventures to become possessed by the Spirit the better to direct the lives of the Voodoo community. Again the human hero has touched the divine and promised to tame the terror in life. Even the Protestants of the area tend, since the decline of British influence, to be the more evangelical Fundamentalists rather than
liturgical Anglicans and Lutherans, and the East Asians of
Trinidad have lost a good deal of the quietism of their Eastern faiths.

As with religion, so with philosophy. The intellectuals
of Middle America have also been cast in a heroic mold.
They fancy themselves people of action more than people of
thought. The Rationalists favor the statist activism of Positivism rather than the free-market Liberalism of the Anglo-
Saxons. Comte is almost always in vogue, Locke almost
never. Whole schools of thought, like that of the Cientificos
in Díaz' Mexico, have been formed to implement the doctrines
of the "planned society" and demonstrate its superiority to
Anglo-Saxon "materialism." Even the Marxists are a different, more heroic, breed who consider Socialism too soft
and too political to be effective. The development of a wide
workers' movement has always taken second place to the discovery of "a new Lenin." The epitome of this heroic attitude was reached in Che Guevara's Guerrilla Warfare, in
which he accuses the Russian- and Chinese-oriented Communist parties of being soft on capitalism. Only the guerrilla hero is the true revolutionary as far as Castro's followers
are concerned, and Che was killed in Bolivia trying to prove
it. Needless to say, the Communist politicians of the cities
do not agree that only those fighting in the mountains are
true Communists, but the guerrillas capture the imagination
of Middle Americans nevertheless. All of this helps to explain the extraordinary appeal of the Mexican Revolutionary
Party and its practical, non-ideological program. The two-
party or multi-party parliamentarianism of Europe has never
been popular in the Caribbean, but neither has a firm ideology
like that of Vicente Lombardo Toledano of the Mexican labor
movement. Even Fidel Castro's appeal could be said to be
more personal than philosophical.

This heroic bent carries over from religion and politics into everyday life and education. University professors are expected to be active in government or business, and students are political activists. At the University of Mexico, or of Puerto Rico, or of Havana, or of the West Indies, active politics is considered a part of the educated person's responsibility. This is what makes the universities so unstable, and so much the concern of the government. Both government leaders and political rebels grow up there. The secondary and elementary schools are likewise making "men of the world," and this has led to some interesting experiments in education. In Mexico, for example, the government has increased the number of teachers by giving them less, though still adequate, training and sending them into rural villages; and other countries like Puerto Rico, Cuba, and Trinidad are doing the same. Even in the family there is pressure to get the brightest children to reach their highest potential so as to improve the lot of family and nation. In this case intellectual attainment is translated into immediate practical benefit through the "intellectual hero." He is a matador with books and pens.

Arts Old and New

The foremost examples of Middle American art--the Indian pyramids and artifacts, the Mexican architects and painters, and the Caribbean dances--are likewise in the heroic dimension. One look at the huge Maya and Aztec sculptures in the Mexican National Museum or one climb to the top of the Pyramid of the Sun at Teotihuacán or the Great Temple at Chichén-Itzá leaves no doubt about the intention of the Indian artists to inspire awe of nature and the gods. The sacred city of Teotihuacán outside Mexico City compares favorably with Angkor Wat as one of the world's great monuments to heroic religion. The Indian handicraft traditions which have come down retain the same flavor of primitive strength, a motif much in evidence in the Ballet Folklorico of Mexico or the cartwheel decorations and colorful costumes of Central America. The strong geometric patterns and primary colors of Indian pottery and weaving reinforce the impression.

The Mexican architects and painters have become world famous for the raw power of their work. The tradition of Spanish baroque churches and public buildings, so obvious on the Zócalo, has given way to the equally impressive "primitive modernism" of the University of Mexico. There the size and grandeur of the baroque tradition has been modified to accommodate the best of contemporary architecture and the superlative accomplishments of the Mexican mural painters. The muralists are following in the steps of the Indian and Spanish colonial masters who decorated the temples and churches of the past. The modern resurrection of the tradition in the House of Tiles and the Palace of Fine Arts led in the revolutionary period to the incomparable works of Orozco, Rivera, and Siquieros. Whether in the form of God's giant hands meeting man's tiny ones in Orozco's Goya-like work or in the writhing El Greco-like bodies of the masses freeing themselves from imperialism in Siquieros' or in the tug of war between the dynamo and the pregnant earth in Rivera's, the effect is the same--a sense of heroic man reaching heights above all reasonable expectations.

It was these muralists who put Mexico on the artistic map. They turned Mexicans from the elitist art of Spanish baroque toward a populist art available to the masses on the walls of public places. They learned their techniques from Cézanne and Picasso, but they found their inspiration in the ancient Indian wall-paintings of Bonampak or the humble decorations of rural Mexican churches. In place of crowds of Mayan nobles or of archangels stand Orozco's Zapatista revolutionaries leaning forward to form a solid "Barricade." In place of a seductive odalisque there is Rivera's sleeping Indian woman whose hand cups a single newly-sprouted corn plant symbolizing the force of life and of revolution. And in his larger public murals Rivera's theme of warm natural forces pushing through cold materialism is carried to its logical conclusion. The famous "Lenin fresco" of the Palace of Fine Arts may place Lenin among the revolutionary heroes, for example, but the point is really the struggle between the oppressive machinery-oriented elites and the corn-growing Indian masses.

The muralists' savior is not some angular Lenin, then, but the monumental Zapatista of Siquieros' "Christ the Worker," with his body from Picasso's classical period, his colors from Spanish Catholic paintings, and his haloed soul from nature and unmerited suffering. He and the bountiful Indians of Rivera's cycle of murals in the Ministry of Education are as inevitable as the newly sprouted corn, nothing more and nothing less than an irresistible force of nature. The muralists have thus captured and joined two of the universal human themes resulting from modernization: tech-

nology vs. nature, and oppression vs. liberation. And
"uprising"--growth--is always the outcome in these revolutionary muralists.

The revolutionary heroism of Rivera, Siquieros, and
Orozco has been by no means the only expression of fervor
among the muralists, however. Juan O'Gorman emblazoned
the exhilaration of the quest for knowledge in Venetian-style
mosaics on the library of the National University and, even
more to the point perhaps, adapted the famous bas-relief
dancers of the Monte Albán culture to add excitement to his
own home in the Mexico City suburbs. Rufino Tamayo con-
veyed a tropical luxuriance through exaggeration of primary
colors such as the reds of watermelon slices. But all of the
muralists have had in common the spirit of the obviously
zealous "Zapata" and "Don Quixote" of Adolfo Best-Maugard.
Inspiration over restraint, Quixote over Sancho--and who is
to say that is not more reasonable than some cramped life
of getting and spending? These muralists have captured the
mood of the sons and daughters of the shaking earth of Middle America. They have kept as far from the pure art-for-
art's-sake of the elite European schools as Thomas Hart
Benton out on the Great Plains has from the New York
esthetes. They have tried to embody the aspirations of the
masses, to picture Quixote's impossible dream. In the process they have created what is called the Mexican Renaissance
or, when the comparison is not with the Italian but the
Spanish painters, Mexico's Siglo de Oro, its "Golden Century."

Middle American music also seems attuned to the impossible, almost as if it were meant to accompany the effort
to get under the low bar in "limbo," the well-known Caribbean calypso dance. Even the bewildering rhythms of the
Guatemalan marimba or the Mexican flamenco guitar pale before the flying fingers on the bongo drum. Those fingers
tattoo the efforts of Caribbean humanity to defy nature and
history and make of backwardness and slavery a tolerable
existence. The frenzies of Caribbean dances mirror the inspirations of the bitter-sweet life immortalized by the Cuban
poet, José Martí: "The wine is bitter, but it is ours." The
same joy-in-sadness is clear in the colored-stucco buildings
and the bright-tinted head scarves of the islanders. The
impression is of the exotic and the superhuman, of something
in defiance of fate. To dance a Caribbean rhythm is to tax
the body, as to live there is to be at risk. The revolutionary
ballad or corrido is probably the best known form of Middle
American music, however, whether of the Mexican or Cuban

variety. Robin Hood stories about Zapata and Villa have become as popular as the gaucho and cowboy songs of South and
North America, for example, and the Fidelistas' song "Guan-
tanamera" even gained fame in the United States. Middle
Americans hope through their underdogs, and mostly in ballad
form.

The writing of Middle America likewise defies fate.
Deep-sweeping currents curl around the hard surface of life
in the most significant works. Rubén Darío, the Nicaraguan
poet who set off the Modernist movement in all Spanish America at the turn of the century, sings a vital American nature
and humanity, and implies that American vitality will someday
reinvigorate European falsity. Miguel Angel Asturias, Nobel
Prize-winning Guatemalan novelist, is even more explicit in
his novel Hombres de Maíz, or Men of Corn (1949), where
he up-dates the myths of the Quiché Mayas' holy book, the
Popol Vuh, and contrasts their humanity with the inhumanity
of the "modernization" of the Europeans and North Americans.
The same theme is to be found in the poems of Aimé Césaire
celebrating négritude (blackness), in Frantz Fanon's studies
of the wretched of the earth, in Juan José Arévalo's fable-
history of United States-Middle American relations called The
Shark and the Sardines, and in the novels of the Mexican
Mariano Azuela. Moreover, anyone who has seen the famous
Mexican actor Cantinflas knows that he somehow makes sense
out of nonsense, sanity out of insanity. Such is the spirit of
Middle America.

Darío is the Neruda of Middle America but in a way
even more important than the Chilean. For he initiated both
the avant garde and engagé elements of Spanish American
poetry in the generation before Neruda. In "The Swan" he
employs the European avant garde poets' symbols for beauty--
the swan, the color blue, Helen of Troy--but contrasts the
classical Latin sense of beauty with the bombast of Wagner's
swan-songs. This and his other early art-for-art's-sake
poems in Azul gave way after the Spanish-American War,
however, to such engagé poems as "Salute to the Optimist."
Darío's striking "Bravo!" for the just-defeated Latins in his
"Salute to the Optimist" echoes the sentiments of the Generation of 1898 in Spain, with the difference that Darío sees
revival building in Latin America and then spreading to Iberia.
But the "great fruitful peoples" will eventually unite like the
branches of the handle of the Roman battle-axe and hurl back
the north European and North American tide.

Like Rodó, Darío sees a revival of culture in the face
of the shopkeeper mentality, of verve in the face of the mundane, or venturesomeness in the face of conformity, of hope
in the face of despair. In Neruda's world, the Andes climb
upward, themselves alive and still self-forming, while the
heirs of Machu Picchu, breathless with wonder and desire
and driven by the same immortal urge pushing up the sierras,
struggle to tack their latest frail habitations ever-nearer the
rising summits. In Darío's world, the peaks are capped
volcanoes threatening to explode. This is not the open, exhilarating, pioneer world of South America but a world of
barely suppressed violence. The words--and the forms,
rhythms, and emotions, for that matter--are not necessarily
trying the death-defying leaps of Neruda. Instead life erupts
suddenly and irresistibly or rumbles earthquake-like deep
within Neruda's plenitude of words from the "dictionary" of
his natural inner drive has become the explosive, liberating,
revolutionary "cry" of the Middle Americans--the so-called
grito. And Darío's "Bravo!" to the optimists of 1898 has
certainly been the most effective grito in the literary arts.

Not that the Spanish-language traditions have been all
that different in Middle America. The Gabriela Mistral or
César Vallejo of Middle America--deeply religious, familial,
emotional--was Amado Nervo, who felt the ceaselessly in-
drawn breath of God tugging at him from eternity. Such
feelings go back to the greats of Spanish Catholicism, including Sister Juana, the poetess of colonial Mexico who has had
much more influence than her analogs in the English colonies,
Anne Bradstreet and Edward Taylor. Lyric naturalism and
eroticism as strong as that of García Lorca's in modern
Spain or Neruda and Ibarbourou's in South America appeared
in the tropical luxuriance of Carlos Pellicer, in the echoes
of oneself heard in the countryside by Jaime Torres Bodet,
and in the immunity to fire of the fabled salamander of Octavio Paz. The oneness of the Spanish cultural world was, in
fact, emphasized when Juan Ramon Jimenez, "Spain's" Nobel
Prize poet (1956), decided to live in Puerto Rico from the
Spanish Civil War on.

The revolutionary tradition of Bolívar in the South and
of the generations of 1898 and 1936 in Spain has been matched
by José Martí, who remarked that each of the words in Free
Verses (pun intended) was half teardrop from the eye, half
blood-drop from a wound. Martí also excelled in the per-
suasive arts of the Spanish tradition, rhetoric and essay,
along with his countryman Fidel Castro and dozens of other

Middle Americans--Reyes and Vasconcelos of Mexico, Hostos of Puerto Rico and the Dominican Republic, Arévalo of Guatemala, among others. They are at least the equals of Azarín and La Pasionaria in Spain or Rodó, Palma, and The Liberators in South America. Yet despite all these similarities, it seems significant that in Middle America many of the vanguardistas called themselves estridentistas, or "strident ones." The emphasis is somehow different, more frightening, more edgy, more passionate, more--well, strident.

That is understandable enough, since Middle Americans confront not only a quaking earth but the two great revolutions of modern Latin America and the direct influence of the Colossus of the North. They are always in some hurricane or other. Hence the engagé is their forte, artistically and politically. Mariano Azuela's Underdogs virtually created the literary indianismo which later spread to the Andes. Azuela's theme, like the muralists', is betrayal of the "Indian revolution" by the citified mestizos, and in The Flies he shows the flight north through Villa country of the ex-maggots as effectively as he pictures the frustrations of the revolutionary Demetrio in Underdogs. The key to the Indianists' thinking lies in Demetrio's response to the question of why such underdogs go on fighting in the face of trickery above and loss of hope below: He throws a stone into a canyon and points out to his doubtful followers how it falls of itself, gathering speed and force.

By comparison, Asturias' indianismo, in El Señor Presidente and Men of Corn, seems almost passive, with the Maya on the defensive against the elite, except that they are only waiting to explode in a grito of their own. Asturias' work has Marxist overtones, but most strictly Marxist literature is more recent and less rooted because less indigenous. Arevalo's fable about the Shark (the United States), the Sardines (the Central American states, featuring the author's native Guatemala), and the self-serving Octopus (law, business practices, and other tentacles) has had enormous influence but is little more than propaganda. Still, a large number of truly great Middle American authors--Carpentier in Cuba, Paz and Fuentes in Mexico, and of course Asturias in Guatemala--are Marxist in the manner of Neruda and García Márquez, only with more fire. Azuela's stone is still gaining speed but has a Marxist twist to it now.

There is another difference between Middle and South

American literature besides the theme of strained silence, and that is the influence of French and English culture as opposed to the sister Iberian culture of Brazil. The French Caribbean, to be sure, has its conservative Catholics following Maritain and its radical Marxists following Sartre and its Surrealists following Breton, approaches not unknown in either Spain or Spanish America. But the two greats of the French Caribbean, Aimé Césaire and Frantz Fanon, are products of the super-rational French schooling and of the Black experience. Césaire, a member of the French parliament for Martinique and one of the great surrealist poets of the French language, somehow found a way to "return to his native land" in his heart of hearts--to Black-Man's Martinique, to his roots in West Africa, to the négritude concept of President Leopold Senghor of Senegal, a fellow poet and member of parliament. Césaire finds the Black's upside-down truth in ironic reversals--in the hurricane rather than the sea breeze, in black midnight instead of the tropical white heat of noon. Someday, or better, some night, Mt. Pelée will finally erupt, tropical blooms will last beyond dawn, and leveling darkness, when all people look alike, will show herself through the surreal senses beyond mere sight. Césaire will then have returned to his native land beyond the tempest, to a cool midnight comfort from the flaming tropical sun, to négritude, "blackness." And, as he said when rewriting Shakespeare's Tempest, Caliban, not Ariel, will be the guiding spirit.

Fanon's Wretched of the Earth seconds that thought, since his experiences as a psychiatrist in Martinique, France, and revolutionary Algeria convinced him that the most wretched--the poorest, youngest, most hated--would explode in liberation first. Hence his Marxism went beyond Lenin and Mao and caused him to look to the Algerian peasant revolutionaries and to the Black Power advocates of the Caribbean and of Africa as the true liberators. Césaire's midnight solidarity and human brotherhood, or even revolutionary solidarity with Castro, was in Fanon's mind a further, far-off stage of the revolt of the wretches.

The appeal of Césaire and Fanon, and of course of Sékou Touré of Guinea, Patrice Lumumba of the Congo, and Senghor of Senegal, extended beyond the French-speaking Caribbean because the "blackness" idea had such wide application in areas where a tiny white minority controlled masses of Blacks. The English-speaking Caribbean assimilated these ideas chiefly through The Black Jacobins (1938), a book written by Trinidadian C. L. R. James long before the African

states began securing independence. James argued that the
Haitian revolutionaries of the Napoleonic era were not blood-
thirsty savages, as European historians charged, but the first
in a long line of Black liberators: first in Haiti, then in
the rest of the Black Caribbean, and finally in Africa itself.
Kwame Nkrumah, later the first President of Ghana, absorbed
these ideas while James was teaching at Lincoln University
near Philadelphia, where many future African and American
Black leaders besides Nkrumah were also students.   By the
late 1950s The Black Jacobins looked prophetic because African and Caribbean Black Power movements had emerged as
both a cultural and political force.

Meanwhile, the purely literary elements of the English-
speaking Caribbean were also moving away from pale imita-
tions of Shakespeare and Dickens toward an indigenous form
of expression.   In place of De Lisser's White Witch of Rose-
hall (1929), a kind of reverse Gone with the Wind depicting
Jamaica as a rum-, vice-, and superstition-ridden environment
for Blacks and Whites, came a new generation of works in
which the West Indies were not alien to the human spirit, but
the writers' true home.   Even the West Indian Whites--Mittel-
holzer in Guyana, Selvon in Trinidad, Drayton in Barbados,
Hearne in Jamaica--saw themselves as something like the
Spanish-world creoles, not quite European, but of course not
quite of the Indies either.   The Blacks have felt more at
home but somehow out of touch with their African origins.
Jamaicans led the way.   Namba Roy painted, sculpted, and
wrote of a Black Albino alienation, and V. S. Reid praised
in The Leopard the stealth of Kenya's Mau-Mau revolutionaries
as useful in restoring West Indian Blacks' identity within.
Although E. R. Braithwaite's To Sir, with Love tried to cope
with the problems of blackness in white London and was made
into a popular movie by Sidney Poitier, Andrew Salkey's
Quality of Violence and Hurricane and Roger Mais' Brother
Man and Black Lightning are more typical of attempts at de-
fining a West Indian Black identity.

The significance of the Black identity movement centered in Jamaica is widely debated.   Its applicability clearly
extends to the other predominantly Black islands, such as
Barbados, where George Lamming's In the Castle of My Skin
shows a remarkable resemblance to Richard Wright's Native
Son and Black Boy in the United States.   But the blackness
theme has less appeal in half-Asian countries farther south,
since in Trinidad-Tobago V. J. Naipaul searches for his roots
in India as earnestly as Cheddi Jagan in Guyana mixes East

Indian consciousness and Marxism. Such overestimation is less frequent than underestimation of the effects of Black pride on the United States and on Spanish America, however.

Claude McKay of Jamaica actually moved to the United States, where he became part of the Harlem Renaissance of the 1920s and 1930s. Wright's novels, plus Ralph Ellison's Invisible Man and the works of James Baldwin, show a clear progress toward the notion that the American South and the New York ghetto are not a backwater and a slum but a separate, Black culture. Such increasing négritude isolated the great Black poet Langston Hughes, who believed it possible to cooperate with White radicals and went into exile in Russia. Most North American Black writers have preferred instead to live in Paris near the center of négritude-in-exile. In addition, a whole generation of Black university students at Lincoln and Harvard also learned C. L. R. James' ideas along with those of Booker T. Washington, the NAACP, George Padmore, and Marcus Garvey. Moreover, W. E. B. DuBois eventually withdrew from the integration-oriented NAACP and spent his last years in Guinea because of the appeal of négritude. The leader of the Black Power movement of the 1960s in the United States, Stokeley Carmichael, a Trinidadian, mocked those who trusted White Christians (as Martin Luther King did) and White radicals (as Eldridge Cleaver did). So the debate continues as to whether United States Blacks can apply the ideas of négritude in a country only ten per cent Black or must cooperate in some way with a White "system."

It would be an exaggeration to say that Black, French, English, and North American influences have created a separate Caribbean form of Spanish American culture, but not much of an exaggeration. The Cuban mulatto Nicolás Guillén is at once one of the best modern Spanish-language poets and a striking example of Black revival, for instance. Like Césaire, Guillén hears tom-toms--in the throb of his heartbeats, in the rhythmic thud-thud-thud of a hoe, in the body-movements of a rumba, in the repeating swirls of a snake, and above all in his onomatopoetic word-roots from Africa. He invents "nonsense"-words which communicate better, he believes, than the "sensible" words of European tongues. On the other hand, Guillén has accepted the Castro revolution and, in a sense, has become its poetic spokesman with such poems as that picturing a tropical "rain of lead" on invading Yankees at the time of the 1961-62 crisis. In fact, this theme of Black-White brotherhood goes back to Guillén's "Two Boys" (1934), in which two famished beggar-boys, one

black and one white, join each other in a "frenzy of man-
dibles" while consuming the castoff garbage of the Havana
rich "like two dogs, one white and one black."

In similar fashion, the Puerto Rican master of the
short story, José Luis González, manages to capture the
special relationship of Spanish to Black and United States culture without sacrificing its Hispanic tone. Alongside typical
stories about cock- and prizefights, honor defended, and
macho extended are "The Porch" and "The Letter." In "The
Porch," an unfeeling white Puerto Rican describes in a weekend porchside chat how his son was saved by having him
nursed by a Black Puerto Rican woman when his wife could
not produce enough milk--and, offhandedly, how the negra's
son died for lack of her milk. In "The Letter," a Puerto
Rican in New York writes a glowing but illiterate letter to
his mother on the island, promising to bring her up soon--
and then goes to the post office steps to beg for a stamp.
Such a superlative combination of Spanish American dignidad,
and of Middle American expectations of sudden luck, would
be hard to match. Such a combination is the very stuff of
which Middle American revolutionary ideals are made.

Revolutionary Ideals

As South America preserves the Americas' original
pioneer ideals, as North America preserves their original
utilitarian ideals, so Middle America preserves their original
revolutionary ideals--those of French Jacobinism. Middle
American Quixotes and Sanchos seem less drawn to South
America's frontier expansiveness than to the Siamese-twin
images of the long-suffering martyr and the messianic revolutionary. The martyrs include the Indians, the slaves and
ex-slaves of the Black Caribbean, the oppressed and wretched
of the earth in general, and of course the Sardines threatened
by the Shark. The messiahs include Toussaint, Hidalgo,
Zapata and Villa, Castro and Che, and the contemporary
Black Jacobins of Africa and the Caribbean. Middle Americans believe the United States has abandoned the true French
democracy of its origins for a fake democracy of the British
type. They feel closer to the South Americans but believe
themselves superior in revolutionary zeal and virtue because
they have been longer and more seriously oppressed. Among
the Europeans, only the anti-Franco forces of the Spanish
Civil War have captured the imagination of Middle Americans,
since European radicals, including the Communists, lack the

required spice of charisma. Middle Americans, even fairly well-to-do people, identify instead with the Third World revolutionaries of Algeria, Angola, Vietnam, China. They think of themselves as part of the strategy of "freeing" the Southern Hemisphere from the "oppression" of the Northern Hemisphere. They believe themselves to be politically "southern" though geographically north of the equator. They believe all the Americas were once devoted to the liberté, egalité, and fraternité of the French Revolution, and that now only they are fully committed.

"Liberty" thus means something different to North and Middle Americans. In the United States and Canada, it means what the Constitution (1789) and the British North America Act (1867) guarantee, namely, individual rights of action and opinion and ownership, protection from government, live-and-let-live pluralism of race and class and creed. There is a "vertical mosaic" in which corporations, churches, and other institutions operate as freely as individuals. In Middle America, however, libertad generally implies a "horizontal mosaic" of groups and individuals interacting through government. It is assumed that the Church, or the corporations, or the unions, or individuals would deprive each other of their liberties without legal intervention. So Middle American revolutions, following the French, have set out to control the Church, the landlords, and the industrialists to protect the People. Likewise, the law codes, based usually on the Code Napoléon, define the relations among individuals, classes, and castes rather than allowing the courts to settle disputes through jury trials. Experiments with the Anglo-Saxon approach in Puerto Rico, the Dominican Republic, and the Commonwealth islands may eventually replace the notion that government protects against others with the idea that one's church, the press, and guarantees of inalienable rights help one to protect himself against government. As yet, however, the French conception of liberty remains predominant. Libertad means that private oppressors are tamed by a government of the People.

"Equality" in Middle America therefore tends to imply a leveling-down of the rich and powerful, not a North American leveling-up. Perhaps that is only natural in an area where inequality is still so evident. Igualdad implies that all should get ahead together or not get ahead at all. What concerns Middle Americans is the oppressing minority rather than the oppressed minority. That makes some sense in feudal or just-modernizing societies with tiny but powerful elites. The not-so-different radical doctrines of Jefferson (French equality) and Jackson (frontier equality) had their greatest influence in the United States whenever and wherever the same circumstances seemed to prevail, at least until the triumph of Northern industrialism after the Civil War. But now North Americans usually voice certain fears about such doctrines: that they offer no guarantees against tyranny of the masses; that they hinder the process of stabilizing and modernizing; that the individual's worth is lost in the common cause. Middle Americans do not accept the contention that the urge which topples one tyrant raises a twin. They believe that only positive government can generate equality. The doctrine that the best government is negative government to protect the individual or, at most, provide equality of opportunity is not believed in most of Middle America. Hence the United States' argument that both Fidel Castro and his mirror-image Tacho Somoza have mistreated political opponents because of an excessive desire for and fear of equality falls on deaf ears. Middle American idealists yearn for a utopia of political, economic, and social equality and are disappointed that they have not achieved it.

"Fraternity" promises Middle Americans what the melting pot used to promise North Americans, namely, E pluribus unum, a solution to divisiveness. But here the reality is even less of the dream than with liberty and equality. One reason is that the Iberian revolutionary tradition was as hostile to state centralism as it was receptive to liberty and equality. The French were Jacobins, the Iberians anarchists--that is, region- or community-oriented. And Middle American countries have always been collages of peoples (like Spain) rather than relatively homogeneous nations (like France). Centralizing efforts have therefore always succeeded about as well as they have in Spain, which is not at all. National solidarity is consequently mostly a myth. Nevertheless, revolutionary solidarity still has the strong appeal it did in the times of Miranda and Martí. The torch has of course passed from the Jacobins, Jefferson, and Juárez to the Marxists and Black Power advocates. Moreover, there is a contradiction these "parties of the people" have not been able to resolve, the contradiction between class war and caste solidarity. Marxists insist that national and racial attachments will evaporate in the fraternal heat of the revolution. Black liberators are as skeptical of the need or wisdom of multi-racial fraternity as Zapata was. Their "brothers" and "sisters" are not the same as the Marxists' "comrades." Neither Napoleon nor Lenin ever solved this problem, and Castro has likewise failed to spread the revolution to other households. All this said, however, the ideal of freedom's fraternity still has strong appeal in Middle America.

North Americans have always thought freedom's fraternity consisted of the nations of the Western Hemisphere, and the Monroe Doctrine embodies that notion. Generations of Latin Americans also accepted this Western Hemisphere ideal--Bolívar, Juárez, even Martí in the early days, for example. But two things changed Middle Americans' minds: first, the United States' imperialism in Middle America after 1898; and second, the United States' alliance with the West European imperialist nations in the cause of "democracy"--items closely interrelated, of course. Middle Americans do not see Winston Churchill as a democrat but as an imperialist. In their minds the United States has broken the fraternal bonds of freedom by siding with the imperialists. Some Middle Americans think of the break as a temporary separation countered by occasional back-home visits in the form of the Good Neighbor Policy and the Alliance for Progress. They still believe in the Western Hemisphere ideal. Other Middle Americans, usually more radical, think of the break as permanent, and point to C. I. A. interventions, unequal economic relations, and other un-brotherly actions as evidence. They no longer believe in the family of Western Hemisphere nations. Instead, they want to join the family of Southern Hemisphere nations in a strategy designed to reverse the trends of the twentieth century. They believe their brothers are in the poor countries of the Third World. Most would include the South Americans in the fraternity but not the North Americans, though there are doubts about Brazil.

Perhaps, then, it is more accurate to think of the Americas as a community rather than as a family or a fraternity. Middle America may then be considered a somewhat down-at-the-mouth neighborhood at the intersection of two great thoroughfares. The intersection of the east-west superhighway and the north-south residential street (that is, the Canal area) is a commercial zone with a rather high rate of both blue- and white-collar crime. The superhighway (the Canal approaches) is carefully policed, although recklessness and lawless behavior are not unknown. The intersection has cops on the beat but is potentially quite dangerous. Along the sides of the residential street in both directions, the buildings (the Caribbean-rim nations) run from adequate to nearly uninhabitable, and security is sometimes weak. But every building has a penthouse, elegant or no, and several overcrowded and impoverished floors leading up to it. On one side of the street live the Asians, on the other the Africans, and in the penthouses are the Europeans and their servants. The corner houses one block north and one block south (Mexico, the United States South, Venezuela, Trinidad-Tobago) are the most elegant, though they, too, have some grim lower floors. Many of the houses are owned by people across town, but some of the penthouse owners manage or even own the rest of the building. Visitors are everywhere-- passers-by, tourists, and shoppers.

The relationships in such a neighborhood are predictable. Nearly everyone resents the ownership and interference of outsiders such as the Europeans, and Middle Americans well understand the sentiment originating in Dixie: "Yankee, go home." Many fear, though some welcome, the overtures of non-owners like the Russians. The richer houses tend to be drawn together by common economic and social interests: the oilmen of Houston and Caracas know each other well; Venezuelan shoppers in Miami have as counterparts New Orleans tourists; and California and Mexico, or even New York and San Juan, also in a sense exchange populations. The poorer tenants want the houses sold or given to their inhabitants, or their rents lowered, so tensions between the penthouses and the lower floors tend to spill out onto the streets. The United States quarrels with Cuba in part because rich quarrels with poor within each country, and similar agonies of racial tension exist within and among Commonwealth nations. Racial and language affinities soon become involved house to house and floor to floor. The in-betweens of class and caste are hesitant to choose sides. Mexico and Venezuela may identify with the wealthy United States and the Spanish-speaking Cubans. Trinidadians may feel both Black and British. On the other hand, basement-dwellers may look to their fellows across town, as may penthouse-owners. So the neighborhood teeters on the brink of decay and dependency for lack of community feeling, and no one escapes the impact of South, North, and Middle America on each other. The Caribbean is still "the sea of the New World," a veritable Mediterranean of cultural cross-currents.

PART III

LATIN AMERICA'S IMPACT

Chapter 7

THE BIG DITCH

Panama assures Latin America a large role in international affairs. When Balboa topped the peak in Darién in 1513 and saw the Pacific, he inaugurated the first period of Panama's importance. There Pizarro launched his conquest of the Incas. There the Spanish galleons from Pacific and Atlantic swapped cargoes by having them portaged across the isthmus. There the Spanish colonists jumped off on their harbor-hopping conquests of South and North America. There enterprising buccaneers and the rival navies of England, France, and Holland tried to cut the main artery of the Spanish empire. There, finally, industrial power and revolutionary politics closed off the bloodstream of Spanish wealth and power. By the 1790s the Spanish could not overawe the British and French in the Caribbean, and even the Russians and the upstart North Americans joined in to claim "Spanish" territory in western North America. The die had been cast, and by the 1820s the Spanish Empire was a shambles. Panama was in the hands of the Spanish revolutionaries--specifically, of Simón Bolívar, who opened the second period by suggesting a Pan-American Congress there to join the revolutionary American states, north and south, in a democratic alliance against reactionary, monarchical Europe.

Bolívar's dream was not to be. The Panama Congress (1823-26) was an end, not a beginning. There certainly seemed to be a need for an alliance of all the democracies, what with Napoleon's revolutionary forces defeated in Europe and the Holy Alliance making noises about a reconquest of the "anarchists" of the Americas as well. But the Middle and South Americans, fearing Bolívar's Gran Colombia as much as Spanish reconquest, went their own way rather than join in a union of all the Americas. The United States, fearful of the British and its own planter class in the South, decided to consolidate its gains and issued the Monroe Doctrine (1823) instead. Bolívar went into retirement muttering that trying to govern the Americas was like plowing the sea--and the struggle began for control of Panama.

For a time, the great powers tolerated the "neutral" solution of Colombian ownership. But the North American conquest of California brought Panama and its neighbors to renewed prominence as the quickest route to the Gold Rush and to the Pacific coaling stations for the new navies, thus reviving great power rivalries in the area. The British at first tried to restore Napoleonic power in Mexico, then to have Ferdinand de Lesseps build a canal for the Colombians --and failed in both instances. The Germans moved in as far as Venezuela and the Virgin Islands, only to have United States Presidents Cleveland and Wilson threaten war over the former and buy the latter before Kaiser Wilhelm could. By that time the warhawk Teddy Roosevelt had engineered a revolution in Panama so that he could have a canal engineered, and by 1914 the Big Ditch had opened.

In Panama's third phase the United States has predominated. The epicenter of Panama's worldwide influence has been the canal and the surrounding Canal Zone. Every moment of every day and night each of the double locks is stairstepping two ships between the oceans, one ship up toward the Pacific and one down to the Atlantic. Like a global force field the Canal draws ships in along the shipping lanes, idles them in concentric circles at its openings, and eventually passes them through. Tolls are cheap, and ships of all nations may cross in peace and war, although great carriers must list to clear the pumphouses and some of the biggest ships, especially the oil-carrying supertankers, cannot squeeze through.

Surrounding the Canal and isolating it from the Republic of Panama is the Zone, a miniature homeland for the United States technicians who have run the Canal Company since 1914. The Zone has "extraterritoriality." The Zonians get paid in and spend dollars, live under United States laws, and send their children to United States schools. More than a quarter-million North Americans have lived and worked in the Zone by now, and their "third nationalism" affects Canal relations as surely as do Panamanian and United States nationalism. Most are justifiably proud of the Canal's record of reliability and are convinced that United States control of the Canal, the Zone, and the Company is good for Latin America, the hemisphere, and the world as well as the United States--and even Panama.

Hence the Zonians' children in Balboa High School, which is within sight of downtown Panama City, have always learned the North American version of the Canal's history: that the United States had a sacred duty to create the Canal, that the Canal runs better in United States hands than it ever could in the hands of Panama, that United States interventions in Central America and the Caribbean to protect approaches to the Canal have been fully justified, and, most important of all, that the Canal and the Zone belong to the United States because the 1903 Treaty specified that the North American colossus acts "as if it were sovereign" there. Four generations of these American students have come to believe ardently that the Monroe Doctrine guarantees the preservation of democracy in the Western Hemisphere, and that the Canal guarantees the Monroe Doctrine. To them there has never seemed any contradiction in having the Southern Command of the United States armed forces in the Zone, nor in its running a "jungle warfare school" for Latin American armies and police. It was therefore the most logical thing in the world to respond to rising Panamanian and Latin American criticism of Canal "colonialism" by raising the United States flag above the Panamanian flag on Balboa High School, thus symbolizing American sovereignty. That was in 1964.

The outcry was immediate in Panama City: riots, assaults on the Zone fences, gunshots, dead Panamanians, and deeper resentment of the Canal throughout the Panamanian Republic. For Panamanians' view of the Canal has always differed greatly from the view of the students at the high school in the Zone named for the discoverer of the Pacific. In Panama City there has been no doubt that the 1903 treaty was a fraud because no true-born Panamanian signed it; that the Canal has always benefited the United States more than Panama as a result of low tolls; that it has been an insult to Panamanians working for the Canal Company to pay them lower wages, keep them in inferior positions, and suggest they could never run the Canal effectively; and that, far from being the sovereign of an American canal in Panama, the United States is but a colonialist tyrant occupying a strip through the Panamanian heartland, intervening anywhere a threat to United States dictation arises, and training mercenaries at the warfare school. The Balboa High School incident therefore became the match that lit the powderkeg of resentment stored up in Panama and, in a 1968 coup, brought General Omar Torrijos to power on a program of changing the Canal Treaty.

The 1964 flag riots seem in fact to have opened a fourth phase in Panama's world role, a phase that epitomizes Latin America's coming of age. Panama's role has changed in two ways exactly parallel to the changes in the rest of Latin America. First, Panama has moved out of the shadow of the United States, partly as a result of the general decolonization movement around the world and partly from a return to the Good Neighbor Policy in Washington. The Southern Command has been absorbed into the Western and Eastern commands in San Diego, California, and Norfolk, Virginia. Panamanians have been made managers in the Canal Company, advanced in pay and position, and trained to run the Canal in the future. And a new treaty, the Treaty of 1977, promises to have Canal and Zone in Panamanian control by the year 2000. By that date Panama would, in effect, have much the same "allied" relationship with the United States that many other countries do, that is, one based on military base-arrangements and strategic cooperation. The second hemisphere phenomenon is the increased interest of Latin American countries in each other and in other parts of the world, as opposed to their concerns with the United States. Panama under Torrijos thus emphasizes Latin and Third World interests such as control of national assets, solidarity of poor nations, and national development--in a word, draws the dividing-line of international politics between the North and the South, not between the East and the West.

Whether Panama's world role will also be altered has been an issue in changing its hemisphere status. Will the Canal run efficiently? Will it remain open through thick and thin? Will tolls be kept low? Certainly the United States or "colonialist" solution no longer seems workable. And equally certainly the Panamanian or nationalist solution seems the only viable alternative. That is, hemisphere and international organizations such as the OAS or the UN have no real claim. Yet the legitimate interests of the hemisphere and the world are undeniable. And so the Panama Canal is taking its place with other land and water passages under national control and international guarantees--like the Dardanelles, Suez, the St. Lawrence, the Rhine, and the passes of the Alps, Himalayas, and Andes. As elsewhere, some of the international guarantees will be formalized in treaties and agreements. Others will be merely tacit understandings as to what will be tolerated. Meanwhile, the ships continue to funnel in and out of Colón and Panama City, stairstep between the seas, and fan out along the lines of the maritime force field as if some eternal quake were centered in Panama. And recognition of the importance of Latin America in world affairs spreads with the tremors. When in June, 1978, Presidents Torrijos and Carter exchanged the documents ratifying the new treaty, the assembled heads of state from across the Americas were acutely aware that the event signaled a new era in hemisphere and world affairs.

Chapter 8

HEMISPHERE IDEALS

The Democratic Hemisphere

The signing of the Panama Treaty of 1977 in Washington harked back to the more idealistic elements of the Western Hemisphere tradition. President Carter saw himself returning to the Good Neighbor Policy of Franklin Roosevelt, with former Presidents Nixon and Ford acting as precursors the way Coolidge and Hoover did. The thirteen years of United States-Panamanian negotiations since the 1964 flag riots had finally ended a dangerous confrontation in precisely the manner Roosevelt had reversed Big Stick diplomacy and interventionism. For their part, President Torrijos and his negotiator, a descendant of one of those who made the 1903 Treaty, saw themselves undoing the fraudulent results of two generations before and restoring the equality of the two halves of the hemisphere.

This theme of re-democratization or re-equalization was echoed by Latin American heads of state of many persuasions. The United States, they emphasized, was finally accepting the "Panamanian revolution," as it had previously accepted the Mexican Revolution and, some implied, would accept the Cuban Revolution in due time. The Mexicans, however, refused to come to the signing because the Cubans were not invited. The Argentines, at the other extreme, also refused to come because of hemisphere criticism of General Videla's regime despite the fact that an Argentine, Orlando Orfila, figured prominently at the signing as OAS president. Chile's General Pinochet, who overthrew Allende in 1973, came--and was pointedly snubbed by men of the word like Gabriel García Márquez. The ghosts of Miranda, Bolívar, Monroe and Martí must, each in its own way, have been pleased with the much-disputed theme of the signing ceremonies because it was their theme: hemisphere democracy, equality, and solidarity.

198

The Panama Treaty of 1977 has in effect re-defined
the meaning of the word "democratic" as it applies to the
ideals of the Western Hemisphere. As President Torrijos
said on the day of the plebiscite for ratification in Panama,
the United States has agreed to stop "spanking" its neighbors.
And two-thirds of Panama's voters in the plebiscite supported
this view of the treaty as an advance in egalitarian democracy among the nations of the hemisphere. There is much of
Simón Bolívar's ideal of cooperation among Western Hemisphere nations in Panama's--indeed, in Latin America's--
view of the treaty. The Canal will belong to Panama, but
its benefits will accrue to all nations of the hemisphere and,
to a lesser extent, of the world. To be sure, in some Latin
American eyes the "second treaty," which guarantees the
permanent neutrality of the Canal and thus implicitly the right
of the United States to intervene to protect that neutrality,
smacks of Big Stick interventionism. There is even a clause
granting United States ships "expeditious" (presumably, first
in-line) transit rights in time of crisis. Hence much of the
Monroe Doctrine's balancing of United States-Latin American
cooperation against other goals recurs in the 1977 arrangements.

But in the main the treaties constitute a long leap in
the direction of renewed Western Hemisphere egalité and
fraternité. No matter how much Bolívar and Monroe dis-
agreed regarding the degree of cooperation necessary in the
1820s, they agreed on the special democratic destiny of hemisphere nations--as do the proponents of the 1977 treaties.
The Panama settlement of 1977 reflects the same division of
opinion concerning North-South cooperation, but the basic
ideals of Bolívar and Juárez, or of Monroe and Lincoln, have
been reaffirmed in the manner of the 1820s and 1860s.

Two major groups oppose the treaty's view of the
hemisphere's democratic destiny, however. The first emphasizes liberté--liberal democracy--more than equality and
fraternal solidarity. It is a mistake to suppose that this is
merely the Anglo-Saxon form of democracy and is therefore
but a vestige of colonialism. Some of the opposition is
without doubt the result of a belief that Latins are too passionate for the give-and-take compromises of liberal democracy, a new and equally insulting leyenda negra of sorts.
Yet there is also more than a little indigenous liberal democracy in Latin America, a native emphasis on parliamentarianism, equality before the law, and jury trial that goes
back to Miranda. Its adherents see some inconsistency be-

tween the drive for human rights in Latin America and the
arranging of the Panama settlement with the authoritarian
government of ex-general Torrijos, which came to power by
overturning the elected government of Arnulfo Arias and now
restricts political liberties. "Why was it not possible to
settle with the constitutional government that preceded Torrijos?" they ask. "Will it be more or less possible to encourage a return to constitutional government throughout the
hemisphere after rewarding Napoleonism?" they inquire.
Some have convinced themselves that restoring legality among
nations of the hemisphere will encourage legality among citizens. Others still oppose the caudillo tendencies implicit
in the Panamanian settlement.

The other opposition group follows Martí rather than
Miranda and looks toward hemisphere revolutions as part of
a world revolution. Some say this group follows Marx more
than Martí, but that is too easy an explanation because it
neglects forces inside the hemisphere in the search for devils
outside. Some North, South, and Middle Americans of a
radical bent see the term "Western Hemisphere" as without
meaning unless it can continue to mean "revolutionary hemisphere," the source of a constantly expanding democratic
destiny. Many Latin Americans still have the notion of
democratic "manifest destiny" possessing North Americans
in the mid-nineteenth century. For those who have given up
on the United States as a source of support for progress in
Africa's Black nations, Fidel Castro is a more credible
Western Hemisphere hero than a United States President who
tries to advance human rights in Africa. "Revolution" is
still a very good word in Latin America, and the concept of
revolution is at least as strong as, and probably stronger than
the concept of a Western Hemisphere with a common history
and common interests. Revolutionaries oppose negotiating
with "imperialists" on such matters as the Canal. But the
hemisphere ideal nevertheless seems predominant in the
emergent Canal Settlement.

The rise of the Western Hemisphere ideal in part explains its later strengths and weaknesses. Napoleon's defeat
at Waterloo in 1815 is the key. Before that the United
States and Latin American revolutionaries had much in common. They both belonged to the "French party," the party
of revolutionary democracy opposed to the monarchies of
Britain and Spain. Napoleon even tried to "liberate" Britain
and Iberia as well as Italy, Germany, and Russia, and succeeded in Spain if not in Portugal. In the United States there

was no question which side the country was on in the French
Revolutionary Wars, merely whether revolution was best
served by staying neutral as Washington's party wanted or by
fighting the British tyrant as the Jeffersonians thought.

In Latin America, which only got revolution ignited
when Napoleon occupied Spain in 1808, the fire had scarcely
begun to flare when the flames were damped down in Europe,
so Bolívar and San Martín still had their half-hemisphere to
win in 1815. For the North Americans things were only
slightly different. The United States had held its own in the
War of 1812 with the British, losing Washington for a time,
but holding New Orleans, which is to say Louisiana, when it
counted. Yet now there was no Napoleon knocking at Britain's
back door hawking revolution. Hence North Americans still
saw British reconquest right around the corner, and Latin
Americans feared Spain in the same way, since the British
navy was expected to support the Spanish legions against god
less revolution in accordance with the Holy Alliance. The
hemisphere of revolution was still loosely united, unrecog-
nized by European nations because all of Europe and its
colonies had been "restored," by treaty at least, to the kings.
In 1815, the American nations were still frightened enough to
hang together in common revolutionary purpose lest the kings
cross the Atlantic make good these claims to their colonies.

Then the British changed their tactics to "divide and
rule." They decided to weaken their opponents in Europe
and America by turning the revolutionaries loose on the
French and Spanish empires (but not France and Spain) instead of their own. By this means they could protect British
possessions in Canada and the Caribbean and, with a German
alliance added, bring Latin Europe to heel for generations.
The Latin American revolutionaries accepted this deal with
alacrity. British warships maintained an embargo on United
States trade with Europe and the Caribbean, but let the gun-
runners through to Latin America instead of bringing Spanish
soldiers to douse the revolutionary flames. The Spanish
Empire in America thereupon collapsed by the mid-1820s.

The North Americans were at first suspicious of the
British deal. After all, since 1776 the British had invaded
twice, used the Indians in the Northwest (and Aaron Burr in
Louisiana) to try to set up counter-revolutionary states,
burned the capitol, intrigued with crown sympathizers, seized
assets, blockaded ports, and embargoed trade. Besides,
United States citizens felt strong revolutionary responsibilities

toward their brothers in Canada and the British Caribbean at least, and some toward their Latin cousins of the Americas as well--though the Blacks of Haiti and the Indians of Mexico and Peru raised doubts. So in the end the terms proved too good to resist: a desperately-desired respite from war; the acceptance of the United States view of the 1783 treaty of independence; the disarmament of the Great Lakes; the calling-off of Britain's Indian allies; an understanding that Louisiana was American; and a tacit agreement not to encourage pro-British factions. The United States won everything except the lifting of the embargo, the settlement of property rights on land taken from Loyalists, and the recognition of the now far-flung borders. The United States had made it; Latin American states--as yet, at least--had not.

Such was the beginning of the end of revolutionary solidarity as the core of the Western Hemisphere ideal. Interests diverged, with the United States' interests becoming more natioanl than revolutionary. Hence the collapse of Bolívar's Pan-American Congress (1823-26). At that point no Western Hemisphere state had been recognized as "legitimate," since democracy, then called "republicanism," was still illegal except in the American hemisphere. But some were more equal than others already, and therefore had more to lose by continued revolutionizing. Moreover, there seemed to be a difference as to how far the writ of revolution should run. Could the planters of the American South make a compact with the Blacks of Haiti? Could the frontier Indian-fighters of Indiana find a common cause with Gran Colombian mestizos? And most important of all, how could an English-speaking nation that had just annexed the Spanish colony of Florida in 1819--and Louisiana, once Spanish, before that--have common interests with Spanish-speaking Americans claiming to be the legitimate heirs to Spanish lands? Thus began the contentions over the Spanish Empire that were to surface in Texas, California, the Philippines, Cuba, and Puerto Rico as British divide-and-rule tactics succeeded.

The implications of the 1815-26 arrangements were not at once obvious, save that there would not be a United States of all the Americas as Bolívar's idealists wanted. The original Monroe Doctrine (1823) was still quite a revolutionary document, saying as it did that the monarchists should add no territory in the New World in return for American revolutionary governments giving no active support to their European confrères. Yet it represented a metamorphosis of the

Western Hemisphere idea in two respects. It emphasized separate development of the revolutions of the Americas, that is, support for rather than union with the Latin revolutions on the part of the United States. And it softened the revolutionary stance so that it was more defensive than offensive, more inclined to national or continental revolution than to generating a world-wide revolutionary surge. The best defense had become, in United States calculations, simply a good defense, not a good offense. Democratic isolationism was born in the peculiar form known as Manifest Destiny, according to which the United States should revolutionize the continent but not the world. The gap between North and Latin Americans concerning the definition of "revolution" widened.

Yet the United States kept returning to its revolutionary origins. In fact, the British "settled" with the North Americans three times before it worked--in 1815-26, 1842-40, and 1870-72. The first was blown away when the radical Andrew Jackson outdistanced the "pro-British" Whigs, nationalized the property Britons had invested in the Bank of the United States, and turned the Irish and French Canadian undergrounds loose on Canada and the frontiersmen on Texas and Oregon. By the late 1830s there was revolutionary brawling on every border. The outcome was the Whig settlement of the Canadian border from Maine to Oregon, the taming of the Irish Fennigans by harsh legal action, and, in return, the annexation of a "Texas" stretching to Oregon itself.

Then Jackson's hot-eyed protégé James Polk reneged by grabbing half of Mexico and, contrary to the British view of the Monroe Doctrine, allowing the European revolutionaries of 1848 to recruit volunteers, raise money, and buy arms in the United States. Gold fever and determination to find enough land to make a slave state for every free state even brought Cuba and Central America under Manifest Destiny as defined by these "radical Democrats." So the British overreacted when the Civil War threatened to split the United States apart and sided, however briefly, with the French and Spanish in an attempt to stop the southward expansion of the North Americans by re-installing the Hapsburgs in Mexico and seducing the Confederacy into a pro-British stance. But in 1870-71 the Washington Treaty buried the Anglo-American hatchet for good, by settling the Americans' claims for reparations for destruction by the British-built Confederate warship Alabama and by granting arbitration of all future disputes. The two sides of the Atlantic began to speak of "the history of the English-speaking peoples."

Latin Americans naturally saw all this as aggressive democracy at best on the part of the United States, and some began to utter the hated word "colonialism." But not all the changes of direction affecting the Western Hemisphere ideal took place in North America. The West Europeans, for example, broke free of reactionary monarchism after 1848 and set up a competing center of democratic ideals. As early as 1833-34, the British had abolished slavery and begun democratization of the electoral process, and from then until World War I they made steady if slow progress in reform and in establishment of their Asian and African empire to replace the thirteen colonies of North America. The French took revolution--and the civilizing imperialism of a benevolent despot--as their ideal and became the only republican great power. Italy and Germany crawled toward modernity, Russia and Turkey remained reactionary, and Spain bled itself worse than France in the struggle of Conservatives and Liberals. The Latin Americans, having lost the first flush of revolutionary idealism without cracking the solid front of army, landlord, and Church, were searching for new democratic approaches, both in the Western Hemisphere and in Europe.

1898 settled the issue in favor of Latin democracy because many Latin Americans saw in the United States victory over Spain colonial collusion among the anglosajones against "lesser breeds" as defined by the new Social Darwinism. No matter that the United States was quarreling incessantly with the British over the treaties assuring equality and neutrality in the Central American isthmus. No matter that the North Americans claimed to be obliged to pick up the pieces of the crumbling Spanish empire lest the Germans do so. No matter the fact that the Anti-Imperialist League in the United States prevented outright annexation of the Philippines, Cuba, and Puerto Rico. What Latin Americans saw was the humiliation of Latins by Germanics, the putting-down of Latin political and cultural sympathies, and the latest round of United States expansion at the expense of the Spanish Empire. They remembered the loss of Florida, Texas, and California and, in contrast, how Canada and the British Caribbean remained untouched even in the crises of the British Empire in 1837 and 1867. To them, Teddy Roosevelt's ride up San Juan Hill in 1898 led to the 1903 Panama "aggression" and all the interventions of Dollar Diplomacy and Roosevelt Corollary days because anglosajones were reading too much Darwinian racism.

Hence the turn-of-the-century lines of debate in Latin America over the meaning of "democracy" as a Western Hemisphere ideal. For every reincarnation of Bolívar and Sarmiento who admired the anglosajones' brand of democracy, there was a copy of Rodó or Darío insisting that only Latin democracy would do, that is, the revolutionary democracy of France and Spain or, better yet, a specifically Latin American form. The true democratic connection was thought not to be with the North Americans, who were shopkeepers at heart, but with the Latins of Europe, who still possessed the vital spirit associated with the best of democracy. The Monroe Doctrine, altered by the Roosevelt Corollary to say that the United States should intervene anywhere in the Americas to protect democracy and stability, found itself confronted by the Drago Doctrine, in which the Argentine foreign minister emphasized separate paths to democracy, equality among hemisphere nations, and the right to national self-determination without threat of intervention from Europe or North America. The Argentines were speaking for Latin America, and the adjective "Latin" had, for perhaps the first time, taken on real meaning.

The Latin Connection

Latin Americans did not simply discover "Latin democracy" in 1898. It was a counter to the Anglo-American notion that democracy originated in the German tribes, grew up in English and American county governments, and came of age in the English-language constitutions. And it had long been building, mainly in France, where it was known as the "Napoleonic ideal." In this view democracy was Roman, not Germanic, since it originated in the plebes of the Roman Republic, survived the neglect of Roman emperors and Middle Age kings, and re-emerged in 1789 to find a concerned and committed champion of the people in Napoleon. Waterloo was thus a disaster, not a step forward, for democracy. Hence the Latin area's kings were said to have sold out to the reactionaries of East Europe and the fake democrats of the English-speaking world after 1815, and were therefore resisted by true revolutionaries like Garibaldi, whose red shirts fought reaction in Uruguay as well as Italy.

This ideal of Latin democracy had no real meaning until after the Revolutions of 1848, which produced a Second French Republic, then a new Napoleon, then by 1871 a Third French Republic. The new French attempt at revolution was

none too successful, what with a war lost to a resurgent
Germany, an economy less rich in industrial might than its
Anglo-Saxon competitors, and constant internal conflicts
stirred up by monarchist conservatives and ultra-revolutionary
Anarchists and Socialists. But it was an alternative to the
Anglo-Saxon claim of a Germanic monopoly on democratic
government. So Latin Americans, believing that the United
States had sold out true democracy to side with the British,
likewise began to look to Latin Europe rather than the West-
ern Hemisphere for their democratic inspiration.

The appeal of Roman-based democracy was not just an
ethnic appeal, however. It claimed to be more community-
minded than Anglo-Saxon Liberalism. The Code Napoléon,
the basis for most Latin American law, was more color-
blind and more social welfare-oriented than the protect-the-
citizen-from-government constitutions of the English-speaking
countries, for example. In the clash of liberty with welfare,
the Latins, European and American, preferred welfare as
more humane, more caring, less merchant-minded. In the
United States, this "French school," led by Henry Adams of
Mont St. Michel and Chartres fame, lost out to the dog-eat-
dog "Germanic school" of Teddy Roosevelt. In Latin America sentiment went the other way.

Latin democracy also claimed to be more "scientific"
and "logical" than the life-is-a-jungle school of John Stuart
Mill and Herbert Spencer in the English-speaking nations.
August Comte's Positivism allowed for benevolent and wise
leadership and cooperative ventures, whereas the Utilitarianism of Mill and Spencer deified competition, at least as
Latins saw it. Comte's disciples in Latin America, as in
Latin Europe, saw mankind progressing from superstition to
philosophy to science--to higher modes of thought, to truth,
if you will--by abandoning the base motives of cutthroat competition, not deifying them. "Sociology" and savagery could
not, must not, go together as the Utilitarians claimed. For
all their differences Botelho de Magalhães in Brazil, Lastar-
ría in Chile, and the Cientificos in Mexico agreed that
Anglo-Saxon democracy was unfeeling and "philosophical,"
not savage, perhaps, but at best only half civilized. Latin
was better.

The only problem was the "imperialism" of European
versions of Latin democracy. Not that at this stage "imperialism" was quite so negative a concept as in the United
States, since in Latin America it called forth images of

Rome, Napoleon, and differing peoples united in equality under one law. But Latin American leaders were definitely divided on the political, as opposed to the social and cultural, responsibilities of Positivists. They more or less agreed that the elites had a responsibility for providing the wherewithal to the population and for upgrading the general level of education and the arts--in a word, for advancing civilization, for progress. But did progress also imply central political control, which is to say nationalism over federalism, or even something, be it called imperialism or cosmopolitanism, over nationalism?

The Argentines, Chileans, Venezuelans, Andeans, and French Caribbeans, and above all the Brazilians, said no to centralizing nationalism, with many, such as the Uruguayans, opting for something in between, and with all under challenge from the opposite camp domestically. In Mexico, Díaz (centralizing nationalist) and the Revolutionaries of 1910 (federalists) set the country aflame over this issue, among others. And beyond this quarrel over whether patria chica could be as civilized as patria lay the issue of cosmopolitanism. Did the nations have to be forced to cooperate by some kind of Napoleonic "imperialism," or might they eventually catch up with Bolívar and choose a less narrow view; or should they even go their separate ways? The experience with Napoleon III's Bonapartism in the Maximilian episode in Mexico in 1862-67 had soured Latin America on that alternative, and Bolívar's ideal lived at best a quiet existence-- until 1898, that is. For it was then that the Anglo-Saxon alternative also lost its anti-imperialist advantage once and for all.

Nationalism seemed to be the logical response to the 1898 debacle, except that no Latin American nation seemed a match for the Colossus of the North. Moreover, the United States was not, in Latin American eyes, active in a solely nationalistic way itself, but was instead joined in at least an Anglo-Saxon, and perhaps a Germanic, alliance to make the world over in a blond image. The result was a surge of Hispanic pride, a tidal wave of artistic achievement on both sides of the Atlantic by the so-called Generation of 1898, and a confused series of half-cultural, half-political movements centered on hispanismo. The French connection became, for a time, the Iberian connection. Whereas the Parnassians and Symbolists of France had dominated artistic life before 1898, Darío, Rodó, Lorca, Picasso, Neruda, Casals, and Dalí held center stage for fifty and more years afterward in Spanish America. French culture, such as Surrealism, still counted, but it was not popular to become nearly so French as Hérédia (Cuban), Lautréamont (Uruguayan) and, for a time, Darío (Nicaraguan) had before.

Whereas the Paris Commune radicals had inspired the restless Spanish American idealists before 1898, it was Martí, Sandino, the Mexicans, and, after World War I, the Spanish Republicans who came to express their democratic yearnings. Nationalism existed, was perhaps primary. But there was also something larger, grander--the ideal of a Spanish-language democracy, or at least a Spanish American democracy, and at best an all-Latin or even a world democracy. So the League of Nations must not sanctify the Roosevelt Corollary theory of intervention. The League should admit Brazil and a Spanish American nation to the security council as a gesture of equality instead of perpetuating Northern Hemisphere dominance in the world body. Such was the extent of Latin American pride by the 1930s.

But since then Hispanic solidarity has stumbled along as a rival to the Western Hemisphere ideal for several reasons. The most important reason was the collapse of its democratic base as a result of the demise of the republics of Portugal and Spain. The Salazar (1922-1974) and Franco (1936-1975) governments in Iberia rebuilt the barriers between the Old and New hemispheres in the Hispanic world. Refugees from the Spanish Civil War revitalized the more east-west division of conservatives and democrats as opposed to the north-south divisions of colonialists and colonizers in the landscape of the Latin American mind. Picasso and Casals vowed never to set foot in Franco Spain, for example, as did Neruda's generation in the Americas. Latin Americans were impressed when United States citizens of the Abraham Lincoln Brigade fought with Latin American volunteers against Franco, and when the New Deal government of the United States discovered the Good Neighbor Policy in its anxieties over Fascism.

The debate between Fascism and democracy was fierce in some parts of Latin America where the Latinisms of Franco and Mussolini, or even the anti-Americanism of Hitler, carried force. On balance, however, Latin American leaders preferred the Monroe Doctrine to the Nuremberg Laws and saw the choice in almost those terms, namely, as a choice between evils. They accepted Good Neighborism because of the mutual defense promised by the Declaration of Panama

(1939), the renewed equality implied by the Pan-American
Conferences and acceptance of the Mexican Revolution, and
the commitment to development demonstrated by the Muñoz-
Tugwell and Batista-Welles efforts under way in Puerto Rico
and Cuba--and promised to others by the Four Freedoms
Speech of President Roosevelt. The Canal and the Corollary
were therefore put aside for the duration of World War II.

Another major reason for the decline of Hispanic unity
has been that nemesis of every cosmopolitan movement, nationalism. When Portugal turned authoritarian in 1922, for
example, Brazilians set out to be more "progressive" than
the mother country both culturally and politically. Equality
with the great and super powers, and superiority in comparison with its Spanish American neighbors, has been the
Brazilian goal ever since. Such a goal is no more consistent
with the ideal of hispanismo than with that of Western Hemisphere unity. In fact, it has so alarmed the Argentines, who
in the 19th century were Latin America's most potent nation,
that their own Peronist nationalism has been exaggerated.
Such power-shifts have not been the only disruptive nationalist
forces, however. The Mexican Revolution's revolt-of-the-
masses, Indianist nationalism, is a form that is difficult to
square with a democracy of, by, and for Latins. Black
nationalism is also contrary to the ideal of a Latin democracy. And of course Marxism denies any meaning to nationalist feelings, Indian, Black, or Latin. So the heyday of
the Hispanic ideal began to wane shortly after World War I
as a result of the turning of time in the direction of Good
Neighborliness, renewed revolution and nationalism, and
global ideological currents.

But the Latin ideal refuses to pass into the dark. In
the late 1960s President De Gaulle tried to revive the French
version. In France and Europe, he tried to rejoin Left and
Right to head off what he saw as the madness of the Anglo-
Saxons in confronting communism; in the Americas, he called
for a Free Québec and hinted at an accommodation stretching
from Castro to Catholic conservatives--all to stop what he
viewed as the Anglo-Saxons' interventionist madness from
Vietnam to Santo Domingo. Moreover, in the middle 1970s,
with Salazar and Franco gone and Portuguese and Spanish
socialists and liberals in their places, the 1898 version has
new appeal. Yet, in the main, nationalism still overshadows
any cosmopolitan idealism, including the revived Good Neighborism of the United States. Napoleon III's pan-Latin propaganda has meanwhile left us with the inaccurate label "Latin
America" for a Red, White, and Black continent.

Good Neighbors

The United States' recalling of the Good Neighbor Policy in signing the 1977 Panama treaties reiterates a belief in the common interests of all Western Hemisphere nations. Indeed, Franklin Roosevelt and the New Dealers who formulated the policy in the 1930s saw a common concern with defense, development, and democracy--the same interests emphasized by the Carter government in concluding the treaties, approaching an accommodation with revolutionary Cuba, and re-thinking economic relationships with Latin America. The issue, in so far as this manifestation of the Western Hemisphere ideal is concerned, then, is whether sufficient common interest exists in these "Three Ds" on both the North and Latin American sides to restore and maintain neighborliness. In the revolutionary era, there was no need to speak of good neighborliness, since it was required by a common terror of the Holy Alliance, a common need for national development, and a more or less common interpretation of democracy. By the time the Good Neighbor Policy was promulgated, there was some reason to doubt that the Three Ds meant the same thing or were equally important for all sides--which was why the policy had to be stated, of course. Now, many Latin Americans question whether clear "national interests" are not more pressing than the common interest. Do the Americas really have the Three Ds in common?

Just before and during World War II the need for a common defense certainly seemed convincing. The Latin American military of that period finally accepted the Anglo-American doctrine that in modern times the basic struggles have been between land-powers in the heartland of Eurasia and the sea-powers of Europe and Asia, with the allies of each joining in. In this view, the aim of Eurasian powers has been to unite the "heartland" by alliance or conquest and divide the "rimland," and the purpose of the rimland democracies to do the reverse. Thus the Western Allies won World War I by dividing Russia and China from the German-speaking powers and by maintaining the support of their colonies or, in the case of the United States, their former colonies. In World War II, so the argument ran, Churchill would do the same by allying with Stalin and Roosevelt and Chiang and by maintaining the support of the emerging democracies of the crumbled or crumbling empires. The Latin Americans were obviously to be counted in the Atlantic Alliance part of the global struggle, but as partners, not as subordinates of the bad old Big Stick days. Hence the Pan-

American conferences of the late 1930s and early 1940s, the declarations of solidarity, the "mutual defense treaties, " the military bases to protect the Canal and its Caribbean and Pacific approaches, the training and equipping of hemisphere soldiers to fight in Europe, and the pressure on non-conformists like Argentina's Perón. The idea of a mutual defense definitely carried meaning.

Still, the Latin American response was complex. For one thing, fascist sympathies--of either the Franco, Musso-lini, or Hitler variety--did exist in some countries, mainly because of the Axis powers' anti-imperialist claims. Vargas' decision to crush the local fascists and join the Allied effort was politically courageous, since a neutrality like Perón's would probably have been less unpopular, especially among his home state's large German population. And without the Brazilian bases, the African front was inaccessible to the Allies, the uranium of the Congo might have gone into a German A-Bomb, or the South Atlantic might have become a German lake, thus encouraging Perón and others to weaken the "Atlantic front. " The same kind of relationship, though less critical, existed on the west coast of Latin America with respect to Japanese power, of course. And almost everyone in Latin America had trouble accepting the alliance with the Russian Communists. For another and much more significant thing, the distinction between mutual defense and imperialism was not very clear, what with Churchill vowing not to preside over the dissolution of the British Empire and thus blurring the question of whether Latin Americans were playing the role of the autonomous Canada or the colonial Bahamas. Yet most Latin Americans looked the other way while the United States obliged Colombia to purge the German pilots from its civilian airline lest they compromise the Canal's defenses, worked to isolate the Perón government, and maintained and enhanced the power gained in 1898 and 1903.

After World War II Latin American governments agreed to extend the mutual defense concept in the Rio Treaty (1948). The resulting organization of American States (OAS) took its place alongside NATO, CENTO, AND SEATO in the globe-circling line of "containment" against Communism posited by United States strategy. Like the Koreans and the West Germans, Latin American forces bought their arms from the United States, had their officers trained in the United States or the jungle warfare school in the Canal Zone, and were advised in the field by United States armed forces personnel. Yet from the outset the OAS was divided over the notion of containment, specially after it led to renewed North American intervention in Guatemala (1954), Cuba (1961), and the Dominican Republic (1965-66). Hemisphere solidarity melted. In 1954, the Latin Americans somewhat reluctantly looked away during Eisenhower's Guatemalan affair; after the Bay of Pigs in 1961, only Kennedy's Alliance for Progress promise of rapid development could hold the line; and in Santo Domingo, the Johnson Doctrine that the United States must intervene anywhere in Latin America to prevent "another Castro" dropped stillborn into a poisonous climate of North-South tensions. Latin Americans were uneasy because they viewed themselves as pawns in the global power game of the Vietnam War era. They feared a Johnson Doctrine for the United States in Latin America, a Brezhnev Doctrine for the Russians in East Europe in the 1968 Czech crisis--in other words, "spheres of influence" like those of Big Stick power-balancing. The containment walls began crumbling.

The United States, like the Russians on the other side, saw "subversion" as the cause of the destabilization. Latin Americans instead saw the Kennedy-Johnson responses to a decade of revolutionary changes in the Third World and of civil rights and anti-war protests in the United States--that is, the United States' combination of slow-moving reforms with counter insurgency, support for conservative military regimes, and, if necessary, direct intervention--as a betrayal of Good Neighborism. The Guevara-inspired radicals looked to an alliance of a North American underclass of Black Power and Chicano rebels with a world underclass of Third World peoples to bring down the capitalist-imperialist "system," no matter how timid the support of their presumed Russian Communist allies. "Many Vietnams," some of which would be in Latin America, could, in Che's vision, coalesce into the long-awaited world revolution. The guerrilla would ignite the peasant, and the peasant the worker--Che to China to Kremlin, so to speak. Che's opponents, supported by the United States, naturally responded in kind.

The Kennedy attempt at seducing Latin America away from world revolution thus gave way to sterner stuff by the Johnson government. First came support for Brazil's conservative 1964 revolution in return for joint United States-Brazilian intervention in the Dominican Republic, a parallel to the Indonesian about-face of 1965 that led to Indonesian support for the Vietnam War. Then came replacement of middle class by military regimes in much of Latin America,

again as in Asia and, for that matter, Africa. And finally
came vigorous counter-insurgency efforts, particularly in
strategic Bolivia, where Che and his guerrilla band were
hunted down and killed by Green Berets and the Bolivian army
in 1967--because moderates had lost out to polarized forces
in Bolivia as elsewhere in the Vietnam decade. Any hope of
a common defense seemed to have evaporated in the heat of
mutual hostility.

The development issue has likewise changed since the
heyday of the Good Neighbor Policy, though perhaps only half
way. The issues are still the same: separate paths to
development, and the means to development. The expectations,
however, are very different on all sides--higher, for one
thing, and more contradictory, it seems, for another. The
"appeasement" of revolutionary Mexico in the 1930s epitomized
the Good Neighbor Policy's stance on development. The New
Dealers simply accepted the Mexicans' determination to follow a path to development that included nationalization of
foreign property, redistribution of land, and centralized planning. Not only did the New Dealers accept the collapse of
the Dollar Diplomacy strategy of forcing Latin Americans to
pursue "sound" financial policies. When Mexico's first really
radical president since the Revolution, Cárdenas, set out to
implement the new development plan to the full and seized
United States citizens' oil property in the process, the New
Dealers also accepted the verdict despite North American
conservatives' pressures for intervention. That was in 1938,
with Hitler starting on his rampage in Europe. Franklin
Roosevelt had decided that to fight across town required
friendships in the neighborhood. "Appeasement" had to succeed in Latin America if it was to be rejected in Europe.
It did, and it was, and the war was won. But the means
for development did not flow to Mexico until after World War
II, when President Alemán, a conservative in economics by
Latin American standards, came to power.

For the United States had another element in its diplomatic strategy: teaching the superiority of the "market
system" by example in Cuba and Puerto Rico. Hence the
experiments with massive North American aid, advisers like
Welles and Tugwell, United States-supported political "revolutions" featuring Batista and Muñoz Marín, and special advantages in trade such as the Cuban sugar quota and Puerto
Rican tariff preferences. The message was clear. The
United States would abandon the Big Stick and Dollar Diplomacy so as to allow separate paths to development; but North

American generosity would flow only, or at least mainly, to adherents of the market system, middle-class democracy, and electoral government. Neighbors, after all, should not litter, and totalitarianism was worse than litter in a community of democratic nations. And in the main Latin Americans seemed to agree. The Mexicans under Alemán came around in 1946, and the Venezuelans under Betancourt's Acción Democrática in 1948, for instance. North Americans seemed responsive, too: The Philippines were freed in 1946; the Europeans were encouraged to free India and Indonesia; and Truman's Point Four Plan agreed to continue "Operation Bootstrap" in Puerto Rico--indeed, to do something like it throughout the "free world." Democracy seemed genuinely on the march in Latin America except, perhaps, in Perón's Argentina as North Americans saw it, and in Cuba and Puerto Rico from the Latin American point of view.

In Cuba, the abrogation of the Platt Amendment in 1934 was followed by the failure to transfer power from Batista's military regime to a constitutional government led by Grau San Martín in 1944, and from then on things went sour. Batista turned tyrant, the economy returned to the chains of sugar plantationism and casino depravities, and rich Cubans and North Americans benefited most. On July 26, 1953, a band of middle-class Cuban idealists led by young Fidel Castro attacked the Moncada Barracks where Batista had jailed his critics, eventually escaped to exile in Mexico, and set off a quantum change to the applause of North American liberals. In Puerto Rico, the Muñoz miracle also ran into criticism as the economy settled into beach hotels and ball gloves, more Puerto Ricans were drafted to fight in Korea, and the vast numbers of nuevoyorkeños (or nuevorriqueños, "Nuyoricans") found work harder to come by because of Mainland depressions. Independentistas heroized their leader, Pedro Albizú Campos, attempted to assassinate President Truman in 1950, and did kill several members in the chamber of the United States House of Representatives in 1954--and were sentenced to life imprisonment. In Puerto Rico many saw them as martyrs. The portraits of Good Neighborly development had been slashed, whether beyond repair no one could say.

The United States determined to patch everything up and, in the process, seemed to Latin Americans to distort the images even more. The North American theory of development was stated by Walt W. Rostow, adviser of presidents, in The Stages of Economic Growth (1963). Commu-

nism was a "disease of the transition" between the take-off
into and the success of modernization, because during the
transition the masses had to sacrifice to pay for new machinery, and because in the early stages the masses benefited
less than the new technicians, professionals, and businessmen of the emerging middle classes. Conclusion: it may be
necessary to maintain political stability during the transition
in order to assure economic growth. Hence the intervention
in Vietnam--and in Guatemala, Cuba, and the Dominican Republic. Hence the support for middle-class or even military
governments where necessary, as in post-1964 Brazil. Hence
the manipulation of World Bank aid policy through the United
States' predominant voting rights in the bank. Hence the
selective use of aid and trade to reward the stabilizers and
punish destabilizers. The epitome of this approach was the
Hickenlooper Amendment, by which the Congress obliged a
cutoff of aid to any country seizing United States citizens'
property, an exact reversal of Andy Jackson's nationalizing
of British assets in the United States and a long way from
the oil crisis settlement with Mexico in 1938.

More and more Latin Americans answered in kind,
with "dependency theory." The modernization process, they
argued, created dependencia without and within unless the
tendency for the rich to get richer and the poor poorer was
actively countered by government action favoring the poor.
Rapid evolution through reform, or even revolution, was
essential to prevent the permanent impoverishment and power-
lessness of the masses outdistanced by the moderns. Latin
American revolutionaries called for drastic measures for
combating dependencia. They called for isolation from the
industrialized Western countries by refusing aid, trade, and
investments so as to avoid the economic "neo-colonialism"
they saw replacing the political "colonialism" of prior decades.
And they called for "popular" governments committed to redistribution of both old and new wealth so as to rectify ancient and prevent future "internal colonization." Latin American moderates rejected the revolutionaries' notions of a
"second revolution" to prevent dependencia but insisted on
strong action against external economic forces: limitations
on foreign ownership and on removal of profits from the host
country; requirements that nationals be given preference over
foreigners in jobs; trade agreements to stabilize the prices
of export products; favorable treatment in United States markets; more and better aid arrangements, preferably multilateral rather than bilateral ones so that there could be no
political strings attached. In a word, most Latin Americans

came to deny the North American notion that, despite different patterns of growth, all nations, and especially Western Hemisphere nations, had a family resemblance so far as development was concerned. Americans to the south no longer saw their development in the North American mirror called "stability."

The 1950s showed rapid polarization, as witness these events. 1952: The Bolivian Revolution led to a vast redistribution of land to the Indians, a reallocation of power benefiting the tin miners in particular, and economic stagnation rather than development. The two super-powers of the Cold War were too preoccupied with the Korean War and the McCarthy and Stalin crises at home to worry about the Bolivians' sharing-out of continued poverty, although worries in Washington concerning the Andes matched those in the Kremlin concerning Poland and East Germany. 1954: Jacobo Arbenz lurched Guatemala leftward at a crucial time. The Eisenhower government, having outwitted McCarthyism and arranged an armistice in Korea, was busily pursuing a settlement in post-Stalin East Europe and watching the death-agonies of French colonialism in Vietnam. President Eisenhower overruled Secretary of State Dulles' suggestion of intervention in Vietnam, but the Guatemalan "communist beachhead" was too near the Canal and was smashed. 1956-59: Eisenhower's idea of a settlement with Khrushchev on the basis of spheres of influence, disarmament, and summit diplomacy shook apart because of the Hungarian and Mideast crises, the contrails of Sputniks and U-2s, and the collapse of the British and French empires in Africa.

Then came the Cuban Revolution. Liberals in the United States saw Castro as the just avenger against the Batista dictatorship--and also saw the Eisenhower government, or rather the conservative faction around Vice President Nixon, as supporters of the big-business types bloating Batista. Meanwhile, the Vice President's visit to Venezuela in 1958 despite the Jiménez dictatorship's suppression of Acción Democrática led to Nixon's being stoned, and to further polarization in Latin America and the United States on the issue of exactly what "democracy" ought to mean. United States policy on Cuba thus staggered right down the middle: no end of government arms shipments to Batista; no suppression of underground support for Castro. So Fidel Castro won. But the hoped-for return to the United States brand of development in Cuba did not materialize. Instead, Washington and Havana fell to quarreling over all the Three Ds. Was

Cuba undermining the defense of the hemisphere at the moment when Sputnik had demonstrated a "missile gap" between Russian and United States preparedness? Was the July 26th movement communist rather than nationalist in its land reform and industrial development programs? Was Castro a dictator suppressing Cuban liberties or a charismatic leader? The gap between Latin and North American opinion on such matters widened.

The early 1960s brought the crisis--and a partial turn-around. On the one hand, the Kennedy administration embraced the Cold War doctrines posited by the Truman and Eisenhower administrations--containment, the arms race, subversion, and nation-building. On the other hand, definitions were changed. Containment included more bridge-building and less threatening brinkmanship; the arms race meant matching every weapon and strategy from H-Bombs and ballistic missiles to hand-to-hand combat; subversion called for counter-insurgency--all as a means of avoiding escalation toward the big bang. And it was Castro Cuba that became the focus of these sentiments.

Early efforts at accommodation between Ike and Fidel had failed in 1960. So the Cubans seized United States assets, and the CIA began supporting Cuban exile raids--and planning an invasion. The U-2 spy plane was downed, the Eisenhower-Khrushchev summit collapsed, both super-powers returned to more radically opposed positions, and Kennedy was narrowly elected over Nixon--while the training of the Cuban exile army proceeded in Nicaragua with President Somoza's blessing. Upon taking office in January, 1961, Kennedy busied himself with catch-up ball in the space game, the African decolonization tangles in Algeria and the Congo, and the heating-up of the Berlin issue by Khrushchev--and let the Bay of Pigs invasion be launched on the basis of CIA promises of popular Cuban support and cheers from all of Latin America. Then, because of the failure of the invasion, he paid the price for neglecting his own low-profile strategy. The Bay of Pigs assured Castro's popularity in Cuba, weakened the United States' position in all of Latin America, and opened a wedge for Russian penetration of the Western Hemisphere.

Kennedy then turned good neighbor, because he was on the defensive, according to some, but because he had a view of nation-building not unlike that of the New Deal, according to others. Not only did Kennedy make amends for the Bay of Pigs by ransoming the remnants of the exile army with medicines and equipment sent to Cuba and by purging the CIA, State Department, and Pentagon hotspurs. He also followed a course suggested before by Latin American moderates like Frei in Chile and Kubitschek in Brazil, in launching the Alliance for Progress and in hinting at the acceptability of Christian Socialist and Social Democratic parties as hemisphere democrats. It seemed that the days of withdrawing marines, encouraging reforms, and backing near-radical democrats were back. Moreover, it made sense in terms of the Kennedy domestic policy of support for Martin Luther King's freedom rides in the South, César Chávez' farm workers' strikes in California, the New Frontier's war on poverty, and, not coincidentally, the Catholic reformism of Pope John XXIII.

Here was a socially conscious Irish Catholic President of the United States searching for a middle way between reaction and revolution in Latin America. The assassinated Trujillo was replaced by the Socialist Juan Bosch in 1962 in the Dominican Republic; support flowed to Frei's Christian Democrats in Chile and their counterparts elsewhere; the leftward drift of Brazil under Quadros and Goulart was winked at. Only Cuba and the Strongmen, like the crazies and the Klan in the United States, seemed actively opposed to such a course. If election of reformers had contained Europe's crazies after World War II, why not in Latin America during the 1960s? Figueres, as critical of the Bay of Pigs as of Castro earlier, approved. De Gaulle's France, marching to the same Catholic reformism as it freed itself from colonialism in Algeria and Vietnam, applauded the end of Anglo-Saxon blindness and foresaw a new era of North-South cooperation against a tide of <u>Communist</u> imperialism. Yet it was not to be.

The Kennedy claim to the title of Good Neighbor was challenged by Latin Americans of an increasingly independent persuasion, particularly by Fidel Castro. To North Americans the "missile gap" and "space race" seemed to favor the Soviet Union, the Berlin crisis appeared to confirm Communist ambitions in Europe, the Congo tangle seemed less decolonization than subversion, the decay in Vietnam advertised the problems of containment in Asia--and Castro seemed to have broken the containment barrier in the Americas by challenging United States notions of defense, development, and democracy. There were certainly Latin Americans who shared the North American view, enough, in fact, to cause imposition of an OAS quarantine of Cuba. Yet in hindsight it is clear that all but the most ardently conservative governments, such as Nicaragua's, had chosen the lesser of two evils, that is, United States leadership over Cuban, or perhaps Russian, leadership. The moderates--Figueres of Costa Rica, Betancourt of Venezuela--took sides only partially and in fact criticized participation in the Cold War as irrelevant to Latin American interests. The Mexicans refused to take sides at all and did not participate in the Cuban quarantine. North Americans and their clients might talk of making a better revolution. Russians might talk about a second, or socializing, revolution. But most large Latin American nations decided to make their own revolutions, nationalist revolutions. And while the Cold Warriors' attention was focused on Vietnam, they did. The result has been an increasing independence of South from North and an increasing influence of Latin Americans on their North American neighbors. The remarkable thing is that this turning of the tide has been so relatively lacking in violence--though violent moments there have been, and one near-fatal moment during the Cuban Missile Crisis.

Chapter 9

THE WORLD

Revolutionary Urges

Sunday, October 28, 1962--that was the morning President Kennedy and Premier Khrushchev pulled the world back from the nuclear abyss by agreeing to end the Cuban Missile Crisis. Two weeks earlier U-2 photos had revealed that launching sites were being built in Cuba for Russian intermediate-range missiles that could reach the eastern half of the United States with nuclear warheads. The United States charged that the missiles upset the balance of power in the world, intruded Old World influences into the hemisphere of the OAS, and encouraged revolutionary instabilities in the Americas. The Soviet Union and Cuba denied the existence of the missile sites at first and then charged that their existence was necessary to protect Cuba from another invasion like that at the Bay of Pigs.

The world held its breath as the United Nations debated the issue in public and the diplomats negotiated in private. Meanwhile, the sites neared completion as Russian ships began delivering the missiles to Cuban posts. The United States then blockaded Cuba to prevent delivery of more missiles and prepared to invade and dismantle any sites made operational. Threatening notes were exchanged as Russian ships approached United States blockade vessels off Havana harbor. Then the Russians sent via a reporter an informal message suggesting removal of the Cuban missiles in exchange for removal of United States forces from Turkey. Cuba, feeling abandoned, shot down a low-flying United States reconnaissance plane to re-heat the crisis. But with the invasion order already given and United States ships preparing to prevent arrival of additional missiles at any cost, the Russian vessels stopped before reaching the blockade, and a deal was made: the missiles out of Cuba--and no mention of the missiles in Turkey. In short, no war, but no peace either. A decade of revolutionary urges had begun.

That Sunday Latin America also took its place, once and for all, in the world arena. Before that, preliminaries-- mere parades before the aficionados. After that, the approach of the moment of truth--a role in the "world revolution" of the second half of the twentieth century. Throughout the 1960s the assumption in much of Latin America was that the proper role was as leader, or one of the leaders, of South against North, colonized against colonizer, with the Havana-Washington clash as the symbol. The major motif was therefore one of confrontation between "revolution" and "counter-revolution." The climax came in the period 1966-68 with the Tet offensive in Vietnam, the student uprisings in Europe, riots in the United States, and the rapid rise and fall of Che Guevara's Bolivian offensive.

Yet by the 1970s another motif, nationalist strength, had come to dominate North-South relations. In Latin America, Brazil's "miracle" had brought the southern colossus to the threshold of great power status. Oil politics had emphasized the reversal of roles for suppliers like Venezuela and consumers such as the United States. On the world scene, the Vietnam confrontation had given way to United States-Soviet détente and to talk of a similar accommodation between Cuba and the United States as well. The sixties seem, in retrospect, to have been a transition decade in which the stage was cleared for "interdependence" on the basis of equality, that is, for confronting, not each other, but the new issues of a world grown small. Cause has become challenge.

From the Latin American perspective, the 1960s revolution had Cuban, hemispheric, and world dimensions--concentric rings of revolutionary energy, if you will. The Cubans' own view of the revolution changed with circumstances, however. In its first two years the Castro revolution had strong nationalist elements and seemed so much like the Mexican revolution that the United States assumed that a Good Neighbor accommodation might be possible. Fidel deemphasized the export of revolution to other parts of the hemisphere, isolated the Communists in the 26th of July Movement, and tried to strike a bargain with the United States by suggesting that nationalized property be paid for by the sale of more sugar. The Eisenhower government muted its criticism in hopes of mellowing the Castro regime, held off on approaching the OAS for anti-Cuban sanctions, and pursued its goal of "peaceful coexistence" with the Soviet Union. Yet the Cuban-United States polarization continued in the face of Communist influence on the one hand, and of Cuban refugees and sugar interests on the other. The collapse of coexistence, the Bay of Pigs, and the Missile Crisis then "radicalized" both sides.

Cuba drew the logical conclusion from Russia's cautious support in the 1961-62 confrontations, however, and played the hemisphere card. A Communist model with a Latin face was pursued to encourage hemisphere nations to undertake radical solutions themselves. Che Guevara became Economics Minister and tried to push the guerrilla-revolution concept over into development matters. "Moral incentives"--revolutionary fervor--took the place of better pay as the driving force, and Fidel joined the sugar harvest (zafra) along with the other leaders and the school children. The Latinness of Cuba's revolution was clear in the people armed, the leaders doing manual work, the emotional as opposed to material motivation, the charismatic leadership, the oneness of party and people, and the gaiety at rallies and sporting events. It was nothing like the sour, controlled materialism of East Europe. It may have looked the same to North Americans, but Latin Americans saw it differently--and responded. The Armageddon of revolution and counter-revolution seemed at hand. It was to be insurgency against counter-insurgency, guerrilla against Green Beret, South against North.

The Cubans were thus ready to take credit for any hemisphere revolutions. The Russians and their sympathizers denied, however, that Latin America, or any Third World area, was "ripe for revolution." And they pointed to the seeming successes of the Kennedy plan for a better revolution via Catholic reformism, the Alliance for Progress, the Peace Corps--and the Green Berets. So there was a split between the Cubans and the Russians, though not a wide one because both wanted revolution despite the Russian reluctance to proceed openly. But then Kennedy was assassinated, and President Johnson turned to active resistance rather than reform as a means of stopping hemisphere revolution. In Communist ideology, reform means that the opposition is strong, resistance that it is desperate, so peaceful coexistence was further de-emphasized by the Cubans while the hemisphere heated up. Thus the Russians and the North Americans began unintentionally to give the Cubans credit for the hemisphere's revolutions--by blaming them.

Latin Americans in general saw the world revolution differently than did the super-powers or Cuba. The Brazilian crisis of 1960-64, for example, was seen as only partially a question of radicalism. To Brazilians themselves, the crisis seemed to represent the culmination of the tensions that had been mounting since "politics" had driven Vargas to suicide in 1954. That is, it reflected the regional tensions associated with development of the West and Northeast at the expense of the Center and South and the class tensions associated with aid to the masses but paid for by the classes already benefiting from development. To Brazil's neighbors, the 1964 "Brazilian revolution" seemed to present a dilemma. It stabilized a volatile ideological situation threatening to disrupt their own fragile politics, but it continued--indeed, accelerated through the Brazilian miracle--the development of Brazilian economic and military strength Yet to committed revolutionaries and counter-revolutionaries alike, the foreign policy result of the Brazilian Revolution seemed clear. Instead of Quadros and Goulart moving toward an arrangement with the non-aligned bloc or accommodation with the genuinely revolutionary forces, the post-1964 military governments adopted a policy of entente with the United States and hostility toward Leftist revolutionaries. It was thus assumed that United States and Brazilian nationalism could be reconciled.

The revolutionaries' interpretation of the United States-Brazilian entente seemed to be confirmed in the Dominican crisis of 1965-66. There Juan Bosch's social democratic government, elected in 1962 at the height of Kennedy reformism, had been overthrown by a military junta which then found itself confronted with a revolt by constitutionalistas. When the rebels took over Santo Domingo's central city and neared the United States embassy, the marines were called in to "protect American lives" and "prevent another Castro"-- and the Brazilians came along despite the fact that other OAS members would not. Eventually, the situation was stabilized. The revolutionary and counter-revolutionary Dominican leaders were persuaded to go into exile. The moderate Joaquín Balaguer, the caretaker president from the assassination of Trujillo to the election of Bosch in 1961-62, was elected, partly because Bosch withdrew after charging that the elections were rigged. The Brazilians and North Americans then ended the intervention in 1966. But President Johnson also enunciated the hard-line Johnson Doctrine that declared the right of intervention to prevent revolution, and Juan Bosch adopted the equally hard-line notion that "Pentagonism" had so duped the Anglo and Brazilian people that they could not see the harm they were doing Spanish American democracy or, for that matter, Vietnamese democracy. The United States-Brazilian military entente seemed confirmed, and so did the drift of Spanish American reformers toward revolution as the only route to democracy.

The Cubans decided the time had come. At least Che did, since he went underground to apply his doctrine of guerrilla warfare to the hemisphere. Had the Sierra Maestra--the poorest, racially most oppressed region of Cuba--not furnished the spawning-ground of the Cuban Revolution? Then the Bolivian Indians--the poorest, racially most oppressed people of Latin America--would do the same for the Latin American Revolution. How Fidel felt about the Guevara offensive is not clear, since his outwardly lukewarm support may have been designed to mollify the hesitant Russians. Che's former comandante may secretly have sympathized with the Chinese strategy of "many Vietnams" and "the city vs. the countryside," but like the Russians the Cubans gave little overt military support to the revolution. Only Che talked and acted like a Maoist attempting to stir up a peasant revolution. Actually, his inspiration was not China but Algeria and Cuba, where the guerrilla freedom-fighter had preceded the awakening of revolutionary consciousness in "the wretched of the earth." So Che went to the wilds of Bolivia to fight for freedom after the cityish Dominicans had shown that they could not shake off oppression.

1966-68 was the time the Western Hemisphere--and the world--almost blew up. The Russians could not afford to let the Maoist peasants or the Vietnamese and Guevarist guerrillas seem more revolutionary and therefore felt obliged to give some support, though not enough to precipitate a direct confrontation between the super-powers. But revolutionary China, having broken with the Soviet Union in 1961 in order to make its own A-Bomb, continued to vie for leadership of the world revolution and for power until, in 1968, the two Communist giants had troops engaged in small-scale combat along the Ussuri River and the Russians actually made plans for a preventive war aimed at dismantling China's atomic facilities before they became operational. Meanwhile, the United States, convinced that the tide of revolution had been turned in Indonesia and Brazil in 1964-65, was determined to contain Communism in Vietnam and elsewhere until the first generation of post-World War II revolutionaries died and the radical tide receded, a policy which led the French to withdraw from NATO. As an alternative, President De Gaulle set out to create a Third Force independent of the "Anglo-Saxons" and the "Russians, " that is, a third bloc that would appeal to the Chinese, the continental Europeans, and smaller client-states of the super-powers, whether in East Europe, the Western Hemisphere, or the former colonies.

Such was the atmosphere when the Guevara offensive set out to create "other Vietnams" in Latin America. Che and his guerrilla band began their revolutionizing in the Bolivian montaña. At the same time, Catholic radicals of a dozen countries took Pope Paul's Development of Peoples to mean that revolution was a holy war against materialism. Cityside guerrilla movements sprang up in Latin America as in all the Atlantic world, and long-democratic governments like Uruguay turned to militarism when confronted by such urban revolutionaries. Castro and Venezuela's Acción Democrática leaders got into a shouting match over whether Cuba was subverting Venezuela, but the Communist Party of Venezuela, which was legal and Russian-oriented, supported the government instead of the guerrillas. Amidst this furor, the Bolivian army, having seized power, tracked down and killed Che Guevara with the help of United States military advisors.

That was in 1967, the year of the Six-Day War in the Mideast. It was the year after the Tet Offensive in Vietnam. And it was the year before the Russians crushed Czechoslovak "liberal Communism, " the Americans elected a seemingly die-hard anti-Communist president, and the French students' and workers' rebellion rocked West Europe's post-World War II settlement and threatened De Gaulle's third way alternative. The remnants of Che's guerrilla band escaped to Chile, where they received asylum, heroes' treatment in the press of much of Latin America, and support from Chile's leading radical, though one who believed in ballots more than bullets--Salvador Allende. Any notion of a Third Force seemed out of the question at that moment.

The Multipolar World

In hindsight that seems nevertheless to have been precisely the moment that Latin Americans began to have some real success in pursuing their own third way, either because they finally decided to do so, or because the United States was preoccupied with Vietnam and home-grown troubles, or, more likely, because of the worldwide power shift

associated with a "multipolar" as opposed to the "bipolar"
world of the Cold War era. It was as if the balance-of-
power arrangement in which Russia crushed Czech restlessness in its sphere of influence and the United States did the
same in the Dominican Republic--and in which a Brezhnev
Doctrine took its place as the mirror image of the Johnson
Doctrine -had the effect of galvanizing most Latin Americans'
determination not to choose sides. They did not opt for
De Gaulle's "Latin alliance" either, however, though his 1967
trip to Québec and Latin America to offer his aid in securing
independence from the Anglo-Saxons sent tremors through the
OAS alliance similar to those preceding the French withdrawal from NATO in 1965. His "Vive l'amérique latine!" had
less force than his "Vive le Québec libre!" a few days before
in Montreal because Latin Americans were not looking for a
new Napoleon III to aid them. They were not looking for any
new European-led third way, in fact. They were looking for
a way of enhancing their own national interests--if necessary,
by working with any outside interests.

The evidence was unmistakable. In the economic
sphere, Figueres--who had lectured Castro as he lurched left
or moved in Russian missiles, and then had tut-tutted the
North Americans as they ran rightward in the period of the
Bay of Pigs and the Dominican intervention--announced that
Costa Rica would step up its relations with the Russians and
other East Europeans in order to convert them from tea to
coffee, thereby expand Latin Americans' coffee market, and
reduce economic dependence on the United States. Moreover,
Latin American countries were already ousting the United
States from West European markets for clothing, auto parts,
and other easily manufactured goods. Latin American trade
with Japan likewise rocketed upward. By the early 1970s
more than half of Latin America's trade was with countries
other than the United States, an enormous change by any
standard.

In political terms, home-grown radicalism revived in
many places: in 1968 in Peru, where General Velasco Al-
varado's revolutionary junta began to pursue an updated
Indianist modernism; in 1970 in Chile, where Salvador Allende was elected president on a platform of radical Latin
socialism; in the mid-1970s in Argentina, where Perón returned to power by popular demand in an effort to restore
his brand of Catholic radicalism; from the late 1960s on in
Jamaica, where Prime Minister Michael Manley began talking
of social engineering in positive terms; at about the same

time in some other Caribbean islands, where Black Power movements gained support. Diplomatically, Latin America's political coming-out meant the recognition of China and Cuba, as had the French Third Force initiative. Most of the neo-radical governments took the plunge and thus signalled the North Americans that more and more Latin Americans favored the Mexican strategy of serving as a bridge between the factions in the Cold War.

The United States at first interpreted Latin Americans' third-way initiatives as a betrayal of containment rather than a step toward world interdependence, however. The first Nixon administration, following the balance-of-power theories of foreign policy adviser Henry Kissinger, hardened its anti-Communist line in Southeast Asia by invading North Vietnamese support areas in Cambodia and Laos in 1970--and also set itself in direct opposition to Allende. The great power of Latin America, according to the Nixon-Kissinger view, was anti-Communist Brazil, and in 1969 the United States President declared, "As Brazil goes, so goes Latin America," thus infuriating the Spanish American states, especially those bordering on the Portuguese-speaking giant.

There was talk of an iron-ring alliance of Brazil's neighbors, even the conservative ones, if the United States-Brazilian entente went too far. So the overthrow of Allende in September 1973, the result of a military coup led by General Pinochet and welcomed by both Brazil and the United States, was not celebrated in most of Spanish America, nor in West Europe. For the slain Allende represented the electoral alternative--revolution by ballot--advocated by Europeans and Latin Americans throughout the post-World War II period. North American efforts to suppress such a revolution rather than to draw off the radical infections through surgically-exact reforms seemed to many United States allies to be an aberration unworthy of one of the leaders in two World Wars for democracy's sake. It smacked of spheres-of-influence power-balancing. And revelations of CIA skulduggery, not only against Allende but also against Castro during the "Kennedy thaw" of 1962-63, seemed to confirm the unfeeling nature of United States policy.

Yet by 1973 the stance of the United States had already begun to change toward a détente in which the great powers were to patch up their differences so as to manage the world's foreign relations better. Ideological rivalries--the free world vs. the Communists--were to be forgotten except in areas of vital interest. Thus the second Nixon administration shelved its quarrel with Mao's China, but merely began to "Vietnamize" the Indochina War. Likewise, the Kissinger plan secured the help of the Soviet Union in ending the Arab-Israeli war of 1973, yet insured that dissidents in East Europe would not receive support and encouragement from the West. Accommodation among the world's great powers, control at home and in one's sphere of interest--that was the formula for détente.

But the equation began not to equal out. The accommodation worked, though it required several changes of government in China after Mao's death to preserve it and left a taste of gall among allies of both the United States and the Soviet Union. The law-and-order-at-home part also prevailed, though the Watergate fallout cost the Nixon-Kissinger element dearly. What did not work was the spheres-of-influence scheme. The North Vietnamese did not negotiate a peace and accept buffer-zone status, but absorbed all of Vietnam. Other Europeans began to follow the French strategy of establishing relationships with any and all states including "clients" of the super powers. The East Europeans and Cubans began, in other words, to set a course more independent of the Russians. The same was true with respect to United States policy in so far as West Europeans were concerned--and Latin Americans, too.

Major changes were signaled by the Iberian, southern African, and energy crises of the 1970s. Within a period of five years, both Portugal and Spain had their authoritarian leaders die, lost the remnants of their empires, and began to move toward European multi-party democracy. In Portugal, there was considerable agony because after Salazar died (1972) his immediate successors tried to preserve conservative institutions and the African colonies in the face of strong revolutionary forces in Lisbon and Angola. In Spain, the transition was smoother because before Franco died (1975) he designated King Juan Carlos as his successor, and the king soon forced the conservatives to give way to more liberal elements. The reactions of the super-powers were predictable. The United States, following the Kissinger balance-of-power theory, set out to keep the Communist parties illegal; the Soviet Union, following the doctrine of opposition to Social Democratic reforms as the chief threat to true revolution, likewise resisted "Eurocommunism."

Nevertheless, the West European formula of legalizing

Communists prevailed, and the opportunity for Portuguese and Spanish governments with Communist ministers to join the Common Market (and perhaps, eventually, NATO) was not ruled out, despite the United States' strenuous opposition. After all, almost nothing could prevent French or Italian "Eurocommunists" from such participation if they were elected. Although Socialist governments emerged in Iberia, the Communists, led by Cunhal in Portugal and Carrillo in Spain, moved toward legal electoral and governmental status because the European formula called for above-ground rather than under-ground parties. Even Leftist leaders from Spanish Civil War days, such as "La Pasionaria," returned from exile.

So Latin Americans again had a European model of Latin democracy based on Catholic and Socialist sentiments. But Latin American reaction to the Iberian revolutions varied with local ideology and with reaction to the colonial crises of Portugal and Spain in Africa. The Cubans, like the Russians, gave only limited support to Cunhal in Portugal and tried to ostracize Carrillo but, unlike the Russians, sent troops to help the radicals secure control of Angola and Mozambique. The Brazilians granted asylum to Portuguese conservatives but recognized the new regimes in Angola and Mozambique rather than follow the hostile United States line and lose all influence in areas of such vital interest. Some of the smaller conservative states did echo the United States' criticism of Cuban revolutionizing in southern Africa (and later in Ethiopia, too). And some few radical Latin Americans applauded the Cuban efforts. Yet most Latin Americans, officials and citizens, seemed to prefer the new Iberian third way--reformist, non-imperial, committed to world interdependence on the basis of mutual interest. They applauded Spain's relinquishing of Spanish West Africa and wished Portugal had done the same with her African colonies. Above all, they applauded Pope John Paul II's 1979 visit to Latin America to foster a Catholic alternative to revolution and reaction.

One good reason for the altered attitudes of many Latin Americans was the partial reversal of economic roles highlighted by the energy crisis. The spectacle of Latin American states--Venezuela and Ecuador--participating in manipulation of oil prices by the Organization of Oil Producing and Exporting Countries (OPEC) in order to persuade the United States to alter its energy policy and its policy toward Israel after the 1973 Mideast war made the new relationship quite clear. Any supposed solidarity with this so-called

"Southern Hemisphere strategy" of Asians, Africans, and Latin Americans should not be exaggerated, however, since the oil states are not like other Third World countries. Besides, the Venezuelans and Ecuadoreans (and the Nigerians) defied the Arab oil boycott and sent oil to the United States. Nevertheless, Venezuela's nationalization of oil property, renegotiation of oil contracts, and defiance of the United States Congress' threats of economic retaliation against all OPEC states seemed part of the emergence of the Southern Hemisphere. Certainly it was taken as such by other Latin Americans--by states with new-found oil such as Mexico and Peru, by states considering formation of a coffee cartel to follow the OPEC example, and by the Latin American members of the Group of 77, a Third World organization designed to get maximum economic benefit out of resources.

And it is equally certain that it was taken as such by the United States. In the face of political weakness, energy troubles, and the growing multipolarity of the Western Hemisphere, the Kissinger foreign policy after the Watergate-forced resignation of President Nixon became one of interdependence, and the concessions granted probably contributed to the defeat of interim President Ford by a Democrat in the 1976 election. But when President Carter signed the Panama Treaty initiated by the Nixon-Ford administration, both Ford and Kissinger aided the Democrats in the efforts at ratification. Only the emphasis was different in the Carter verion of what Kissinger had called a "Good Partnership" Policy. Like the Good Neighbor Policy, this was a bipartisan initiative, as was the conservative opposition to such "appeasement" in Latin America and to "giving away" the Canal. The Kissinger aim, however, was like Herbert Hoover's--to tie Latin Americans to the United States' policies with bonds of self-interest such as tariff preferences, aid agreements, and minimal political and security concessions. The Carter aim, in contrast, seemed even broader than Franklin Roosevelt's--to settle all the outstanding North-South political issues in the Western Hemisphere and to forge new economic relationships consistent with the emerging interdependence of the hemisphere and the world. More importantly, President Carter's list of outstanding political issues seemed closer to Latin Americans' own list.

Panama came first on everyone's list, including Kissinger's, but Carter's and the Latin Americans' lists had Cuba next--and demanded less of the Cubans in return for détente. In effect, the Latin Americans forced the lifting of the OAS sanctions against the Cubans in 1976 by threatening to vote a change without the United States. At that time the United States decided to make the best of a lost cause and voted to end ostracism of Cuba, leaving only Brazil and a few hard-line Spanish-American states in opposition. But the Kissinger Good Partner Policy viewed Cuban hard-lining in Africa as contrary to interdependence and demanded withdrawal of Castro's forces before proceeding toward détente, only to find most Latin American states proceeding anyway. Carter policy, without reversing the earlier demands, led to a lifting of the United States trade embargo and the opening of negotiations on almost everything except Guantánamo and Africa, in hopes of drawing the Cubans toward a more moderate line or of convincing the Latin Americans that the U. S. was more reasonable than Cuba. A movement toward accommodation of the Cuban Revolution, similar to the earlier acceptance of the Mexican Revolution, began despite continued confrontations on the issue of Russian troops in Cuba.

A corollary of Cuban détente was alteration of the Brazilian entente. Kissinger's post-1973 plans for a partnership of all Latin Americans to reduce the danger of spreading revolution was one thing; Carter's reconciliation with the Spanish Americans quite another. For the Carter plan called for an end to the tilt toward Brazil or, better, a shift from overt anti-Communist power politics to something much more compatible with "Latin" egalitarian reformism. The reaction was immediate. The United States and Brazil were soon quarreling over a number of issues: about the Communist issue, of course, but also about the nuclear power plants Brazil wanted to buy from West Germany, about whether human rights were adequately respected in Brazil, about trade issues, and about Brazil's relations with her Spanish-American neighbors. Brazilian patriots were nevertheless convinced that there was really only one issue, the unwillingness of the United States to accept the fact that by century's end, Portuguese-speaking America might become a super-power if present growth continues. Most Brazilians simply could not fathom a policy in which the United States assigned equal importance to relations with Brazil and with some much smaller Western Hemisphere nation.

The Carter policy of stressing human rights was also a departure from Kissinger warnings about criticizing the internal affairs of other states, and akin to the "democratic morality" stressed by many Latin Americans. Others besides the Brazilians--the Chilean junta which ousted Allende,

and even some moderate leaders--were agitated because they
believed the United States' president had undermined Latin
America's need for "management" and "discipline" rather
than "politics." Yet the majority of Latin Americans seemed
sympathetic to the more committed stance of the Carter administration in the racial crisis in Rhodesia and South Africa,
the minority rights movement in the United States itself, and
human rights in political dictatorships of all persuasions.
Support for the underdog is what the Latin Americans read
in the Carter foreign policy. They read a respect for the
weak as well as the strong, a decline in balance-of-power
geopolitics, and increased concern with such priority issues
of an "interdependent" world as arms control and development.

Latin Americans' lists of outstanding political issues
have usually included two other entries--Puerto Rico and
United States minority relations affecting migrants from Latin
America. Puerto Rican-United States matters actually include
both issues. The commonwealth status of Puerto Rico was
not conclusively settled by the 1951 plebiscite, though tension
was clearly lessened and the United States no longer had to
report to the United Nations as if Puerto Rico were a trust
territory. After the retirement of Muñoz Marin (1964), the
debate over Puerto Rico's status began to heat up again,
mainly as a result of Puerto Rico's suffering all the pains
1960s United States politics was heir to, including anti-
Vietnam riots at the university in 1968.

Mainline Puerto Rican politics oscillated between the
commonwealth and statehood alternatives--Muñoz, then statehooder Ferré, then commonwealther Hernández Colón, then
statehooder Romero Barceló as governors--while the independentistas garnered much sympathy but few votes. Another
plebiscite in 1967 confirmed the 1951 results, in fact. In-
dependentista leader Albizú Campos died in 1965, but in the
virulent years of the late 1960s, Castro tried to bring the
Puerto Rican issue before the United Nations decolonization
committee, and in the early 1970s other Latin American
states began to vote with the Afro-Asian bloc, thus raising
the serious possibility of open United Nations debates on the
matter. Despite continued bombing incidents by Puerto Rican
nationalists in North American cities, the Carter administration then sent a signal of goodwill by commuting the sen-
tences of the independentistas who had attempted to kill President Truman in 1950 and attacked the House of Representatives in 1954. The hero's welcome the independentistas received in San Juan and the refusal of the most popular, Lolita

Lebrón, to rule out violence have to be placed alongside the
mainline debate over statehood in order to comprehend Puerto
Rican realities--and possible hemisphere and world reactions
to the colonialism issue.

Puerto Ricans are unique among Latin American minorities in the United States in that commonwealth status
exempts them from immigration laws. Until the mid-1960s
this distinction was not particularly important, since Mexican
braceros were welcomed for migratory fieldwork until 1964
and no quota on Western Hemisphere immigrants existed until
1968. Under these circumstances, Spanish Harlem in New
York City and its equivalents in other East Coast cities
came to include Dominicans and Colombians (and in nearby
Black ghettos, Haitians and Jamaicans) as well as Puerto
Ricans. In Florida were the "little Havanas" of the Cubans
of both pre- and post-Castro times. In the Southwest were
the Mexican-Americans--some hispanos descended from pre-
United States hacendados, some dirt farmers from peones of
earlier times, some migrant workers and town menials descended from braceros who may or may not have become
United States citizens. Spanish-speakers totaled between five
and ten per cent of the population of the United States. And
after the laws of 1964 and 1968, many of them became "illegal aliens"--except, of course, for the Puerto Ricans, who
were and are United States citizens.

Puerto Ricans, along with other culturally independent
ethnic groups, played a special role in United States minority
affairs by failing to "integrate" into the melting pot. Cultural pride was demonstrated in several ways. Island figures
such as "Doña Fela," long-time mayoress of San Juan, were
always highly visible on Puerto Rican Day in Mainland communities, as were the popular music and literature of the
common people (jíbaros). Puerto Rican migration was very
often circular--back "home" after a stretch of work or a
career. By the 1970s net migration was toward Puerto Rico,
in fact. This marked difference from other Spanish-speaking
immigrants to the United States was no doubt due to the assured citizenship status, to the fact that pensions and public
assistance would go farther on the island than the Mainland,
and to the integrity of a culture tight-knit enough to survive
the shock of "exile." Puerto Ricans who had achieved economic success in Mainland culture nevertheless felt both the
pull of jíbaro culture in the schools and the resentments
caused by racial misunderstandings and discrimination--so
much so that the ethnic "revolution" against the melting-pot

concept in the United States found Puerto Ricans in the forefront.

The so-called "Latin American revolution" has thus
had its impacts on United States domestic as well as foreign
relations, the most notable being the radicalization of minority movements during the 1960s. At the beginning of the
decade, a kind of liberal crusade led by the Kennedys' reform Catholics, Martin Luther King's Southern Christian
Leadership Conference, and AFL-CIO's campesino organizers
such as César Chávez had launched a North American version
of Vatican II's Catholic reformism under the Great Society
banner. But despite continuing work on civil rights, the war
on poverty, and educational opportunity programs, the Johnson administration was carried into confrontation with the
minorities and the young by its world anti-Communist crusade.

The "student revolt" which began with the Free Speech
Movement in 1964 at the University of California in Berkeley
soon adopted Che Guevara's notions of world-wide rebellion
against "the system" and confronted the Johnson forces at
the 1968 Democratic party convention in Chicago even though
the president had withdrawn from candidacy. Blood flowed,
Democratic candidate Humphrey was defeated, and Republican
President Nixon took office in 1969 determined to crush radicalism at home and abroad. And his administration saw the
aspirations of minority groups as part of the "revolt" and
set out to isolate them and the students from their Catholic
and labor allies, infiltrate and disrupt their organizations,
and discredit their leaders. Joining minorities to mainstream "middle America" was no longer the goal.

Latin American radicals gladly took credit for, and
tried to encourage, both youth and minority radicalism. In
his 1961 visit to the United Nations, for example, Fidel
Castro managed to get himself thrown out of a posh downtown hotel near U.N. headquarters, allegedly for holding
cockfights in his room, and then moved uptown to the jazz-
famous Hotel Teresa in Harlem to symbolize his solidarity
with Blacks and Puerto Ricans. A good deal of explicit
Marxist radicalism emerged in Black communities as a result of Stokeley Carmichael's, Eldridge Cleaver's, and the
Black Panthers' Fanon-inspired Black Power ideology. Black
Jacobinism and separatism, plus solidarity with the world
revolution in Vietnam and elsewhere, was in; "co-optation"
by White liberals through desegregation was out. Riots in the
Black ghettos of United States cities--the Watts section of

Los Angeles in 1965, Detroit in 1967, and many places after
the assassination of Martin Luther King in 1968--seemed to
confirm the revolutionary drift. "The counter-revolution
struck" was the Black Nationalists' explanation of Dr.
King's murder just after he had announced his opposition to the
Vietnam War and promised a more active, but still nonvio-
lent, confrontation with the "system." It was clear that even
liberal groups like the SCLC, the NAACP, and the Urban
League were becoming responsive to the "Black is beautiful"
slogan in order to avoid being accused of selling out.

The Spanish-speaking community seemed to be moving
in the same direction, especially after the assassination of
Robert Kennedy, the "minorities' candidate" in the 1968 election. In addition to the heightened feelings among Puerto
Ricans caused by drafting islanders for the Vietnam war,
there was rising disenchantment among Mexican Americans,
who were increasingly called "Chicanos" even though some
considered the term misleading or insulting. Rage peaked
with the assassinations of King and Kennedy in mid-1968.
César Chávez, the "theology of liberation" leader among the
Chicanos, was in the midst of the California grape strike.
La Huelga had been declared in 1965 in Delano, California,
and the campesinos responded to Chávez' grito with "Viva la
huelga! Viva la causa! Viva César Chávez!" The strike,
the cause and Chavez seemed to represent la raza even
though Chávez still asked for Anglo help through AFL-CIO
support, boycotts, and liberal democratic political action.
He fasted, prayed, and lived with the campesinos, that is,
maintained his moral authority by sacrificing more than they
did. But he also reached out to King, Kennedy, and other
leaders of the liberal crusade. And he approached the
Puerto Ricans and Cubans of the New Jersey truck farms
and the Florida citrus groves. There was one success: the
importation of Mexican braceros to undercut his efforts was
ended by law (if not in fact) in 1964. But there were no
contracts with the growers in California, New Jersey, or
Florida. And then King and Kennedy were killed just before
the riotous election of 1968.

Radicalism was in the wind--because of the situation,
and because of the Latin American concept of a bronze continent. In New Mexico in 1963 Reies Tijerina, a Protestant
preacher, had revived the notion that the nuevo mexicanos
and the tejanos, the Spanish-speakers on the land before the
Treaty of Guadalupe-Hidalgo (1848), should still own their
property. For the better part of a decade Tijerina and his

alianza occupied courthouses, made citizens' arrests of un-
cooperative law officers, and were arrested in turn. The
titles remained as they were despite the ambiguities of the
Spanish land-grants and the treaty, but the United States West
was inflamed. The Brown Berets of the urban barrios,
modeled on the Black Panthers of the ghettos, adapted their
wretched of the earth doctrines to accommodate their feelings
of solidarity with the submerged Bronze Continent. Then
came an imaginative leader--Rodolfo "Corky" González, ex-
prizefighter, poet, ex-party-worker for Denver's Democrats.
In 1968, at the height of the time of troubles, he declared
that "Aztlán," named for the sacred place of origin of the
Aztec (and Mexican) nation, included the Chicanos. The
Aztlán concept was vague, like the Blacks' concept of a Republic of New Africa in the United States South, but it tied
the "Chicago nation" to its Indian and Latin roots.

Such cultural reinforcement, rather than political action, has been the major effect of the Latin American revolution on North American minority relations. Political dis-
sent has diminished with more minority opportunities, the
signing of contracts in the fields, the election of the more
sympathetic Carter government, and the calmer atmosphere
after the Vietnam war. But ethnic and cultural pride has
grown and spread from Blacks and Chicanos to Italians, Poles,
and others. Blacks have naturally focused mainly on Africa--
as in Alex Haley's Roots, the saga of a Black family from
capture in Africa to the cities of 20th-century North America.
Next on the ladder of pride has come the Black experience in
North America--rewriting the history of slavery and emancipation, the Civil War and civil rights, and the Harlem Ren-
aissance--and creating such "liberation literature" as that of
Imamu Baraka (LeRoi Jones) and Nikki Giovanni. But in
third place stands Caribbean culture. New York and other
large North American cities now maintain round-the-clock
radio programs featuring Jamaican music, including the popular reggae. Caribbean as well as African styles are part
of the "Black is beautiful" movement. Immigration from
both English- and French-speaking islands continues despite
the 1968 barriers. There is some opposition to the growing
influence of Caribbean "soul" in the Black community--by the
Black Muslims who see in it the corruption caused by White
materialism, and by Black Christians who also see moral
decay in its excesses. Yet all agree that one aspect implied
by "soul"--the aspect of Black pride--is beautiful in Africa,
the Caribbean, or the ghetto.

Spanish-speakers have had more direct cultural con-
tacts with Latin America than have Blacks. Once the ideological divisions diminished, the common culture surfaced.
Among Mexican-Americans, the descendants of pre-Anglo
hacendados have made common cause with campesinos and
youth from the barrios in securing bilingual education laws
to protect the language and culture. Corky González' plan
for a Chicano university is controversial because some oppose such separatist approaches as ghettoization, but bi-
lingualism in the lower schools is widely accepted. "Chicano
literature" has also appeared. The "Spanish-speaker" label
imposed by Anglo culture remains a problem because it obscures the attachments to Mexico, Puerto Rico, Cuba, and
other countries. But Siquieros' murals of the 1930s, which
were painted over after the New Deal in an excess of
Chamber-of-Commerce zeal, have been restored in the Southwest by Mexican experts at the insistence of Chicanos.
Nuyoricans who regret their loss of Puerto Rican culture
send, or take, their children back to the island to be educated. And Miami's Little Havana, despite divisions between
pre- and post-Castro immigrants, maintains a certain cuban-
ismo. Not only Spanish-speaking pride, but pride of nation
and even of patria chica, can and must be preserved, Hispanics believe, despite attempts at "integration" and continuing ideological differences.

The fact that ghetto and barrio have become a home
and not a slum in the minds of Black and Spanish-speaking
minorities is more than a challenge to United States domestic
politics. It also represents a challenge to the most important
North American concept of Western Hemisphere affairs after
the Monroe Doctrine--the "Canadian model" of Good Neighborism. United States citizens rightly point to the strength
of the Canadian relationship: peaceful settlement of a border
now long stable and demilitarized; mutually advantageous economic relations; and a mutual commitment to democracy and
progress. But North Americans have tended to take the
Canadian relationship for granted--and, since Big Stick domination has long since gone out of fashion, aim at building
the same relationship with Latin America. But Latin Americans, United States minorities, and French Canadians see a
flaw in that relationship, the so-called "melting pot" concept.
"Integrating" into a basically Anglo-Saxon concept of democracy and progress has little appeal to them in domestic or
foreign relations. Thus the French Canadians' demand for
greater autonomy in Canada and the potential hidden in the
Gaullists' Third Force concept. Latin Americans, and mi-

norities within the United States and Canada, are now among those demanding many roads to democracy. What started as a revolutionary concept in the hemisphere and the world has become accepted doctrine almost everywhere, however. The melting pot and the unitary hemisphere have disappeared and pluralist democracy has become one of the foundation stones of the emerging "world system"--for which the Latin Americans can take more than a little credit.

World Issues

The energy crisis of the early 1970s not only confirmed the increased importance of Latin America and other Southern Hemisphere nations in world affairs. It also called attention to changes in the nature of world affairs caused by post-industrial issues. Throughout the era of industrialization, nations have sought armed strength, economic and population growth, and educational and political advance. But post-industrialization now seems to require control of the arms race, recognition of economic and demographic limits, and restraint with respect to media and state manipulation of citizens--at least in highly developed countries. In Latin America, however, industrialization and post-industrialization must proceed together. Educated Latin Americans definitely recognize that interdependence extends beyond politics. But they also recognize that their mid-range societies cannot afford to compete openly with advanced economies or slow their growth before creating viable and equitable internal patterns. In fact, Latin America has almost the full range of social situations, from pre- to post-modern, and is therefore a kind of laboratory for both internal and external interdependence. Latin Americans therefore participate in the world's most up-to-date issues from perspectives as varied as those of super-powers and ministates, jet setters and stone-agers.

The arms race or nuclear proliferation issue is typical. Most Latin American states have signed the Nuclear Non-Proliferation Treaty (1963), and all have supported the treaties that forbid armaments in space, on the seabed, and in Antarctica. The most significant non-signatories of the non-proliferation agreement are Brazil and Argentina, although Cuba and Chile have not signed either. Most Latin American states have signed the Treaty of Tlatelolco (1968) forbidding nuclear weapons in Latin America, but again Brazil and Argentina have not put it into force. Many advanced Latin American countries do have the scientific know-how to operate or even to build nuclear weapons. What they lack is the technology and the fuel, and, perhaps, the desire. In the late 1960s and early 1970s the Brazilians and Argentines, with United States help, developed several small nuclear power plants and, in the case of Argentina, a small reprocessing plant without United States help. Ecuador, meanwhile, has discovered uranium and has agreed to have United States firms extract it. Hence the technology and the fuel may soon be available in Latin America.

The first major crack in the Latin American nuclear non-proliferation shield came as a result of the energy crisis, which caused oil-short Brazil to order from West Germany eight nuclear power plants and the uranium enrichment and reprocessing facilities to fuel them. The International Atomic Energy Agency, which was set up to monitor non-proliferation, approved the sale, but the United States tried to stop the West Germans from fulfilling the contract as soon as President Carter took office in early 1977. Brazilians suspected that the North Americans were more concerned with black-balling them as members of the nuclear club than with the threat of terrorists stealing plutonium or the instability of a world with more and more nuclear powers. In any case, the United States could not undermine the agreement. The West Germans insisted on selling, and the Brazilians on buying. Nuclebras, Brazil's government-owned nuclear energy agency, set about making the country a member of the nuclear club in energy, but not, Brazilian leaders promise, in weaponry.

Brazil's decision to seek initiation to the nuclear club received a sympathetic hearing from oil-desperate countries such as West Germany and France, Japan and India and Egypt, Australia and Israel and South Africa. The Germans and French also wanted to sell the technology, the Australians and South Africans the fuel. Indeed, many energy specialists, including those in the United States, have argued that every country except the oil-rich Arabs, Indonesians, Nigerians, North Sea states, and possibly the Venezuelans, will have to play the nuclear energy game. In fact, the United States admitted as much in the quarrel over the German-Brazilian deal (and similar French contracts with several Asian nations) and sought only to restrict the fuel processing, not the nuclear power plants.

Processing ought, in this view, to be considered more

like nuclear weapons than like power plants because re-
processed fuel could be diverted to make weapons, indeed
had been diverted when India used its Canadian-built processing plant to provide material for its bomb in 1975. Only
"senior" members, so to speak, should have weapons and
processing facilities, and not even they should have hot-
metal "breeder" reactors capable of producing more weapons-
grade plutonium than they consumed. The United States led
the way in cancelling its hot-metal breeders in favor of
safer but less efficient light-water breeders as a sign of
good faith, but only succeeded in dividing the club members,
including its own scientists, more. Meanwhile, the Soviet
Union and China continued building plants (including breeders)
of their own but kept close control over fuel processing and
weapons in Communist countries. The continental Europeans
began building breeders and sold processing plants, and
smaller countries began gearing up.

The consequences were immediately apparent in Latin
America. Since Brazil could soon build weapons if it chose,
the larger Spanish-American states, especially its long-term
rival Argentina, began to consider the nuclear strategies
more seriously themselves, so as to be in a position to
compete if necessary. Two additional issues affecting the
hemisphere also surfaced. First, what if some Western
Hemisphere nation such as Brazil became disenchanted
enough to reject the United States' "nuclear umbrella" of
protection in favor of its own nuclear security force, as
President De Gaulle of France had in the 1960s? Second,
what if one of the nations near the United States such as
Mexico or Cuba began developing processing or even breeder
facilities to keep its options open? In other words, what if
the potential military balance were to be changed in a manner not foreseen by the Monroe Doctrine--that is, from
within the hemisphere?

Meanwhile, the smaller, less-developed nations of
Latin America watched helplessly as club members and candidate members wrangled over the virtues of interdependence,
separate development, and competition for uranium supplies
from South Africa and Australia, or over the relative advantages of nuclear equipment from Europe, the United States,
or the Soviet Union. And most Latin Americans became
impatient with the slow progress in disarmament on the part
of the nuclear powers in such forums as the Strategic Arms
Limitation Talks (SALT). Why, they thought, if others are
to have nuclear weapons, should Latin Americans not have
them as well?

Technological nationalism has extended far beyond the nuclear issue, of course. Increasingly, Latin Americans see their national independence threatened by lack of control over the technologies of defense and of development. Conventional armaments, for instance, have raised several concerns besides the primary questions of internal stability and relative strength vis-à-vis potential external threats. The major concern has been for independence of action in security matters. Few Latin American nations have gone in the Cuban direction and secured arms from Communist powers, though the post-1968 military-populist government in Peru considered doing so. Yet quite a few, including Peru, have turned to the French so as not to be too dependent on the North Americans, and some have begun to produce their own spare parts and strain their own maintenance personnel as a hedge against dependency.

In addition, it is only a matter of time until many Latin American countries can, like the Europeans and Japanese, produce and repair their own conventional arms, which could give them the option of independent action already available to Israel and South Africa. This world-wide movement toward a multipolar international security system has become evident as a result of China's military independence of the Soviet Union, France's production of its own weapons and strategies, and even rumblings within NATO and the Warsaw Pact. Attempts to have the United States and the Soviet Union cooperate to control arms sales could unintentionally push Latin Americans and other strong Southern Hemisphere nations in the direction of military multipolarity rather than restraint in armaments. The Venezuelans and Argentines and Peruvians will not sit by idly and watch the Brazilians outstrip them, for example. Nor will the Peruvians, Chileans, or Bolivians allow each other to gain an advantage in the sensitive War of the Pacific area which joins them together. In Middle America, North American influence has kept this issue below the surface except in Cuba, but it exists nonetheless in muted rumblings.

Another serious concern has been the effect of heavy armaments expenditures on development in Latin America. Revolutionaries contend that such militarism is merely the essence of a desperate, dying order. Others contend that militarism is rooted in the Latin American psyche, that it is necessary to provide the stability for development, or that military civic action programs are the cheapest way to build roads and educate citizens. Some Latin Americans

argue that they are affected even more by the hard realities
of modern technological warfare. First, the Atlantic and
Pacific moats have been bridged by planes and missiles as
surely as they have in the Northern Hemisphere, thus undermining Latin American as well as North American security.
The world grown smaller has also grown less secure for
every nation. Second, all modern militaries cost more because of technological advance--and also cost proportionately
more in developing countries with fewer resources. Latin
Americans are therefore on a security treadmill running ever
faster, and always much faster than the rich North Americans, to avoid being disarmed by default.

Many Latin American nations, especially the smaller
non-revolutionary ones, therefore see no hope of secure
development without taming the arms race everywhere, assuring everyone a secure fuel supply, and mediating diplomatic disputes--in other words, without genuine interdependence. Brazil differs very little from its smallest, poorest
confrères in supporting United Nations efforts at achieving
general disarmament, for instance, since long-term security
and development seem to depend on such arms control. But
neither Brazil nor any other nation anywhere will make unilateral concessions without guarantees of security and development. And since either one or the other, or both, cannot
be assured yet in most instances, the arms race continues--
at great cost.

Unfortunately, the technology for development also
costs more, and proportionately more, so that in twentieth-
century Latin America development is harder than it was in
the nineteenth-century United States. Because citizens expect more before considering themselves well off, the hurdle
to modernization is higher. Because other nations are more
advanced, the competition is also faster. Yet Latin Americans of every status tend to be as positive toward technology
as North Americans, and perhaps more positive. The
British-French Concorde supersonic airliner was accepted
eagerly in Brazil while being denied landing rights in most
of the United States, for instance. Plastic hairbrushes,
rubber-soled sneakers, and ready-made clothes find their
way to tribes in the wilds. Television comes to the cantina
in all but the remotest villages, and battery-powered radios
fan out to isolated individuals beyond the reach of gasoline-
powered electric generators. City folk yearn for refrigera-
tors and mod furniture, the latest style of clothing or wrist-
watches, and a motorcycle or an automobile. The rich go

in for personal airplanes and an elegant office in the latest highrise, plus a bit of stock in some flourishing enterprise building construction equipment or farm machinery. If Latin America is to go through the stages of exploiting the land, conserving parts of the wilderness in national parks, and eventually protecting the environment as happened in North America, stage two has scarcely begun.

Latin Americans have been most concerned with the kind of technological dependency the Grangers objected to when the railroads crossed the Great Plains. The Ocean Treaty negotiations at the United Nations in the mid-1970s illustrated the complexities of this issue of "technological imperialism"--and of the ecology vs. economy issue--in a developing area. In a sense, it all started with anchovies and tuna in the icy Peru or Humboldt Current and the fact that ships from the United States, the Soviet Union, and Japan were taking more fish than the Latin Americans, who could not compete with the sophisticated sonar devices and netting techniques of the great Pacific maritime powers. For, late in the 1960s, the anchovies almost disappeared altogether, tuna catches began to decline, and Peru and Ecuador decided to enforce their 200-mile offshore fishing limit. "No license, no fishing" was the rule. Since the United States accepted only a twelve-mile limit, conflicts occurred, ships were seized, and the entire question of ownership of the ocean's resources soon came before the United Nations. The result was the convening of a Law of the Sea Conference to write an Ocean Treaty. The Peruvians and Ecuadorians entered into the negotiations determined to maintain the 200-mile limit as a way of preserving "their" resources and, almost incidentally, the viability of the fish population of the Peru Current.

The offshore limit issue actually proved to be among the least difficult during the several negotiating sessions on the Ocean Treaty. While awaiting agreement on a treaty, the United States declared its own 200-mile limit because the Russians, the Japanese, and the West Europeans were depleting the fisheries of the North Atlantic, too. The West Coast fisherman in the United States objected that they had been sold out to the interests of the East Coast, and the Eurasian fishing powers regretted the restrictive licensing the treaty mandated for the Americas' waters. But after some intense over-fishing in anticipation of stricter limits (and a "cod war" between Iceland and Britain), the new licensing system went into effect in the Americas even before

the signing and ratification of a treaty. Peru owned its anchovies, Ecuador its tuna, the United States its hake, Canada
its mackerel, Iceland its cod.

Nor did the security issue plague the treaty talks. It
was agreed that the territorial limit would differ from the
fishing limit--that is, would be set at twelve miles rather
than two hundred--in order to avoid overlapping ownership in
narrow waters such as the English Channel, the Malacca
Straits and the passages between the Caribbean islands.
Latin Americans and other Third World countries at first
argued that only wider national waters could prevent electronic
surveillance and naval bombardment. But carrier-based
planes had really made such objections academic, and the
narrower limit was written into the treaty. In addition, the
principles of freedom of the seas were rather easily reaffirmed for both the open seas and for those narrow seas
without special arrangements like those affecting the Dardanelles and the mouth of the Baltic.

The sticking point in the Ocean Treaty talks concerned
open-sea resources--the oil, manganese, and other materials
of the sea floor and the fish of the open ocean. It was clear
that resources within twelve miles belonged to the shore nation, and agreement was reached to extend ownership to the
two hundred miles insisted on by the Latin Americans because the United States and other great powers saw advantages in it for themselves. But though the Latin Americans
generally saw eye-to-eye with other Western Hemisphere nations on the 200-mile territorial limit, they wanted a whole
world approach to the open oceans. The Latin Americans
have regarded the open ocean as the remaining natural patri-
mony of humankind--the means of cutting land-locked nations
in on the sea's wealth, the bankroll for Third World development, something to be preserved for future use--and therefore as the "property" of the United Nations. But the United
States and other high-technology powers have argued that access to deep sea resources depends on competition that encourages deep-mining, deep-drilling, and deep-fishing in-
ventions, capital investment, and proper organization. The
issue of technological imperialism thus surfaced again (and
was helped along by revelations that the United States'
Glomar was not just for grabbing manganese nodules off the
Pacific floor but for lifting a sunken Russian submarine to
aid CIA intelligence as well). Negotiation or ratification of
the Ocean Treaty may well founder on this problem, since
it has always seemed to sum up the differences in de-

velopment strategy between developed and developing countries.

In one respect the concept of "free use" of the sea
has divided the Americas and the world along other lines,
however. The United States, and developed countries in
general, have shown increasing concern since World War II
over pollution of the seas. United Nations agreements speci-
fying areas for release of bilge, controlling ship construction
to prevent spills, and establishing punishments have been
supported by most of the great maritime powers. Yet flag-
of-convenience states such as Panama (and Liberia) continue
to allow non-complying ships to register, while other nations,
including the United States, most often look the other way to
please shipowners and hesitate to ban such ships from their
own ports. In heavy-traffic harbors and near the Canal, the
sea has become a sewer. Developing countries say that they
cannot afford better ships and blame the greed of shippers
and of great maritime nations for most of the damage. Developed countries blame flag-of-convenience hiding-places for
undermining reform efforts. Meanwhile, unsafe super-tankers
threaten more huge oil spills, smaller craft leak toxic chem-
icals, and globs of such wastes sail the Gulf Stream and the
Peru Current on round-the-world voyages. Moreover, efforts
to protect nearly extinct or otherwise special sea-creatures
such as whales and porpoises have encountered even more
complex responses which often place the United States and
Europe as protectionists vs. Russians and Japanese opposing, so that developing nations, including Latin America,
could tip the balance if they become environmentalist in outlook.

Latin Americans are beginning to rise to the challenge
of balancing development against long-term environmental
realities, especially with regard to their role as special cus-
todians of the Amazon, Antarctica, and endangered species.
The Amazon's ecological importance is now recognized as
meriting the title Portuguese explorers gave it--O Rio Mar,
or "The River Sea"--since it generates as much as one-
fourth of the earth's oxygen supply because of its size and
the luxuriance of its plant growth. It is home to 100,000
species of plants and animals, including 145-foot-tall roses,
350-pound catfish, and an ever-increasing number of humans
and bulldozers threatening, at their present rate of progress,
to destroy most of this tropic sea of water and wildlife by
century's end. Where generations of explorers--Cabral,
Orellana, de Vaca, Humboldt, Teddy Roosevelt, Fawcett--
went to find wilderness, there are now cities of 350,000

(Manaus), paved highways, and vast projects for burning away
tropical hardwoods to make way for tree farming of faster-
growing species. But the Amazon is politically almost unique
as well, since it belongs essentially to one nation, Brazil.
It is not like the Great Lakes or Great Plains of North America, which require international cooperation for their protection, but like the steppes or Lake Baikal in the Soviet Union.
And Brazil is just entering into a serious debate about the
ecological consequences of the vast program of "national integration" (roads, settlement, etc.) being undertaken in the
Amazon.

The debate is very much like that on conservation in
the United States early in the twentieth century. Idealists and
citified easterners favor conservation and protection of the
Indians, whereas outback westerners see their future in exploitation of the Amazon's resources. There are other similarities as well. The preponderance of opinion in Brazil is
clearly for growth, and the interference of international
forces--in this case, the United Nations--in the Indians' be-
half is deeply resented. Most Brazilians believe that FUNAI,
the Indian office, is providing the best possible solution by
creating reservations such as the one in Xingu National
Forest, and that environmental projects like "Man and the
Biosphere" headquartered at Humboldt Scientific City will
hold off environmental disaster by preventing clearing too
close to the rivers. But a growing minority of educated
Brazilians, prompted by international studies, fear that ero-
sion will clog the rivers anyway, that the photosynthesis
cycle will be disrupted and earth's climate altered, that
numerous species will become extinct, and that whole cultures
of Indians will disappear. Meanwhile, Brazilian rural police
struggle in vain to maintain law and order amid endemic
frontier violence.

The Antarctic issue is somewhat different--more like
the problems of the Great Lakes and Great Plains, the Mediterranean, or the great northern forests and tundra around
the other Pole. Like the Amazon, Antarctica is almost as
large as the United States and plays an enormous role in
world climate. But in this case Argentina and Chile, the
Latin American countries with greatest interest and responsibility, have been joined by ten other nations, including the
two super-powers, in an international agreement to make the
whole continent an example of worldwide cooperation. The
thirty-year Antarctic Treaty (1959) not only forbids weapons
and wastes, but also provides for cooperation in the search

for resources, a search which has revealed the probability
that oil and uranium exist. Helicopters flying from the
United States' base at McMurdo Sound to survey every inch
of the continent with radiation equipment have found "hot"
readings near Taylor Glacier, for example, much as the
Brazilian surveying agency has found non-radioactive minerals
in the Amazon by using satellite readings made available by
the United States. Will the ban on territorial acquisitions in
Antarctica hold if vast mineral deposits exist, particularly
since the controls will have to be renewed in 1989? The
treaty nations and the international scientific community have
already begun efforts to prevent such a "gold rush."

Meanwhile, Latin America's ecological role is being
altered by changes in its economic role. Historically, Latin
America's role in world economic affairs has been like that
of the rest of the Western Hemisphere, that is, to serve as
a "great frontier" of under-utilized resources ready to absorb
excess populations and level up the social order by benefiting
the lower classes of the New and Old Worlds. In contrast
to North America, South America continues to play the role
of great frontier to a certain extent, since open land is still
available, the doors to immigration are still open, and opportunities for quick wealth are many. Middle America, like
North America, long ago lost its openness in terms of free
land. But both Middle and South America are just beginning
to benefit from the "second frontier"--mechanization of agriculture and large-scale industrialization. The abuses of
North American robber baron days and the concomitant opportunities for getting rich quick are now evident in much of
Latin America. Argentine grain moguls, Brazilian soy-bean
giants, Mexican chain-store supermen, Venezuelan oil
magnates--such are the new-rich Rockefellers, Fords, and
Hearsts of Latin America. But the open opportunities, that
is, the Western Hemisphere or frontier qualities, have probably always been less in Latin than in North America and
are shrinking rapidly.

The Southern Hemisphere school contends that Latin
America's economic future depends on solidarity with other
developing countries now that the "myth" of open opportunity
has been exploded. In this view, the reason for difficulties
in Latin American growth is a history of exploitation and
dependency both longer and deeper than in North America.
No sooner had Latin America broken free of Iberian economic
domination in the mid-19th century than it found itself confronted with the prospect of becoming the tropical garden and

open-pit mine of the North Americans. No sooner had the North Americans been dislodged from the land and the mines than they, the Europeans, and the Japanese overwhelmed the infant industries of Latin America with cars, TVs, tractors, planes, and computers--with retail goods rather than foreign ownership, that is. Hence Latin America has joined the recent "economic revolution" because the Southern Hemisphere strategy (control of national resources, re-direction of aid and investment, and diversification of trade) seemed suited to an economic future in which growth could no longer be assured by the new wealth of under-used resources. New partnerships were sought with the Communist states in trade, with the Group of 77 in Third World economic matters, with the Afro-Asian bloc in United Nations affairs, and with each other in the political and economic organs of the Western Hemisphere.

The success of the Southern strategy in Latin America is a matter of definition. If improvement in the position of South vs. North is meant, there was considerable success. Local control of resources proceeded through nationalizations in Peru, Venezuela, Jamaica, and (despite Allende's fall) Chile, and even more through stricter controls over new investment. Aid and investment were secured on terms more favorable to Latin America by drawing on the Swedes, Japanese, and Arabs as well as from the larger countries of West Europe and from the United States; by arranging more multilateral aid from the World Bank than bilateral aid from the northern countries; and by weakening United States influence over the World Bank and Western Hemisphere economic bodies. Trade advantages were secured by turning to additional trading partners (which is what caused the United States to have less than half of Latin American trade for the first time in the early 1970s); by challenging the most-favored-nation clause in trade treaties so as to protect Latin America's infant industries from unfair competition by developed economies; and by insisting on tit-for-tat trade deals with the economic giants, deals secured by partnership in cartels such as OPEC, if necessary. Yet if success means a "new economic order" was formed, there was no real success. For Latin America remained part of the Atlantic World system--pegged to the dollar or pound, trading mostly with the Europeans and North Americans, trying to get a piece of the economic action. Latin America became part of the world economic system, but still mainly as part of a regional unit.

The economic elements of the United States' Good Partnership Policy were a response to these transformations in Latin America. The Rockefeller Report (1969) had summed up the policies of a generation of North Americas: containment of communism through military intervention and economic stimulation; encouragement of private United States investment along with retaliation against nationalization; and trade and aid policies to help friends and harm foes. But after the oil crisis of 1973 Secretary of State Kissinger announced a new set of principles: non-imposition of United States "political preferences" in Latin America; prior consultation on all matters by means of conferences of foreign ministers; and reformation of aid and trade policies. The United States shifted politically, of course--toward accommodation on Panama if not Cuba, toward criticism of human rights violations in Chile if not in Brazil. But the shift was also economic--to end the dispute with Mexico over Colorado River water, to settle on compensation for nationalized property in Peru rather than enforce the Hickenlooper Amendment, and, unfortunately as it turned out, to arrange "trade preferences" in the Trade Act of 1974.

The Trade Act seemed reasonable from the North American perspective, almost a return to the plans of James G. Blaine, father of the Pan-American Congresses of the 1880s, for a system of planned economic advantages among Western Hemisphere nations. But to modern Latin Americans it appeared that the United States was trying to punish the Latin American members of OPEC, to arrange a new system of tariff incentives to hold Latin American nations in orbit around the United States, and to continue to isolate Cuba. So the Latin Americans broke off the "North-South dialogue," cancelled the next conference of hemisphere foreign ministers, and began lifting the ban on Cuba, symbol of the Southern strategy.

The Latin Americans' adherence to the Southern strategy can be over-drawn, however, since the real aim is national development on the part of each country by whatever means seem suitable. There are undoubtedly Southern Hemisphere circumstances in many Latin American nations, and some sort of "dependency strategy" to break the connection between dependency and backwardness is as natural as it was in the United States South and West before the sunbelt states began drawing abreast of the snowbelt in industry, education, and the like. In Latin America there will continue to be nationalization of foreign-owned (and domestic-owned) property in order to achieve land reform, control of oil and mineral resources, and planning of transportation and communications facilities. There will be legal restraints on new private investment to restrict export profits, assure training of local workers, and re-cycle money into further development. There will be an insistence that aid come through international agencies like the World Bank and the Inter-American Development bank--and that the United States' influence over these bodies be diminished--so as to assure a minimum of political interference in national planning. But the United States has more or less conceded these points under the Good Partnership Policy of Kissinger and his successors. These are the old issues, some still inflamed, to be sure, but probably on the wane.

The new issues are larger, harder--something beyond Western Hemisphere optimism and Southern Hemisphere pessimism; what might perhaps be called a new global realism. The over-riding question is "How does this or that Latin American country fit into the emerging world economy?" After dependency, this lack of an isolationist alternative, similar to that of the 19th-century United States, is the most significant difference in North and South economics in the Western Hemisphere. Hence the responses to the world economy are sometimes quite surprising.

Take the heated issue of the multinational corporation, for example. The most widely accepted interpretation in Latin America at the moment is that this is a North vs. South matter from beginning to end--that GM in the United States and Shell in The Netherlands are the new conquistadores and robber barons. But multinationals also "export jobs," so that Mexico manufactures the electronic components of many North American TVs and calculators, components previously manufactured in the Great Lakes region. Is that neo-imperialist exploitation of low-cost Mexican labor, scab-labor manipulation of United States workers, or development? Moreover, Latin Americans--few and rich, to be sure--own stock in multinationals, hold skilled positions in them, participate, though minimally, in the world economy. Still, most Latin Americans' relationship with multinationals is probably Southern--that is, one of buying dear and selling cheap, or, in the imaginative plan put forward by Latin America's new economic organization, SELA, of trying to set up Latin American-owned multinationals to compete with the Northern giants. Bunge Corporation, the Argentine grain giant, is already a world economic power, in fact. Yet the

long-term interest of Latin Americans, like that of all
"world citizens, " is to turn the multinationals to democratic
purpose before a scientific world elite has secured a monopoly on wealth and power.

Global money questions--banking, exchange, trade,
capital--also confront Latin American economies with problems beyond those of early-industrialized nations. The bank-
ing district in Panama, a kind of Wall Street or Beirut of
Latin America, is much resented by proponents of the Southern strategy. They see the solution of Latin American economic problems in higher real return for raw materials
going out and lower real outlay for equipment coming in, and
blame the branches of the big Northern banks headquartered
in Panama for stacking the monetary system against the
Third World. Thus a Brazilian cruzeiro, a Guatemalan
quetzal, and a Mexican peso buy less and less of a German
motor or a Japanese auto. But there are counter-currents
of opinion about "exported inflation" because the prices of
Northern goods climb due to high prices of oil and raw materials from the South, and about "exported unemployment"
because Northern recessions and austerity measures mean
fewer imports from the South. Thus many Latin American
economists, particularly in the United Nations Economic
Commission on Latin America (CELA), look to a mutually
advantageous "indexing system" to solve the difficulties. A
ton of steel, for example, would be equal to an agreed number of barrels of oil or bags of coffee independent of what
happens to the currencies. This monetary law-and-order
question is at least as controversial and important as that
concerning multinationals.

The third difference in Latin American vis-à-vis
earlier North American development is that it requires more
social transformation than economic stimulation--bluntly, a
less laissez-faire approach. To be sure, there is still more
than a little conflict over the merits of centralized planning,
Marxist or nationalist, as witness the Chilean agonies in the
Allende and Pinochet era. There is also more than a little
truth in the notion that the Latin tradition is more social
than individual. In other words, Latin Americans believe
they must progress together rather than separately, either
by national evolution (nationalism) or class revolution (Marxism); that social amenities rather than mere wealth determine the good life; and that the exclusively economic approach to success is cold and vulgar. Yet these attitudes,
however vital they may still be to understanding Latin Amer-

ican development patterns, are giving way to a conviction that the developing world is caught up in a race between population growth and development, something never faced, at least to the same degree, by nations achieving development before the population explosion caused by the inexorable "revolution" in sanitation, medicine, and nutrition. The crucial economic challenge before Latin America in the late twentieth century is therefore whether it can become one of the producers rather than a consumer of the world's goods, by reducing its baby boom. If the North's role is to protect the future by restraining production, the South's role is to restrain reproduction--so that its production can catch up.

To fulfill this role Latin America will have to transcend the optimistic myth of a Western Hemisphere available to fuel endless economic growth. This great frontier myth, which motivates Latin Americans as much as North Americans, runs counter to the recognition of limits required by a post-industrial world economy. It obscures the necessity of doing more with less through restraint in the matter of riches and of babies. So at such mid-1970s international meetings as the Environment Conference in Stockholm, the Food Conference in Bucharest, and the Population Conference in Rome, the United States and Latin America were sometimes on the same frequency, and sometimes not.

Both Latin and North Americans at these meetings recognized that limits will be essential for the future of the Americas. Likewise, none of the Western Hemisphere nations reacted to the energy crisis as vigorously as oil-starved West Europe or Japan because the Americas are still more or less self-sufficient in energy. On the other hand, the limits to be adhered to were not the same in North American and Latin American schemes. North Americans wanted their Southern neighbors to become self-sufficient and develop by controlling population increases--and conveniently neglected the effects of the United States' standard of living. Latin Americans wanted their northern neighbors to scale down their riches--and conveniently neglected the effects of Latin American population growth. Mutual lack of comprehension and cooperation thus prevented a plan for rational development in the Western Hemisphere, and the United States began to throw up immigration barriers against the demographic pressures from Latin America, while the Latin Americans tried to force resource conservation and economic austerity on the United States by price manipulation through cartels such as OPEC.

A pessimistic Southern Hemisphere myth becomes involved here--on both sides. North Americans fear an over-populated and poverty-stricken South will necessarily prove to be hostile. Latin Americans, or Southern strategists, at least, contend that the North wants merely to hold down revolutionary pressures within countries and between the rich and poor hemispheres. This difference over which comes first, revolution or population control, dominated the Food and Population conferences and prevented agreement on all but the most technical subjects, such as the best form of contraception if one were to be used. This is a matter on which many Latin American Communists and Catholics agree, the former for reasons of revolution, the latter for reasons of morality, self-control, and concern for unborn humanity. So in Latin America birth control is often viewed as an act of selfishness and a lack of social concern rather than as an act of social responsibility. Yet the use of contraceptives is on the increase in most Latin American countries, even in the countries where they are still illegal. Still, population growth remains Latin America's most significant development problem and is increasingly recognized as such by Latin Americans.

The Interdependence Ideal

Commitment to other aspects of economic development on the part of Latin American elites also seems assured now, although both Western and Southern strategists have voiced doubts. Since the 1950s even conservative governments have come to regard development as a necessary condition for stability. Educated wage-workers are to replace the illiterate peons, industrial plants are to supersede haciendas, and the profits of a money economy are to grow out of subsistence agriculture. The idea of progress has taken hold. The debate now is not about whether but how, about internal colonization vs. institutionalization. "Colonization" is the code-word of radicals. It means that rational development will require a less elitist approach to development--higher wages, better education and health programs; if necessary, expropriation of land and nationalization of major industries. Otherwise there will be no true nation but internal colonies of oppressed castes and classes. "Institutionalization" is the code-word of conservatives. It means that national development will require discipline--more saving than consuming, less social overhead (education, health) than economic reinvestment (roads, factories), less politicking and more

law and order. No doubt the outcome will be a compromise:
something between maximum consumption and maximum investment, between maximum and minimum educational and
health benefits, between optional and intolerable class and
caste divisions. But the road toward progress has already
been taken, and the destination will come into view if population and consumption pressures can be surmounted.

Arrival could in fact be more rapid if developed
countries, most particularly the United States, were to help
fuel the journey. The Carter administration policy does in
fact promise some additional advance over the Kissinger plan,
since the prevailing notion, originated in a think tank called
the Trilateral Commission, holds that the crucial connection
is not North-South in the Western Hemisphere or East-West
across the Atlantic but among the democracies wherever they
are found. As far as Latin America is concerned, that
seems to mean not only dropping the political quarrels over
Panama and Cuba. It also seems to mean furthering human
rights and economic justice. If so, the Latin American-
United States dialogue on dependency may take on a new tone.
It might even lead to renewed Atlantic World relations badly
damaged in the Cold War era. Certainly the Atlantic World's
developed countries and Latin America have much to provide
each other--capital from the former and raw materials from
the latter, for instance. But an interdependence on the basis
of equal advantage is as much as can be expected. That
means "energy independence" on the part of the United States
is less likely than exchange agreements with the oil states
of Latin America and other continents. Likewise, the Latin
Americans' "import substitution" development strategy, which
aims at home production rather than import of as many goods
as possible, will require trade agreements which are fair to
both the South and the North.

Both South and North will have difficulty creating such
a relationship, the Latin Americans because Southern strategists think it ties them to crass consumerism, the North
Americans because the Chamber of Commerce and the AFL-
CIO see in it a surrender of profits and of jobs. Without
such an interdependent solution between developed and developing nations, the future of democracy on the world scene
does appear doubtful, however. With the envisioned cooperation of Europe, Japan, and the United States to revive the
democratic alternative in the Third World by reforming the
North-South relationship, on the other hand, much progress
seems possible. There is a danger that North Americans

will expect too much of the return to the Good Neighbor notion of willingness to profess and practice equality and justice.
Latin Americans will not be easy to convince after years of
alternating Cold War confrontations and what the Nixon administration called "benign neglect." There is also a danger
that Latin Americans will expect the benefits of a new North-
South relationship to substitute for the need for population
control and tough economic measures. Thus North Americans will be hard to convince that equal return for equal effort has become the rule. And even a new North-South
interdependence within the Western Hemisphere will be less
of the story than it would formerly have been, and rightly
so.

A continental alternative has been created because
Latin Americans are more and more important to each other
in political, economic, and cultural terms--which means that
the United States is, relatively, less important. Consider
the diplomatic consequences: for the United States pressure
for lifting the blockade against Cuba and re-writing the Canal
treaty; solidarity on oil, trade, oceans, and other development questions; movement toward a "neutral" position in
Cold War matters. There are also diplomatic consequences
within Latin America. Chief recent examples, besides
Brazil's relations with contiguous nations, have been the
Belize dispute, the "Soccer War" between El Salvador and
Honduras in 1969, and the continuing hostility among Peru,
Bolivia and Chile over the War of the Pacific territories.
The United States has been active in all these matters through
the OAS, but Latin American states have been more active
still. The Soccer War was settled by OAS arbitration. The
Belize dispute, in which the independence of former British
Honduras was challenged by both Mexico and Guatemala, has
been tamped down for the moment by similar means. A
race against the hundred-year deadline set by the War of the
Pacific treaty for providing Bolivia an outlet to the sea was
started in a like manner. The most telling event of all,
since it directly affronted both the United States and Brazil,
was the Spanish-American states' break with the tradition of
selecting a citizen of a small nation as the head of the OAS
when their votes elected Orlando Orfila, an Argentine, as a
signal of opposition to the great power ambitions of any
colossus in the hemisphere.

So despite setbacks, as when Latin American Common
Market efforts to see to it that some nations produce autos
and others TVs broke down, the down-home, continental al-

ternative to the Western Hemisphere idea has made progress.
Besides that, there are two other "regional" alternatives,
the Southern and the European. The Southern alternative has
held the attention of a generation of Latin American diplomats.
But the revolutionary school of Southern Hemisphere strategists such as Castro is not the only school. From the time
of the Bandung Conference (1955), many Latin Americans
have preferred the non-aligned Southern strategy of Tito's
Yugoslavia, Nasser's Egypt, revolutionary Algeria, and independent India. That was the policy of Quadros in Brazil
before Goulart began turning toward the more revolutionary
alternative and the military turned back Westward. Many
other Latin American states have also oscillated among these
alternatives. Since the collapse of the Brazilian-United States
entente, the Brazilians have begun to follow what might be
called a third or nationalist Southern strategy designed to
maintain Brazil's influence in Africa whatever Cuba or the
United States does. And Spanish-American states have also
pursued nationalist Southern policies to encourage trade with
Africa even while standing clear of the diplomatic tangle between Cuba and the United States in Africa. The problem,
however, is that Latin America has all too few manufactured
goods to sell in Africa or Asia and that those are mostly the
goods many Third World countries want to produce for themselves under the import-substitution scheme.

The other regional connection, that with European nations of either Cold War ideology, therefore carries more
economic, but perhaps less political, logic. Latin Americans have always had strong ties with West Europe in economic and cultural matters, albeit with colonialist overtones.
The Third Force concept of Gaullist France, despite the fact
that it failed of immediate effect, may prove viable in a
broader context. Brazil and other conservative Latin American states have gravitated toward connections with Germany,
the moderate Latin Americans toward the social democratic
nations of Europe such as Sweden. The Iberian revolutions
of the '70s have removed a barrier to cooperation with that
part of Latin Europe. And most Latin Americans have followed the North American lead--and sometimes anticipated
it--in building bridges to and arranging détente with East
Europe politically and economically. The Third Force alternative would require further shifts (to the left in Europe and
to the right in Latin America) in order to put an end to the
rancor left by imperialism, but the Gaullists' so-called
"natural alliance" among the Europeans, Chinese, and Latin
American-African-Asian bloc against the two super-powers

makes some economic and political, not to mention military, sense. North American approaches to China--and concessions to Europe and to Latin America--are in part responses to such a contingency.

The corridors of power lead to many rooms now, not just two, and Latin Americans are among those adopting a newly independent foreign policy line. Examples are many: Cubans leading the Russians (and the Chinese, for that matter) in revolutionary fervor; Latin American anti-revolutionaries defying the United States on détente and human rights issues; Latin American moderates pushing the revolutionaries and counter-revolutionaries toward an accommodation on Panama, Cuba, and trade; alliances with the Arabs in oil matters and with the Black Africans in southern Africa; and solidarity with the Palestinians and against Israel in the United Nations. This independence is not especially anti-United States. Only Cuba recognized Vietnam so long as the United States was at war there, for example. It is independence--better, genuine interdependence--instead of hostility. And that is the mark of the new multipolar world. Weaker states can pursue an independent course because weak is not that weak any longer, particularly in the case of the larger states of Latin America. The Russians cannot take the heartland for granted, nor the North Americans the rimland--especially Latin America.

The North American ideal for Latin America has become the same as for postwar Europe. Military agreements like NATO's should protect it, a Marshall Plan arrangement should develop it, and a Fulbright exchange program should share the common culture. That is indeed a step up from the client status Latin America shared with East Europe during the Cold War. But whether such a Good Partnership will meet the requirements of Latin Americans better than the other alternatives depends on the nature of world circumstances. The old problems--security, dependency, cultural respect--are just now being addressed, and not all that convincingly, by the new democratic alliance around the world. And the new problems--disarmament, post-industrial limits, the world culture of the electronic media--are already being felt. Hence the crucial question is the same for all, Latin Americans eventually included: "Can the world's problems be handled within the nation-state system at all?" In Latin America, as everywhere but above all in the developing world, this question has two parts--the relationship of the nation to its own units on the one hand, and to the units to which it belongs on the other. Many Latin Americans are questioning whether the "North American model" or the "European model" of nationhood suits their circumstances.

The importance of nationalism in Latin America is far greater than in post-World War II Europe. Development requires great efforts at drawing together castes and classes to get at the nation's resources, gather taxes, raise an army, run the trucks and buses and planes, and educate the children. The proper comparison is not with the reconstruction of post-war Europe but with the construction, or development, of the United States in the late 19th and early 20th centuries. Brazilians must develop the Amazon and Peruvians the altiplano-- and draw the Indians into the nation in the process. Argentines and Mexicans and Jamaicans must mechanize agriculture and build industries--and initiate semi-literate peasants into the educational mysteries of machine culture in the process. Latin American leaders must reach the masses through patriotic sentiment, revolutionary fervor, or charismatic ideology in order to produce the minimum of national will for development--and establish a communications system of telephones, radio, and television in the process.

And they must hurry far more than the North Americans had to. So their nationalism is centralized, socially conscious, more interested in a positive state doing something than in a negative state designed to protect individual rights. Something like the conquest of the Great Plains by the railroad-builders and the throwing-up of Chicago by the captains of industry is furiously at work in Latin America but is much more state-sponsored. It is encouraged by tariffs, subsidies, government sponsorship--all the paraphernalia of North American development. But it also includes land reform, government ownership of resources, civic action programs by the army, or whatever else might work. Latin Americans, Africans, and Asians understand each other on these points that North Americans and Europeans have largely forgotten. Development hurts, especially if you get a late start or begin at a disadvantage. And nationalism is at least a partial cure, for it mobilizes the nation to meet the crisis of development as if the crisis were a war. Development is Latin American nations' moral equivalent of war in the late 20th century. They are part of the world-wide effort to rectify the imbalance of the North and South hemispheres in terms of development. And the nationalist solutions they develop are closely watched by other nations confronted with the same problems. Neither European nor North American

nationalism seems a proper model for development to most
Latin Americans.

Yet the limitations of nationalism in an interdependent
world are evident throughout Latin America. Few countries,
Brazil being the chief exception, can afford the luxury of believing in extensive progress through national efforts alone.
Latin American nations are most often too small, too weak,
or too principled to have great-power illusions about complete independence of action. Their aim is a relative independence from the military, economic, and cultural domination
which has been their historic lot. And they have pursued international, supranational, and transnational routes to that
end.

Internationally, they have sought alliances and agreements which seemed most profitable in each circumstance.
Some have followed the Western Hemisphere alternative:
hence the OAS, the Alliance for Progress, and cultural cooperation. Some have chosen the European alternative: hence
deals with the European Common Market, continued immigration, and Third Force sentiments. Some have considered the
Eastern strategy: hence Cuba's shuttling between the Russians and the Chinese, everyone's trade and diplomatic con-
tacts from Arabia to Japan, and the encouragement to tourists
from the East. Many have attempted various Southern methods: hence the popularity of Arab Socialism, Indian neutrality, and the African market. And most have combined elements of all these with commitment to the United Nations and
other international bodies. Latin America has contributed its
fair share of the United Nations' world citizens, including
Felipe Herrera, the Chilean mastermind of the Economic
Commission on Latin America. Latin Americans have been
instrumental in the work of agencies such as the World Health
Organization and UNESCO. The World Conference on Women,
one of the most significant United Nations human rights efforts, was held in Mexico City in 1975.

In contrast, Latin America's response to "supranation-
alism" and "transnationalism" is uncertain. The supranational common markets for Latin America, Central America,
and the Andean states have yet to take hold in the manner of
the European experiment despite some successes on tariffs
and currencies. All the Americas' experiences with supranational confederations have been poor, from Bolívar's Gran
Colombia and the Central American Confederation to the
scheme designed to include the British-speaking islands after

independence, unless Brazil, Canada, and the early United States be counted. And Latin Americans have also generally stood at arm's length from transnational bodies such as corporations and, with a few notable exceptions, have played the role of poor relations in the world's artistic and scientific communities. But such isolation has nearly disappeared now. There are Latin Americans among the political and managerial groups of the "world system." There are Latin Americans in crucial places in the world scientific community. And above all there are Latin Americans in the first ranks in film, music, and literature--above all, in literature.

What the so-called "Boom" in Latin American literature contributes on the world scene is a vision of the pluralist reality--the many worlds within a world--hidden in the consciousness of contemporary humanity. That is what has made the new world-class Latin American authors known around the globe. They deal with everyone's reality and thus contribute to interdependence. But they also express the Latin American view of the new reality. They mirror the Latin American ideal of a world of more or less self-contained nations and cultures in a relationship of mutual respect. From one point of view this "fortress" approach might appear to be nothing more than the traditional stance of every developing area, including the early United States. But in Latin America this "small power mentality" has been extended beyond isolationist doubts as to the wisdom of Cuban intervention in Africa or of Brazil's great-power ambitions. For most Latin Americans do not share the ideal of sameness implicit in the Cuban--or the Russian or the North American--worldview. Nor do they share the Brazilian--or the Russian or the North American--view that great power is the most laudable national attribute. Their view of interdependence is not that of a kind of efficient world-machine with all its parts humming in unison. Instead, their view is "organic" or "familial," a vision òf each plant in the world-garden or of each of humankind's many brothers and sisters developing separately and uniquely within an overall family resemblance. Such is the ideal of interdependence expressed by writers of The Boom--and the one which appears in the ascendant in the world, even among the great powers.

The Literary Boom

Many roles have been suggested for Iberian-American

culture in the modern world. Spanish essayist Salvador de
Madariaga explained early twentieth-century cultural realities
in Englishmen, Frenchmen, Spaniards (1928). The English,
he said, were people of action, the French people of reason,
the Spanish--by which he meant all Iberians and Ibero-
Americans--people of passion. As Spain's League of Nations
delegate, Madariaga had in mind the noblest of purposes,
toleration among peoples of different "national character."
He and the other League diplomats would bring about a peaceful world through international understanding and eventual
one-worldism. The man of passion would learn not to de-
spise objective thinking and practical pursuits, the man of
thought not to neglect depth of emotion and pragmatism, the
man of action not to confine himself to rat-race materialism,
and so on. Humans would become whole; peoples would draw
together; the "parliament of mankind" would take root; the
world would know peace, progress, and democracy. The
"Spanish" world would teach its fellows and learn from them.
Then Madariaga's world-to-be held together by humane purpose and industrial progress came apart, and by 1939 he
was in exile bemoaning the collapse of the Spanish Republic
and the League of Nations. Not only had the dream of cultural unity evaporated in the heat of ideology and nationalism.
World War II also made Madariaga's parable on disarmament,
in which the eagle, lion, and bear debate whether to give up
talons, fangs, or hugs first, seem like the utopian folly of
a small-power democrat. Great-power politics had returned.

After the war an Americanized version of this notion
of one-world culture gained popularity because Ibero-America,
especially Mexico, was thought to be able to merge the "rationalism" of the West and the "mysticism" of the East.
Mexican essayists--Education Minister José Vasconcelos
mainly, but in another way Alfonso Reyes and others--had
been suggesting since the Revolution that Ibero-America
could perform a special mediating role in the world, and the
arrival of Asian, Mid-Eastern and African peoples on the
world scene revived the idea just as Vasconcelos himself
was becoming disenchanted with it and returning to his original nationalism. Vasconcelos' ideal of La Raza Cosmica
(world people) moved beyond Madariaga's world cooperation
toward world unity. Biologically, Latin America was amal-
gamating all the races. Psychologically, what began with
Pagan-Muslim-Christian or African-Asian-European mixing
in southern Iberia was being continued in the cultural inter-
actions of Negroes, Indians, and Europeans in Ibero-America.
Politically, then, these "cosmic" Americans were ideally

suited to bridge the differences within and among nations, by setting an example and by mediating international disputes. Eastern magic and Western materialism, Southern love of life and Northern discipline could and would be reconciled in a world-wide melting pot of peoples. A humane materialism would take root, and one cosmic cultural identity would emerge.

Events have gone the other way, of course, and to their credit Vasconcelos and other Latin American cultural leaders were among the first to see that what was needed in the contemporary world was not one homogenized identity but an ability to cope with multiple identities. Such has been the main contribution of the recent Boom in Latin American literature on the world scene. The implicit message of this new generation of Latin Americans is that richness is the major need in the contemporary world. Variety is positive, sameness negative in an increasingly predictable world in which human life is reduced to plastic possessions and routine actions. Every human being and every culture should be multi-dimensional if Kafka-like indifference is to be avoided. "Deadness" is upon us in the form of technology, management, and mass media. But whereas the Europeans usually described the horrors of the emerging "brave new world," the Latin Americans usually set out to hint at the alternatives to such a world. European literary figures, the avant-garde French such as Sartre, Beauvoir, Camus, and Robbe-Grillet included, were dealing with grown-together identities that were coming apart. But the "new" Spanish American novelists who began to emerge during and after World War II--Onetti in Uruguay, Cortázar in Argentina, Donoso in Chile, Vargas Llosa in Peru, García Márquez in Colombia, Rulfo and Fuentes in Mexico, Carpentier in Cuba-- lived in thrown-together cultures striving toward identity. And in a globe thrown together by technology and politics, the Latin Americans' multi-layered view of personality hit home.

Carlos Fuentes has pursued one intriguing passage into this psychic Amazon, and has seen himself reflected in the eyes of others in the labyrinth. Fuentes' experiences have included a boyhood in provincial Mexico, adolescence in Mexico City and various world capitals served by his diplomat-father, and adulthood as a literary giant and diplomat in his own right. Hence he has become all too familiar with the mixed identity of world-personalities. But he believes in a special kind of "permanent revolution"--not

Trotsky's politics, but psychic progress--whereby humanity
grows into its birthright of mutual respect. Somehow humans
hang on to what is good and beautiful in their past while
progressing or developing, as if the Wheel of Fate were rolling uphill of its own momentum. In Good Consciences Fuentes
described how his provincial patria chica lived on in the
grown-up Mexican. In Where the Air Is Clear the hero-heir
of Aztecs, Ixa Cienfuegos, carried on the Indian "conscience"
in modernized Mexico. In Terra Nostra the kings and saints
of Iberia, the conquerors and conquered of Latin America,
and their latest reincarnations elbowed each other for room
in present consciousness. In The Death of Artemio Cruz
revolution pushed its way through the crust of habit in 1810
(Hidalgo and Morelos), 1859 (Juárez), 1910 (Villa and Zapata),
and 1959 (Castro). Age becomes youth becomes age, father
becomes son becomes father, false becomes true becomes
false--in permanent revolution.

Change of Skin is Fuentes' masterpiece on this subject.
Four friends driving from Mexico City to an Easter Vacation
in Vera Cruz become stranded at the Cholula Pyramid, exactly where Cortez and his Indian concubine Malinche mated
and produced "Mexico." The four are quickly dragged into
their "pasts" in this atmosphere. Javier, the Mexican pro-
fessor and diplomat, must face his sterility as an author
and as the husband of Catherine, his Jewish wife from New
York. Catherine must face her flight from Jewishness.
Isabel, Javier's student, must face her lust for anything different, including her German companion Franz and the Beat-
nik leader they encounter. Franz must face the crimes his
architectural creations housed in Nazi times, the child he
abandoned to save his own skin, the woman he disowned because she was Jewish, and his own death, which occurs as
midnight becomes Easter inside the pyramid. In one sense,
this is all "madness" related by Freddy Lambert, an asylum
inmate. In another, it is as deeply true as the Easter
"myth," because the vacationers have been reborn by having
insight forced on them. It is doubtful that on the return to
Mexico City the survivors will turn past Vietnam news on
the car radio to get rock music, as they had coming out.
Past and future have shattered their comfortable present,
exactly what happens when cultures clash in the global community. The names of kings and saints are not accidental,
of course, nor the appearance of Cortez' Christ as Malinche's
Quetzalcoatl. The snake-bird Quetzalcoatl has changed his
skin, Christ has been reborn--as have whole-world people
suffering both past and future shock.

"Life has its limits, but insight does not" is the meaning of the literature of The Boom. Fuentes' symbolic pyramids rise, one on top of the other, every fifty-two years because the Indians believed a new era opens regularly-- because the world, too, changes its skin. But most of the Boom writers have discovered an even more remarkable passage into the unknown continent of the modern consciousness, "magic realism." To them Fuentes seems too political, too historical, too literal, too confined, too un-magical, almost scientific. Their sympathies lie with Gabriel García Márquez and his One Hundred Years of Solitude, in which the imaginary village Macondo and its leading family, the Buendías, re-discover the super-natural and sub-natural. Macondo and the Buendías may be isolated from rational human reference-points, so that normal history and rational thought, even in the labyrinthine forms of Borges or Fuentes, are inconsequential. There is "solitude," aloneness, isolation in the face of this magic, off-the-beaten-track townlet of twenty adobe houses in the Colombian outback. Yet in another sense Macondo and the Buendías inhabit a macrocosm more real, more populated than any city wired to the latest global information sources. Not only is nature back--the cloying, raucous, tropical jungle vortex. The mythic-magic life of the mind submerged by modern rationalism is back, too. Divine madness strikes, and its beneficiary is tied to the village tree as a half-crucified exemplar. The Buendía generations circle around, lost, in their magic backwater. Each new patriarch carries the same name, Colonel Buendía, and each carries the seed of the flaw--the pig's-tail stigma that appears on the "last" heir.

In place of science, García Márquez suggests imagination; for modern solitude, magic. The stripped-down human of science again becomes the fleshed-out human of an expanded consciousness. Hence the popularity and the importance of Fuentes, García Márquez and the other Boom novelists in a managed world starved for enlivening, quasi-religious myths. As for the poets, they have had a lesser role. The best of the older generation--Neruda, Paz, and, in Brazil, João del Melo Neto--have continued to reach toward the ancient verities buried in the "deep structures" of mind and world. Paz has actually gone a step further and tried to explain the literary movement derived from French anthropologist Claude Lévi-Strauss' idea of "structuralism." In a series of books of criticism--The Labyrinth of Solitude, Claude Lévi-Strauss, The Bow and the Lyre--Paz has attempted to explain how the word-smiths might utilize the

myths of primitive peoples to reinvigorate the dream of
reason and its monsters: "Every moribund or sterile society
attempts to save itself by creating a redemption myth which
is also a fertility myth, a creation myth. Solitude and sin
are resolved in communion and fertility. The society we
live in today has also created its myth. The sterility of the
bourgeois world will end in suicide or a new form of creative
participation.... Modern man likes to pretend that his thinking is wide-awake. But this wide-awake thinking has led us
into the mazes of a nightmare in which the torture chambers
are endlessly repeated in the mirrors of reason. When we
emerge, perhaps we will realize that we have been dreaming
with our eyes open, and that the dreams of reason are intolerable. And then, perhaps, we will begin to dream with our
eyes closed." De-mythologize, then re-mythologize--here is
the same message as in Fuentos and García Márquez.

At least one new type of poetry has tried to re-
visualize the receding verities of the contemporary mind.
Nicanor Parra of Chile called it anti-poetry (anti-poesía) because it forced one to be conscious of the loss of "poetry"
in life by going to the opposite extreme of using un-poetic
words, images, moods, and subjects. As water is most
enticing when one is thirsty, so poetry is more desperately
needed as one is deprived of it and love is dearer the more
it is threatened by death. Nasty pigeons in the plaza become angels, then, or death puts on a modern mask and in-
vades our bedrooms as "Spots on a Wall." Human imagination turns the spots into "things vegetal" or "mythical animals" such as "griffons, salamanders, dragons." Hence "in
the wall's cinematography/Soul discerns what body can't
see." The mundane spots are transformed by creative forces
into "men on their knees/Mothers clutching babies/Equestrian
monuments/Hosts lifted by celebrants." Life intrudes as
"genitals joined." And so does death: "But the most mysterious are those/Like atomic explosions." Poetry--epic
emotion--slips through the seemingly sterile, anti-poetic ex-
terior of modern reality.

In Brazil, a group of young poets took yet another
step and suggested in poesía praxis (action poetry) that the
modern invasion of identity has left room for the self only in
a mystifying Paz-like funhouse-turned-torture-chamber. Here,
for example, is Mario Chamie's "TV":

> the glass' transparency/the blind eye's consciousness
> the consciousness in the window/the transparency of
> glass

the people blind from the square/the black eye of the
mass
the square of the blind eye/the mass of the black eye

the glass' transparency
the blind consciousness
the mass before the window
the mass = globe of glass

the square of the black eye
the people = bat-blind eye

not seeing the people selling
black room = its store

not seeing/the selling in the eye of the people
you seeing/the black room of sleeping

Such envisionings of the need for imaginative elbow room as
the world falls in on moderns are intriguing but probably not
so forceful as those of The Boom's novelists.

The influence of The Boom on world culture cannot be
measured any better than, for instance, the impact of North
American jazz. Yet it is clear that the outlook of The Boom
has much in common with the directors of New Cinema--the
Italian New Realists, the French New Wave, and their common ancestor, Buñuel--and that world culture, to the extent
it exists, has been affected more by film than literature because film is more easily "translated" via a few subtitles.
Direct influences abound: Buñuel and Fuentes are friends
and have drawn on each other's work; Antonioni made Blow-Up
from a Cortázar story; Latin American film-makers like
Torre-Nilsson, Santos, and many others form a bridge between Boom writers and European directors. Among indirect
influences, the common origin of The Boom and the new cinema in the literature of alienation (Kafka, Sartre, and, more
recently, Goytisolo in Spain) and the psychology of the un-
conscious (Freud, then Jung, then Lévi-Strauss) is the most
striking.

The methodology of complex "narrative" borrowed
from Joyce, Proust, and Dos Passos has also been refined
by the Latin American novelists in interaction with the film-
makers. In Cortázar's famous Hopscotch, for example, the
book can be read straight through (straight narrative) or according to a special "map" that leaves the reader jumping

back and forth between two pages and the book lacking an "ending" (circular narrative). In other words, the reader puts the "meaning" in, just as he does in an overloaded world of progress (linear time), replays (circular time), memories and hopes piled on present perceptions (layered time), or life-altering moments (stopped or frozen time). As in Blow-Up, the world is what we make of it, a point easily understood in any part of the modern world from Japan to Buenos Aires. Just as in films, "double exposure" is created in The Boom's novels by telling the story over and over from several characters' point of view (see the Japanese film Rashomon) or by writing two separate stories on odd and even lines (see the films of Fellini) or by any of a number of other methods. But the point is the same, namely, to have the film-goer or the reader sense the inrush of images and the outruoh of meaning in a media-rich world.

Spanish American culture is generally not involved in close encounters with other cultures of the Southern Hemisphere in the way the West Europeans have interacted with Asia, the Mideast, and Subsaharan Africa or the North Americans with Latin America. Political affinities, yes; cultural affinities, no--except, of course, in Brazil, where Portuguese African literature influences popular publications and sometimes finds its way onto television. Crazy currents exist. The Boom does not, for example, influence most Communist countries despite its leftist sympathies, because, like other "bourgeois literature," such works are banned by Communist censors in favor of "socialist realism." On the other hand, Brazil has not had much of The Boom because its literature is not in a "world language," because its cultural order does not sanction alienation or "pessimism," and because its citizens and writers do not seem to feel so much of the modern "identity crisis" as yet. The Boom nevertheless sympathizes with the underdog, which appears at first glance to mean the Indian or the Black as before, but on closer inspection turns out to be Camus' stranger or Dostoyevsky's underground man. Despite the political differences, then, The Boom's novelists are much like Solzhenitsyn in their yearning for a meaning beyond materialism. Hence their exotics and savages are in the Northern Hemisphere, whereas the traditional underdogs remain whole. That is what makes Fuentes and García Márquez intriguing and important in the post-modern sense.

The Western Hemisphere connections of the writers of The Boom therefore have a special significance. The minority cultures of the United States--the Blacks and the Spanish speakers--appear in these novels as if they were extensions of the general human condition. They are as healthy as their counterparts in the Caribbean or the Andes in the face of the whittled-down samenesses of melting-pot "rationalism." There is more here than the obvious influence of United States literary giants--Dos Passos, Steinbeck, Hemingway, Faulkner, Mailer--who tackled the problem of identity in a pluralist democracy. Indeed, a certain affinity has always existed between Black writers in the United States and Latin America, since James Weldon Johnson was a consul in Venezuela and Nicaragua, Langston Hughes taught in Mexico, and the Harlem Renaissance of the thirties and forties was based on a Black pride in Caribbean as well as African culture. Arna Bontemps and Countee Cullen were obviously fusing Black experiences everywhere in the Americas, and W.E.B. DuBois' famous epigram, "The problem of the twentieth century is the problem of the color line," seemed to apply south of the Rio Grande and the Florida Strait as well.

But after World War II there emerged another, more important, connection: W.E.B. DuBois, Richard Wright, Ralph Ellison, and James Baldwin were part of the Paris intellectual groups to which writers of The Boom also belonged. Hence it was no accident that James Baldwin's discovery that the uptown New York ghetto dubbed Harlem was not a hovel but a home--that downtown 5th Avenue and Wall Street constituted the real ghetto--came after he had lived among these Paris intellectuals. Nor was it surprising that W.E.B. DuBois discovered in the "African revolution" of Sékou Touré and the négritude of Leopold Senghor and Aimé Césaire a better way of describing his "soul" than he had found at the NAACP in the fifty years he had worked there. Black "soul" was just another way of putting the point Fuentes was making with his Indians, or García Márquez with his "simpletons" in Macondo. "Soul"--depth of emotion--was back.

By way of comparison, the literature of the Spanish-speaking minorities in the United States, whose writers did not travel in Parisian literary circles, was less articulate about the barrio as a true "home." Like Richard Wright's early Native Son, most hispano works were struggling against Anglo culture rather than for their own. But there was a clear progression from Villarreal's nearly resigned Pocho (1959) to the murals, the Casa Aztlán, and the Teatro Campesino in the barrios of the American Southwest, and from early Nuyorican escapism to René Marqués' Truncated Suns and the works of José Luis González in the Puerto Rican sections of East Coast cities. There may never be a Mexican-American or Puerto Rican-American culture of the depth of Afro-American culture, in fact, because of the proximity and strength of the Mexican and Puerto Rican cultures themselves. But the feeling that something like "soul" or salsa ("sauce," the essence of Spanish-Caribbean music) is necessary to leaven an inert rationalism is the same as that of The Boom--and has influenced and been influenced by it.

The outlook of The Boom has also found its way, at least partially, into general North American culture. The Blacks and the Spanish speakers have had an influence, though probably more through music and the dance than through literature. A still larger influence has come from a cultural generation enamored of the "Latin mentality"--from the Beatniks of Kerouac's On the Road, the crazies of Kesey's cuckoo's nest, and Carlos Castañeda's supposed holy man (brujo), Don Juan. The lure of Mexico as a source of emancipation and insight has easily equaled that of Zen among the last generation in the United States. And after stripping away the excesses (since Latin Americans would consider them crude "gringoisms"), one finds a genuine seed of re-affirmation, a wraparound instead of a throwaway culture, community rather than personality, "us" instead of "I"--the new creation myth predicted by Paz. For literary circles in the United States, another exile living in Mexico, Thomas Pynchon, has meanwhile restated the Spanish-French-Italian truths of The Boom with German and North American accents in such novels as Gravity's Rainbow. His point? The human mind must be emancipated from external images so as to be able to re-fill its world with its own, more meaningful, imaginings--exactly The Boom's point.

The Boom is now part of a world-wide attempt to define the new cultural identity created by a globe grown small and noisy, and the attempt was started thanks in large part to the Latin Americans themselves. Whether their insights came because they were on the sidelines during the great events of the twentieth century or whether they are engaging in a kind of underdog parochialism hostile to modern scientism is less important than the fact that the wonders of modernism needed to be questioned. In social terms, many Latin Americans now have a worldview, a very up-to-date worldview, to go with their advances in control over their environment and technology on the one hand and their ever-more-viable institutions on the other. In psychological terms, the rationalist Sancho and the idealist Quixote have reached a modus vivendi that makes it possible to be modern and lively. Or in the poetic terms Latin Americans would prefer, the trees of the Latin American vortex have become well-rooted, though some are in poor and others in choice places, so that a few are likely to become giant mahoganies, others exquisite umbrella pines, others tough and tangled mangroves and cypresses. Latin Americans are increasingly convinced that they have discovered the deep structures and hidden rhythms of their existence--and the world's--and have moved beyond youthful rebellion to strong adulthood. Latin America has come of age but still retains its youthful verve and hope.

SOME SOURCES

Since this book is intended for North American readers, references are confined to items written in or translated
into English, but there are of course Spanish, Portuguese,
or French works either by or about almost every figure
mentioned in the text. The Handbook of Latin American
Studies will list most of the materials in all languages. Beyond that, textbooks in the history, geography, economics,
and culture of Latin America provide beginning bibliographies,
although such lists usually neglect non-Romance languages
other than English. Helen Miller Bailey and Abraham Na-
satir's text Latin America: The Development of Its Civilization (Prentice-Hall, 1960) has handy but partly outdated sections listing standard reference works, map collections, pe-
riodicals, and official publications available in English. The
American Historical Association has two old but useful pamphlets on the bibliography of Latin American history, and
the scholarly journals Hispanic American Historical Review,
Journal of Inter-American Studies, Caribbean Studies, Luso-
Brazilian Review, and Foreign Affairs list and review new
items. The Organization of American States' Inter-American
Review of Bibliography is a major source for new publications.

In conceptual framework the study of the region from
the Rio Grande to Cape Horn ranges from colonialism to
nationalism, conservatism to radicalism, Latin to anti-Latin.
Most texts in English follow an outline similar to that of
Hubert Herring's A History of Latin America (rev. ed.;
Knopf, 1961) or John Fagg's Latin America (3rd ed.; Macmillan, 1977), namely, a treatment of the "Latin" areas in
terms of their Indian, colonial, revolutionary, and national
development. The emphasis is political. The role of the
United States is played up. And the contemporary events of
the non-Iberian areas are neglected. Donald Dozer's Latin
America (McGraw-Hill, 1962) is more thematic than geo-

271

graphic but still political. Víctor Alba's The Latin Americans (Praeger, 1969) asks socioeconomic questions, and Ronald Hilton's book of the same name (Lippincott, 1973) draws cultural conclusions--for the Latins. Alfred Thomas' Latin America (Macmillan, 1956) is an interesting attempt at identifying Atlantic, Pacific, and Caribbean orientations within the general Latin milieu. Indian, Black, Hispanic, north European, and North American interpretations are noted in various places below. Sílvio Zavala's edited History of the New World (Pan American Union, 1961) tries to relate them all. Richard N. Adams and Dwight B. Heath's Contemporary Cultures and Societies of Latin America (rev. ed.; Random House, 1973) surveys the cultural horizon.

THE HISTORY

THEN TO NOW:

The "Life World Library" series has volumes on Brazil (1967), The River Plate Republics (1968), The Andean Republics (1965), Colombia, Venezuela, and the Guianas (1965), Mexico (1966), Central America (1964), and The West Indies (1963), in which photographs add a dimension to the reliable textual material on history and culture. An Encyclopedia of Latin American History (Bobbs-Merrill, 1968) is available, and so is a more general Encyclopedia of Latin America (McGraw-Hill, 1974). But a broad range of interpretive accounts is difficult to assemble in English. Most general works adopt either the sympathetic stance of E. Bradford Burns' Latin America (2nd ed.; Prentice-Hall, 1977) or the Marxist indignation of William Z. Foster's Outline Political History of the Americas (International Publishers, 1957). Among the most gripping narratives is The Red, White, and Black Continent (Engl. trans.; Doubleday, 1966) by the German Herbert Wendt.

Recently the range of interpretations in English has broadened somewhat. In the last generation John Gunther has twice captured the mood in the Americas--once at the height of the Good Neighbor Policy in Inside Latin America (Harper, 1941) and once during the Alliance for Progress crusade in Inside South America (Harper, 1967). Gunther's stance is reformist in the Franklin Roosevelt-John Kennedy sense, which means that he likes Muñoz and Frei but dislikes both Batista and Castro. John Gerassi's The Great

Fear in Latin America (Collier, 1965) sees the situation from a Socialist perspective, and Gary MacEoin's Revolution Next Door (Holt, 1971) presents a radical Catholic viewpoint. Frederick B. Pike's Hispanismo, 1898-1936 (Notre Dame, 1971) offers some insight into moderate and conservative Catholic interpretations. For some fragmentary Latin American views of the history of the Americas, see German Arciniegas, ed., The Green Continent (Knopf, 1944) and Ramón Ruiz, ed., Interpreting Latin American History (Holt, 1970).

Reliable materials on the non-Iberian cultures of Latin America are usually hardest to find because of the brief or non-existent national experience, the deep divisions between colonial and nationalist interpretations, and the polyglot nature of Latin American societies. Hence one finds David A. G. Waddell's The West Indies and the Guianas (Prentice-Hall, 1967) strongly biased in favor of the Commonwealth connection and the Caribbean federation scheme, though this and its companion volumes in the "Modern Nations in Historical Perspective" series constitute the best source for basic information and bibliography on the Caribbean nations. In addition, one must search for many of the alternative interpretations of events in the newspapers and news magazines of the independent nations, of Britain, or of North America--or, better yet, in the writings of the political figures involved. The situation is most difficult for the French- and Dutch-speaking areas, since translations are usually not available. It is notable, for example, that the most wide-ranging coverage in English of the Caribbean Black Power movement of the late 1960s and early 1970s seems to have been in Time and The New York Times--because of the interest in Black Power issues in North America. The other major English-language sources were The Times (London), The Guardian, and The Economist.

Keeping up to date using only English is nevertheless possible because of the newspaper Times of the Americas, despite the fact that it reflects the concerns of its North American business and governmental readership. The monthly Current History publishes one issue per year on Latin America, includes the latest bibliography in English, and furnishes a monthly calendar of events which includes Latin America. North American newspapers with a national circulation or Spanish-speaking interests--The New York Times, The Christian Science Monitor, The Washington Post, The Los Angeles Times, The Miami Herald, etc.--carry articles almost daily. The weekly news magazines Time, Newsweek, and U. S. News and World Report run specials on important events.

But it is necessary to correct for the North American biases of these sources in some way, and for readers of English that probably means consulting Latin America (London) and the NACLA Report of the North American Committee on Latin America because both present writers with Leftist connections in Latin America. Publications of the various Catholic religious orders (e. g. , Orbis Books by the Maryknoll Fathers) or of Protestant missionary groups (e. g. , the Summer Institute of Linguistics) are often quite useful, too. Any of the yearly almanacs will give the bare essentials of the latest demographic, political, and economic data. Who's Who in Latin America (3rd ed. ; Blaine Ethridge Books, 1971) is a little behind the times but is a ready source on important Latin Americans, except, of course, that not all countries treated in this book are covered. The Americas, outlet of the Pan American Union, is far and away the most indispensable English-language source for new information on cultural subjects.

BEFORE INDEPENDENCE:

The history of Indian America is being re-thought as its beginnings are made clearer by the latest archaeological findings, but the general outline presented in Kenneth Macgowan and Joseph Hester, Jr. 's Early Man in the New World (Anchor, 1962) remains true. National Geographic has made available in popular form the newer interpretations of life in the heyday of The Incredible Incas (1973) and The Mysterious Maya (1977). Hans Dietrich Disselhoff's Daily Life in Ancient Peru (Engl. trans. ; McGraw-Hill, 1967) and Alfred Métraux' The History of the Incas (Pantheon, 1969) give a lively but perhaps somewhat idealized view of the Incas which should be compensated for by referring to the Handbook of South American Indians. Interesting contrasts appear in Garcilaso de la Vega's Royal Commentaries of the Inca in the 16th century on the one hand, and the Indianist works by Alegría, Arguedas, and Icaza in the 20th century on the other. Victor von Hagen's Realm of the Incas (Mentor, 1957) and World of the Maya (Mentor, 1960) are adequate short accounts, though one should also consult Philip A. Means' Ancient Civilizations of the Andes (Reprint; Gordian, 1964) and Sylvanus Morley's The Ancient Maya (Stanford University, 1956). For the Aztecs, see R. C. Padden's The Hummingbird and the Hawk (Ohio State University, 1967), George C. Vaillant's The Aztecs of Mexico (Pelican, 1950), or Alfonso Caso's The Aztecs, People of the Sun (University of Oklahoma, 1958). The Handbook of Middle American Indians covers the other Indian peoples of the Caribbean area. The immediate post-Conquest effects on the Indians are clear in The Encomienda in New Spain (University of California, 1950) by Lesley Byrd Simpson, and the longer-range effects in Charles Gibson's The Aztecs Under Spanish Rule (Stanford University, 1964).

The Conquest is described in colonial histories such as Salvador de Madariaga's The Rise of the Spanish American Empire (Free Press, 1947), Charles R. Boxer's Four Centuries of Portuguese Expansion (University of California, 1969), the reprint of Herbert I. Priestley's 1938-39 France Overseas (Octagon, 1966), and Alfred L. Burt's The Evolution of the British Empire and Commonwealth from the American Revolution (Heath, 1956). More exciting are William H. Prescott's classics The Conquest of Mexico and The Conquest of Peru (many editions). Yet more thrilling are the opposing stories of the conquistadores in first-hand accounts like Bernal Díaz del Castillo's True History of the Conquest of New Spain (many editions) and of the Aztec defenders in Miguel Leon-Portilla, ed. , The Broken Spears (Engl. trans. ; Beacon, 1962). Various aspects of the Iberian empires are treated in C. H. Haring's The Spanish Empire (Harcourt, Brace, Jovanovich, 1963) and Empire in Brazil (Norton, 1968), Charles Gibson's Spain in America (Harper, 1966), J. H. Parry's The Spanish Seaborne Empire (Knopf, 1966), William L. Schurz' The Manila Galleon (E. P. Dutton, 1939), and Caio Prado, Jr.'s The Colonial Background of Modern Brazil (Engl. trans. ; University of California, 1967). The most complete one-volume treatment is Bailey W. Diffie's Latin American Civilization: The Colonial Period (Reprint; Octagon, 1967). Some effects of the Indians on the Iberians have been considered in Lewis Hanke's Bartolomé de las Casas (University of Pennsylvania, 1952), Aristotle and the American Indians (Hollis and Carter, 1959), and The Spanish Struggle for Justice in the Conquest of America (University of Pennsylvania, 1949). Some unexpected economic consequences of the Conquest are considered in Earl Hamilton's American Treasure and the Price Revolution in Spain (Reprint; Octagon, 1965).

Reform and independence issues in Ibero-America are covered in Salvador de Madariaga's The Fall of the Spanish

American Empire (Reprint; Collier Books, 1963), William S. Robertson's The Rise of the Spanish-American Republics as Told in the Lives of Their Liberators (Appleton, 1918), and Bertitia Harding's Amazon Throne (Bobbs-Merrill, 1941), not to mention the many biographies of Miranda, Bolívar, San Martín, O'Higgins, Brazil's two Pedros, and others. The diplomatic and military struggles which made Latin American independence possible have been studied in Charles K. Webster's Britain and the Independence of Latin America (2 vols.; Oxford University, 1938), William W. Kaufman's British Policy and the Independence of Latin America (Reprint; Archon, 1967), W. S. Robertson's France and Latin American Independence (Reprint; Octagon, 1967), and Arthur P. Whitaker's The United States and the Independence of Latin America (Johns Hopkins, 1941). The re-intervention of the Spanish in Peru in 1863-66 is criticized in W. C. Davis, The Last Conquistadores (University of Georgia, 1950), and the Hapsburg adventure in Mexico is praised in Egon Caesar Corti, Maximilian and Charlotte of Mexico (2 vols.; Knopf, 1928). For North American views of the rise of United States power in Latin America see Dexter Perkins' The Monroe Doctrine (3 vols.; Johns Hopkins, 1927, 1933, 1937) and Samuel Flagg Bemis, The Latin American Policy of the United States (Harcourt, Brace & Co., 1943). Interpretations of the crucial results of the Spanish-American War are provided in T. P. Greene, ed., American Imperialism in 1898 (Heath, 1955). Needless to say, all these colonialist views are contradicted by Latin American nationalists of the modern period.

MODERN SOUTH AMERICA:

Brazil's history comes alive in E. Bradford Burns' A History of Brazil (Columbia University, 1970), and the bibliography is excellent. Roy Nash's The Conquest of Brazil (Harcourt, 1926) pictures the Brazilian frontier of the early twentieth century. Great detail on the contemporary period can be found in Thomas E. Skidmore's Politics in Brazil, 1930-64 (Oxford University, 1967), Irving L. Horowitz's Revolution in Brazil (Dutton, 1964), and Ronald M. Schneider's The Political System of Brazil, 1964-70 (Columbia University, 1971). The various political forces are analyzed in Burns' Nationalism in Brazil (Praeger, 1968), Emanuel J. DeKadt's Catholic Radicals in Brazil (Oxford University, 1970), and in a special issue of Studies on the Left (Fall, 1964). Rollie Poppino's Brazil: The Land and People (2nd ed.; Oxford University, 1973) is the most complete short

account in scope of time, subject matter, and references.
In fact, this "Latin American Histories Series" provides the
most useful scholarly introduction to Latin America's nations
and when complete, will include companions on Argentina,
Mexico, Bolivia, the Caribbean, Central America, Chile,
Colombia, Peru, Uruguay, and Venezuela. Attempts at pen-
etrating the Brazilian mind include Gilberto Freyre's New
World in the Tropics (Knopf, 1960) and José Honório Rodri-
gues' The Brazilians (University of Texas, 1967). For years
every annual Latin American issue of Current History has
printed an article on Brazil.

James Scobie's Argentina: A City and a Nation (2nd
ed.; Oxford University, 1971) describes the political and
social schizophrenia, but in sympathetic terms. George
Pendle's Uruguay (3rd ed.; Royal Institute of International
Affairs, 1963) provides a British perspective, a remarkable
bibliography, and solid, readable, exciting history up to the
onset of the time of troubles. His Argentina (Royal Institute
of International Affairs, 1955) and Paraguay (3rd, ed.; Oxford University, 1967) complete the picture of the river
republics and need only be supplemented with works reflecting
Latin American viewpoints and others providing more up-to-
date information. José Luis Romero's A History of Argentine Political Thought (Stanford, 1963) reflects the views of
Spanish South America's long-leading state, and such articles
as David C. Jordan's "Argentina's Military Government" in
Current History (February, 1977) bring the more recent
political decline into focus. Madeline Nichols' The Gaucho
(Duke, 1942) tracks the legend which animates Argentines.

The "Pacific republics" have recently come to receive
almost as much attention in English as the "Atlantic republics"
because of the decline of the Europe-centered international
system. Kalman Silvert's Chile (Holt, 1965), Ernst Hal-
perin's Nationalism and Communism in Chile (Massachusetts
Institute of Technology, 1965), and Federico Gil's The Political System of Chile (Houghton Mifflin, 1966) bring the story
outlined in Luis Galdames' A History of Chile (Engl. trans.;
University of North Carolina, 1941) and G. J. Butland's
Chile (3rd ed.; Royal Institute of International Affairs, 1956)
up to the times of Frei and Allende. John Reese Stevenson,
The Chilean Popular Front (Oxford University, 1942) studies
the precursors of today's radicals. Harold Osborne's Bolivia
(3rd ed.; Oxford University, 1964), George Blanksten's
Ecuador (University of California, 1951), and Frederick Pike's
The Modern History of Peru (Praeger, 1967) are good

starting-points for the history of the Indian states. Harry
Kantor describes the importance of the APRA in The Ideology
and Program of the Peruvian Aprista Movement (Octagon,
1966), and David A. Robinson's Peru in Four Dimensions
(American Studies Press, 1964) stands alone among attempts
to relate geography, demography, economy, and government
in the Andes. Dwight Heath's Land Reform and Social Revolution in Bolivia (Praeger, 1969) and E. V. K. Fitzgerald's
The State and Economic Development (Cambridge University,
1976) provide a comparison of Bolivian and Peruvian approaches. Recent NACLA Report and Current History articles
make for interesting comparisons of Allende's and Pinochet's
Chile.

VENEZUELA, COLOMBIA, THE GUIANAS:

The "Caribbean republics" of South America are
joined with the other nations influenced by the Mediterranean
of the Americas in German Arciniegas' The Caribbean, Sea
of the New World (Knopf, 1946). Harry Bernstein's Venezuela and Colombia (Prentice-Hall, 1964) offers information
for a meaningful comparison of the lands of the Spanish
Main. Introductory histories of Venezuela are Guillermo
Morón, A History of Venezuela (Engl. trans.; Roy, 1964)
and Edwin Lieuwin, Venezuela (Oxford University, 1961).
Lieuwin has also published Petroleum in Venezuela (University of California, 1954) on the vital economic subject, and
John Martz' Acción Democrática (Princeton University, 1966)
and Robert Alexander's The Venezuelan Democratic Revolution
(Rutgers University, 1964) chronicle the emergence of democ-
racy. Interesting local colors show through in Robert Gil-
more's Caudillism and Militarism in Venezuela (Ohio University, 1964) and in T. R. Ybarra's autobiographical Young
Man of Caracas (Washburn, 1941). See also Lloyd Rodwin,
et al., Planning Urban Growth and Regional Development
(Massachusetts Institute of Technology, 1969), where Venezuela's Guayana development scheme is described. Stephen
Dodge delineates "Venezuela's Bright Future" in Current
History (February, 1976), and Venezuela Up-to-Date provides
monthly coverage.

John Martz' Colombia (University of North Carolina,
1962) leads a too-short list of histories of Colombia. T.
Lynn Smith's Colombia (University of Florida, 1967) does,
however, provide a more-than-adequate analysis of "social
structure and the process of development," and Orlando

Fals-Borda's Peasant Society in the Colombian Andes (University of Florida, 1955) details the traditional society in process of change. Vernon L. Fluharty's Dance of the Millions (University of Pittsburgh, 1957) analyzes the role of the military in change since the 1930s, and Malcolm Deas explains the balancing-act electoral process in "Colombian Aprils," Current History (February, 1973). First-person accounts and descriptions of local realities are hard to come by in English, although Robert C. West's The Pacific Lowlands of Colombia (Louisiana State University, 1957) captures the feel of a Black area of the mainland of South America and Kathleen Romoli's popular Colombia, Gateway to South America (Doubleday, 1941) reveals an eye for what was unusual in an earlier period.

Much of the best information on the Guianas is to be found in general histories of the Caribbean such as Sir Harold Mitchell's Europe in the Caribbean (Cooper Square, 1963). There are, however, a few specific works worth mentioning, e. g. , Raymond T. Smith, British Guiana (Oxford University, 1962) and Jan H. Adhin, Development Planning in Surinam in Historical Perspective (Stenfert Kroese, 1961). In addition, Cheddi Jagan's Forbidden Freedom (International Publishers, 1954) gives at least one side of the political quarrels in Guyana. Melville and Francis Herskovits' Rebel Destiny (McGraw-Hill, 1934) describes a Black culture in Surinam.

MEXICO AND CENTRAL AMERICA:

Among the most striking single-volume treatments of Mexico in English are Lesley Byrd Simpson's Many Mexicos (G. P. Putnam's Sons, 1941), Henry Bamford Parkes' A History of Mexico (Houghton Mifflin, 1938), and Ernest Gruening's Mexico and Its Heritage (The Century Co. , 1928), although José Vasconcelos' Breve historia de Mexico (Ediciones Cultura Hispanica, 1952) outdoes them all. Charles C. Cumberland, ed. , The Meaning of the Mexican Revolution (Heath, 1967) presents varying points of view on the events and a good bibliography. Biographies of Juárez, Díaz, Madero, Zapata, Villa, and others exist in English. Howard Cline's Mexico: Revolution to Evolution (Oxford University, 1962) leans toward the "evolutionaries. " The fate of the Mexican Revolution is also the subject of Stanley Ross, ed. , Is the Mexican Revolution Dead? (Knopf, 1966), Martin Needler, Politics and Society in Mexico (University of New

Mexico, 1971) and Frederick C. Turner, The Dynamics of
Mexican Nationalism (University of North Carolina, 1968).
Pablo González Casanova's Democracy in Mexico (Engl.
trans.; Oxford University, 1970) praises, and Kenneth John-
son's Mexican Democracy (Allyn and Bacon, 1971) critiques,
Mexican one-party democracy. The notion that modernization
rather than politics is crucial appears in Sanford Mosk's
Industrial Revolution in Mexico (University of California,
1950), and two crucial issues are considered in Raymond
Vernon, ed., Public Policy and Private Enterprise in Mexico
(Harvard, 1964) and Clarence Senior, Land Reform and
Democracy (University of Florida, 1962). Current History
devoted its entire May 1974 and March 1977 issues to the
state of the Mexican nation in terms of politics, economics,
education, social life, and foreign policy. Literary figures
such as Aldous Huxley, Graham Greene, and Erico Verissimo
have written about their fascination for Mexico as well.
Samuel Ramos' Profile of Man and Culture in Mexico (Engl.
trans.; McGraw-Hill, 1963) looks for long-term cultural consequences.

Several good introductions to Central America exist,
e.g., Franklin D. Parker, The Central American Republics
(Oxford University, 1964) and Mario Rodríguez, Central
America (Prentice-Hall, 1965). John D. Martz' Central
America (University of North Carolina, 1959) questions the
reputation of Costa Rica for democracy, literacy, and uniqueness. John and Mavis Biesanz have drawn two good national
outlines, The People of Panama (Columbia University, 1955)
and Costa Rican Life (Columbia University, 1944). Nathan
Whetten's Guatemala (Yale University, 1961) and Alastair
White's El Salvador (Praeger, 1973) capture the social qualities of those countries. Other aging but striking portraits
of the various nationalisms are Vera Kelsey and Lilly Osborne's Four Keys to Guatemala (Funk & Wagnalls, 1943),
W. S. Stokes' Honduras (University of Wisconsin, 1950), and
Chester L. Jones' Costa Rica and Civilization in the Caribbean (University of Wisconsin, 1935). On recent attempts
at unified action, see Carlos Castillo, Growth and Integration
in Central America (Praeger, 1966) and David Ramsett,
Regional Industrial Development in Central America (Praeger,
1969). The major theme of disunity is covered in Thomas
Karnes' The Failure of Union (Arizona State, 1976). C. M.
Wilson's Challenge and Opportunity (Holt, 1941) and Empire
in Green and Gold (Greenwood, 1947) answer the criticisms
of the United Fruit Company in Charles Depner and Jay
Soothill's The Banana Empire (Vanguard, 1935). Thomas P.

McCann's An American Company: The Tragedy of United
Fruit (Crown Publishers, 1976) chronicles United Fruit's
decline. Dwight Heath describes the state of affairs in Central America from time to time in Current History (e.g.,
February, 1970 and February, 1973).

The connection of Central America and the United
States Southwest is emphasized in Herbert Eugene Bolton's
Rim of Christendom (Macmillan, 1936) and The Spanish
Borderlands (Yale University, 1921). The priority of Nar-
váez, Da Vaca, and Coronado over the Winthrops and Adamses
in the history of this part of North America also stands out
in books like The Grand Colorado (American West, 1969)
and John Francis Bannon's The Spanish Borderlands Frontier
(Holt, 1970) The predominant civilizing-Anglos or Manifest
Destiny interpretation of Justin H. Smith's The War with
Mexico (2 vols.; Macmillan, 1919) still appears in most
works printed in the United States, however. The pre-
Panama struggles for Central America are delineated in A.
H. Z. Carr, The World and William Walker (Harper, 1963)
and J. H. Kemble's The Panama Route, 1848-1869 (University of California, 1943). The Panama Canal chronicles in-
clude Gerstle Mack's The Land Divided (Knopf, 1944), Lawrence O. Ealy's The Republic of Panama in World Affairs
(University of Pennsylvania, 1951), and David G. McCul-
lough's The Path between the Seas (Simon and Schuster,
1977). Other United States interventions appear in Neill
Macaulay's The Sandino Affair (Quadrangle, 1967) and Ronald
M. Schneider's Communism in Guatemala (Praeger, 1958).

THE CARIBBEAN ISLANDS:

The conjunction of the United States South with the
Caribbean has not received quite so much attention as the
Central American-United States Southwest connection, though
both appear in Bolton's scheme of Spanish "borderlands. "
John Hope Franklin's From Slavery to Freedom (Knopf, 1967)
includes information on Negroes' history in the Caribbean
(and in Canada) so as to emphasize that the North-South
theme does not end at the United States borders. Strangely,
the more radical Before the Mayflower (rev. ed.; Johnson,
1964), a Black history by Lerone Bennett, Jr., is deficient
on the Caribbean dimension. While there is no adequate
treatment of the southward migration of Black freedmen to
the Dominican Republic or of diehard planters to the Spanish
Caribbean and Brazil, the effects of modern northward mi-

gration on areas as far afield as New York City have received attention in Oscar Handlin's The Newcomers: Negroes and Puerto Ricans in a Changing Metropolis (Harvard, 1959). The formal political and economic connections are the concern of many works, most notably the "Caribbean Conference Series" of A. C. Wilgus and others under the collective title The Caribbean (University of Florida, 1951-1967), Scott Nearing and Joseph Freeman's 1926 Dollar Diplomacy (Reprint; Arno, 1970), and the summary of relations between The United States and the Caribbean (rev. ed.; Harvard University, 1966) by Dexter Perkins. The Journal of Negro History is concerned with race relations and occasionally with Black Power. The notion that the South (Caribbean) and the West (Central America) meet in Texas is discussed in Frank Vandiver's The Southwest: South or West? (Texas A & M, 1975).

The long-independent states of The Greater Antilles are the subject of John E. Fagg's Cuba, Haiti, and the Dominican Republic (Prentice-Hall, 1965), while the smaller states remaining colonies until at least the mid-twentieth century appear in Waddell's The West Indies and the Guianas, as noted above. A subject affecting all the islands comes to the fore in Noël Doerr, The History of Sugar (2 vols.; Chapman and Hall, 1949-50). Selden Rodman has written histories of both Hispaniola nations in Haiti (rev. ed.; Devlin, 1974) and Quisqueya (University of Washington, 1964). Accounts of recent times include Jean-Pierre O. Gingras, Duvalier (Exposition, 1967) and "Progress in Haiti, " The New York Times Magazine (March 12, 1972). Alfred Métraux is more spirited in Haiti: Black Peasants and Voodoo (Engl. trans.; Harrap, 1960). James G. Leyburn's sociological analysis, The Haitian People (Yale University, 1966), is informative, and Melville Herskovits' Life in a Haitian Valley (Knopf, 1937) brings home life's realities.

Cuba's distant past comes out in Charles E. Chapman's A History of the Cuban Republic (Macmillan, 1927) and in Cuba 1933: Prologue to Revolution by Luis E. Aguilar (Cornell University, 1972). Jorge Mañach's Martí (Engl. trans.; Devin-Adair, 1950) and Richard Gray's José Martí (University Presses of Florida, 1962) seek the spirit and the image as well as the man. The social bedrock is exposed in Nelson Lowry's Rural Cuba (University of Minnesota, 1950), Fernando Ortiz' Cuban Counterpoint: Tobacco and Sugar (Engl. trans.; Knopf, 1947), and Ramiro Guerra y Sánchez' Sugar and Society in the Caribbean (Yale University,

1964). Wyatt McGaffey and Clifford R. Barnett's Cuba: Its
People, Its Society, Its Culture (HRAF Press, 1962) attempts
an overview. A positive interpretation of United States influence in Cuba is Russell Fitzgibbon's Cuba and the United
States, 1900-1935 (Russell & Russell, 1964), and a critical
view is Philip Foner's A History of Cuba and Its Relations
with the United States (2 vols.; International Publishers,
1962-63).

Interpretations of the Cuban Revolution include Fidel
Castro's own History will Absolve Me (Lyle Stuart, 1961),
the Marxist view of Leo Huberman and Paul M. Sweezy's
Cuba: Anatomy of a Revolution (Monthly Review, 1961),
Theodore Draper's middle-class-charismatic-leader approach
in Castro's Revolution (Praeger, 1962) and Castroism (Praeger,
1965), the Communist-menace view of Irving P. Pflaum's
Tragic Island (Prentice-Hall, 1961), and the another-road-to-
modernization treatment of Ramón Ruiz' Cuba: The Making
of a Revolution (University of Massachusetts, 1968) and Car-
melo Mesa-Lago's Cuba in the 1970s (University of New
Mexico, 1974). Lee Lockwood's Castro's Cuba, Cuba's Fidel
(Macmillan, 1967) and Herbert L. Matthews' Fidel Castro
(Simon and Schuster, 1969) are first-hand observations which
see both Cuban and revolutionary elements in the líder máximo. Daniel Cosío Villegas' Change in Latin America (University of Nebraska, 1961) is a comparison of the Mexican
and Cuban revolutions by a leading Mexican historian, and
the same two revolutions are compared with others world-
wide in an attempt to assess The Politics of Violence
(Prentice-Hall, 1968) by Karl Schmitt and Carl Leiden.
Hugh Thomas' The Cuban Revolution (Harper, 1977) is a vast
compendium of events, and Boris Goldenberg's The Cuban
Revolution and Latin America (Praeger, 1965) speculates on
the hemispheric appeal of Fidel and Che which will be noted
below.

Kal Wagenheim's Puerto Rico (Praeger, 1970) is
remarkable for its attention to matters like telephones, news-
papers, and slang as well as history, politics, and the arts.
It has a chronology of events, and its annotated bibliography
lists other general works in English such as the passionate
Gordon K. Lewis, Puerto Rico (Monthly Review, 1963). The
"Muñoz revolution" is the subject of Thomas Aitken's biog-
raphy of Munoz entitled Poet in the Fortress (New America
Library, 1964), Henry Wells' The Modernization of Puerto Rico
(Harvard University, 1969), Thomas Mathews' Puerto Rican
Politics and the New Deal (University of Florida, 1960),

Charles T. Goodsell's Administration of a Revolution (Harvard, 1965), and Rex Tugwell's The Stricken Land (Doubleday, 1947). Puerto Rico's connections with the other islands concerns Arturo Morales Carrión in Puerto Rico and the Non-Hispanic Caribbean (University of Puerto Rico, 1962), and the other political alternatives from statehood to independence are discussed in Robert W. Anderson's Party Politics in Puerto Rico (Stanford, 1965). James and Dorothy Bourne's Thirty Years of Change in Ten Selected Areas of Puerto Rico (Cornell, 1964) shows the tension between change and tradition in Puerto Rico and thus serves as a counterpart to Oscar Lewis' controversial La Vida (Random House, 1966). The bilingual Interamerican Review/Revista Interamericana supplements the Caribbean Review and the San Juan Star as contemporary sources.

John H. Parry and Philip M. Sherlock's A Short History of the West Indies (St. Martins, 1956) has the best reputation among histories of the newly independent or still-dependent islands of the Caribbean chain. More detail on the smaller entities appears either in Europe-oriented works like Sir Alan Burns' The British West Indies (Bobbs-Merrill, 1951), W. Adolphe Roberts' The French in the West Indies (Bobbs-Merrill, 1942), and Philip H. Hiss' Netherlands America (Duell, Sloan and Pence, 1943), or in very specific treatments such as John and Dorothy Keur's Windward Children (Royal Van Gorcum, 1960), Michael Craton's A History of the Bahamas (Collins, 1962), and David A. G. Waddell's British Honduras (Oxford University, 1961). The larger English-speaking islands have received more attention, Jamaica in Samuel and Edith Hurwitz' Jamaica (Praeger, 1971) and Trinidad-Tobago in Eric Williams' History of the Peoples of Trinidad and Tobago (Praeger, 1964). Harold Mitchell updates events from time to time in Current History, e. g., in "Islands of the Caribbean" (February, 1970).

Interesting comparisons of development policies emerge from older works such as A. Curtis Wilgus, ed., The Caribbean: British, Dutch, French, United States (University of Florida, 1958) and Mary Proudfoot, Britain and the United States in the Caribbean (Faber and Faber, 1954). There is no adequate treatment of the clash between Black Power and other radicalisms in the Caribbean, although the range of ideas can be deduced from C. L. R. James' The Black Jacobins (Vintage Books, 1963), Eric Williams' Capitalism and Slavery (University of North Carolina, 1944), Franz Fanon's The Wretched of the Earth (Grove, 1963), and

Michael Manley's The Politics of Change (Howard University, 1975). Older works such as Melville J. Herskovits' The Myth of the Negro Past (Harper, 1941) deal with Blackness if not with Black Power. Famous writers have reacted to the Black Caribbean in such works as Alec Waugh's Hot Countries (Literary Guild, 1930) and V. S. Naipaul's The Middle Passage (Macmillan, 1963).

THE FOUNDATIONS

LAND, TOOLS, AND PEOPLE:

Theodoro Miller's Graphic History of the Americas (Wiley, 1969) is a remarkable collection of historical and contemporary maps and graphs. His one page of graphs on demographic and social patterns (p. 59) speaks volumes. Preston E. James' geographies, especially the interpretive Introduction to Latin America (Odyssey, 1964), tie land and human together extremely well. Robert West and John Augelli's Middle America (Prentice-Hall, 1966) captures the cultural dimensions of the Caribbean-rim lands and describes the phenomena associated with "shatter belts." Moreover, popular magazines such as National Geographic and Smithsonian seldom neglect the flora, fauna, and exotica of Latin America for long. Travel accounts, old and new, also reveal much about the land and people. So one should not overlook either the tour-books--Fodor, Michelin, etc.--or such works as John Stevens' Incidents on a Travel in Yucatan (1843), Charles Darwin's Journal (1839), and Theodore Roosevelt's Through the Brazilian Wilderness (1914).

The numerous investigations of the science and technology of the Incas and Mayas run the gamut from close scientific studies of the Caracol at Chichén Itzá in Science (June 6, 1975), through Peter Tompkins' speculative attempt to repeat Gerald Hawkins' feat of decoding Stonehenge in Mysteries of the Mexican Pyramids (Harper, 1976), to the fanciful theories about the Nazca figures in Von Däniken's works on "ancient astronauts." As for the rise of industrial-era technologies, Watt Stewart's Henry Meiggs (Duke, 1946) shows a North American railroad baron at work in the Andes, and Richard Graham, Stanley Stein, and Warren Dean have analyzed the onset of modernized cotton and coffee manufacturing in Brazil. Modern Latin American science and technology are considered in volume 21 of the Guide to World

Science (Francis Hodgson, 1975), and some aspects of the
influence of technology on Latin American development are
analyzed in Science, Government, and Industry for Development (University of Texas Latin American Institute, 1975).
Marvin Alisky has considered the Mexican experience with
airlines (Mexican-American Review, October, 1966) and radio
(Journalism Quarterly, Winter, 1954).

The various Indian groups are covered in the famous
Handbooks of North, Middle, and South American Indians or
in specialized monographs by anthropologists like Ralph Beals
and Robert Redfield. Among the best demographic and social accounts for Mexico and Central America, both in terms
of over-view and for its bibliography of anthropological and
sociological materials, is Eric Wolf's Sons of the Shaking
Earth (University of Chicago, 1959). Nothing quite so good
exists for the whole of South America, though T. Lynn Smith's
Brazil: People and Institutions (Louisiana State University,
1963) presents an extraordinarily complete portrait of the
Southern colossus. Lucien Bodard's Green Hell: Massacre
of the Brazilian Indians (Engl. trans.; Outerbridge and Dienst-
frey, 1972) treats a contemporary issue contentiously. Many
lesser items are interesting for their treatment of special
issues of acculturation, e.g., Ray B. West's The Law of the
Saints (Viking Press, 1957) for its view of defenses against
assimilation; Carolina María de Jésus' Child of the Dark
(Dutton, 1962) for its look at Brazil from the viewpoint of a
Black woman in the city underclass; and Harold Courlander's
The Drum and the Hoe (University of California, 1960) for
its picture of African cultural remnants in Haiti.

Slavery and its aftermath deserve special mention.
Almost all the important works are represented or cited in
such edited "comparative histories" as Laura Foner and
Eugene Genovese's Slavery in the New World (Prentice-Hall,
1969), which is radical, and Richard Frucht's Black Society
in the New World (Random House, 1971), which is more
widely representative. Everyone should read some slave-
narratives from a collection like that of Arna Bontemps'
Great Slave Narratives (Beacon, 1969). Charles Wagley and
Marvin Harris' Minorities in the New World (Columbia University, 1958) reports six case studies, some of which provide a local view not available in more general works like
Florestan Fernandes' The Negro in Brazilian Society (Columbia University, 1969) and Eric Williams' From Columbus to
Castro (Harper, 1971). A close comparison of Gilberto
Freyre's The Masters and the Slaves (Engl. trans.; Knopf,

1956), Frank Tannenbaum's Slave and Citizen (Vintage, 1946), and Gunnar Myrdal's An American Dilemma (Harper, 1962) is instructive concerning the differing definitions of Blackness in Iberian, French, and British culture-areas. Carl Degler's Neither Black nor White (Macmillan, 1971) tries to compare Brazilian and North American racial progress, and Herbert Kelin's Slavery in the Americas (Quadrangle, 1967) provides an even closer comparison of Virginia and Cuba. Consultation of works by the Black Power writers such as Lerone Bennett, Jr. and Stokeley Carmichael has become crucial, however, because of the recent radicalization of interpretations of the Black experience in the Americas. Moreover, a Latin American version of Roots has yet to be written.

Thorough accounts of the "new immigrant" experience in Latin America seem to be lacking, too. A Latin American Oscar Handlin has not appeared, and the onset of "ethnic liberation movements" like those described in Daniel Moynihan and Nathan Glazer's Beyond the Melting Pot (Massachusetts Institute of Technology, 1963) has not yet occurred. Even the otherwise excellent Race Mixture in the History of Latin America (Little, Brown, 1967), by Magnus Mörner, makes only passing reference to this immigration (pp. 127-88), although Morner's excellent bibliography summarizes the work done so far on immigrant Latin Americans as disparate as the Italians, Poles, Germans, Jews, and Japanese.

ECONOMICS AND POLITICS:

The view of the modernization process followed here is drawn from Mahbubul Huq's The Poverty Curtain (Columbia University, 1976), Robert Heilbroner's The Future as History (Harper, 1960), and Daniel Lerner's The Passing of Traditional Society (Free Press, 1958). Reform of Latin America's rural regime appears in its various manifestations in Rodolfo Stavenhagen, ed., Agrarian Problems and Peasant Movements in Latin America (Anchor, 1970), and there are many classic studies or rural life in various countries, e.g., Nathaniel Whetten's Rural Mexico (University of Chicago, 1948) and Frank Tannenbaum's Mexico, the Struggle for Peace and Bread (Knopf, 1950). Thomas L. Smith, ed., Agrarian Reform in Latin America (Knopf, 1965) and Ernest Feder, The Rape of the Peasantry (Anchor, 1971) spell out the alternatives in land-use patterns, old and new, conservative and radical. The question of whether dependencia creates a "backwash" which keeps Latin America agricultural is raised in Gunnar Myrdal's Economic Theory and Under-developed Regions (Duckworth, 1957) and James D. Cockroft et al., Dependence and Underdevelopment (Anchor, 1972). The former Brazilian Minister of Planning, Celso Furtado, has also argued this thesis in Economic Development of Latin America (Engl. trans.; Cambridge University, 1970) and Obstacles to Development in Latin America (Engl. trans.; Anchor, 1970). Keith Griffin's Underdevelopment in Spanish America (Massachusetts Institute of Technology, 1969) attempts to explain the "economic inferiority" in terms of trade, investment, and other mysteries.

The status of modernization in Latin America concerns Victor L. Urquidi and his collaborators in Latin America in the International Economy (Wiley, 1973). Urquidi's The Challenge of Development in Latin America (Engl. trans.; Praeger, 1964) still has some value as well. Many studies of individual countries' economies have been written from various points of view: for instance, Furtado's The Economic Growth of Brazil (Engl. trans.; University of California, 1968), Enrique Pérez López, et al., Mexico's Recent Economic Growth: The Mexican View (University of Texas, 1967), and Laura Randall, An Economic History of Argentina (Columbia University, 1977). An older but useful series of reports by the International Bank for Reconstruction and Development includes, among others, The Economic Development of Venezuela (Johns Hopkins, 1961) and The Economic Development of Jamaica (Johns Hopkins, 1952). Michael Nelson's The Development of Tropical Lands (Resources for the Future and Johns Hopkins, 1973) outlines Latin Americans' debates concerning the development potential of their tropical regions. Inter-American Economic Affairs and various United Nations and Organization of American States publications compare Latin American development with that of other areas.

The workplace situation and the interaction among groups in the modern sector are detailed in Stanley Davis and Louis Wolf Goodman's Workers and Managers in Latin America (Heath, 1972). Serafino Romualdi describes the Latin American labor unions from the perspective of a North American labor ambassador in Presidents and Peons (Funk & Wagnalls, 1967), and Robert Alexander analyzes the labor movements in critical areas in Labor Relations in Argentina, Brazil and Chile (McGraw-Hill, 1962) and Organized Labor in Latin America (Free Press, 1965). Víctor Alba's Politics and the Labor Movement in Latin America (Stanford,

1968) contrasts Latin American unions with North America's "non-political" unions. Frank Safford's The Ideal of the Practical: Colombia's Struggle to Form a Technical Elite (University of Texas, 1976) is a fine example of recent efforts to come to grips with the crucial question of skills, and Brain Drain (U. S. Government Printing Office, 1974) is an effort by the United States Congress to understand the loss of skilled workers and professionals by developing areas. Seymour Martin Lipset and Aldo Solari, eds. , Elites in Latin America (Oxford University, 1967) and Philip M. Hauser, ed. , Urbanization in Latin America (International Documents Service, 1961) deal with two crucial social consequences of modernization. It is instructive to compare Spanish America's modern elites with those of Canada described in John Porter's The Vertical Mosaic (University of Toronto, 1965) because French- and English-speaking areas of the Caribbean have elements common to both Canada and Spanish America.

Robert Alexander's Latin American Politics and Government (Harper, 1965) covers the Latin American political situation from a reformist parliamentary perspective. Irving L. Horowitz, ed. , Latin American Radicalism (Vintage, 1969) does the same from the perspective of the revolutionary left, nationalist, religious, or Marxist. Paul E. Sigmund, ed. , Models of Political Change in Latin America (Praeger, 1970) compares the Mexican, Bolivian, Cuban, Brazilian, Argentine, Venezuelan, Colombian, and Chilean approaches. The contrast in the democratic successes of Mexico and Venezuela can be considered in L. Vincent Padgett's The Mexican Political System (Houghton Mifflin, 1966) and Frank Brandenburg's The Making of Modern Mexico (Prentice-Hall, 1964) on the one hand and John Martz and David Myers' edited Venezuela: The Democratic Experience (Praeger, 1977) on the other. Comparison of charismatic regimes in general is undertaken in Jean Lacouture, The Demigods (Engl. trans. , Knopf, 1970), and Richard Bourne's Political Leaders of Latin America (Penguin, 1969) analyzes the careers of Guevara, Stroessner, Frei, Kubitschek, Lacerda, and Eva Perón as examples of Latin American leadership styles. Richard E. Feinberg's The Triumph of Allende (New America Library, 1972) analyzes the mixture of revolution and democracy in the Chilean Revolution. Kalman Silvert suggests that Latin America may be The Conflict Society (American Universities Field Staff, 1961) in terms of political style. The "exile system" is evident in Charles D. Ameringer, The Democratic Left in Exile (University of Miami, 1974).

The impact of the 1960s time of troubles can be seen in thinking about the role of the military and of violence in Latin American statecraft. Militarism and violence were considered passing phenomena in Tad Szulc's Twilight of the Tyrants (Holt, 1959) and in Edwin Lieuwen's Arms and Politics in Latin America (Rev. ed.; Praeger, 1961), and then seen as more permanent features in Lieuwen's Generals vs. Presidents (Praeger, 1964) and in Richard Gott's Guerrilla Movements in Latin America (Doubleday, 1971). Che Guevara's diaries of the Cuban and Bolivian guerrilla movements are more informative than Guerrilla Warfare (Engl. trans.; Monthly Review, 1961) itself, and Arturo Porzecanski's Uruguay's Tupamaros (Praeger, 1973) criticizes the urban guerrilla outcome of the Guevarist approach. A contemporary French analysis of the influence of the myth of Che Guevara in Latin America is Jean Lartêguy's The Guerrillas (Signet, 1970).

Analysis of the use of the armed forces in "civic action" programs by regimes of every sort appears in John J. Johnson's The Military and Society in Latin America (Stanford University, 1964), which serves to balance Johnson's analysis of the role of civilian professionals in Political Change in Latin America: The Emergence of the Middle Sectors (Stanford University, 1958). Most of all these themes are covered by the selections in Robert D. Tamasele, ed., Latin American Politics (rev. ed.; Anchor, 1970) though the North American leanings should be considered in the light of MacEoin's Revolution Next Door or Horowitz's Latin American Radicalism. The backward look at a 1920s revolt in a Mexican village from a local viewpoint in Paul Friedrich's Agrarian Revolt in a Mexican Village (rev. ed.; Chicago University, 1977) lends a certain objectivity to the phenomenon of political violence by analyzing the motives of the "political middleman." The Catholic center is the subject of Edward Williams' Latin American Christian Democratic Parties (University of Tennessee, 1967).

MANNERS AND MORALS:

Oscar Lewis' Tepoztlán (Holt, 1960) and Life in a Mexican Village: Tepoztlán Restudied (University of Illinois, 1951) build on the earlier investigations of the village by Robert Redfield in Tepoztlán, A Mexican Village (University of Chicago, 1930). The Rohrschach studies, field investigations of everything from sexual views to economic status, and clear cultural descriptions in these works can be supplemented by such literary approaches as Arturo Barea's Lorca: The Poet and His People (Engl. trans.; Evergreen, 1949), which tackles the vexed questions of Spanish attitudes toward death and sex, and also by such technical approaches as Rogelis Díaz-Guerrero's Psychology of the Mexican Culture and Personality (University of Texas, 1975), which analyzes the Americanization of those Iberian themes in a scientific manner. Lewis' other studies, namely, the previously noted La Vida, Five Families (Basic Books, 1959), and The Children of Sánchez (Vintage, 1963), are as good as any in English on the subject of daily existence in Latin America, although some consider them unsympathetic to the "Latin mentality" and insulting to "Latin culture." José Yglesias' books, besides In the Fist of the Revolution (Pantheon, 1968), are The Goodbye Land (Pantheon, 1967) and Down There (World, 1970). Many other close-to-the people studies exist, e. g. , Charles Wagley's Amazon Town (Knopf, 1964), Stanford Gerber, The Family in the Caribbean (University of Puerto Rico, 1968), Edith Clarke, My Mother Who Fathered Me (2nd ed. ; Allen and Union, 1966), Judith Blake, Family Structure in Jamaica (Free Press, 1962), and the Herskovits' Trinidad Village (Knopf, 1947). Life in the still-untamed Mexican jungle is the subject of Paul Record's journalistic Tropical Frontier (Knopf, 1969). Evelyn Stevens has assessed the prospects for "women's liberation" in Latin America given machismo in The Western Political Quarterly (December, 1965) and The Journal of Marriage and the Family (May, 1973).

The folkways, folklore, holidays, rituals, names, gestures, and recreations of Latin Americans are often covered in the "Blaine Ethridge Reprints Series" of older studies such as Richard N. Adams' Cultural Surveys of Panama, Nicaragua, Guatemala, El Salvador, and Honduras (1938), Dorothy Kamen-Kaye's Venezuelan Folkways (1947), Charles F. Gosnell's Spanish Personal Names (1938), Walter Larden's Estancia Life (1911), and Frances Toor's Mexican Popular Arts (1939). This last is based on articles from the periodical edited by Toor and Diego Rivera, Mexican Folkways, and serves as a partial substitute for the needed translation of the Spanish works of "Dr. Atl, " father of muralism. There is no substitute for the study of Brazilian festivals and traditions by Alexander José de Mello Moraes, though the Pan American Union has published pamphlets on the folkways of most of the Americas' republics. D. Lincoln Canfield's East Meets West South of the Border (Southern Illinois,

1968) is an extraordinary personal interpretation through
"essays on Spanish American life and attitudes" and covers
everything from language to jai alai and sexual mores. Lav-
inia Dobler's National Holidays Around the World (Fleet,
1968) keys major patriotic events, and Edward T. Hall's The
Silent Language (Doubleday, 1959) and The Hidden Dimension
(Doubleday, 1966) compare Latin Americans' gestures and
conceptions of time and space with those of others, especially
with those of North Americans. George M. Foster, ed.,
Contemporary Latin American Culture (Selected Academic
Readings, [1965]) presents anthropological articles on the
patrón relationship, spiritualism, drinking, curanderismo,
and other interesting sidelights of culture. The Time-Life
"Foods of the World Series" volumes on The Cooking of Spain
and Portugal (1969) by Peter S. Feiblemann, Latin American
Cooking (1968) by Jonathan N. Leonard, and The Cooking of
the Caribbean Islands (1970) by Linda Wolfe give both recipes
and cultural insights.

LIFE OF THE MIND:

The best of the general intellectual histories of Latin
America is undoubtedly Arciniegas' Latin America: A Cul-
tural History (Engl. trans.; Knopf, 1968), although it should
be supplemented by Jean Franco's The Modern Culture of
Latin America (Praeger, 1967) for the twentieth-century ele-
ments. Others include W. Rex Crawford's A Century of
Latin American Thought (Praeger, 1944), Stephen Clissold's
Latin America: A Cultural Outline (Colophon, 1966), and
Latin American Thought by Harold Eugene Davis (Louisiana
State University, 1972). Pedro Henríquez-Ureña's Concise
History of Latin American Culture (Engl. trans.; Praeger,
1966) provides about the only treatment in English of Latin
American scientists, plus an excellent bibliography of sources
in English on most cultural matters except religion. Intel-
lectual histories of various countries have been written,
notably Fernando de Azevedo's Brazilian Culture (Reprint;
Hafner, 1971) and João Cruz Costa's A History of Ideas in
Brazil (University of California, 1964). In order not to
exaggerate the "high culture" elements it is important to
refer to Arciniegas' last chapter, "Appointment with Necro-
mancy," and at least some of a number of items on the persistence of magic, voodoo, and "deep structures": Maya
Deren's Divine Horsemen: The Voodoo Gods of Haiti (Chel-
sea, 1970); Ari Kiev's Curanderismo (Free Press, 1968);
and Claude Lévi-Strauss' famous works on "structuralism"

inspired in part by his Latin American researches, especially
Tristes Tropiques (Engl. trans.; Criterion, 1961) and The
Savage Mind (Engl. trans.; University of Chicago, 1966).

The mainstream of modern Catholic thought in Latin
America and elsewhere is clear in I. M. Bochênski's Con-
temporary European Philosophy (Engl. trans.; University of
California, 1956) or in greater depth in the New Catholic
Encyclopedia. The outlet of the Maryknoll Fathers, Orbis
Books, has published a good deal on the "theology of liberation," including Enrique Dussel's History and the Theology of
Liberation (1977) and the works of Nestor Paz and Dom Helder Câmara. Ralph Woodward, Jr., Positivism in Latin
America, 1850-1900 (Heath, 1971) and Luis Aguilar, Marxism
in Latin America (Knopf, 1968) are edited collections of modern secular thinkers. Leopoldo Zea's The Latin American
Mind (University of Oklahoma, 1963) dwells on the importance
of Positivist principles in Latin American thought. It is a
pity that Zea's Spanish work in the "Pensamiento de America"
series has not been translated, since it would make the views
of Latin American philosophers much better known. Some
of the academic pensadores have received attention, however,
in Aníbal Sánchez Reulet's Contemporary Latin American
Philosophy (University of New Mexico, 1954) and in Patrick
Romanell's Making of the Mexican Mind (University of Notre
Dame, 1952).

Church and State in Latin America (rev. ed.; University of North Carolina, 1966), by J. Lloyd Mecham, raises
crucial questions about the public mind in Latin America in
times past. Frederick B. Pike has addressed the same issue
for recent times in The Conflict Between Church and State in
Latin America (Knopf, 1964) and Religion, Revolution, and
Reform (Praeger, 1964), the latter in co-authorship with
William V. D'Antonio. The vexed relations of religion and
revolution which inspired Graham Greene's sympathetic treatment of the Cristeros in The Power and the Glory (many editions) continue throughout Latin America, but The Religious
Dimension in the New Latin America (Fides Publishers, 1967),
edited by John Considine, indicates a movement toward change
for God's sake in Catholic culture. John Tate Lanning's
Academic Culture in the Spanish Colonies (Oxford University,
1940) is useful background for the survey of contemporary
education in Latin America outlined in the relevant sections
of Donald K. Emmerson's edited Students and Politics in
Developing Nations (Praeger, 1968). Harold Eugene Davis
has attempted to plot Social Science Trends in Latin America

(University Press of Washington, 1950), and Joseph Kahl has
interpreted the work of three contemporary sociologists in
Modernization, Exploitation, and Dependence in Latin America
(Transaction Books, 1976). As yet, however, there are many
more works like Mariano Picón-Salas' elegant treatment of
the colonial period in A Cultural History of Spanish America
(Engl. trans.; University of California, 1964) than there are
studies of ascendant movements such as modern education and
fundamentalist Protestantism. There is, however, a study of
a Black Power sect in Jamaica, The Rastafarians (Beacon,
1977) by Leonard E. Barrett.

Literary histories exist in plenty. Enrique Anderson
Imbert's Spanish American Literature (Engl. trans.; Wayne
State University, 1963) and Arturo Torres-Rioseco's The Epic
of Latin American Literature (Engl. trans.; University of
California, 1970) carry the Spanish-American story up almost
to The Boom, whereupon Luis Harss and Barbara Dohmann's
Into the Mainstream (Harper, 1967) picks up the thread. The
Review of the Center for Inter-American Relations, the Latin
American Literary Review, and Hispania, and sometimes the
New York Times Book Review, provide up-to-date translations
and critical assessments. There is also a Latin American
Theater Review which covers the spectrum well, and for
earlier plays see Behind Spanish American Footlights (Uni-
versity of Texas, 1965) by Willis K. Jones. No one who
wants to capture the temper of The Boom can neglect D. P.
Gallagher's elegant Modern Latin American Literature (Oxford, 1973), John Brushwood's The Spanish-American Novel:
A Twentieth Century Survey (University of Texas, 1975), or
Walter Langford's The Mexican Novel Comes of Age (University of Notre Dame, 1971). Manuel Bandeira's Brief History
of Brazilian Literature (Engl. trans.; Brazilian-American
Cultural Institute, 1964) is a thorough listing, but Samuel
Putnam's Marvelous Journey (Knopf, 1948) and Erico Verissimo's Brazilian Literature (Greenwood, 1945) reach deeper
into the Brazilian consciousness. Frederick Ellison's treatment of the Northeastern novelists (University of California,
1954) furnishes the link with the past which Harss provides
for Spanish America, and the Luso-Brazilian Review does
some articles on contemporary writers. Standard reference
volumes such as World Authors (Wilson, 1975) include famous
Caribbean authors, and Caribbean Review and Journal of African Studies occasionally print articles on Caribbean culture.
Kenneth Ramchand's West Indian Narrative (Nelson, 1966)
can serve as a starting point for the English-speaking areas,
and Norman Shapiro's Négritude (October House, 1970) for

the French-African connections. But for well-known writers in every culture the best source is the "Twayne World Authors Series" or some equally good biography. Guides to movements are David and Virginia Foster, Modern Latin American Literature (2 vols.; Ungar, 1975) and especially David Foster's Dictionary of Contemporary Latin American Authors (Arizona State, 1975).

Pal Kelemen's Art of the Americas (Crowell, 1969) attempts to summarize the ancient and Hispanic elements and even presents a comparison with the Philippines. Leopoldo Castedo's A History of Latin American Art and Architecture (Praeger, 1969) is also useful. Gilbert Chase's Contemporary Art in Latin America (Free Press, 1970) and A Guide to the Music of Latin America (Pan American Union, 1962) are indispensable. For insight into the influence of Latin Ameri can traditions on the United States, see José E. Espinosa's Saints in the Valleys (University of New Mexico, 1967) and Americo Paredes' With His Pistol in His Hand (University of of Texas, 1958) on the santo and corrido traditions of the Borderlands. Paredes has also published the bilingual A Texas-Mexican Cancionero (University of Illinois, 1976). The Pan American Union's "Art in Latin America Today" series includes a volume on most independent nations. E. Bradford Burns' Latin American Cinema (University of California at Los Angeles, 1975) opens up the world of film, and Vernon Young's On Film (Quadrangle, 1972) offers some speculations on how Latin American film-makers compare with the Europeans, North Americans, and Japanese. Francisco Bullrich's New Directions in Latin American Architecture (Braziller, 1969) presents the work of famous contemporary Latin American architects such as Niemeyer, Villanueva, and O'Gorman, complete with many photographs and a good bibliography. The Mexican Muralists (Crown, 1960), by Alma M. Reed, is a good interpretation, and Antonio Rodríguez, A History of Mexican Mural Painting (Engl. trans.; Putnam, 1969) provides a wealth of mythic and social detail as well as excellent reproductions.

THE IMPACTS

HEMISPHERE PATTERNS:

Lewis Hanke, ed., Do the Americas Have a Common History? (Knopf, 1964) asks the right question and presents

some standard answers by both Latin and North Americans.
One of the traditional answers, that the vast resources of
the Americas provided the wealth necessary for democracy,
is the theme of Walter Prescott Webb's The Great Frontier
(Houghton Mifflin, 1951). The more modern answer, that
concern must be shown for military threats to democracy
from outside the hemisphere, plays a large part in Arthur
P. Whitaker's history of The Western Hemisphere Idea (Cornell University, 1954). Norman Graebner's Empire on the
Pacific (Ronald Press, 1955) implies that the frontier democracy of North Americans had already become incompatible
with hemisphere solidarity by the time of the Mexican-
American War, and Samuel Flagg Bemis' The Latin American
Policy of the United States (Harcourt, 1943) embraces the
late-nineteenth-century concept of Anglo-American parliamentary democracy rather than the Jefferson-Bolívar view of
hemisphere Jacobinism. Julius Pratt's The Expansionists of
1898 (Quadrangle, 1964) and Robert Beisner's Twelve Against
Empire (McGraw-Hill, 1968) tell the two sides of the resulting United States debate over imperialism for democracy's
sake. Recent efforts designed to show that the Anglo-
American entente after the Spanish-American War was an
imperialist deal rather than a democratic front have been
made in William A. Williams' The Tragedy of American
Diplomacy (Dell, 1972) and Walter Lafeber's The New Empire
(Cornell, 1963), but Barbara Tuchman's The Zimmerman
Telegram (Viking, 1958) suggests that there was a German
threat during World War I.

The oscillation between intervention and neighborliness
during the period of the World Wars eventually led to such
works as Making an Inter-American Mind (University of
Florida, 1961) by Harry Bernstein in addition to the traditional histories by Bemis, Perkins, and others. Studies of the
Good Neighbor Policy run from quarrels over its origins in
Edward Guerrant's Roosevelt's Good Neighbor Policy (University of New Mexico, 1950) and Alexander DeConde's Herbert Hoover's Latin American Policy (Stanford University,
1951) to questions about its meaning in Donald Dozer's Are
We Good Neighbors? (University of Florida, 1959) and his-
torical summaries like Bryce Wood's The Making of the Good
Neighbor Policy (Columbia University, 1961). The defense
issue is treated in J. Lloyd Mecham's The United States and
Hemisphere Security (University of Texas, 1961), Stanley
Hilton's Brazil and the Great Powers, 1930-1939 (University
of Texas, 1975), and Alton Frye's Nazi Germany and the
American Hemisphere (Yale, 1967). The Pacific sun rises

and sets in Anita Bradley's Trans-Pacific Relations of Latin
America (AMS Press, 1942) and C. Harvey Gardner's The
Japanese and Peru (University of New Mexico, 1975). The
development issue as it affected Mexico appears in Howard
Cline's The United States and Mexico (rev. ed.; Atheneum,
1963) and J. Richard Powell's The Mexican Petroleum Industry (University of California, 1956). The offspring of the
democratic issue and the hemisphere idea is described in O.
Carlos Stoetzer's The Organization of American States
(Praeger, 1965). The animadversions of Arevalo's The Shark
and the Sardines (Engl. trans.; Lyle Stuart, 1961) take legal
form in Non-Intervention (Southern Methodist University,
1956) by Ann and A. J. Thomas, Jr.

The Cold War period reheated the issue of intervention
summarized by both Latin and North Americans in C. Noalo
Ronning, ed., Intervention in Latin America (Knopf, 1970).
Galo Plaza's Latin America Today and Tomorrow (Acropolis,
1971) presents a case for the North-South connection implicit
in his role as Secretary-General of the Organization of American States. Jerome Levinson and Juan de Onis argue in
The Alliance that Lost Its Way (Quadrangle, 1970), however,
that the interamerican advance foreseen by The Alliance for
Progress (Princeton, 1966) of J. Warren Nystrom and Nathan
Haverstick has collapsed. C. Wright Mills' Listen, Yankee
(McGraw-Hill, 1960), Haynes Johnson's The Bay of Pigs
(Norton, 1964), and Robert Kennedy's Thirteen Days (Norton,
1971) register the tremor set off in hemisphere affairs by
the Cuban Revolution. Some interesting general accounts
also emerged from the re-thinking of hemisphere relations:
Thomas L. Karnes, ed., Readings in the Latin American
Policy of the United States (University of Arizona, 1972),
which quotes policy-makers from Jefferson and Adams to
Castro and Figueres on every crucial issue of hemisphere
policy; Edwin Lieuwen, U.S. Policy in Latin America (Praeger,
1965), which reflects United States military concerns; and
above all, Federico G. Gil, Latin American-United States
Relations (Harcourt, 1972), which puts Latin Americans'
relations with each other into perspective and is probably the
best account of interamerican affairs from the new, co-equal
standpoint.

Several previously cited volumes by Dexter Perkins,
Arthur Whitaker, Howard Cline, Federick Pike, et al., in
Harvard's "American Foreign Policy Library" have detailed
the North American interests and perceptions. Spanish
American Images of the United States (University of Florida,

1977) have also been updated by John T. Reid. Latin Americans' interests in each other and in Third World areas have come to the fore in Harold E. Davis, et al., Latin American Foreign Policies (Johns Hopkins, 1975), Carlos A. Astiz, ed., Latin American International Politics (Notre Dame, 1970), and Luigi Einaudi, ed., Beyond Cuba (Crane, Russak, 1974). Wayne A. Selcher's The Afro-Asian Dimension of Brazilian Foreign Policy, 1956-72 (University Presses of Florida, 1974) provides evidence of Brazil's special interests in the Third World, and his and Jordan Young's articles on Brazil's super-power ambitions appear in Intellect (June, 1977). Stephen Clissold's Latin America: New World, Third World (Praeger, 1972) sets forth the larger choices confronting the hemisphere nations.

THE GLOBAL DIMENSION:

The North American view of the role of Latin America in the so-called "world revolution" is presented, with a bibliography, in Chapters 8 and 9 of Gil's Latin American-United States Relations. The strategy of reform as a response to revolution is advocated in Charles O. Porter and Robert J. Alexander's The Struggle for Democracy in Latin America (Macmillan, 1961), and a more rigid strategy in the later Rockefeller Report on the Americas (Quadrangle, 1969). The uncertain relations of Cuba and the Communist giants are the subject of Andres Suárez, Cuba: Castroism and Communism (Massachusetts Institute of Technology, 1967). The range of Marxist-revolutionary sympathies in Latin America is obvious not only in the works of Che Guevara and Frantz Fanon but also in David Caute's biography Frantz Fanon (Viking, 1970), Juan Bosch's Pentagonism (Grove, 1968), Régis Debray's Revolution in the Revolution (Engl. trans.; Grove, 1967) and The Chilean Revolution: Conversations with Allende (Vintage, 1971), Jay Mallin's edited volume "Che" Guevara on Revolution (Delta, 1969), and George Lavan's similar Che Guevara Speaks (Grove, 1967). Two somewhat unusual pieces are also instructive on the Marxists: Gabriel García Márquez, "The Death of Salvador Allende," Harper's (May, 1974), and J. Gregory Oswald, Soviet Images of Contemporary Latin America (University of Texas, 1970). For the change from stand-fast to evolutionary North American attitudes in the 1970s, see Thomas Weyr, "Our Crumbling Role in the Americas," The American Legion Magazine (July, 1975); Francis P. Kessler, "Kissinger's Legacy: A Latin American Policy," Current History (February, 1977); and

Thomas J. Knight, "Détente in Latin America?" Intellect (March, 1976).

The technological, environmental, and population issues are so current that most available information is in the popular or semi-popular press or in global works such as William R. Kintner and Harvey Sicherman's Technology and International Politics (Lexington Books, 1975). T. Lynn Smith has analyzed the crucial food-population issue in The Race Between Population and Food Supply in Latin America (New Mexico, 1976), however. Some of the purported impacts of technological dependency have been considered in a NACLA Report entitled "Electronics: The Global Industry" (April, 1977) and in Alan Wells' analysis of television's images in Latin America called Picture Tube Imperialism (Orbis, 1976). The Amazon's importance and the possible dangers inherent in Brazil's westward expansion are discussed in Robert Campbell's analysis of the biosphere of the Americas (The Smithsonian, September and October, 1977) and in Loren McIntyre's "Brazil's Wild Frontier" (National Geographic, November, 1977). More general environmental issues emerge in an article by Mary and Laurance Rockefeller entitled "How South America Guards Her Green Legacy" (National Geographic, January, 1967). The Foreign Policy Association's annual Great Decisions booklets also present analyses of interdependence issues (e. g. , on the oceans in 1977). Alfonso García Robles' The Denuclearization of Latin America (Carnegie Endowment, 1967) and Nuclear Proliferation (Foreign Policy Association, 1976) address the problem of moving from the petroleum to the plutonium era. Scientific American and Science publish occasional pieces on energy and population, e. g. , in "Brazil: Energy Options and Current Outlook" (Science, 14 April, 1978). Noël Mostert's Supership (Warner, 1976), Anthony Sampson's The Sovereign State of ITT (Stein and Day, 1973), and James Petras, et al. , The Nationalization of Venezuelan Oil (Praeger, 1977) raise questions about multinational corporations' role in Latin America and elsewhere. Nicolás Sánchez-Albornoz' The Population of Latin America (University of California, 1974) confronts the question of too many.

THE CULTURAL CONNECTIONS:

The major influences of the Latin American worldview are evident in the "underdog" cultures of the Americas. The connections of Africa, the West Indies and North America

are exhaustively detailed in Harold Cruse's The Crisis of the
Negro Intellectual (Morrow, 1967), so that various national-
isms and radicalisms of North American Harlems come
clearer in light of the influence of Garvey, McKay, Césaire,
Carmichael, Innis, and other West Indians. E. David
Cronon's biography of Garvey and his movement, Black
Moses (University of Wisconsin, 1955), is also revealing,
along with "The Jamaican Experiment" (Current History,
February, 1978). The important French-speaking connections
are considered in James Baldwin's report on the 1956 Paris
Conference of Negro-African Writers and Artists in Nobody
Knows My Name (Dell, 1961). The West Indian and African
influences on intellectuals such as W. E. B. DuBois, Richard
Wright, Langston Hughes, Paul Robeson, and others are
doubtlessly the most important Black currents flowing north-
ward, but the racial symbolism from Brazil is also clear in
Ebony's occasional articles (see "Does Amalgamation Work in
Brazil?", July, 1965). Likewise, Raymond Sayers' The
Negro in Brazilian Literature (Hispanic Institute in the United
States, 1956) makes for interesting comparisons with North
American literature. The Red Power sympathies behind pop-
ular books such as Dee Brown's Bury My Heart at Wounded
Knee (Holt, 1971) come from within North America or from
the Indianist writings produced in Mexico and the Andes, but
David Driver's The Indian in Brazilian Literature (Hispanic
Institute in the United States, 1942) gives a third perspective.

The advent of ethnic pride among Spanish-speakers in
North America produced a number of political works which
indicate the Latin American inspiration, among Mexican-
Americans in particular. See, for instance, Chicano Power
(Dutton, 1974) by Tony Castro, La Raza (Harper & Row,
1969) by Stan Steiner, Sal si puedes (Dell, 1969) by Peter
Matthiessen, and The Chicanos (Penguin, 1971) edited by Ed
Ludwig and James Santibañez, all of which are more or less
radical. The Mexican Americans (Prentice-Hall, 1970), in
the "Ethnic Groups in American Life Series," and Wayne
Moquín, ed., A Documentary History of the Mexican Ameri-
cans (Praeger, 1971) are historical and moderate. Philip D.
Ortego's anthology We Are Chicanos (Pocket Books, 1973)
offers some selections from the emerging literature of the
Chicano movement. Studies of "Boricuans" include, besides
La Vida, Beyond the Melting Pot, and The Newcomers,
Francesco Cordasco's Puerto Ricans on the United States
Mainland (Rowman, 1972) and Dan Wakefield, Island in the
City: The World of Spanish Harlem (Houghton Mifflin, 1959).
The "Ethnic Groups in American Life Series" also has vol-

umes on Puerto Ricans, Blacks and Indians. Miguel Algarín and Miguel Piñero have provided a unique collection of Nuyorican Poetry (Morrow, 1975). Harold Alford's The Proud Peoples (McKay, 1972) covers the entire Spanish-speaking community in North America from colonial times to militant times and furnishes short biographies of famous figures in an appendix. John H. Burma's 1954 Spanish-Speaking Groups in the United States (Reprint; Blaine Ethridge, 1977) presents an older, more cultural view. Theodore Anderson and Mildred Boyer, eds., Bilingual Schooling in the United States (Reprint; Blaine Ethridge, 1977) has essays on education in various ethnic communities and on the history of bi-lingualism in several countries of the Americas.

In time the claim that Latin Americans' multi-dimensional view of reality is just what is required in a too-rational global culture may supersede the claim that the major appeal will always be confined to the minority cultures of the Americas. What Octavio Paz' The Labyrinth of Solitude (Engl. trans.; Grove, 1961) does to outline a Spanish American view of contemporary reality, for example, his Claude Lévi-Strauss (Engl. trans.; Delta, 1967) does to outline a new "myth" applicable to global realities. Moreover, to complement the claims of Paz and earlier Hispanics such as Rodó, Madariaga, and Vasconcelos, a number of North Americans have voiced support for the "Latin" view of multi-faceted emotionalism rather than "Anglo-Saxon" rationalism. See, for example, F.S.C. Northrop's chapter on the reconciling power of Mexican thought in The Meeting of East and West (Macmillan, 1946), James Michener's hymn to Hispanic love of life in Iberia (Random House, 1968), and Michael A. Weinstein's effort at spelling out the philosophical underpinnings in The Polarity of Mexican Thought (Pennsylvania State University, 1976). To my knowledge, there is no general treatment of the mutual inspirations of the North Americans Faulkner, Hemingway, Dos Passos, Kerouac, Burroughs, and Pynchon on the one hand and The Boom's writers on the other. Yet the success of Carlos Castañeda's Journey to Ixtlán (Simon and Schuster, 1972) indicates the potential buried in the appeal of the non-rational in the Americas. That such yearnings are not new in Latin America is evident in the collection of papers entitled Artists and Writers in the Evolution of Latin America (University of Alabama, 1969).

INDEX